Toward a Unified Psychoanalytic Theory

This book aims to integrate different psychoanalytic schools and relevant research findings into an integrated psychoanalytic theory of the mind.

A main claim explored here is that a revised and expanded ego psychology constitutes the strongest foundation not only for a unified psychoanalytic theory but also for the integration of relevant research findings from other disciplines. Sophisticated yet accessible, the book includes a description of the basic tenets of ego psychology and necessary correctives and revisions. It also discusses research and theory on interpersonal understanding, capacity for inhibition, defense, delay of gratification, autonomous ego aims and motives, affect regulation, the nature of psychopathology; and the implications of a revised and expanded ego psychology for approaches to treatment.

The book will appeal to readers who are interested in psychoanalysis, the nature of the mind, the nature of psychopathology, and the implications of theoretical formulations and research findings for approaches to treatment. As such, it will also be of great value on graduate and training courses for psychoanalysis.

Morris N. Eagle, Distinguished Faculty, New Center for Psychoanalysis in Los Angeles; Senior Scholar, York University, Toronto; Fellow of the Royal Society of Canada; recipient of the Sigourney Award; former President of the Division of Psychoanalysis of the American Psychological Association; author/editor of 8 books; author of more than 150 journal articles and chapters.

PSYCHOLOGICAL ISSUES

The basic mission of *Psychological Issues* is to contribute to the further development of psychoanalysis as a science, as a respected scholarly enterprise, as a theory of human behavior, and as a therapeutic method.

Over the past 50 years, the series has focused on fundamental aspects and foundations of psychoanalytic theory and clinical practice as well as on work in related disciplines relevant to psychoanalysis. *Psychological Issues* does not aim to represent or promote a particular point of view. The contributions cover broad and integrative topics of vital interest to all psychoanalysts as well as to colleagues in related disciplines. They cut across particular schools of thought and tackle key issues, such as the philosophical underpinnings of psychoanalysis, psychoanalytic theories of motivation, conceptions of therapeutic action, the nature of unconscious mental functioning, psychoanalysis and social issues, and reports of original empirical research relevant to psychoanalysis. The authors often take a critical stance toward theories and offer a careful theoretical analysis and conceptual clarification of the complexities of theories and their clinical implications, drawing upon relevant empirical findings from psychoanalytic research as well as from research in related fields.

Series Editor David L. Wolitzky and the Editorial Board continues to invite contributions from social/behavioral sciences such as anthropology and sociology, from biological sciences such as physiology and the various brain sciences, and from scholarly humanistic disciplines such as philosophy, law, and ethics. Volumes 1–64 in this series were published by International Universities Press. Volumes 65–69 were published by Jason Aronson. For a full list of the titles published by Routledge in this series, please visit the Routledge website: www.routledge.com/Psychological-Issues/book-series/PSYCHISSUES

'Morris Eagle has an integrative mind that is in a class of its own within psychoanalytic theory and beyond. This book accurately integrates almost all developments in the last decades into the best established framework of psychoanalytic science and advances an exciting new vision of contemporary psychoanalysis remarkable not just for its clarity but for opening fresh clinical vistas. A virtuoso achievement of great value to our community.'

– **Peter Fonagy,** *Professor of Contemporary Psychoanalysis and Developmental Science*

'In this impressive and scholarly contribution, Morris Eagle breathes new life into ego psychology. A resuscitation effort is quite timely as ego psychology has gradually been edged out of psychoanalytic discourse and replaced with themes derived from object relations, self psychology, attachment theory, and relational approaches. The author makes a splendid argument for how an updated and more comprehensive approach to ego psychology may be more user-friendly than the partial theories that seem to be more popular today. He points out that a unified psychoanalytic theory of the mind must rest on the placement of a "personal element", the "I", at the center of the theory. In this regard, he reminds us that our subjective experience is the core of true ego psychology. I highly recommend this extraordinary new book to all those who care about the future of psychoanalysis.'

– **Glen O. Gabbard, MD,** *Training and Supervising Analyst, Center for Psychoanalytic Studies in Houston*

'Along with four co-edited books, this is Morris Eagle's fifth authored book, another classic. His lifelong line of research comes full circle. In this book, he confronts a central issue of our field today: the possibility of a unified psychoanalytic theory, the foundation for which, he convincingly argues, should be a corrected, revised, and expanded ego psychology. Here the *fil rouge* that characterized all his previous books and papers is more evident than ever: he is not satisfied with remaining at the theoretical level, where we know he excels; he relentlessly connects psychoanalytic theory and clinical issues to theory and research from related disciplines. No doubt, this book will be a reference point for the entire psychoanalytic community, will be translated in other languages and will be used as a vital source for graduate courses and education and train-ing programs in psychoanalysis.'

– **Paolo Migone, MD,** *editor of the journal* Psicoterapia e Scienze Umane

'In this dazzlingly brilliant and breathtakingly bold new book, Morris Eagle, psychoanalysis's most astute theoretician and critic, shares his gripping vision of a revitalized ego psychology that draws on the latest discoveries in the psy-chological sciences while attending to the aspirations of psychoanalysis to be a comprehensive science of human meaning. There was a time when one heard the complaint that ego psychology is unexciting and shallow relative to other branches of psychoanalysis. To the contrary, drawing on philosophy as well as psychology to illuminate a new understanding of the ego, Eagle shows that a fully realized ego psychology offers the necessary dynamic center at which all psychoanalytic perspectives meet in forming human experience. Eagle resuscitates ego psychology through arguments of enormous scope and erudition. Drawing on the latest research in multiple psychological disciplines, he offers a profound prescription for the future of clinical theory that places the human subject – Freud's "ego" – at the heart of an integrative study of the mind and its meanings. Psychoanalysis has displayed its own death instinct in recent decades, splintering into narcissistically defended enclaves each of which holds itself out as the "true" psychoanalytic theory, leaving the field unable to present a common vision or an integrated empirical and theoretical research tradition that can make a credible claim to be taken seriously as part of the larger multi-disciplinary psychological/cognitive/neuropsychiatric science of our time. One wants to say to psychoanalysis: Enough already with the many blind men feeling different parts of the elephant! Open your eyes and see that the parts exist within an integrated whole, and that the essence of that whole is the human ego and its many influences and meanings. This book will finally put to rest the suspicion that psychoanalysis is incapable of dynamic new theoretical advances and will open a pathway for psychoanalysis to realize its natural place as a protector of the importance of meaning in a world more and more focused on biological underpinnings. His book is a must-read for all those faculty, graduate students, and clinicians – whether in psychoanalysis, clinical psychology, social work, or other psychotherapeutic professions – who want to approach their clients and theories of helping with the broadest and deepest research-anchored vision available.'

– **Jerome C. Wakefield, PhD, DSW,** *University Professor, Professor of Social Work, Honorary Faculty in the Psychoanalytic Association of New York Affiliated with NYU Grossman School of Medicine, Center for Bioethics in the School of Global Public Health*

Toward a Unified Psychoanalytic Theory

Foundation in a Revised and Expanded Ego Psychology

Morris N. Eagle

Routledge
Taylor & Francis Group

LONDON AND NEW YORK

First published 2022
by Routledge
2 Park Square, Milton Park, Abingdon, Oxon OX14 4RN

and by Routledge
605 Third Avenue, New York, NY 10158

Routledge is an imprint of the Taylor & Francis Group, an informa business

British Library Cataloguing-in-Publication Data
A catalogue record for this book is available from the British Library

Library of Congress Cataloging-in-Publication Data
Names: Eagle, Morris N., author.
Title: Toward a unified psychoanalytic theory : foundation in a revised and expanded ego psychology / Morris N. Eagle.
Description: Abingdon, Oxon ; New York, NY : Routledge, 2021. | Series: Psychological issues series | Includes bibliographical references and index.
Identifiers: LCCN 2020058066 (print) | LCCN 2020058067 (ebook) | ISBN 9781032023168 (hbk) | ISBN 9780367767532 (pbk) | ISBN 9781003182863 (ebk)
Subjects: LCSH: Psychoanalysis—Philosophy. | Ego (Psychology)
Classification: LCC BF173 .E1655 2021 (print) | LCC BF173 (ebook) | DDC 150.19/5—dc23
LC record available at https://lccn.loc.gov/2020058066
LC ebook record available at https://lccn.loc.gov/2020058067

ISBN: 978-1-032-02316-8 (hbk)
ISBN: 978-0-367-76753-2 (pbk)
ISBN: 978-1-003-18286-3 (ebk)

Typeset in Times New Roman
by Apex CoVantage, LLC

Contents

Acknowledgments

I want to express my appreciation for the thoroughness with which my wife Rita read and helped organize every chapter in the book. I also want to express my gratitude to Dr. Lauren Jensen for her invaluable skill at ferreting out relevant material and references. This book could not have been completed without her help.

Introduction

Why a book on ego psychology at this time? Although exerting hegemony over psychoanalytic theorizing in the 1950s and 1960s in the United States, its influence has significantly waned (Bergmann, 2000). One consequence of the waning influence of ego psychology is a relative loss of psychoanalytic interest in certain fundamental aspects of psychological functioning that are central to an ego psychology perspective, including the development of reality-testing and the capacity for inhibition and delay. There appears to be little interest and little or no room for these core aspects of psychological life in contemporary psychoanalytic *schools*. This may be less of a problem in the clinical context (although issues of ego functioning are relevant for understanding psychopathology and for treatment). However, it is a major problem if one believes, as Freud did, that psychoanalysis' major claim on posterity lies in its embodiment as a theory of mind rather than as a form of treatment (although, of course, a theory of the mind also carries implications for understanding of psychopathology and for approaches to treatment).

The main theses of this book are, one, that an expanded and revitalized ego psychology constitutes the strongest foundation for the development of a general psychoanalytic theory of mind; two, that an expanded and revitalized ego psychology would, perforce, also constitute the strongest foundation for the development of a unified psychoanalytic theory capable of integrating the perspectives of different psychoanalytic *schools*; and three, that, as Rapaport and Hartmann argued, an adequate psychoanalytic theory of the mind needs to integrate findings from non-psychoanalytic sources. In an important sense, this book constitutes a re-engagement with the abandoned project of psychoanalytic theory as a general theory of the mind

The vision of psychoanalytic theory as a general theory of mind is mainly attributed to the writings of Hartmann and Rapaport on ego psychology. However, it is also present in Freud's writings, not only in the abandoned *Project for a scientific psychology* (Freud, 1950 [1895]), but also in his later writings. Thus, in 1926, Freud wrote that "psychoanalysis is a part of psychology, not of medical psychology in the old sense, not of the psychology of morbid processes, but simply of psychology" (p. 252). He proposed that analytic training include "elements from the mental sciences, from psychology, the history of civilization and sociology, as well as from anatomy, biology, and the study of evolution" (p. 252).

My interest in writing this book was initially sparked by my recognition of a relatively direct line from Freud's conception in the *Project* of the ego as an inhibitory structure to research on delay of gratification, affect regulation, and other executive functions, at the center of which are inhibitory capacities. Thus, although the influence of ego psychology has waned within psychoanalysis, a great deal of research and theorizing is being carried out outside of psychoanalysis that is highly relevant to psychoanalytic theory, in particular, to psychoanalytic ego psychology. The assimilation and integration of this work into psychoanalytic theory would, in my view, contribute to the development of an expanded and revitalized ego psychology that could also serve as the basis for a unified psychoanalytic theory.

There are also personal motives for writing this book. My graduate training began with two years at a remarkable master's program in clinical psychology at the City College of New York (CCNY) that claimed among its faculty Ernst Kris, David Beres, Roy Schafer, Katherine Wolf, Ruth Munroe, and Kurt Goldstein. From there, I entered the psychoanalytically oriented doctoral program in clinical psychology at New York University. I was given a research assistantship at the New York University Research Center for Mental Health, the Co-directors of which were George Klein and Robert Holt. I carried out my doctoral research under the mentorship of George Klein and, following the granting of my doctoral degree, stayed on as a Research Assistant Professor for a number of years. My colleagues at the Research Center included Fred Pine, Donald Spence, David Wolitzky, Irving Paul, and Leo Goldberger and the visiting faculty included David Rapaport, Merton Gill, and Hartvig Dahl. Along with others, I had the good fortune of participating in a remarkable one-year seminar with David Rapaport on Chapter 7 of Freud's *Interpretation of dreams*.

Although much of the research at the Research Center was carried out in traditional psychological areas, (for example, I carried out research on subliminal priming and incidental and intentional memory), it was motivated by its relevance to psychoanalytic issues and concerns. For example, research on the effects of subliminal stimuli on cognition and affect was motivated by an interest in unconscious processes; and research on coping with sensory deprivation was linked to the ego psychology concept of "adaptive regression". The dominant perspective at the Research Center was an ego psychological one and the dominant ethos, one compatible with that perspective, was belief in the vital importance of cross-fertilization between psychoanalysis and psychological research and theory. Virtually everyone at the Research Center had one foot in psychoanalysis and one foot in research and theory in psychology.

Although there are exceptions, to a significant degree, the perspective I have described has essentially disappeared in much of the psychoanalytic literature. That development, I believe, is quite unfortunate and constitutes a significant danger for the future growth, let alone survival, of psychoanalysis as something more than a marginal discipline (See Stepansky, 2009). From a personal perspective, this book represents a kind of completion of a circle, a return to central issues within psychoanalysis that arose during the early formative years at CCNY and the NYU Research Center.

There are ten main interlocking strands I will follow in elaborating and supporting my main theses. The first strand (Chapter 1) begins with Freud's (1950 [1895]) conception of the ego in the *Project for a scientific psychology* as a structure whose main function is *inhibition* of, as he puts it, the flow of excitation from one neuron to another; then turns to Freud's formulation of the basic concept of inhibition in psychological rather than neurological terms following his abandonment of the *Project*; and continues with an account of a body of empirical research and theory dealing with delay of gratification and other inhibitory capacities. The main purpose here is to demonstrate the continuous conceptual (and historical) line from Freud's conception of the ego as an inhibitory structure to current research on delay of gratification and other expressions of executive function, a relationship that has been largely ignored in the psychoanalytic literature. The second strand (Chapter 2) presents the basic tenets of ego psychology. The third strand of the book (Chapter 3) presents the major critiques of ego psychology, including its inadequate account of the role of object relations in psychological functioning and its failure to recognize the capacity for interpersonal understanding as a central ego function. The ego psychology of Freud, Hartmann, Rapaport, and others has relatively little to say about object relations beyond their link to drive gratification; and, along with other psychoanalytic schools, has relatively little to say regarding interpersonal understanding as a fundamental ego function.

The fourth strand (Chapter 4) identifies the necessary correctives and revisions of ego psychology. The fifth (Chapter 5) strand of the book deals with interpersonal reality-testing as an ego function. The sixth strand (Chapter 6) presents a sampling of research on interpersonal and social understanding. The seventh strand (Chapter 7) discusses aims and motives associated with ego functioning. The eighth strand (Chapter 8) deals with psychoanalytic theories of affect and affect regulation. The ninth strand (Chapter 9) presents a sampling of research on affect regulation. The tenth strand (Chapter 10) discusses the implications of an ego psychology perspective for conceptions of psychopathology. The eleventh (Chapter 11) discusses the implications of an ego psychology perspective for psychoanalytic treatment. And finally, the twelfth strand of the book (Chapter 12) addresses arguments for pluralism and presents the case for a revised and expanded ego psychology as the foundation for a unified psychoanalytic theory.

1

Ego psychology in Freudian theory

The concepts of ego and ego function are already present in Freud's earliest writings and play a critical role in his development of psychoanalytic theory. As a central aspect of the *Project*, in which, as Strachey (1950 [1895]) observes in the Editor's introducion to the *Project,* Freud attempted "a description of mental phenomena in physiological terms" (Freud, 1950 [1895], p. 292, Editor's comments), he posited an ego structure, a main function of which is the *inhibition* of the flow of excitation from one neuron to another (Freud, 1950 [1895], pp. 323–324). Although Freud abandoned the *Project*, in his subsequent writings, he retained the central idea of a structure – the ego – that serves delay and inhibitory functions, inhibition now formulated in psychological rather than neurological language. As Strachey (1950 [1895]) writes, "In spite of being ostensibly a neurological document, the *Project* contains within itself the nucleus of a great part of Freud's later psychological theories" (p. 290). Indeed, the birth of psychoanalysis is marked by the introduction of the concept of "defense hysteria" and the "cornerstone" concept of repression, which can be understood as an inhibitory ego process that prevents the emergence of unacceptable mental contents in conscious awareness. Freud (1894, p. 47) also writes that repression is triggered by "an occurrence of incompatibility" between an idea and the ego, which not only marks the introduction of the central role of inner conflict in psychopathology but can also be seen as a proto-formulation of the later id-ego or drive-defense model.

In his later writings, Freud (1926 [1925]) described repressive defenses as essentially inhibitory processes that in response to small doses of anxiety (signal anxiety) keep certain mental contents that, were they to be consciously experienced, would trigger traumatic anxiety. Since Freud's original formulation, repression has been expanded to include not only the inhibition of anxiety-provoking mental contents, but also mental contents that may trigger other negative affects such as depression, guilt, shame, and threats to self-esteem (e.g., Brenner, 2002; Lewis, 1992; Morrison, 1989; Weiss & Sampson, 1986; Cramer, 2006, 2008, 2012). Thus, the essential function of repression and other defenses is to regulate negative affects through inhibitory processes that keep certain mental contents from being consciously experienced.

Capacity for inhibition as a fundamental psychological function

The importance of inhibition as a fundamental physiological and psychological process has a long history. For example, James (1890) wrote that inhibition is "not an occasional accident; it is an essential and unremitting element of our cerebral life" (p. 583). And much before that _Descartes (1649 [1989]) wrote that "if anger makes the hand rise in order to strike, the will can ordinarily restrain it; if fear incites the legs to flee, the will can stop them" (p. 44). As another example of an early interest in inhibition, Ferrier (1876) observed that "besides the power to act in response to feeling or desires there is also the power to inhibit or restrain action, notwithstanding the tendency of feelings and desires to manifest themselves in active motor outbursts" (p. 282). Virtually a description of the relationship between id and ego and anticipating contemporary research on individual differences in inhibitory capacity, Ferrier also wrote, "If the centers of inhibitory, and thereby the faculty of attention, are weak, or present impulses unusually strong, volition is impulsive rather than deliberate" (p. 287). (See Smith [1992] for an extensive history of the concept of inhibition; See also Bari and Robbins [2013] for a brief and very useful review of theory and research on inhibition).

An early inhibitory function that Freud (1900) focused on is the capacity to delay gratification, which he viewed as a hallmark of ego functioning. He speculated that following the experience of satisfaction after being fed, the next time the infant is hungry, s/he hallucinates the breast. Hallucinatory wish fulfillment was for Freud, a quintessential instance of lack of inhibitory capacity, that is, a mode of primary process functioning characterized by a direct path from impulse to immediate discharge. According to this account, because hallucination of the breast does not satisfy hunger, the infant turns to the actual breast, which entails a primitive recognition of means-ends relationships as well as the necessity of delay until one finds an actual need expression of the gradual shift in the course of development from the predominance of the pleasure principle, characterized by immediate gratification and discharge, to the predominance of the reality principle, characterized by inhibition and delay of discharge.[1]

To sum up, for Freud, ability to delay gratification is inextricably linked to one's capacity to function in accord with the reality principle. In contrast to immediate gratification, delay of gratification, including delay of actions taken to achieve gratification, entails planning, assessing the consequences of one's actions, and finding actual objects in reality necessary for gratification. Thus, from a psychoanalytic perspective, the ability to delay gratification is an important marker of the development of the ego and an important marker of intact ego functioning.[2]

Early research on the capacity for inhibition

The seminal idea of the ego as an inhibitory structure generated a good deal of psychoanalytically oriented research in the 1950s and 1960s, a period when the influence of ego psychology was predominant in psychoanalysis, at least in the United States. In one of the earliest papers on the research implications of the concepts of impulse control and delay of gratification, following a review of studies in that area, Singer (1955) concludes:

> The concept of delay or impulse control as a basic ego function affords also a highly significant contact point between psychoanalytic theory and general psychology. More than fifty years after its original pronouncement, Freud's theory of thought development is vigorously alive and beckons toward new vistas of research.
>
> (p. 265)

With the waning of interest in developing a psychoanalytic general theory of mind and, in particular a waning of the influence of ego psychology, these new vistas never materialized, at least not within psychoanalysis.

The central themes running through the research reviewed by Singer were the ideas, one, that there is an inverse relationship between inhibition of action and thought; and two, that the ability to inhibit action is systematically related to thinking, planning, and imaginative activity. Some examples of early studies include the demonstration of a relationship between the ability to inhibit a motor response (e.g., to write as slowly as possible) and the inhibition of a cognitive response (e.g., refrain from giving a learned response in a word association task) (Meltzoff & Levine, 1954); the finding that immobilization of movement is associated with greater readiness to perceive motion in the autokinetic phenomenon and heightened motor activity with less readiness to perceive motion (Goldman, 1953); the finding that, following periods of motor inhibition, a greater number of human movement responses (M) are given on the Rorschach (Meltzoff, Singer, & Korchin, 1953); a lack of planfulness and a relative absence of "normal inhibitory pattern" shown in institutionalized children (Goldfarb, 1945); the finding that "adequate inhibition ability is an important factor in earning a high score on the intelligence test" (Levine, Glass, & Meltzoff, 1957, p. 43); the finding that among emotionally disturbed boys in a residential treatment center, compared to boys who were more capable of responding to a long-term incentive, those boys who were less capable of responding to a long-term incentive tended to experience time as passing more slowly (Levine & Spivack, 1959).

Delay of gratification as an inhibitory capacity

Mischel and his colleagues embarked on an extremely fruitful series of investigations referred to as the Marshmallow test on the correlates of immediate gratification of lesser rewards versus delayed gratification of larger rewards – one aspect of inhibitory capacity. In his earliest 1958 study, Mischel found that in children aged 7 to 9, absence of father was associated with preference for immediate gratification. In his 1961 study Mischel cites Freud's (1922) "theoretical formulations [of] the 'pleasure principle' and the 'reality principle'" (p. 1). In that study involving children aged 12 to 14, preference for delayed gratification was associated with higher social responsibility scores. Also, compared to students in juvenile delinquency schools, a significantly larger number of students in a government elementary school preferred delayed over immediate gratification. The former group of students tended to choose immediate gratification and showed less accuracy in recall of the time of an event (the year of the last national election). Interestingly, as noted previously, although Mischel (1958) refers to Freud's distinction between the pleasure principle and the reality principle as a theoretical context for one of his early studies on delay of gratification, references to Freud drop out in subsequent studies.

The findings of these early studies suggest, one, that capacity to inhibit action is associated with greater cognitive activity; and two, that capacity to delay gratification (an inhibitory process) is associated with more adaptive behavior, including greater planfulness and social responsibility.

Later research on delay of gratification

Since Mischel's 1958 and 1961 studies, many investigations have been carried out on the ability to delay gratification. Later studies on inhibitory capacity include a wide range of concurrent correlates and longitudinal predictors of individual differences in self-control inhibitory behaviors and capacities. Correlates of delay of gratification, self-control, and other inhibitory capacities include better academic performance, fewer reports of psychopathology, higher self-esteem, less binge eating and alcohol use, secure attachment, better interpersonal skills (Tangney, Baumeister, & Boone, 2004; Jacobsen, Huss, Fendrich, Kruesi, & Ziegenhain, 1997; Gillath, Shaver, & Mikulincer, 2005), resiliency and social competence (Eisenberg et al., 2003; and ego resilience (Funder & Block, 1989). Poor ability to delay gratification has also been shown to be associated with borderline personality disorder (Ayduk et al., 2008); gender differences (Bjorklund & Kipp, 1996; Silverman, 2003); and severity of psychological disturbance (Shybut, 1968)

There is a good deal of evidence that the executive function of inhibitory control in children, particularly in tasks involving conflict between dominant and subdominant responses, is significantly associated with performance on theory of mind tasks (e.g., Carlson, Moses, & Claxton, 2004). Carlson et al. (2004) note that what is reflected in theory of mind tasks is being able to hold in mind multiple perspectives (which requires working memory capacity) and inhibition of irrelevant perspectives. Carlson, Davis, and Leach (2005) presented a "Less is More" task to toddlers who must point to a smaller reward (two candies) to receive a larger reward (five candies). Performance on this task was significantly associated with aggregate scores on executive function tasks (which include conflict, delay, and working memory). In a variation of this procedure, children carried out the "Less is More" task with symbolic substitutes (i.e., rocks, dots, and elephant versus mouse) that represented the candies. The fascinating results obtained were as follows: Whereas compared to the real candy treat, the children did not perform significantly better in the rocks and dots conditions, they did perform significantly better in the elephant versus mouse condition. As the authors note, whereas in the rocks and dots conditions the symbols remain closely related to the enticing treat – numerosity remains visually present and salient – in the elephant versus mouse condition, because the symbols are more distant from the real reward, they lead to the greatest capacity for delay.

Similar to the early research, the findings of later research also indicate that capacity for inhibitory control, including capacity to delay gratification, is generally associated with more adaptive behavior and that relative inability to delay gratification is associated with maladaptive behavior.

Longitudinal studies on individual differences in inhibitory capacity

In addition to concurrent correlates of individual differences in inhibitory capacity, a number of longitudinal studies have shown that early individual differences in inhibitory capacity predict various aspects of subsequent development. In one study by Mischel, Shoda, and Peake (1988), children who are about 4.5 years of age who showed a high ability to delay gratification were rated by their parents as more academically and socially competent, verbally fluent, rational, attentive, playful, and able to deal with frustration during adolescence.

In a study carried out by Berman et al. (2013), children who were first tested for delay of gratification at age 4 were re-examined 40 years later on a task that required control over the contents of working memory. In the task, six words were presented for storage in working memory. Participants were instructed to forget three of the six words. A probe word was then presented and participants had to indicate whether it was one of the three words to be stored. Sometimes a "lure" word was presented that was one of the words to be forgotten. The participants' reactions to these words were compared to control probe words that were not part of the six-word set. The results showed that compared to high delayers, low delayers were less accurate on this task and took longer to respond to "lure" than to control words. Berman et al. (2013) also obtained neural responses and report that compared to those classified as high delayers at age 4, low delayers "recruited neural networks less efficiently to achieve the same behavioral outcome" (p. 1375) when tested 40 years later. Berman et al. (2013) also reported the remarkable finding that one could predict with 71% accuracy whether a participant was a high or low delayer from the pattern of the neural data.

Drawing from the same sample as Berman et al. (2013), children who were tested for delay of gratification at age 4 were given a go/nogo task in their mid-40s in which they have to suppress a response to neutral, happy, and fearful faces Casey et al. (2011). The investigators found greater ventral striatal activity in low delayers in their attempt to suppress a response to the happy face, but not to a neutral or fearful face. This was interpreted as demonstrating the greater difficulty of low delayers in suppressing a response to "positive compelling cues" (p. 15001). Casey et al. (2011) note that the ventral striatal area of the brain is implicated in processing of desires and needs, as well as immediate versus delayed choice behavior. They also found "diminished recruitment of the right inferior frontal gyrus, which was involved in accurately suppressing a response" (p. 15001). Notably, the right inferior frontal cortex was associated with a correct inhibition of a response. The authors interpret their findings as indicating the stability of impulse control over time.

Schlam, Wilson, Shoda, Mischel, and Ayduk (2013) reported that performance on a delay of gratification task at age 4 accounted for a significant portion of variance in body mass index 30 years later. Eigsti et al. (2006) found that

> the proportion of time preschoolers directed their attention away from rewarding stimuli during a delay of gratification task was positively associated with efficacy (greater speed without reduced accuracy) at responding to targets in a go/no-go task more than 10 years later.
>
> (p. 478)

This latter finding indicates that capacity to inhibit action (through an attentional deployment strategy) in the context of delay of gratification in childhood is predictive of cognitive control in adolescence. Similar to the Schlam et al. (2013) finding, Seeyave et al. (2009) reported that preschoolers who chose an immediate reward were more likely to be overweight at 11 years of age.

There have been a number of studies which suggest that the relationship between ability to delay and later outcome in various areas of functioning may be more complex than reported in early papers. In a recent paper, Watts, Duncan, and Quan (2018) report the results of "A conceptual replication investigating the links between early delay of gratification and later outcomes" (the subtitle of their paper). Their focus is on the "famous marshmallow study" (p. 1) carried out by Shoda, Mischel, and Peake (1990). Although they successfully replicated the finding of a significant bivariate association between early delay (minutes waited) at 54 months of age and academic achievement at age 15, the strength of the association was "considerably less" (p. 9) than the one reported by Shoda et al. (1990). Furthermore, when variables including family background, home environment, and the children's early cognitive abilities (e.g., letter and word identification, picture vocabulary, memory for sentences) were controlled for, the overall relationship between delay of gratification at 54 months and achievement at age 15 was no longer significant.

For the subsample of children of mothers without a college degree, compared to children who were able to delay for at least 20 seconds, children who were not able to delay for at least 20 seconds did show significantly poorer achievement at age 15. Watts et al. (2018) suggest that with those children who do not wait at least 20 seconds, we are seeing mainly problems with impulse control, whereas with children who can wait longer than 20 seconds, cognitive ability factors play more of a role.

For the full sample of 918 children (including children of both degreed and non-degreed mothers), delay of gratification was associated with concurrent measures of attention, impulsivity (negatively), and self-control. As Watts et al. (2018) note, these results are congruent with Duckworth et al.'s (2013) finding, using the same data as those employed in the Watts et al. (2018) study, that "both self-control and intelligence mediated the relation between early delay ability and later outcomes" (p. 17).

What are the implications of Watt et al.'s finding that when one controls for early cognitive abilities, as well as other factors, delay of gratification at 54 months no longer significantly predicts achievement at age 15? Does it mean that early delay of gratification plays no role in influencing later behavior? Does this finding throw into question the host of findings to the effect that delay of gratification is significantly predictive of later adaptive behavior? I think the answer is that it does not. What the Watts et al. (2018) findings do suggest is that delay of gratification is a marker not only self-control, but also family background, cognitive abilities, and socioeconomic status. I will pursue this latter factor in Chapter 4. It also needs to be noted that the Watts et al. (2018) findings bear mainly on the

Shoda et al. (1990) and not on the remarkable longitudinal findings of the long-term longitudinal findings described previously.

Watts et al. (2018) are aware that a number of studies have "demonstrated that self-control – typically understood to be an umbrella construct that includes gratification delay but also impulsivity, conscientiousness, self-regulation and executive function – averaged across early and middle childhood, predicted outcomes across a host of domains (Moffitt et al., 2011)" (p. 2). Nevertheless, the rationale they offer for focusing on the Shoda et al. (1990) study is that "despite the proliferation of work on gratification delay, and the related construct of self-control, Mischel and Shoda's longitudinal studies still stand as the foundational examinations of the long run correlates of the ability to delay gratification in early childhood" (p. 2). However, the Shoda et al. (1990) study, as well as the Mischel and Shoda's longitudinal studies, are foundational mainly in terms of the time of their appearance and their role in generating a great deal of research in this area, not in any other sense. A consequence of Watts et al.'s (2018) focus on the Shoda et al. (1990) study is that they do not adequately address the discrepancies between their findings and those of other studies in the area.

The Watts et al. (2018) study notwithstanding, the longitudinal studies discussed previously have provided some striking findings on the ability of measures of inhibitory capacity at a young age to predict later behaviors ranging from academic and social competence, cognitive control, obesity, and neural efficiency with regard to the control of the contents of working memory. The findings of the Watts et al. (2018) have alerted us to the fact that delay of gratification is a complex construct and may represent a "marker" for cognitive abilities as well as for self-control. These findings are highly relevant to the general claim of psychoanalytic ego psychology regarding the relationship between adequacy of ego functions and adaptive behavior. (I will pursue this issue further in Chapter 2.)

Factors that influence inhibitory capacity

A number of studies have been carried out on factors that influence one's capacity for delay of gratification, self-control, and other inhibitory behaviors. They include both internally generated strategies (e.g., distracting oneself) as well as external experimental interventions (e.g., experimental instruction to engage in a particular activity) factors, such as strategies generated through external interventions. As an example of the former, there is evidence that toddlers who spontaneously used attentional distraction strategies during a brief separation from mother were able to delay gratification longer for more valued rewards (Sethi, Mischel, Aber, Shoda, & Rodriguez, 2000), suggesting that these strategies are effective in enabling the child to better tolerate various forms of frustration.

As an example of an external factor, there is evidence that, whereas attention to the reward decreases delay, providing an intervention, such as distraction or presenting an image of the reward rather than the actual reward during the waiting period, serves to enhance delay (Mischel & Moore, 1973; Mischel, Shoda, & Rodriguez, 1989). Further, the more distant the symbol is from the actual reward, the greater the delay (Carlson & Zelazo, 2011). These are important findings. For one thing, whereas impulsivity in the presence of the actual reward makes immediate gratification more likely, this is not the case with an image of the reward – one cannot eat an image of food. Also, an image of the reward entails the insertion of intervening cognitive-symbolic processes between the impulse and the reward. The finding that attention to an image of the reward rather than the reward itself serves to support self-control is congruent with Lieberman et al.'s (2007; Torre & Lieberman, 2018) finding that the mere *labeling* of an emotional stimulus serves to dampen amygdala activity and enhance prefrontal cortex activity.

As another example of an external factor, Leonard, Berkowitz, and Shusterman (2006) reported that compared to a control condition, simply a touch on the back of the child accompanying the instruction to wait for permission before eating a candy resulted in preschool children waiting two minutes longer. There is a good deal of evidence that a pleasant touch facilitates social behavior ranging from school children's compliant behavior to restaurant tipping (Crusco & Wetzel, 1984). More directly relevant in the present context, Ogden, Moore, Redfern, and McGlone (2015) reported that a gentle stroking touch resulted in shorter estimates of the temporal duration of a neutral visual stimulus.

As an example of an internal factor, there is evidence that both the child's generalized trust, that is, the extent to which others are viewed as trustworthy, as well as trust in the specific individual promising the future reward, are related to delay of gratification (Ma, Chen, Xu, Lee, & Heyman, 2018). As Ma et al. (2018) note, these results suggest that "there is more to delay of gratification than cognitive capacity" (p. 118). Combining the previous results on the effects of touch with the results reported by Ma et al. (2018), it may be the case that touch influences delay through its enhancement of trust. Kidd, Palmeri, and Aslin (2013) found that delay of gratification is influenced by the child's beliefs about environmental reliability. They note that delay of gratification "may not only reflect differences in self-control abilities, but also beliefs about the stability of the world" (p. 109).

In a summary of factors that enhance delay, Mischel et al. (2011) write that "broadly speaking [effective strategies] involve redirection of attentional focus or altering the cognitive representation of the object of temptation [i.e., cognitive reappraisal]" (p. 253). As an example of the former, simply looking away can enhance delay; and, as an example of the latter, imagining the marshmallow reward as a cotton ball rather than as a tasty treat enhances delay. And as an example of the use of both an attentional and a reframing strategy, focusing attention on the object's non-consummatory features (e.g., its shape) rather than its consummatory features (e.g., its taste) enhances delay.[3]

Representative research on executive functions in cognitive psychology

There is a good deal of research on executive functions other than delay of gratification. The term "executive function" includes a variety of cognitive operations such as ability to shift, working memory, and attentional control. The components of executive function include attentional focus and control; task persistence; working memory; ability to inhibit a prepotent response; ability to shift tasks; ability to delay gratification; impulse control; and regulation of negative affects. As can be seen, there is a goodly degree of overlap between the concepts of executive functions and ego functions. Indeed, earlier research carried out under the rubrics of "ego strength" and "ego weakness" (e.g., Block & Block, 1980) can be viewed as research on executive functions. The studies described earlier on delay of gratification and inhibitory capacity are obvious examples of research on executive functions (and ego functions) having to do with delay of gratification and other inhibitory capacity. In this section, I will describe some additional representative studies on executive functions other than delay of gratification.

Concurrent correlates of inhibitory capacity

Following are some representative examples of studies of concurrent correlates of inhibitory capacity: Inhibitory control in 3- and 4-year-old children was positively associated with their performance on theory of mind tasks (false beliefs; appearance-reality) (Carlson et al., 2004). A significant association was found between inhibitory control of a prepotent response and ability to regulate emotions in 4- to 6-year-old children (Carslon & Wang, 2007). Especially interesting is the finding that optimal emotion regulation is associated with an intermediate level of inhibitory ability (I will return to this issue later in the paper). Scult, Knodt, Swartz, Brigidi, and Hariri (2017) reported that pre-frontal cortical activity during a "cold" (mathematical) task involving working memory was associated with the use of cognitive appraisal in emotion regulation, suggesting a general executive function factor across "hot" and "cold" contexts.

Based on a discriminant functional analysis, Wolfe &and Bell (2004) found that a combination of the independent variables of EEG pattern, heart rate, language, and temperament related to self-control correctly predicted 90% of performance on tasks that tapped working memory and inhibitory control. And finally, in a longitudinal study of children assessed at 3, 4, 7, 11, 14, 18, and 23 years of age, Kremen and Block (1998) reported that personality descriptions of the children in nursery school were significantly associated with assessment of ego control in adulthood.

Kochanska, Murray, and Coy (1997) reported that inhibitory control as a toddler was associated with the development of conscience at school age. Kubzansky, Martin, and Buka (2009) reported a significant relationship between ability to stay focused on a task at age 7 and physical health 30 years later, even when controlling for childhood social environment and childhood health. Similar to Kubzansky et al.'s (2009) finding regarding physical health, Appleton et al. (2011) found that impulsivity versus capacity for inhibition at age 7 was significantly associated with C-reactive protein (CRP; an inflammatory agent) in middle adulthood.

Carlson et al. (2004) found that, compared to the more restrained group, the group that was less restrained on a do-not-touch task as children had significantly lower scores on executive function at age 17. In a longitudinal study of more than 900 children at age 3, Newman, Caspi, Moffitt, and Silva (1997) were able to identify five distinct groups of children based on behavioral observations: well-adjusted, undercontrolled, reserved, confident, and inhibited. Their interpersonal functioning was then assessed at age 21. The findings of interest in the present context are that the undercontrolled children (low inhibitory capacity) showed lower levels of adjustment and greater interpersonal difficulties than any of the other groups. Another interesting finding was that children who were identified as inhibited had at age 21 relatively healthy romantic relationships, better interpersonal adjustment at work, and little anti-social behavior. This finding is of special interest insofar as the major focus of research in this area has been on the correlates of relative failure of inhibition. As I will discuss later, there is little work on the correlates of what might be viewed as excessive inhibition. We do not know the degree of inhibition shown by the group classified as inhibited. (I will have more to say on this topic later).

Moffit et al. (2007) followed a cohort of 1,000 children from birth to age 32, as well as 500 zygotic twins from age 3.5 to age 12. With regard to the first sample, they found that measures of self-control during the first ten years predicted the following outcomes at age 32 even when controlling for socioeconomic status (SES) and IQ, physical health: substance dependence, financial condition, single parenthood, and criminal convictions. As for the 500 sibling pairs, the 5-year-old siblings with poorer self-control were more likely at age 12 to begin smoking, perform more poorly at school, and engage in anti-social behavior.

A number of studies have been carried out on the relationship between parenting style and the child's executive functioning. Meuwissen and Carlson (2015) reported that a father's controlling parenting during play with his 3-year-old was inversely related to the child's composite executive function scores, which included inhibitory control, capacity for delay, set switching, and working memory. Bernier, Carlson, and Whipple (2010) and Matte-Gagné and Bernier (2011) reported that measures of maternal sensitivity, mind-mindedness, and autonomy support when children were 12 to 15 months of age was significantly associated with executive function, including impulse control, when the children were 18 to 26 months of age. Especially interesting is the finding that parental autonomy support was the strongest predictor of the child's executive function. As the authors note, autonomy support facilitates the developmental transition from external regulation to increasing self-regulation. They also found that the child's expressive vocabulary (an internal factor) plays a mediating role in the relationship between maternal support for autonomy (an external factor) and the child's impulse control. This is but one example of the influence of situational and interpersonal factors on ego functions, an issue I will discuss later.

There is evidence that attentional control in infants and toddlers, including the ability to shift attentional focus and to maintain attentional persistence, are associated with less negative emotionality and greater regulation of negative emotions (Rothbart, Ziaie, & O'Boyle, 1992; Wilson & Matheny, 1983; Matheny, Riese, & Wilson, 1985; Kochanska, Coy, Tjebkes, & Husarek, 1998). Building on this work, Belsky, Friedman, and Hsieh (2003) reported that although negative emotionality at 15 months predicted lower social competence at age 3, this was true only for those children who were low in attentional persistence (during play). In other words, whereas low attentional persistence is a risk factor for the effect of negative emotionality on social competence, high attentional persistence is a protective factor in modulating the effects of negative emotionality on social competence. In the present context, the point to be made is that greater control of attention deployment, as manifested in attentional persistence, is associated with lower negative emotionality and a higher level of social competence. Thus, we see an association between a basic ego function – control of attention deployment – and adaptive behaviors (See Singer & Sincoff, 1990, for a conception of defense in terms of deployment of attention; See also Rapaport, 1951, p. 699, for a similar conception).

Although I am not suggesting any direct or indirect influence, one can see a thematic red thread from the early focus on ego strength and ego weakness to research on executive functioning in cognitive psychology. Both perspectives share an emphasis on investigating functions necessary for adequate adaptation. This shared theme opens up the potential enrichment of both disciplines through the assimilation of findings on executive functions into ego psychology; and in the reverse direction, through the enrichment of research and theory on executive functions provided by the psychoanalytic focus on effective and dynamic factors (e.g., unresolved conflict; early emotional trauma) on executive function.

Can inhibitory behavior be maladaptive?

As we have seen, virtually all the research on delay of gratification deals with the maladaptive correlates of failure to delay gratification. And in virtually all of the studies discussed, inhibitory capacities such as delay of gratification and self-control, are found to be predictive both of other con-current adaptive behavior (e.g., social competence) and adaptive behavior later in life. That is, greater self-control (e.g., longer period of delay) is consistently shown to be more adaptive than lesser self-control or under-control (e.g., shorter period of delay). These findings provide support for a fundamental proposition of psychoanalytic ego psychology regarding the adaptive value of the ego function of inhibition of immediate discharge, which allows the individual to plan and consider the reality consequences of his or her actions, an important aspect of reality-testing.

There is, however, virtually no research that deals systematically with the question of whether an excessive delay of gratification can be maladaptive. In one study on the relationship between observations of children at age and assessments at age 21, Caspi, Moffitt, Newman, and Silva (1996) reported that the investigators were able to reliably classify the children into one of five groups, the following three of which are of special interest: undercontrolled, inhibited, and well-adjusted (the other two groups were confident and reserved).

Although the relationships were modest, children who were classified as undercontrolled and inhibited at age 3 were most likely to be diag-nosed with a psychiatric disorder at age 21 and were the most severely impaired by this disorder. Undercontrolled children were more likely to be diagnosed with antisocial personality disorder as adults, more likely to be convicted of a violent offense, and more likely to be repeat offend-ers. Inhibited children were more likely to be diagnosed with depression (but not anxiety) and, unexpectedly, were also more likely to be convicted of a violent offense as adults. However, this was true only for boys who, compared to the undercontrolled group, were more likely to be one-time offenders. Other findings include the following: undercontrolled boys were more likely to have alcohol dependence as adults; both undercon-trolled and inhibited boys were more likely to have alcohol-related prob-lems as adults; both undercontrolled and inhibited children made more suicide attempts as adults. Remarkably, undercontrolled children were 16.8 times more likely to make suicide attempts as adults compared to the well-adjusted children; and inhibited children 6.5 times as likely.

This is one of the few studies that includes not only undercontrolled impulsive children, but also inhibited children. The finding that inhibited children are more likely to have problems in adulthood is especially inter-esting from an ego psychology perspective. It suggests that it is not only relative lack of inhibition and control (i.e., impulsivity) that is maladaptive, but also *excessive control and inhibition*. The far greater emphasis in the literature is on impulsivity and undercontrol, perhaps because failure of inhibition and self-control is a more obvious social threat than excessive inhibition and self-control. However, from an ego psychology perspective, either extreme is maladaptive and reflects some form of ego impairment. It is *ego flexibility*, that is, the capacity to disinhibit as well as inhibit that is adaptive.

From a psychoanalytic perspective, insofar as delay to the point of failure of gratification is pathological, a question that would arise is whether there is a degree of inhibition that impairs capacity for gratification and capacity to act and is therefore maladaptive rather than adaptive. As far as I am aware, there are no parametric studies in the research literature treating inhibitory behavior as existing on a continuum ranging from undercontrol to over-control, which would allow one to address the question of whether "over-control" is as maladaptive, albeit perhaps in different ways, as under-control. For example, does an inverted U curve describe the adaptive nature of degree of control?

I am familiar with only a few studies that focus on the maladaptive aspects of excessive inhibition. In one study Pinto, Steinglass, Greene, Weber, and Simpson (2014) reported that obsessive compulsive personality disorder (OCPD) show an "excessive capacity to delay reward . . . and is associated with perfectionism and rigidity" (p. 653). They conclude that the delay of gratification "component of self-control lies on a continuum in which *both* extremes (impulsivity and over-control) contribute to psychopathology" (p. 653). Dombrovski et al. (2010) found that, whereas low-lethality suicide attempts were associated with immediate gratification, high-lethality suicide attempts were associated with greater delay of gratification. Also, "better planned suicide attempts . . . were associated with willingness to wait for larger rewards" (p. 138).

There are familiar figures in literature for whom excessive delay inhibits gratification and for whom excessive inhibition, often in the form of ruminative thought, inhibits action toward a goal. They include, for example, Shakespeare's Hamlet, who is paralyzed by his inability to act; the protagonist in Henry James' *Beast in the Jungle*, whose life passes him by as he waits for the great event to occur; and Melville's *Bartleby the Scrivener*, whose refrain of "I'd rather not" expresses a refusal to act on virtually every occasion. In the real world, every clinician has encountered patients whose behavior patterns include such features as excessive inhibition and delay, relative failure to experience pleasure and gratification, and failure to take action in the pursuit of goals. Indeed, from a classic psychoanalytic perspective, neurosis is understood more as a problem of excessive inhibition, over-socialization, and relative inability to experience gratification due to conflict, guilt, and anxiety than a problem of failure of inhibition. Consider, for example, anorexia nervosa, which is marked by a pathological inhibition of normal eating behavior and feelings of hunger. Or consider individuals whose conflicts, anxiety, and guilt in relation to sexual impulses leads to inhibition of sexual feelings and a relative incapacity to experience sexual gratification or what Freud (1912 [1957]) referred to as "psychic impotence" (p. 180). These phenomena entail *excessive* inhibition rather than incapacity for inhibition.

What over-controlled individuals appear to have in common with under-controlled individuals is an *impairment* in the flexibility of the inhibitory function, even if the impairment is expressed at opposite ends of the control continuum and is associated with different maladaptive consequences (e.g., externalizing versus internalizing problems). For over-controlled individuals, it is, perhaps, misleading to speak of *capacity* or *ability* to inhibit or delay gratification, which suggests some degree of choice. In fact, many over-controlled individuals cannot help but inhibit or delay. From an ego psychology perspective, such behavior reflects ego rigidity as opposed to ego flexibility, the latter implying the capacity for either immediate gratification and action or delay of gratification and inhibition of action as a function of the adaptive context. Another way to put it is to say that ego flexibility implies both a capacity for delay, inhibition, and control as well as a capacity for gratification and relinquishment of inhibition and control. This is in contrast to both the individual who cannot control, delay, or inhibit as well as the individual who cannot relinquish delay, control, and inhibition, that is, who can do nothing but delay, control, and inhibit. In extreme cases, such individuals appear to forgo any experience of gratification and any effective action toward a goal.

From an ego psychology perspective, ego strength is equally reflected in an ability to *relinquish* control as well as to exert control. Implicit in the concept unfortunately labeled "regression in the service of the ego" (Kris, 1952) is the idea that it is ego *flexibility* regarding control that is adaptive in contrast to either under-control or over-control.[4] I will have more to say regarding the issue of ego flexibility in Chapter 2.

Notes

1 There is no evidence that infants actually hallucinate the breast when hungry. Indeed, immediately after birth, infants show the rooting reflex, that is, automatically turn their face toward the stimulus and make sucking movements when their lip or cheek is touched. The notion of hallucination of the breast is best understood, not as an actual event, but as a metaphor for the idea of immediate gratification.

2 Although, as is evident in his emphasis on delay of gratification, Freud's focus is on the inhibitory function of the ego, reality-testing and adaptive behavior entail more than simply inhibition. As we will see in Chapter 2, ego psychology identifies a range of ego functions that play an important role in adaptation to the environment.

3 One might think of what Mischel et al. (2011) refer to as altering the cognitive representation of the tempting object, as well as focusing attention on non-consummatory features of the tempting object as analogous to the defense of intellectualization. Or perhaps one should say that these strategies are specific examples of how intellectualization is implemented.

4 I say "unfortunately" because of the pathogenic connotations of the term "regression". The ability to relinquish ego control has little necessary connection to regression.

2

Psychoanalytic ego psychology
Basic tenets

The emergence and hegemony of ego psychology in the United States

Wallerstein (2002) writes that "the roots of ego psychology trace back to Sigmund Freud's *The Ego and the Id* (1923) and *Inhibitions, Symptoms and Anxiety* (1926)" (p. 135). Although it is in *The Ego and the Id* that the foundation for an ego psychology is clearly delineated, I think the roots of ego psychology can be traced back earlier. The concepts of ego and ego functioning are present early in Freud's writings and play a critical role in his further theorizing. The formulation of an incompatibility between an idea and the ego and the role of repression in the development of "defense hysteria" can be seen as a pre-drive proto-formulation of the later id-ego and drive-defense model.

It is with the advent of drive theory, along with the formulation of a structural model of the mind, as reflected in Freud's 1923 *The Ego and the Id* and 1926 *Symptoms, Inhibitions, and Anxiety*, that an explicit and delineated conception of the ego and ego functions is established. Freud (1923) writes:

> We have found the idea that in each individual there is a coherent organization of mental processes; and we call this his ego. It is to this ego that consciousness is attached; the ego controls the approaches to motility . . . it is the mental agency which supervises all its own constituent processes.
>
> (p. 17)

An ego psychology perspective was then developed further by Anna Freud's 1936 *The Ego and the Mechanisms of Defense*, where the primary emphasis is on the ego function of defense, as well as by Hartmann (e.g., 1939), Rapaport (e.g., 1959), and others.[1] As Wallerstein (2002) observes, an ego psychology perspective "maintained a monolithic hegemony over American psychoanalysis" (p. 135) "through the 1950's and 1960's, and even into the 1970's" (p. 144).

Central tenets of ego psychology

The ego as an organ of adaptation

According to Hartmann (1950), "the estrangement with reality, so characteristic of the id of the human" (p. 79) requires the development of "a specific organ of adaptation" (Hartmann, 1948, p. 52) – the ego. Like Freud, Hartmann (1950) refers to both the ego's superordinate organizing function as well as specific ego functions such as delay of discharge, anticipation of danger, and relative "independence from the impact of present stimuli" (p. 75).[2] As Friedman (1989) has pointed out, it would be a mistake to attribute to ego psychology the proposition that adaptive behavior is always characterized by rationality. Rather, as a superordinate organizing structure, the ego organizes non-rational trends such as habits, traditions, and drive impulses that "trend in some way toward our purposes" (p. 538).

It is important to note that Hartmann does not limit the concept of adaptation to the realistic satisfaction of drives, but also includes the importance of adapting to the larger society. He writes that "the crucial adaptation man has to make is to the social structure, and his collaboration in building it" (Hartmann, 1939, p. 31). However, as we will see, Hartmann does not take the next step of developing the implication that the social nature of adaptation requires that ego functioning include interpersonal and social understanding, that is, interpersonal reality-testing. He also recognizes that "the social locus . . . of the individual codetermine[s] the possibilities of adaptation and also regulate in part the elaboration of the instinctual drives and the development of the ego" (p. 31). Far more than Freud, Hartmann recognized and wrote about the role of the larger society in ego functioning and the nature of adaptive requirements. It is my impression that this aspect of Hartmann's writings is relatively neglected.

Ego psychology as a foundation for a general theory of the mind

Hartmann's vision of psychoanalysis was not simply (and not primarily) as a form of treatment, but also and perhaps mainly as a general theory of mental functioning. He attributes a similar perspective to Freud when he refers to a "trend in the work of Freud and many of his followers, which aims at the more comprehensive conception of analysis as a general psychology" (Hartmann, 1950, p. 77). A central expression of that ambition is seen in the prominence given by Hartmann to an adaptive point of view as a fundamental perspective of psychoanalytic theory. For Hartmann and other ego psychologists, the emphasis on adaptation led naturally to a focus on the ego and ego functioning (p. 82). As an "organ of adaptation", the ego mediates between the pressures of immediate discharge and the adaptive demands of reality, which requires delay and planning.[3]

Ego autonomy from drives

From an ego psychology perspective, in order to carry out its adaptive function adequately, the ego must be free of excessive influence from the peremptory pressures of the drives for immediate blind discharge. As A. Freud (1945) put it in somewhat extreme form, the ego must become as reliable as a "mechanical apparatus" (p. 144) if it is to control unruly drive impulses, which, if acted upon, may be inimical to the adaptive interests of the individual. One can see the logical path from the focus on adaptation to the positing of ego autonomy. Implicit in the notion of ego autonomy is the seemingly paradoxical idea that in order for ego functions to be successful in meeting our needs in a realistic way, they must be relatively autonomous, that is, relatively free of excessive influence from needs and drives. In the language of ordinary discourse, one would say that assessments of reality must not be contaminated by wishful thinking driven by drive aims. This consideration is central to the concept of ego autonomy. Thus, at the heart of Hartmann's and other ego psychologists' concept of ego autonomy is the idea that if the ego is to gratify drives in a realistic and adaptive way, it must function relatively autonomously of the influence of drives.

According to a structural perspective, a primary impediment to adaptive ego functioning is its embeddedness in conflicts surrounding forbidden sexual and aggressive wishes. In the further development of ego psychology, it articulates a logical implication of this model by defining intact ego functioning in terms of relative autonomy from the conflict surrounding drive-related wishes. Thus, the assumption made in ego psychology, as reflected in the terms "ego autonomy" and "conflict-free spheres of functioning", is that, ideally, adaptive ego functioning is characterized by relative freedom from influence by wishes and desires and from enmeshment in conflict. Such autonomy allows reality-oriented rather than wishful thinking (that is, thinking that is contaminated by wishes and desires) or defensive thinking (that is, thinking reflecting the contamination of thought motivated by the avoidance of negative affect).

Hartmann posits two forms of ego autonomy: primary and secondary.

Primary autonomy

As we have seen, according to Freudian theory, reality-testing, a primary ego function, emerges only because hallucinatory wish fulfillment does not succeed in leading to drive gratification. For example, Freud (1900) writes that thinking, including a grasp of the means-ends relationship between drive and object (or stated differently, between desire and actions and the objects necessary to gratify desire) develops when it becomes clear that hallucinatory wish fulfillment does not serve to gratify desire or need. However, according to Freud, thinking is only a roundabout or detour means of gratifying desire and need. Freud (1900) writes that

> all the complicated thought-activity which is spun out from the mnemic image to the moment at which the perceptual identity is established by the external world – all this activity of thought merely constitutes a roundabout path to wish-fulfillment which has been made necessary by experience. Thought is after all nothing but a substitute for a hallucinating wish.

> (pp. 605–606)

The clear implication is that were we living in a science fiction world in which wishing makes it so, that is, would be sufficient to gratify desire, we would never develop the capacity for thinking.

Hartmann (1939) recognized that the problem with this formulation is that it fails to take account of the fact that certain "inborn apparatuses"

(p. 49) such as the capacity for thinking, motility, perception, and memory, develop and mature at a predictable rate in "average expectable environmental conditions" (p. 46) independently of drive gratification.[4] That is, he recognized that Freud's formulation left no room for the existence of "inborn apparatuses" that are adapted to reality and that develop according to maturational processes in a wide range of environments. These "inborn apparatuses", according to Hartmann, have a *primary autonomy*. Hartmann (1939) developed this idea further by stating, in discussing the relationship between "the needs for self-preservation" and the external world, that "the reality principle in the broader sense would historically precede and hierarchically outrank the pleasure principle" (p. 44). On this view, one would have to say that hallucination of the breast is not likely to be an accurate description of the infant's early feeding behavior.[5]

Secondary autonomy

Secondary autonomy refers to functions and behaviors that may have arisen in the context of conflicts surrounding drive impulses (e.g., defenses), but have achieved autonomy from their original context and function. For example, intellectual interests that may have originated in the context of intellectualization as a defense but are now pursued in their own right. It will be recognized that the concept of secondary autonomy bears a strong family resemblance to Allport's (1937) formulation of "the functional autonomy of motives" (p. 141), which also states that, although arising in one context, a given behaviour may come to serve a function that is relatively independent of its original function.

Different ego functions

As we have seen in Chapter 1, the main ego functions that Freud identified are the ability to delay gratification, reality-testing, and defense.

With the advent of ego psychology, a number of attempts were made to identify and assess different ego functions. One of the most systematic and ambitious attempts was made by Bellak and his colleagues. Based on a standardized 2-hr. interview or sessions of psychodynamic psychotherapy, clinicians rated ego functions of schizophrenic, neurotic, and normal individuals (Bellak, Hurvich, & Gediman, 1973) as well as changes in ego functioning following psychodynamic combined with drug therapy

(Bellak et al., 1973). Following is a list of 12 ego functions identified by Bellak and Meyers (1975):

(1) Reality-testing
(2) Judgment
(3) Sense of reality
(4) Regulation of control of drives
(5) Object relations[6]

(6) Thought process
(7) Adaptive regression in the service of the ego (ARISE)
(8) Defense function
(9) Stimulus barrier
(10) Autonomous function
(11) Synthetic function
(12) Sense of mastery and competence

In attempting to assess "structural change" in treatment, a number of researchers (e.g., Zilberg, Wallerstein, DeWitt, Hartley, and Rosenberg (1991) developed a set of scales of "psychological capacities", some of which bear a strong family resemblance to ego functions. They include "self-esteem"; "self-organization"; "commitment to reality"; "affect tolerance"; "impulse regulation"; and "effectance and mastery". As we will see, many of the ego functions identified in ego psychology are similar to those described as executive functions in cognitive psychology. Indeed, the terms "executive functions" and ego structure both refer to organizing processes in the personality.

The concept of ego strength

Influenced by the emergence of ego psychology, a good deal of research was carried out on the development of scales of "ego strength", which can be seen as precursors of research on executive function in cognitive psychology. The most well known of these early projects was Barron's (1953) attempt to measure "ego strength" through a scale derived from the Minnesota Multiphasic Psychological Inventory (MMPI). Karush, Easser, Cooper, and Swerdloff (1964) attempted to evaluate "ego strength" from clinical interviews. However, their categories were overly impressionistic and were not especially useful for a systematic exploration.

A good deal of research has been carried out linking ego strength to a wide range of behaviors.[7] Barron (1953) suggested the possible use of ego strength as "a predictor in any situation in which an estimate of personal adaptability and resourcefulness is called for" (p. 327). Following are some representative examples of studies on ego strength: Barron (1953) demonstrated that the MMPI-derived measure of ego strength specifically predicted response to psychotherapy. In a series of studies investigating the relationship between Barron's ego strength scale and physiological responsivity (as measured by skin resistance, finger blood volume, heart rate, and muscle potential responses to sound), Roessler, Alexander, and Greenfield's (1963), Greenfield, Katz, Alexander, and Roessler (1963), and Alexander, Roessler, and Greenfield (1963) found that high ego strength was associated with greater magnitude of physiological responses. Pfaehler and Roessler (1965) that high ego strength was associated with "significantly greater blood glucose volume" (p. 431). Based on Barron's ego strength scale, Milner's (1988) developed his own ego strength scale which was able to discriminate between nurturing parents from parents engaged in child abuse. Lees-Haley (1992) reported that an MMPI scale of ego strength contributed to the detection of spurious PTSD claims. Bagby, Taylor, and Parker (1988) demonstrated an inverse relationship between ego strength and alexithymia.

More recently, a number of studies have been carried out on what has been referred to as *ego depletion*, that is, fluctuations in ego functioning associated with different organismic conditions and behaviors. The basic hypothesis proposed by Baumeister and his colleagues (e.g., Baumeister, Brataslavsky, Muraven, & Tice, 1998) is that, like a muscle, mental resources can tire and become depleted as a function of various conditions and behaviors (e.g., fatigue, extended effort, prolonged suppression of emotion, etc.). According to Baumeister and his colleagues, the consequences of such depletion include impairments in various areas of ego functioning, including self-control. As an example of this phenomenon, Kahan, Polivy, and Herman (2003) found that the depletion of ego strength undermines dietary restraint.

There is a good deal of controversy in this area generated by failures to replicate findings. In a meta-analysis of 83 studies on the effects of ego depletion on task performance, Hagger, Wood, Stiff, and Chatzisarantis (2010) found "no significant effect sizes . . . for ego depletion on effort, perceived difficulty, negative affect, subjective fatigue, and blood glucose levels" (p. 495). No evidence of ego-depletion was also reported by Lurquin et al. (2106). (See, however, Baumeister & Vohs, 2007.)

As a final example of research on ego functioning, Watson and Clark (1984) reported that diverse personality scales, including trait anxiety, neuroticism, and ego strength, essentially measure "the same pervasive and stable trait" (p. 465), namely *negative affectivity*, which the authors describe as the "experience [of] discomfort at all times and across situations, even in the absence of overt stress" and the tendency "to dwell on the negative side of themselves and the world" (p. 465). From an ego psychology perspective, pervasive negative affectivity can be understood as an impairment in the fundamental ego function of affect regulation. As noted in Chapter 9, pervasive negative affectivity is also viewed as a general factor common to a wide range of psychopathology.

As can be seen from the preceding account, the psychoanalytic concepts of ego functions and ego strength have stimulated a good deal of psychological research. With the waning of the influence of ego psychology, much of this research, particularly research on ego strength, came to a virtual halt. However, as we will see in Chapter 4, outside the domain of psychoanalysis, research and theory are flourishing in the area of *executive functions*, a concept that bears a close family resemblance to the concept of ego functions.

Hartmann's main contributions to the project of developing psychoanalysis into a general theory of mental functioning lay in: (1) the explicit addition of an adaptive point of view as a fundamental perspective to psychoanalytic theory, which generated a broadened conception of the ego and ego functions; (2) the introduction and development of the concept of ego autonomy; (3) setting the stage for the further delineation of different ego functions and the facilitation of research in this area; (4) the implication that the adequacy of ego functions, including the degree and range of "conflict-free" functioning, are central criteria for assessing degree of psychopathology versus mental health; and (5) the additional implication of ego psychology that ego strengthening, operationally defined as the enhancement of various ego functions, is an overriding aim of psychoanalytic treatment.

The waning of ego psychology

Central concepts of ego psychology were never accepted by some analysts, including Continental and Latin American analysts who viewed it as introducing essentially *non-motivational* factors into psychoanalytic theory and thereby diluting a psychoanalytic perspective. The positing of the "conflict-free" sphere of the ego and of the autonomy of the ego from drives, with the implication that adaptive ego functioning is characterized by relative freedom from influence by wishes and desires and from enmeshment in conflict, was unacceptable to these analysts.

After the mid-1970s, psychoanalytic interest in the concept of ego functions as well as in ego psychology in general waned. Indeed, when I recently asked a representative group of psychoanalysts to identify five or six core psychoanalytic concepts and formulations, not a single respondent named ego functions [Eagle, 2018a). The waning of the influence of ego psychology coincided with the emergence of new psychoanalytic *schools*, such as self psychology, object relations theory, and relational psychoanalysis, which replaced the dominance of ego psychology. For the most part, these new *schools*, which are more closely tied to the clinical situation and, perforce, narrower in scope, essentially relinquished the aim of Freud and the ego psychologists to develop a general theory of mind. One consequence was a markedly reduced interest in concepts and formulations, such as reality testing and delay of gratification, that addressed vital areas of mental functioning. Another consequence was a loss of interest in research on ego functions.

Another related reason for the waning influence of ego psychology lies in its origins and theoretical location in an id-ego model of the mind. With the rejection of drive theory as a common theme shared by the newer psychoanalytic *schools*, it became more difficult to maintain a theoretical focus on the ego, a main function of which, according to classical theory, is the control and channeling of drive impulses. One consequence of the rejection of drive theory was that the id-ego or drive-defense model as the basis for a psychoanalytic theory of mind was replaced by object-relational "units" (e.g., Kernberg, 1976); ego structures as internalized objects "units" (Fairbairn, 1952); self-selfobject "units" (Kohut, 1984); and "relational configurations" "units" (Mitchell, 1998).

The *coup de grace* was given to ego psychology in a series of papers by Brenner (e.g., 2002) arguing for the abandonment of structural theory.

These papers had special significance in view of the fact that Brenner, along with Arlow (Arlow & Brenner, 1964), was one of the architects of structural theory. A central point of these papers was that, as far as the clinical data are concerned, all we have is conflict among wishes and aims and compromises between these conflicting wishes and aims. In effect, Brenner was advocating the return of psychoanalytic theory to its earliest days, reflected in the concept of "defense hysteria", in which the core ideas are one, that we harbor wishes and desires that conflict with our sense of self and moral values and that would trigger distressing affects if consciously experienced; two, that these wishes and desires are therefore barred from conscious experience; and three, that we find compromises among conflicting aims. For Brenner (2002), clinical classical psychoanalytic theory is primarily a *motivational* theory (Eagle, 2012). That is, experience and behavior are the product of the interplay between different aims, viz., the wish to gratify certain desires (which Freud believed were primarily sexual) and the wish to avoid the distressing affect that the conscious experience of these desires as well as the attempt to gratify them would entail. From this perspective, there are only wishes in conflict with each other and compromises among these conflicting wishes. Although Brenner (e.g., 2002) eschewed the structural model of psychoanalytic theory and limited psychoanalytic theorizing largely to conflicting aims and compromises among these aims, in stressing the adequacy of compromise formation, he is implicitly invoking ego functioning insofar as degree of adequacy of compromise formation is clearly attributable to the adequacy of functioning of some structure or agency of the personality.

Notes

1 Gray (e.g., 1994) and his colleagues (e.g., Busch & Joseph, 2004; Sugarman, 2006, 2007) and others have formulated a contemporary ego psychology, one, however, that is primarily limited to the clinical situation. I will discuss their work in Chapter 11.

2 Inhelder and Piaget (1958) describes aspects of cognitive development in similar terms; Loewald (1951) also conceptualizes the ego structure in terms of its organizational and integrative function. He writes: "The ego mediates, unifies, integrates because it is of its essence to maintain, on more and more complex levels of differentiation and objectification of reality, the original unity" (p. 11).

3 In the context of Freudian theory, one would refer to the need to replace immediate discharge, as reflected in hallucination of the breast (the pleasure principle) with delay and turning to the actual breast if the hunger drive is to be satisfied (the reality principle).

4 Rapaport (1956 [1967]) understood ego autonomy not only in terms of relative independence from drives, but also in term of relative independence from the environment. The latter form of ego autonomy is relevant to findings showing that delay of gratification

is enhanced by one's ability to distract one's attention away from the reward as well as findings having to do with task persistence in the face of distracting cues.

5 Freud (1914) himself suggested that self-preservative needs, being fed, for example, are primary and that libidinal pleasures are anaclitic upon these primary needs. He writes that "the sexual instincts are at the outset area attached to the satisfaction of the ego instincts; only later do they become independent of these, and even we have an indication of that original attachment in the fact that the persons who are concerned with a child's feeding care, and protection become his earliest sexual objects" (p. 87). Thus, sexual gratification originally "leans" upon the self-preservative need to be fed. One way of understanding this is to recognize that, in the course of evolution, satisfaction of self-preservative needs are pleasurable and, therefore, part of our motivational system. However, this did not lead him to relinquish his speculation regarding the hallucination of the breast.

6 Although Bellak and Meyers (1975) include object relations as an ego function, as we will see, they were not viewed as an ego function in the ego psychology theory of Hartmann.

7 The studies on delay of gratification and inhibitory control discussed in Chapter 1 can be seen as studies on ego strength.

3

Critiques of ego psychology

Classic and romantic vision

A useful framework in which to view critiques of ego psychology is to locate them in the broad historical framework of the tensions between what Strenger (1989) refers to as "the classic and romantic vision of psychoanalysis". According to Strenger, the perspectives of Freud and "American ego psychology" (p. 593) reflect the classic vision of psychoanalysis, whereas "the romantic vision began to evolve in psychoanalysis with the ideas of Sandor Ferenczi. . . [and] was taken up by Michael Balint. . . [and] developed further in the British object-relations school" (pp. 593–595).

Strenger also writes that the classic and romantic visions "can be placed historically . . . in the conflict between the more rationalist streak of the enlightenment and the romantic reaction against it" (Strenger, 1989, p. 595). Strenger cites Kant's emphasis on the rational and the need to transcend our animal nature as a clear expression of the classic view and Rousseau's valuing of spontaneity, the uniqueness of the individual, and "the richness of [one's] subjective experience" (p. 595) as an equally clear expression of the romantic vision.

Critiques of ego psychology reflect the tensions between these two visions, as expressed in a set of concerns, including the fear that, in its excessive emphasis and valuing of control (over our animal nature), rationality, and adherence to the reality principle, ego psychology's vision of ideal psychological functioning is essentially that of an adaptive mechanism, one that leaves little room for the recognition and valuing of the positive role of spontaneity, passion, and desire in psychological life.

In this chapter, I present various critiques of ego psychology, some more justified and some less justified. The most far-reaching and general critique of ego psychology lies in the objection to Hartmann's project of developing psychoanalytic theory as a general theory of the mind.

Critique of the project of ego psychology as a general theory of mind

The dominant view of psychoanalysis, both within the psychoanalytic community and in the larger culture, lies in its claim that it uncovers aspects of oneself – desires, wishes, emotions, motives, and aims – that one has difficulty confronting and acknowledging and therefore keeps from conscious experience. The uncovering of these aspects of oneself is carried out through interpretation of a wide range of the individual's behavior and productions, including dreams, free associations, transference, slips of the tongue, transference reactions, and symptoms. This takes place largely in the clinical treatment situation, but also outside that situation in the context of applied psychoanalysis. In both contexts, the psychoanalyst and the psychoanalytically informed commentator or critic, armed with knowledge of theory, intuitive abilities, and personal analysis, took on the mantle of a *menschenkenner*, who could unravel hidden meanings, not only in the context of treatment, but also in such domains as literary products, works of art, psychobiography, and political behavior. The role of *menschenkenner* and decoder of hidden meanings accorded the psychoanalyst and the psychoanalytic critic a good deal of status and prestige in our culture over many years. For example, with regard to the former, it was not that long ago that many chairs of departments of psychiatry were psychoanalysts.

For many psychoanalysts, the advent of ego psychology, with its austere and abstract language, its emphasis on function and adaptation rather than hidden meanings, its openness to findings from non-psychoanalytic disciplines, and its ambition to develop psychoanalysis into a general theory of the mind, constituted a threat to what in their minds represents the core of psychoanalysis, namely, the uncovering and interpretation of hidden aims, intentions, and meanings. The project of developing psychoanalysis into a general theory of the mind was viewed by critics as misplaced ambition, beyond the proper boundaries of psychoanalysis and, ultimately, inimical to its identity and future.

Clinical theory versus metapsychology

In the 1960s and 1970s a number of papers appeared in which the authors argued that the core of psychoanalysis lay in its clinical theory and that its metapsychological formulations could be abandoned without any significant loss to psychoanalytic theory. (e.g., Gill, 1976; Holt, 1976; Klein,

1976). According to the view of these authors, the focus and language of clinical theory referred to purposes, meanings, and intentions from the point of view of the subject, whereas the metapsychological formulations employed the natural science language and concepts of energy, forces, and mechanisms. Insofar as the ego psychology of Hartmann and A. Freud employed the language of energy (e.g., "neutralization" of libido), mechanisms (e.g., "defense mechanisms"), and function (e.g., "ego functions"), the critique of metapsychology could be and, indeed, was directed toward ego psychology. For example, Klein (1976) wrote: "perhaps the most unfortunate interpretation of function . . . is the tendency to consider it in an entirely *non-motivational* sense" (p. 153, emphasis in the original). (As we will see, this is a justified criticism.)

The preceding critique of ego psychology essentially centers on the question of the boundary of psychoanalytic theory. Those who argue for the self-sufficiency of the clinical theory view psychoanalysis as a circumscribed theory concerned primarily with desires, aims, intentions from the subject's point of view, with data obtained mainly from the clinical situation.[1] The ambition of ego psychologists, such as Hartmann and Rapaport, to develop psychoanalysis into a general theory of mind with ego psychology as its foundation, which would require the integration of findings from non-psychoanalytic sources, was rejected by those who argued for the self-sufficiency of the clinical theory. According to Klein (1969 [1970]), "proceeding in this direction, ego psychology becomes indistinguishable from traditional academic psychology" (p. 522), with its view of explanation in terms of "mechanism" rather than "in terms of purpose" (p. 524). Klein (1969 [1970]) calls for psychoanalysis to "shed all pretenses of offering a nonteleological, mechanistic picture of ego processes" (p. 524) and to

> restrict the scope and terms of ego theory to the level of motivational explanation that brought psychoanalysis into being in the first place – an endeavor exclusively concerned with understanding behavior in relation to psychological dilemma, conflict, task, and life history.
>
> (p. 524)[2]

He also writes, with regard to the issue of conceiving ego functions in terms of "process explanations" rather than in terms of aims and purposes that "proceeding in this direction, ego psychology becomes almost indistinguishable from traditional academic psychology . . . it is certainly not psychoanalytic" (p. 157).[3]

As another example of rejection of Hartmann's ambition, Edelson (1985) writes that, unlike a general psychology of mind which is primarily concerned with

> conscious mental states, [which are] causal relations among conscious mental states [that] are caused by intrinsic features of the environment of the organism [and] the various capacities of the mind that enable the organism to carry out at least some of the various kinds of action[,]
>
> (p. 577)

the proper domain of psychoanalysis are unconscious mental states. He also writes that "the psychoanalytic aim is to make comprehensible intentional mental states the analysand finds incomprehensible" (p. 586). He also writes:

> Psychoanalysis has its *raison d'etre* in the investigation of the phenomena and the treatment of the disorders that are expressions in conscious mental life of causal interrelations among unconscious mental states, rather than the investigation of causal relations between conscious mental states and environmental stimuli.
>
> (p. 583)

Edelson also writes that because the domain of psychoanalysis is limited to the relationships among various unconscious internal states, it goes beyond its proper boundary when it concerns itself with functions and capacities. He writes: "psychoanalysis as a theory of motivation is to be distinguished from a theory about one or more psychological capacities – perception, memory, cognition, or language" (pp. 585–586). In short, Edelson appears to believe that the appropriate context for psychoanalytic theorizing should be limited to the clinical situation.

Guntrip (1969) takes a position similar to Edelson's and Klein's. According to Guntrip, Hartmann's (1939) conception of the ego as an "organ of adaptation" (p. 50) and an accompanying set of delineated ego functions that serve adaptation belongs to general psychology and is "far removed from clinical psychopathology and psychoanalysis as a basis for psychotherapy" (Guntrip, 1969, pp. 404–405). Although Guntrip is surely aware of the adaptive role of ego functions in psychological life identified by Hartmann, he believes that concern with them lies outside the boundary of psychoanalytic theory, the main role of which, according to Guntrip, is to provide a basis for understanding psychopathology and carrying out psychotherapy.[4] That is, he is not denying the existence of ego functions identified by Hartmann. Rather, he is stating that only certain aspects of mind, those that provide a basis for psychoanalytic psychotherapeutic work, lie within the boundary of psychoanalysis.

The preceding depictions of both general psychology and psychoanalysis are overly narrow and do not reflect the actual state of affairs in either domain. With regard to the former, although, at the time that Guntrip and Klein made their comments, it may have been the case that a psychological theory of the mind was primarily concerned with conscious mental states and processes in academic psychology, this is no longer the case. Cognitive psychology is largely concerned with the influence on conscious mental states (and behavior) of environmental factors as well as (inferred) internal mental processes *that are out of awareness*. Indeed, as Fodor (1983) writes, "all psychologically interesting cognitive states are unconscious" (p. 86). And Lakoff and Johnson (1999) write that one of three "major findings of cognitive science [is that] thought is mostly unconscious" (p. 3) (See also Wakefield, 2018.) Although the kinds of unconscious processes of interest to general psychology and psychoanalysis may differ in certain respects, both include concern with the role of unconscious processes in conscious experience and behaviors.

As is clear from the preceding comments, Edelson, Klein, and Guntrip take the position that psychoanalysis should be limited to its clinical theory (i.e., experience-near concepts applicable to the clinical situation) and should eschew any explanatory accounts that entail reference to "functions", "process" and "mechanisms".[5] Although this may be appropriate in the in the context of ongoing treatment, a question that arises is whether any psychoanalytic theory, including its clinical theory, which purports to explain human behavior can be limited solely to discourse in terms of aims, purposes, and motives. As the philosopher Black (1967) writes: "As soon as reasons for actions have been provided, an inquiring mind will want to press on to questions about the provenance and etiology of such reasons" (p. 656). In other words, although appeal to the agent's reasons and motives as explanation may suffice in the context of everyday interaction and discourse, they constitute phenomena that require explanation themselves. Further, as Black (1967) suggests, the latter explanatory account need not be limited to the discourse that employs the same language used in describing the phenomena themselves (see Eagle, 1980, 1984 for a fuller discussion of this issue).

The idea that one can separate psychoanalytic clinical formulations and processes from some general theory of the mind is questionable. As Rubinstein (1997) has cogently argued, the formulations and assumptions of an apparently strictly clinical theory are often implicitly based on a general theory of the nature of the mind. At the very least, clinical formulations cannot contradict what we know about psychological and neural functioning and remain tenable. Further, as Rubinstein has demonstrated, the dependence of clinical formulation on general theory goes beyond that minimal requirement. For example, many psychoanalytic clinical interpretations assume the validity of the general principle of motivational determinism, or, as Rubinstein (1976, 1997) puts it, the general hypothesis that "all observable and unobservable activities in which a person may be said to engage are motivated consciously or unconsciously" (p. 342). As another example, as Rubinstein (1975, 1997) notes, the attribution of an unconscious wish to a patient rests on assumptions regarding the existence of unconscious processes. In short, a radical dichotomy between clinical formulations (and techniques) and a theory of mind is untenable.

Even if it were possible to limit the theory of psychoanalysis entirely to its clinical context, restricting psychoanalytic treatment to the descriptions provided by Edelson and Klein would appear to such processes and outcome goals as corrective emotional experiences, strengthening the therapeutic alliance, feeling empathically understood, softening the harshness of the superego, internalizing representations of the analyst, experiencing the therapist as a secure base, improving the patient's capacity for gratification, enhancing quality of object relations, enhancing tolerance of anxiety and frustration, strengthening ego functions, reaching more adaptive compromise formulations, and so on. In short, Edelson's and Klein's conception of psychoanalysis, even if limited to a form of treatment, is too narrow and does not adequately reflect the range of aims that characterize current psychoanalytic treatment. And even if one accepted Guntrip's view that psychoanalytic theory should be limited to providing a basis for psychotherapeutic work, it is not at all apparent that a concern with ego functions is irrelevant to carrying out psychoanalytic psychotherapy.

A central issue here comes down to the degree to which one's vision of psychoanalysis is that of an entirely separate discipline situated at a great distance from and unsullied by other disciplines, or as a discipline that, to at least some significant degree, can and should be integrated with and enriched by other disciplines. It is not clear what great virtue lies in insisting on psychoanalysis as an entirely separate discipline (and all that that implies, including separate training institutes, loyalty to this or that "school", and limitations on one's perspective). That has led to the current state of marginalization of psychoanalysis. A call for increased integration between psychoanalytic and non-psychoanalytic theories and perspectives, however, comes with some important caveats. With all their difficulties and problems, psychoanalytic theories have addressed significant and vital human issues and have generated important insights – that is their great strength. This must not be relinquished or attenuated. Far too often, non-psychoanalytic research has been preoccupied with methodology *per se* rather than with the question of how best to account for the phenomena under investigation, and at the cost of neglecting vital human issues. This is far less the case today than during the period in which preoccupation with operationalizing and controlling variables resulted in psychological research largely concerned with the behavior of rats in mazes. However, in my view, there continues to be an over-concern with methodology at the cost of compromising ecological validity (Kazdin, 2006).

However, one also needs to keep in mind that psychoanalytic theorizing has had its own serious problems, for example, arbitrary interpretations of unconscious meaning and attributions based on little or no evidence of any kind. Thus, in order for increased integration between psychoanalytic and non-psychoanalytic theories to constitute a desirable goal, both the non-psychoanalytic and psychoanalytic perspectives and approaches need to do a great deal of work. For non-psychoanalytic perspectives, the challenge is to become more open-minded and flexible in their attitudes toward methodology and, perhaps most important, more concerned with ecological validity as a primary value in empirical research. For psychoanalytic perspectives, the challenges include greater recognition of the need for evidence and critical thinking in formulating clinical hypotheses and theories as well as greater openness to findings from other disciplines.

The criticism that ego psychology minimizes the importance of drive theory

Despite the rejection of Freudian drive theory reflected in the emergence of object relations theory, self psychology, and American relational psychoanalysis, there is a body of thought, associated largely with French psychoanalysis that continues to view drive theory as the core of psychoanalysis. From that perspective, any theoretical formulation that rejects or minimizes the significance of drive theory is seen as threatening the very existence of psychoanalysis. For these theorists, ego psychology represents precisely such a set of theoretical formulations. The most articulate spokesperson of that perspective is Green (2000) who writes "that to say that one can put the ego on a par with the id is inconsistent because it is a major hypothesis of Freud that the id dominates the ego . . ." (p. 248). He repeats this criticism in his statement that

> my main objection to Hartmann was that he thought he could provide a sounder image of the mind if he turned his back to the viewpoint of the overpowerful influence of the id. There is no vantage point from the ego in psychoanalysis, because if you have a vantage point from the ego you lose the essentials of psychoanalysis.
>
> (p. 251)

Why would a vantage point from the ego entail losing the essentials of psychoanalysis? Implicit in Green's position is the fear that a de-emphasis on the id threatens what for him is the primary focus of psychoanalysis: interpreting and making comprehensible unconscious aims, desires, wishes, and fantasies, the source of which is the id. For Green, any departure from that task is tantamount to losing "the essentials of psychoanalysis". Hence, Green (2000) concludes, "Hartmann did a lot of harm to American psychoanalysis" (p. 251).

Green is not alone in taking this position. In an edited book entitled *Infantile sexuality and attachment*, Widlocher (2002) writes that "seeking the expression of infantile sexuality [the source of which, of course, is the id] in what the analysand is saying and thinking is undoubtedly one of the fundamental aspects, if not the foundation itself, of the psychoanalytic approach" (p. 27). In the same edited book, Scarfone (2002) writes:

"Infantile sexuality . . . is not a separate object within the field of psychoanalysis . . . It is the very object resulting from the territory marked out by the Freudian method" (p. 97). Similar to Scarfone, Squires (2002) argues that, although attachment theory has made interesting contributions, Bowlby's neglect of infantile sexuality "leads him to overlook the complexity of [the infant-mother] bond, to deny its ambivalent erotic nature, and to conceal the elements of unconscious fantasy formulation" (p. 139). Thus, each in his or her way, Green, Widlocher, Scarfone, and Squires, reject any clinical or theoretical formulation that denies or minimizes the primacy of the id. For them, an emphasis on adaptive functions entails the risk that psychoanalysis would lose its distinctiveness as a psychology of the id and would take its place alongside other perspectives and disciplines (such as cognitive or developmental psychology) that include an emphasis on the nature, adequacy, and adaptiveness of various cognitive (or ego) functions.

The fear that openness to findings from other disciplines would be destructive to the distinctiveness of psychoanalysis is reflected in what appears to be Green's (1992) position that *any* findings from non-psychoanalytic sources are not relevant to psychoanalysis. Thus, he distinguishes between the "real" child, that is, the child who is investigated in developmental research, and what he refers to as the "true" child of psychoanalysis and rejects the idea that findings from developmental psychology have any relevance for understanding the latter. It is clear from the context of Green's comments that what he means by the "true" child of psychoanalysis is the child's inner world *as inferred from the analysis of adult analysands*. Although such inferences may be therapeutically useful in the analysis of adults, they cannot serve as adequate data for a theory of psychological development or a theory of the mind. However, Green does not appear to have an interest in either. In short, insofar as for Green, ego psychology entails one, a de-emphasis on the id; and two, an openness to findings from non-psychoanalytic disciplines (e.g., developmental psychology), it represents a danger to his vision of psychoanalysis.

In a certain limited sense, the fears of Edelson, Green, Widlocher, and the others regarding the "dilution" of psychoanalytic identity may be justified. That is, insofar as ego psychology does share with cognitive psychology and attachment theory a common focus on function and adaptation, there will be integrations and blurred boundaries. However, one can see that as a strength rather than a problem insofar as it facilitates mutual enrichment between disciplines and encourages an expansion and reformulation of both ego psychology and cognitive psychology. Further, a focus on function and adaptation does not preclude attention to wishes, desires, and meanings.

Ego maturity is essentially a defensive adaptation to mad environment

In a paper on Michael Balint's attitude toward ego psychology, Bonomi (2003) writes that "a fundamental premise of [Balint's] work was Ferenzci's distrust for the structural model, which praised the maturity of the ego and verbal, social, and adaptive abilities" (p. 219). Indeed, according to Bonomi, Ferenzci viewed "ego maturation as a trauma derivative" (p. 219), by which he seems to mean that the adaptations required by a mature ego represent a response to a mad environment and "a surrender of one part of the personality" (Bonomi, 2003, p. 235). Ferenczi's mistrust and rejection of ego psychology were also based on his view that it is a form of metapsychology not especially relevant to clinical work – a criticism, as we have seen, that is echoed by others (See Bergmann, 2000).

Bonomi points out that Ferenzci and Balint were reacting to a classical perspective in which a prerequisite for undergoing an analysis was a sufficiently high level of ego maturity that would allow the analysand to form a transference relationship and to receive insight generating interpretations. Indeed, in Bonomi's words, "the capacity to gratify the analyst [i.e., by demonstrating a high level of verbal ability] was both the unspoken criteria [sic] on which the preselection of the analysands was made to fit the classical technique" (Bonomi, 2003, p. 225) and forced "the patient to remain at the Oedipal level during the whole treatment" (Balint, 1968, p. 99). In short, for both Ferenzci and Balint, ego maturity and the adaptations it entails reflect "sheltering structures" (Bonomi, 2003, p. 219), and are essentially equivalent to what Winnicott (1960) referred to as a "false self", that is, a self of social compliance.

Ferenczi's and Balint's critique of the concept of adaptation rests on an erroneous equation of conformity and compliance with adaptation. From an evolutionary perspective – one that is clearly the framework for Hartmann's emphasis – adaptation has little to do with compliance or conformity. The main criteria for the assessment of particular adaptations include, above all, their survival value and relatedly, the degree to which they serve to meet our fundamental needs.

The modes of conceptualization of ego psychology are inadequate for the study of object relations

One of Guntrip's (1969) far-reaching criticisms of ego psychology is that its "basic modes of conceptualization and orientation [are] inadequate to the study of man as a person whose be-all and end-all of existence is his relational life with other persons". To be faithful to this core aspect of life, according to Guntrip, only "object relations terminology is adequate" (p. 391).[6] These criticisms overlook the fact that, although one's object relational life is undoubtedly a central aspect of one's existence, the adequacy of one's ego functioning in a variety of areas in one's life is also of great moment to most people. Concerns with one's ego functioning, and intense feelings about one's functioning, are often an important focus of psychotherapy, including psychoanalytic psychotherapy. Surely, an account of certain impairments in ego functions, for example, loss of reality-testing or presence of hallucinations, require more than "object relations terminology". And, just as surely, just as the quality of one's object relations influences the development of one's ego functioning, so similarly, does the adequacy of one's ego functions influence the nature of one's object relations. And finally, there are central aspects of existence, such as values, ideals (Kohut, 1984), passionate interests, and fulfilling one's talents and abilities, that are not exclusively object relational in Guntrip's sense, but that are nevertheless central to and give meaning to one's life (See Eagle, 1981; Storr, 1988).

Rejection of ego autonomy

Green (2000) writes that Hartmann's concept of neutralized energy "supports the idea of the autonomous ego as safe, escaping the primary influence of the bodily needs, affects, passion, and desire" (p. 108). This is not a justified criticism. Green fails to understand here what Hartmann means by ego autonomy and overlooks the consideration that, if the ego is to *serve* bodily needs and desire well, it must have a significant degree of freedom from wishful thinking. Thus, Hartmann is not suggesting that the autonomous ego escapes bodily needs. Indeed, some degree of ego autonomy is necessary if the ego is to adequately meet bodily needs. The seeming paradox is that, if the ego is to be able to gratify bodily needs and desire, it must not be excessively influenced by these needs and desire. This insight is at the core of Freud's (1900) distinction between the pleasure principle and the reality principle as expressed, for example, in his contrast between hallucinatory wish fulfillment and gratification through means-ends interactions with objects in the external world. In short, Green does not give recognition to the consideration that gratification of needs and desires requires, in important respects, some degree of autonomy of ego functioning from the very needs and desires it is serving.

What is striking about the preceding critiques of ego psychology is that, for the most part, they are based not on the argument that its formulations are not supported or contradicted by the available evidence, but rather on such grounds as: they dilute psychoanalysis; de-emphasize primitive aggression and sexuality; put the ego on a par with the id and thereby contradict Freud, and so on. These criticisms are more sociological and political in nature rather than directed to the degree of empirical (including clinical evidence) support for the theoretical formulations of ego psychology.

I turn now to a set of more justified criticisms and shortcomings that need to be addressed if ego psychology is to serve as a foundation for a general psychoanalytic theory of the mind.

Reification and jargon

Before I discuss more substantive criticisms that have to do with theoretical content, I want to address a general problem that characterizes much of psychoanalytic writing, especially Freudian theory and ego psychology, namely, the tendency to reify abstract theoretical constructs. In both Freudian theory and ego psychology, the abstract concepts of id, ego, and superego are discussed as if they were homunculi that strive, have aims, and do things. As examples of such reification, Freud (1915b, p. 122) refers to the source, object, and *aim* of instincts, as if instincts could have aims; *to "evil impulses" in the id for "which the poor ego feels responsible"*; to the superego as an "agency" that enforces and prohibits, and as "the vehicle of the ego ideal by which the ego measures itself" (Freud, 1914, p. 93). In all of these examples, Freud refers to hypothetical components of the personality as if they were mini-agents who have aims, feel things, and have responsibility.[7] Although I use the "standard" terms of id, ego, and superego as well as other hypothetical terms (e.g., internal objects) throughout this book, it needs to be made clear that these terms are metaphors and do not refer to concrete entities. There is perhaps little wrong with writing metaphorically about theoretical entities as if they were homunculi so long as we are aware of the *as-if* nature of our formulations. However, too often, we forget the as-if nature of the theoretical formulations and refer to the concepts in these formulations as concrete entities in the world. As the philosopher Alston (1977) writes: "It is all too easy to postulate a little man inside who does the integration and the self-observing".

Freudian theory, among others, has come dangerously close to succumbing to this temptation. But in overreaction to such excesses, self-theorists have tended to deny, or at least ignore, the fact that there is an agent who does the integrating as well as the perceiving, the thinking, the desiring, the fearing, and so on – viz., the *person*, the *human being* whose behavior, thought, and feeling is being studied. To be sure, there is no ego or self or self that acts as an entity that is distinct from the remainder of the personality (Allport, 1955), "but there is a self that *is* the person" (pp. 65–66; emphasis in the original).

I want to qualify the preceding argument with regard to the concept of ego. To the extent that the concept of ego is understood as a component structure of the personality, along with the concepts of id and superego, the criticism of reification holds with regard to the concept of ego. However, the problem of reification is significantly mitigated when the term ego is understood as I or person. Understood this way, it is not reification to speak of the ego (i.e., I or person) desiring, thinking, feeling, and so on. In contrast, we do not say that ids or superegos think, feel, and act because we recognize that only persons think, feel, and act. Indeed, such locutions are built into our everyday language of I desire, I think, I feel, I act. The importance and implication of this fact of our language should not be dismissed or minimized as simply a matter of grammatical structure. For, as Wittgenstein (1966) has observed, language reveals the "forms of life" in which it is embedded.

We also recognize that biologically based instinctual systems, such as sex, aggression, attachment, hunger, thirst, *influence* what I desire, think, and feel. These factors have their impact through influencing what we, as persons, desire, think, and feel. It is, above all, because of the superordinate status of the I as person that it is a revised ego psychology that constitutes the strongest foundation for a unified psychoanalytic theory. In such a theory, it is the I or person who is at the center of interest. And in such a theory, much of the focus is on identifying and understanding the various factors – inner and outer, biological and social, early and concurrent – that influence the development and functioning of the person. Thus, and somewhat ironically, despite the austere, impersonal, and experience-distant language of Hartmann (and other ego psychologists), more than any other psychoanalytic perspective and to the extent that one understands the ego as the I or person, a revised ego psychology places the person at the center of its concern. This is not to say that theoretical explanation in a revised ego psychology needs to be limited to the phenomenal language of experience. Indeed, it will not be. What it should be able to do is make clear its links to what the person experiences, thinks, and feels, and the actions s/ he takes.

The problem of reification is often accompanied by the twin problem of jargon. Both are well represented in much of Hartmann's writings. Let me provide some examples:

According to Hartmann (1939) the things

> that we know about thinking [includes] its being energized by desexualized libido, its conjectured relation to the death instinct . . . its dependence on the cathectic conditions, its facilitation or inhibition by the superego and by drive and affect-processes, and so on.
>
> (p. 59)

> It is likely that part of the energy which the ego uses is not derived (by way of neutralization) from the drives but belongs from the very first to the ego.
>
> (Hartmann, 1964, p. xiv)

> Neutralization of energy is clearly to be postulated from the time at which the ego evolves as a more or less demarcated substructure of personality.
>
> (Hartmann, 1952, 1964, p. 171)

> In speaking of various shades of desexualization or deaggressivization one has to think of two different aspects. One may refer to different modes or conditions of energy, and this energic aspect of neutralization

may partly coincide with the replacement of the primary by the secondary process, which allows of any number of transitional states.

(Hartmann, 1950, 1964, p. 131)

It is difficult to know what to make of these (and many other similar)
passages. The problem with them is not that they attempt to provide
explanatory accounts of clinical and other data. That is what theoretical formulations are supposed to do. The problems lie in the fact that,
for the most part, the preceding formulations are pseudo-explanatory
rather than actually explanatory. They do not seem to refer in any discernible way to phenomena in the real world. Or, if they do, Hartmann does little to indicate how they do. Also, many of these presumed
explanatory accounts are circular in nature. For example, how does one
know when ego functions are employing neutralized energy (whatever
that is)? Answer: When they are conflict-free. What enables conflict-
free functioning? Answer: the employment of neutralized energy. I single out Hartmann's writings because the focus of this book is on the
revision of ego psychology. However, much of the psychoanalytic literature needs to undergo a cleansing process in which jargon is rewrit-
ten in ordinary discourse. In those instances where it does not seem
possible, one has good reason to question the value of the theorizing.
(See Leites [1971] undeservedly ignored [as well as Stoller's intro-
duction] attempt to clarify meaning in Hartmann's as well as in other
psychoanalytic writing.)

Object relations in ego psychology: 1) ego psychology does not recognize the relative autonomy of object relations from drives

Although ego psychology accords autonomy from drives to ego functions,
it does not do so with regard to object relations. Rather, it retains the classical view that, along with ego functions, the primary function of the object
and of object relations is drive gratification. For Freudian theory as well
as for ego psychology, the object remains "the thing in regard to which the
instinct achieves its aim" (Freud, 1915b, p. 122). Indeed, as noted earlier,
implicit in classical theory is the idea that were we living in a science
fiction world in which mere wishing would make it so, that is, in which
actual objects were not necessary for drive gratification, we would never

develop object relations or even a concept of an external object. Thus, as is the case for thinking, object relations are a roundabout or detour route to drive gratification.

Freud (1915b) stated that the drive and the object are initially separate. That is, it is the nature of drives that their sole tendency is immediate, blind discharge. The recognition that objects are necessary for drive gratification and that objects become connected to drives, thus initiating our relationship to objects comes only with experience. Freud (1915b) also writes that our initial relationship to objects is one of hatred (due to its disturbance of the infant's presumed Nirvana state). He writes: "At the very beginning, it seems, the external world, objects, and what is hated are identical" (p. 136). However, hatred is overcome and object relations are established by our recognition that objects are necessary for drive gratification. The object then becomes "the thing in regard to which the instinct achieves its aim" (Freud, 1915b, p. 122). In short, it is the infant's experience of the object's role in satisfaction that establishes object relations and that transforms hatred of the object to love of the object. Although, as we have seen, Freud (1915b) writes that the drive and the object are initially separate, given the logic of Freud's formulations, it would be more accurate to say that early in development, there is no object; there are only drives pressing for discharge.[8]

Consistent with the preceding view of the origins of object relations, both Freud (1916–1917, p. 329) and Anna Freud (1960) write that the mother's provision of pleasure during her ministrations constitute the basis for the infant's attachment to her. However, the pleasures provided during the course of the mother's ministrations are primarily *sensual pleasures* associated with stimulation of the infant's erotogenic zones, the kind of pleasure that does not easily fit into a drive reduction model. To acknowledge this would suggest that it is not only or primarily drive gratification that motivates the infant's turn to the object. The way out of this dilemma is to assimilate sensual pleasures associated with stimulation of the erotogenic zones to a drive model by arguing that insofar as oral and anal impulses can be thought of as linked to "partial instincts" pleasures associated with stimulation of the oral and anal zones entail reduction of what one might refer to as partial drives. This is quite forced insofar as the experience of sensual pleasure hardly fits Freud's conception of pleasure as essentially equivalent to a quantitative reduction of excitation due to build-up of instinctual tensions.[9]

Evidently, for ego psychology to grant autonomy of object relations from the drives would constitute too radical a departure from a classical theory in which the very definition of the object is the thing in regard to which the instinct achieves its aims, in which the mind is a discharge apparatus and in which objects and object relations are established primarily because they are necessary for drive discharge (gratification) to take place. Indeed, from this perspective, there is no object without the drives. It is the need for an object in order to achieve gratification that, in an important sense, creates the object as an object of desire. Thus, the step of granting object relations autonomy from drives was never taken.[10]

The claim that all behavior, including object relations are, either directly or indirectly, in the service of drive gratification was also a dominant point of view for many years not only within but also outside the psychoanalytic context. One clear expression of that view is the proposition of Hullian drive-reduction theory that the infant's attachment to the caregiver is based on the latter's role in gratification of the hunger drive. Hull (1943, 1951) argued that, due to the mother's role in the reduction of the primary hunger drive, she took on secondary reinforcement properties for the infant. That is, due to its role in hunger reduction, food is a primary reinforcer, and because of her association with the primary reinforcer, the caregiver acquires secondary reinforcement properties, a formulation virtually identical in structure to the Freudian account of the basis for the early object relations.

Object relations and ego psychology: 2) ego psychology does not adequately recognize object relations as the milieu for the development of ego functions

As we have seen, the primary concern of ego psychology, as reflected in its concepts of primary and secondary ego autonomy and conflict-free sphere of functioning, is the relationship between ego functions and drives. Virtually nothing is explicitly said regarding the relationship between object relations and ego functions beyond Hartmann's (1939) statement that ego functions will develop normally in an average expectable environment. However, although ego functions may develop relatively autonomous of drives, they do not develop autonomously of object relations. Indeed, object relations are the very milieu in which ego functions develop.

It surely would have been obvious to Hartmann that the maturational processes that the concept of primary autonomy refers to take place in an environmental milieu, in particular, in a social and object relational milieu. Hartmann's implicit acknowledgment of this fact is expressed in his formulation that the primary autonomy of certain ego functions (i.e., their maturational timeline) requires an "average expectable environment". Hartmann is stating here that primary ego autonomy, that is, the maturational unfolding of certain ego functions, can only take place in a set of environments that do not go outside a certain range. In effect, he is saying that in a particular range of environments, ego functions will develop in a certain predictable way. Thus, Hartmann puts on hold the question of the kinds of environments, including object relational environments, that are necessary for the development of ego functions. In short, the criticisms of ego psychology that it does not adequately accommodate object relational phenomena is entirely justified (e.g., Guntrip, 1969; Marcus, 1999). More specifically, it does not adequately account for the role of object relations in the development as well as in the ongoing operation of ego functions. This is clearly an aspect of ego psychology that is deficient and that requires revision and correction. I will address this issue more fully in Chapter 4.

Ego psychology places excessive emphasis on control of id impulses

Critiques of structural theory and an ego psychology perspective go back many years in the history of psychoanalysis, even before the development of a systematized ego psychology found in the writings of Hartmann and Rapaport. As early as 1922, Ferenczi and Rank's (1924 [1956]) wrote that psychoanalysis "had become overly scholastic" (Makari, 2008, p. 253). This criticism anticipated the later claim that the emphasis in ego psychology on autonomy and control read like a description of the obsessive character's experience and ego functioning (Loewald, 1952).

A major critique of ego psychology was launched by Apfelbaum (1966) in what has become a classic paper. As Apfelbaum (1966) observes, according to both Freudian theory and ego psychology, id impulses represent a major threat to the integrity of the ego. As A. Freud (1936) puts it, there is a "primary antagonism" between "timeless" id impulses and the ego (p. 172). Hence, on this view, because they are not subject to change and because they represent an ever-present threat, the only adaptive way of dealing with instinctual impulses is, along with renunciation and sublimation, enhanced ego control. In short, from this perspective, a primary criterion for adaptive functioning is ego control over timeless, asocial, and infantile instinctual impulses. And a primary goal of psychoanalytic treatment is enhancement of such control. As we will see, this view needs to be re-examined as does the id-ego model on which it is based.

Are drives cut off from reality?

Hartmann (1948) writes that in contrast to animals, for whom instincts serve as a reliable guide to adaptive behavior, in humans, instinct is cut off from reality. Hence, an "organ of adaptation" – the ego – is necessary for adaptation to reality. This suggests the view that instinctual drives and drives aims, so to speak, left to their own devices, are inherently maladaptive. Given the way natural selection works and given the fact that the evolutionary conception of adaptation entails an environmental niche (reality) to which the behavior (or structure) is adapted, it seems highly unlikely that drives and drive aims are inherently maladaptive. What is likely is that an organizing structure, one that integrates various aspects of the personality, is necessary for adaptive functioning. This is also likely to be the case for animals above a certain level of complexity. Finally, as biologists have long informed us, in animals as well as humans, drive behaviors are not simply endogenously generated, but are triggered by external stimuli (e.g., Beach, 1976). Hence, it is unlikely that, for animals above a certain level of complexity, instinctual drives alone would suffice for adaptive behavior. In short, the claims that instinctual drives that have been selected for in the course of evolution are cut off from external reality and therefore that drive aims are inherently maladaptive do not seem tenable.

Interpersonal and social reality-testing as a fundamental ego function

Given its emphasis on adaptation, and given our social nature, it is striking that ego psychology has relatively little to say regarding ego functions that have to do with one's capacity to understand the other, that is, with one's "mind-reading" ability, as well as with one's understanding of the social "rules" and cues that govern interpersonal and social interaction in one's culture or sub-culture. The capacity for interpersonal understanding is not included by Hartmann among the inborn apparatuses that have the status of primary autonomy. For social animals who live in a social world, this ability is at least as crucial as understanding and acquiring knowledge and skills in relation to the physical world. Indeed, for social animals, even the latter knowledge and skills are embedded in social interactions and processes. Given our social nature, we need to broaden the conception of ego functions so that it includes not only physical and intrapsychic reality but what one may refer to as social or interpersonal reality-testing.

In contrast to the very active research in this area outside psychoanalysis, there is little within psychoanalysis of a systematic nature that addresses what I refer to as interpersonal reality-testing, that is, the processes through which one person gets to routinely understand the actions, intentions, feelings and thoughts of another person. The focus in psychoanalytic theory is primarily on *failure* to understand another. And when there is a focus on understanding the other, it is generally on the other's unconscious mental states. This is a striking lacuna for any theory that purports to provide an account of how the mind works. In view of the fact that we are social creatures and live in a complex social world, reality-testing in regard to the interpersonal and social world is at least as critical an adaptive requirement as the reality-testing and controlling functions emphasized by ego psychology (as well as work on executive function). Any adequate conception of the ego function of reality-testing needs to include our ability to understand others in interpersonal and social interactions. Chapters 5 and 6 will be devoted to a fuller discussion of this vital issue.

Aims and motives associated with ego functioning

Although ego psychology recognizes the relative autonomy of ego functions from drives, it continues to accept the assumption of classical theory because the source of motives, desires, and aims, directly or indirectly, overtly or covertly, linked to drive gratification, there are no distinctively motives, desires, and aims associated with ego functioning. To put it another way, whereas the id is the source of motives, aims, and desires, the ego is a structure with a set of functions that mediate these motives, aims, and desires. This is seen quite clearly in Anna Freud's (1945) insistence that in order for the ego to serve as a conduit for satisfaction of basic aims and desires it must function as accurately and reliably as a "mechanical apparatus" (p. 144). This statement is but an extreme version of the general view of ego psychology that the ego functions as a structure or apparatus that controls, channels, and operates to meet instinctual needs, but is not associated with aims and motives of its own. At best, Hartmann (1939) allows ego "interests" (*Ich interesse*), but no full blown motives, desires, and aims.

Criticisms of this sharp dichotomy between motives, desires, and aims, on the one hand, and ego functions, on the other hand, appear quite early in the history of psychoanalysis. For example, Hendricks, 1943) posited an "instinct to master" (p. 561) and White (1959) referred to a "feeling of efficacy" (p. 297) accompanying competent functioning. He also contrasted what he referred to as the "viscerogenic" motives associated with Freudian theory with the "neurogenic" motives associated with ego functioning. In short, the failure of ego psychology to recognize the motivational aspects of ego functioning is a shortcoming in the theory that requires correction and revision. Efforts in this direction will be pursued in Chapter 7.

No adequate motivational theory of affects in either classical theory or ego psychology

Given the centrality accorded to the pleasure principle, one would think that classical psychoanalytic theory, as well as ego psychology, would place an overriding emphasis on affects as primary motivational factors in psychological functioning and behavior. However, that is not the case, at least not in any straightforward way. One reason is that pleasure and unpleasure in Freudian theory are not conceptualized as affective feelings, but rather are understood in terms of build-up and discharge of excitation. Pleasure and unpleasure are embedded in a theoretical network that includes the principle of constancy and the conception of the mind (and the nervous system) as a discharge apparatus. This is also the case with regard to Freud's references to affect. In his early writings, Freud equates "quota of affect" with "sum of excitation" and view affects as "corresponding to processes of discharge" (Freud, 1915a, p. 178).[11]

Freud recognizes that there is no one-to-one correspondence between increase and diminution of excitation and *feelings* of pleasure and unpleasure and is aware that build-up of excitation can be experienced as pleasurable and discharge of excitation can be experienced as unpleasurable.

With regard to the former, Freud (1920) writes that there "is not a simple relation between the strength of feelings of pleasure and unpleasure and the corresponding modifications in the quantity of excitations". He speculates that "the factor that determines the feelings is probably the amount of increase or diminution in the quantity of excitation *in a given period of time*" (emphasis in the original) (Freud, 1920, p. 8).

With regard to the latter, Freud (1924 [1961]) notes that "it cannot be doubted that there are pleasurable tensions and unpleasurable relaxations of tension" and then cites "sexual excitation" as "the most striking example of a pleasurable increase of stimulus" (p. 160). Therefore, Freud (1924 [1961]) writes,

> pleasure and unpleasure [here Freud is obviously referring to pleasurable and unpleasurable feelings] cannot be referred to an increase or decrease of quantity [which we describe as "tension due to a stimulus"], although they have a great deal to do with that factor. It appears that they depend, not on this quantitative factor, but on some characteristic of it which we can only describe as a *qualitative* one.
>
> (p. 160, emphasis added)

Freud then goes on to speculate that this qualitative factor may be due "the rhythm, the temporal sequence of changes, rises and falls in the quantity of stimulus" and concludes with "We do not know" (p. 160).

As far as I know, Freud does not pursue this issue of the qualitative nature of pleasure and unpleasure any further. One consequence of continuing to view affect in a quantitative context is that Freud's main focus is on the affect of anxiety, which, insofar as it lends itself to conceptualization in terms of build-up and diminution of excitation, easily fits into a drive-theory framework. Thus, despite acknowledging the existence of a qualitative factor in the experience of pleasure and unpleasure, Freud does not go on to recognize, let alone elaborate, the motivational role of affective feelings unrelated to drives. Direct and or indirect drive gratification remain the primary motivational force in behavior. There is little room in this theoretical formulation for a motivational role for affects (as feelings) that are unrelated to instinctual gratification/discharge of excitation. This theoretical formulation remains essentially unchanged in ego psychology. For example, there is not a single entry for affects or emotions in the index of Hartmann's (1939) classic *Ego psychology and the problem of adaptation*.[12]

Before ending this chapter, I want to note a core problem of ego psychology identified by Greenberg and Mitchell (1983). They observe that, although Hartmann's work points the way to further developments, his theoretical formulations regarding the ego and ego functions are "too narrowly based. . . [particularly in terms of its close relation to the drives, on the one hand, and the problem of physical survival, on the other] to provide the breadth of integrative capacity required" (p. 268). I would agree with the suggestion implied in their comment that, in order for ego psychology to serve as the basis for a unified psychoanalytic theory, it would need to sever its "special connection" to drive theory. Given the central place that drive occupies in Freudian theory, this would have meant too radical a break with the classical id-ego model, something Hartmann was not prepared to do. It is ironic that, as noted earlier, that although one of the criticisms of ego psychology was its neglect of drive theory, its real problem is its failure to free itself of its close connection to drive theory.

Notes

1 See Eagle (1985) and Rubinstein (1976) who argue against the ideal of a self-sufficient clinical theory.

2 Apart from the issue of proper boundaries for psychoanalytic theory, as we will see in Chapter 7, I think that Klein is correct in observing that, in his exclusive focus on ego mechanisms and functions, Hartmann overlooks the motivational aspects of ego functions. I take up this issue in Chapter 7.

3 Klein's program of research at the New York University Research Center for Mental Health was almost exclusively concerned with empirical investigation of perceptual, cognitive, and affective processes that are relevant to a psychoanalytic theory of the mind. This makes it all the more odd that he would take the discussed theoretical position.

4 As we will see later, ironically, Guntrip (1969) describes psychopathology mainly in terms of "ego weakness".

5 This position contrasts with Ricoeur's (1970) observation that what is distinctive about at least Freudian psychoanalytic theory is that it is a theory of both meaning and mechanism. One could argue that any adequate theory of the mind will include both meaning and mechanism as well as the relationship between the two.

6 The abstract style of Hartmann's language render his formulations to appear far removed from subjective experiences and the clinical situation. However, despite Guntrip's favorable assessment of their theories, this is also true of Klein's and Fairbairn's writings. The language of, for example, life and death instincts, good breasts and bad breasts, urethral attacks, and so on, employed by M. Klein and the language of libidinal ego and anti-libidinal ego, primary unitary ego, splits in the ego, and so on, employed by Fairbairn are certainly as far removed from subjective experience as Hartmann's concepts of ego functions. In all these cases, to the extent that it is possible, one can try to identify and describe the kinds of behavioral and subjective experiential correlates

of these more abstract concepts; Another of Guntrip's criticisms of ego psychology is that it fails to address the "whole person" (p. 402). It is not clear, however, what Guntrip means by "whole person". Nor is it evident that any theory, ego psychology or object relations theory, addresses the "whole person".

7 Perhaps more than any psychoanalytic theorist, Schafer (1976) recognized and launched an effort to confront the problem of reification in psychoanalytic theorizing in his *A New Language for Psychoanalysis*. Whatever one's views regarding the overall success of Schafer's project, he was correct in his recognition of the pervasive problem of reification in much of psychoanalytic theorizing.

8 This is not entirely the case. For in Freud's own speculative formulations, the infant's presumed hallucination of the breast entails a connection between a wish and an internalized representation of an object, the breast. Hence, the object is psychologically present, even if as a fantasied object, even in the case of hallucinatory wish fulfillment. After all, Freud could have proposed that hallucinatory wish fulfillment consists in the magical experience of *satiety* in response to the experience of hunger tensions (see Eagle, 2011). Of course, the hallucination of satiety would be highly maladaptive in that it would provide no developmental pathway to the adaptive experience of learning that one needs an actual object in the external world to experience the reduction of hunger tension and would therefore threaten survival.

9 Interestingly, G.S. Klein (1976) suggests that we replace the term "infantile sexuality" with infantile sensuality"; Indeed, as I will return to later, only at one point in his writing – in a footnote, no less – does Freud (1924) acknowledge that pleasures possess a *qualitative* aspect that can be experienced independently of the quantitative factor of discharge of excitation. Indeed, he writes that pleasure can be experienced even when there is an *increase* rather than a decrease in quantity of excitation or tension. However, Freud goes on to say that he cannot go any further with a theoretical understanding of pleasure as a qualitative experience. It is clear that the reason this is so is because, in Freudian theory, pleasure and the pleasure principle are totally embedded in a quantitative framework, as reflected in the core ideas of the mind as a discharge apparatus and the constancy principle, ideas he never relinquished. In short, there is little room in Freudian theory for the ordinary concept of pleasure as a qualitative sensual phenomenon. The only point of convergence between Freud's metapsychological concept of pleasure and the ordinary experience of pleasure is when the particular pleasure experienced is due to reduction of tension. Other experiences of pleasures unrelated to tension reduction cannot easily be accommodated in the Freudian metapsychological theory.

10 Even when Freud (1914) writes in *On Narcissism* that "one must love [the object] in order not to fall ill" (p. 85), this is so, according to Freud, because one must divert excessive libido from the ego on to the object. In other words, from a metapsychological point of view, cathecting the object is adaptive because it avoids the danger of the ego being inundated with excessive excitation.

11 Following Damasio (2003), I use affect to refer to *feelings* and reserve emotion to include physiological processes and overt behaviors. On this view, whereas emotions can be unconscious, affects are always conscious. Because Freud often employs "emotions" to refer to feelings, his argument that emotions cannot be unconscious is equivalent to the position taken here (See Wakefield, 1992).

12 It is not only ego psychology that does not have an adequate theory of affects, but also other psychoanalytic schools. For example, despite the importance given to regulation of self-esteem in self psychology, there is not a single entry for the terms "affect" or "emotion" in Kohut's 1984 book. Nor does Kohut directly address the issue of the motivational role of affects. A similar situation characterizes the treatment of affects

in relational psychoanalysis. Again, there is not a single entry for the terms "affect" or "emotion" in Mitchell's 1993 book. Greenberg and Mitchell (1983), however, do refer to affect and emotion, mainly to the work of Freud and to Sandler (!991), the latter presenting a theoretical perspective that provides a central motivational role to "feeling states" (p. 188). (I will pursue Sandler's important contribution in Chapter 4.)

4

Correctives and revisions

In the previous chapter I described the major criticisms of ego psychology. Among those criticisms, I identified those that I believed to be justified and that therefore called for necessary correctives and revisions of ego psychology. In this and ensuing chapters, I discuss these necessary correctives and revisions. I devote separate chapters for each of the following areas requiring correctives and revisions: interpersonal understanding; ego motives and aims; and a theory of affects.

Object relations and drives

In Chapter 3, I noted the (justified) criticism that, although ego psychology recognizes the relative autonomy of ego functions from drives, it does not recognize the relative autonomy of object relations from drives. In a passing statement that was never integrated into his drive theory, Freud (1912) comments that the "affectionate current" is older than the "sensual current". He writes that

> the affectionate current is the older of the two . . . it is formed on the basis of the interests of the self-preservative instincts and is directed to . . . those who look after the child . . . It corresponds to *the child's primary object choice* [original emphasis]. We learn in this way that the sexual instincts find their first objects by attaching themselves to the valuations made by the ego instincts, precisely in the way in which the first sexual satisfactions are experienced in attachment to the bodily functions necessary for the preservation of life.
>
> (pp. 180–181)

Freud's remarks here reflect the recognition that object relations are the matrix for the unfolding of instincts.

Strikingly, Freud suggests in these remarks that object relations, reflected in "the child's primary object-choice" and assigned to the "self-preservative" or ego instincts initially develop independently of the gratification of the partial instincts of infantile sexuality. Only later in development do the sexual instincts attach themselves to the valuations made by the self-preservative or ego instincts. This formulation appears to contradict Freud's own claim as well as Anna Freud's (1960) that the infant becomes attached to caregiver due to the role she plays, respectively, in the discharge of tensions and excitations associated with the hunger drive and the sensual pleasures associated with erotogenic zones.

The ideas that the "affectionate current" precedes the "sensual current" and that "the child's primary object-choice" is inextricably linked to the self-preservative or ego instincts are entirely congruent with Bowlby's (1969) positing of a primary attachment instinctual system linked to survival. Indeed, had Freud pursued the line of thought described here, his model of the mind might have looked very different than the id-ego model. (See Silverman, 1991, who writes that "the concept of the self-preservative instincts. . . [provides] an explicit object relations motivational system equal to drives" (p. 169).) However, Freud neither developed nor integrated the implications of his comments into his existing theory. The recognition that object relations are the milieu for the development and expression of drives was left for others.

One such contributor was Modell (1975), who writes that "object relations provide the setting for the normal unfolding of the instincts of the id" (p. 63). Modell also writes that unlike the gratification of sexual and aggressive motives, the gratification of object relational motives require the "fitting in of specific responses from other persons" (p. 64).[1] And as Sandler (1976, 1981) insightfully pointed out, an instinctual wish entails a desired response from the other. For example, an exhibitionistic impulse implies a wish for an observer to observe what one has exhibited.

More than any other ego psychologist, it is Loewald who most clearly formulates the autonomy of object relations from drives. Indeed, according to Loewald (1971), it is the object relational milieu that makes possible the development of instincts, when the latter is understood as a *psychological* factor in psychological life. He writes: The "transformation, the organization of instincts *qua* psychic forces, comes to pass, I maintain, through interactions within the mother-child psychic field" (p. 119). He adds: "[T]he object . . . contributes crucially to the organization of instincts *qua* instincts" (p. 120). In another paper, Loewald (1972) writes that "instincts . . . are to be seen as relational phenomena from the beginning and not as autochtonous forces seeking discharge" (pp. 321–322). Loewald's recognition of the primacy of object relations has led Chodorow (2004) to describe his theoretical positions as "intersubjective ego psychology" (p. 207).

In both the psychoanalytic and non-psychoanalytic contexts, the rejection of a drive-reduction model resulted in a more adequate account of the origin and nature of object relations. As we have seen in the previous chapter, according to both Freudian theory and ego psychology, the origin as well as the function of object relations are entirely linked to drive gratification. As we have also seen, the claim that all behavior, including object relations, are in the service of drive gratification is also at the center of Hullian drive-reduction theory. It was skepticism toward the secondary reinforcement theory of infant-mother attachment that motivated the classic Harlow (1958) study, a main finding of which was that infant monkeys formed an attachment bond to a terry cloth surrogate mother despite the fact that the wire surrogate mother was the source of food. The drive-reduction secondary reinforcement theory of object relations could not withstand the evidence provided by the Harlow study as well as other ethological evidence (Bowlby, 1969).

In the psychoanalytic context, the first theoretical step toward the emergence of an object relations theory was taken by Klein (1952, 1975), who argued that there is no drive without an object and that some image of the object and relationship to the object (the breast) is there from birth on. Other early expressions of the positing of the autonomous status of object relations include Ferenczi's (1988) and Balints'(1937, 1960) concept of "primary object love", Hermann's (1976) positing of a clinging instinct; Fairbairn's (1952) insistence that "libido is object-seeking rather than primarily pleasure-seeking" (p. 82); and Bowlby's (1969) positing of a separate instinctual attachment system.

With the possible exception of Klein, who continued to retain drive theory, all the others, despite different theoretical language, proposed an inborn and autonomous object relational instinctual system. Furthermore, the kind of instinctual system they posit is markedly different from the Freudian conception of either drive or instinct which, modeled after the hunger and sexual drives, is characterized by periodic build-up and discharge of tension and excitation. Thus, for both Bowlby and Fairbairn, the foundation of object relations is an inborn motivational system independent of drive reduction. Thus, paralleling the argument of ego psychologists, such as White and Hendricks, that certain motives and behaviors (e.g., desire for competence and mastery) develop and influence psychological functioning independently of drive reduction was the argument of object relational theorists, such as Bowlby and Fairbairn, that object relational motives and behaviors also develop and influence personality functioning independently of drive reduction.

As Polan and Hofer (1999) observe, despite the "minimization of secondary reinforcement in most formulations of human filial attachment . . . the oral stimulation of sucking and the provision of milk play a powerful role in forging the rat pup's ties to its mother" (p. 163). Given the fact that rats and humans are both mammals, I do not think that we should rule out any role for hunger reduction in the formation of infant-mother ties.

To sum up, just as ego psychology recognized the relative autonomy of ego functions from drives, in a revised ego psychology, the relative autonomy of object relations from drives is recognized.[2] The insights generated by object relations theory need to be incorporated into a revised and expanded ego psychology.

Object relations and the development of ego functions

As noted in Chapter 3, Hartmann (1939) writes that ego functions will develop autonomously in an average expectable environment. The clear implication is that, in non-average expectable environments, the development of ego functions may show a different trajectory (e.g., may be less autonomous). However, Hartmann does not further elaborate the nature of an average expectable environment or the effects of non-average expectable environments on the development of ego functions. Instead, this issue is left to be elaborated and examined by others. In effect, Hartmann puts on hold considerations of the role of different object relational environments on the development and nature of ego functioning.

One of the main themes that runs through Guntrip's (1969) book is that object relational experiences between infant and mother constitute the ground for ego development. Although the term "ego" is not included in the title of Guntrip's book, it appears in four chapter headings, whereas the term "object relations", which is in the title of the book, appears in three chapter headings. The point here is that Guntrip's 1969 book is as much concerned with ego functions as with object relations. Or to put it more precisely, Guntrip is concerned with the influence of object relations on ego functioning. Thus, in an important sense, one can view Guntrip's theoretical formulations as pointing the way to an expanded and revised ego psychology. It is true that the ego functions on which Guntrip focuses are quite different from those of primary interest to Hartmann. Thus, whereas Hartmann is concerned with the ego functions of delay of gratification, reality-testing, synthetic function, planning, thinking, and so on, Guntrip focuses primarily on more object relational or social ego functions (e.g., ego relatedness). However, here too, Guntrip's formulations can point to an expansion of the nature of ego functions to include the assessment and negotiation of interpersonal and social reality. (I will pursue this issue later.)

Guntrip's (1969) concern with ego development and ego functions is reflected in the centrality he assigns to the concept of "ego weakness". He writes that "the basic ego weakness . . . is the tap-root of all later problems" (p. 207). He also refers to the "inability of the weak infantile ego to stand its guard and cope with outer reality" (p. 102), a description quite compatible with the concepts of ego strength and ego impairments in ego psychology.[3] However, unlike what one would find in Hartmann's writings, the last half of the Guntrip sentence reads "in the absence of adequate maternal support" (p. 102). Thus, despite Guntrip's – as well as others'[4] – claim that at an object relations approach is incompatible with ego psychology, it is apparent that the important recognition that the early object relation milieu influences the development of ego function can be easily integrated into an expanded and revised ego psychology.[5]

Kohut is correct in observing that ego psychology in its current form does not adequately accommodate the crucial role of the selfobject in facilitating ego functions such as self-soothing capacity and sense of continuity of the self in time. He is mistaken, however, in his understanding of the concept of ego autonomy. It refers to the ego's autonomy from drives, not from object relations. As I have noted earlier, Hartmann paid little attention to the role of the object and of object relations in the development and maintenance of ego functioning. As we have seen, he put that issue on hold by referring to an average expectable environment necessary for the development of ego functions but did not address the question of the specific nature of that environment. However, Kohut is clearly not correct in arguing that "the armamentarium of even the most sophisticated ego psychology" cannot adequately account for the development of such ego function as the capacity for self-soothing and sense of continuity of self as well as for the role of object relations[6] in the development and sustenance of those ego functions. As I have tried to show in Chapter 3, there is no inherent reason that ego psychology cannot be revised and expanded to incorporate the extensive findings on the role of object relational environments in ego functioning. Kohut himself has provided precisely such an account in his description of a self psychology perspective on agoraphobia. Kohut (1984) presents a clinical vignette of a woman whose mother

> was apparently not able to provide a calming selfobject milieu for the little girl which . . . would have been transmuted into self-soothing structures capable of preventing the spread of anxiety. It is this structural deficit, the deficiency in calming structures . . . that necessitates the presence of a companion . . . who temporarily replaces the missing structure and its functions.
>
> (p. 30)

The gist of what Kohut is describing here can be stated quite simply in the terms of the relationship between an object relational milieu and ego functioning. Because mother was apparently not consistently available for comforting and soothing when the little girl was distressed, she, the little girl, did not have the experiences necessary for internalizing an adequate self-regulation capacity. In the language of a "sophisticated" ego psychology, one would say that due to an inadequate object relational milieu (the specific features of which can be described), the little girl never developed an adequate capacity for affect regulation. In the language of attachment theory, because mother was not available as a comforting safe haven and secure base, particularly during efforts at exploration (which are likely to elicit distress), the little girl was never able to internalize these functions.[7]

Kohut seems to imply that only self psychology can provide a fully adequate account of agoraphobia, an implication that justifies the need for a separate school. The fact, however, is that there is little or nothing in Kohut's account of agoraphobia, which is substantively different from say, attachment theory or a "sophisticated" ego psychology account that it requires a separate psychoanalytic school in order to do justice to the clinical phenomena. Indeed, a revised and expanded ego psychology, one that adequately recognizes the influence of object relational environments on the development of ego functions (including the ego function of affect-regulation), is eminently capable of doing justice to all the phenomena described by Kohut's account of agoraphobia.

The point here is that Kohut did not attempt to build on extant theory and try to construct a more sophisticated ego psychology. Instead, he simply asserted that "even the most sophisticated ego psychology" could not adequately account for the processes and phenomena with which he was primarily concerned. Only a new self psychology would suffice. Thus, a new psychoanalytic school is born. However, if one is interested in integration and a unified theory, one's efforts would go toward incremental revision and building of extant theory rather than toward the development of a new psychoanalytic school. The latter would be justified if the phenomena it identifies were susceptible to an adequate theoretical account only through the development of a new psychoanalytic school. This has not been shown to be the case met by either self psychology or other psychoanalytic schools.

Experience-Near versus Experience-Distant formulations

One of the frequent criticisms of ego psychology is the excessive distance from phenomenal experience of its concepts and formulations, which is often contrasted with the more experience-near concepts of other psychoanalytic schools such as self psychology and object relations theory (e.g., Guntrip, 1969). This criticism can be understood in two different ways: One meaning, which, it appears, is what Kohut and Guntrip have in mind, is that the theoretical formulations of ego psychology are distant from patient's experiences. This is very likely the case. Concepts such as self-cohesiveness come closer to capturing one's subjective experience (i.e., of feeling centered versus fragmented) than, say, reference to neutralized energy. Similarly, consider the contrast between a formulation that refers to the patient's lack of empathic mirroring in childhood versus one that refers to a relative failure in some aspect of the patient's ego functioning.

This criticism, however, reflects a misunderstanding of the nature of theoretical accounts. The function of theory is to explain experience, not

to duplicate it. Among other features, an adequate theory attempts to identify the processes and mechanisms that underlie experience rather than
capture the phenomenological "feel" of experience. However, that does
not necessarily mean that it has greater theoretical explanatory value than
a more experience-distant and more abstract concept or formulation. One
should not equate clinical usefulness with explanatory power. One cannot
reasonably require that a theoretical formulation employ the same language or capture the feel of experience. Its function is, rather, to provide
an explanatory account of experience (see Schlick [1925 (1985)] on the
distinction between experience and knowledge).

Another way of understanding the criticism that ego psychology concepts are excessively experience-distant entails the more serious problem that many of Hartmann's concepts and theoretical formulations lack
empirical referents, a general criticism that, as we have seen, has also been
directed to Freudian metapsychology (e.g., Gill, 1976; Holt, 1976; Klein,
1976). This is not the appropriate place for a discussion for this complex
issue (see Eagle, 1980; Rubinstein, 1976 for a rebuttal of this criticism).
Suffice it to say that this criticism is justified in regard to many of Hartmann's (and Freud's) theoretical formulations and concepts. However, it
does not follow that the problem lies in their failure to capture the phenomenal feel of experience. That is not the work theoretical accounts are
intended to do. In short, experience-near versus experience-distant is not
the issue. The issue is lack of explanatory power.

Inside versus outside perspective

Paralleling the experience-near versus experience-distant distinction is
one between inside and outside perspectives. It has been argued that,
because the domain of psychoanalysis is subjectivity, the object of its
inquiry as well as its explanatory accounts need to be from the inner perspective of the agent. Further, the argument goes, whereas a theoretical
perspective from the outside may be interesting in its own right, it is not
legitimately part of psychoanalysis as a discipline. On this view, findings from neuroscience or cognitive psychology or attachment theory,
for example, would be seen to have little relevance to psychoanalytic
theorizing. As we have seen in Chapter 3, this is the position taken by
Scarfone (2002), who argues that findings from attachment theory have
no relevance to psychoanalysis, as well as by Green (2000), who argues

similarly, that findings from developmental psychology are essentially irrelevant to psychoanalysis.

Once again, we need to take account of the different requirements of the clinical and theoretical contexts. There would be widespread agreement regarding the overriding importance of employing discourse from the inner perspective of the agent (i.e., his or her psychic reality) in the clinical situation. However, insofar as a theoretical formulation represents an attempt to provide an *explanatory account* of the individual's psychic reality, there is no reason for its discourse to be limited to the language of subjective perspective. Indeed, it is phenomena from the agent's subjective perspective that require explanation. One is reminded of Black's (1967) comment in regard to explanation in terms of the agent's reasons and motives. He writes: "As soon as reasons for actions have been provided, an inquiring mind will want to press on to questions about the provenance and etiology of such reasons" (p. 656). In other words, although appeal to the agent's reasons and motives as explanation may suffice in the context of everyday interaction and discourse, reasons and motives constitute phenomena that require explanation themselves. Further, as Black (1967) suggests, the latter explanatory account need not be limited to discourse or formulations from the agent's subjective perspective (see Eagle, 1980, 1984 for a fuller discussion of this issue).

Research on the influence of different environments and object relational factors on ego functioning

There is now much that we know regarding the influence of various environmental factors, including object relational milieu, both on the development of as well as on concurrent ego functioning. We no longer need to put this issue on hold; we can now identify specific environmental factors that influence development, including development of ego functioning. There is evidence of the effects of child maltreatment on a wide range of outcomes, including impulsivity and risk behaviors in young adulthood (Hallowell et al., 2019), neuroendocrine functioning (Cicchetti & Rogosch, 2001), physical health, and a wide range of psychopathology (Keyes et al.,2012; Conway, Raposa, Hammen, & Brennan, 2018). Further, different forms of maltreatment seem to have equivalent negative consequences (Snyder, Young, and Hankin, 2017). We know that poverty, which is likely not the averagely expectable environment Hartmann may have had in mind, influences development of ego functions, including their maturational pace as well as their adequacy. We also know that there are protective factors that moderate the negative effects of harsh environments on development. And finally, we also know from research on infant-mother attachment, that more subtle environmental factors *within* the range of averagely expectable environments influence development, including the development of ego functions, even if in ways that are more subtle than is the case in grossly deviant environments.[8]

Ego functions and socio-economic status

There is a good deal of evidence that different socio-economic environments influence the development of self-control as well as other ego functions. One of the findings in the earlier noted Watts et al. (2018) study is that children who waited the full 7 minutes in a delay of gratification task were from higher income families than children who did not wait the full 7 minutes; and also that a larger percentage of children who waited less than 20 seconds were from lower income families. This is but one of many findings that short-term choices, including choice of immediate gratification, and valuing the present over the future are associated with childhood low socioeconomic status (SES) (e.g., Griskevicius et al., 2013).

This research can be thought of as picking up on the unfinished business left by Hartmann with regard to the relationship between environmental factors and ego development. As we have seen in Chapter 1, there is a great deal of evidence that compared to delayed gratification for a larger reward, selecting immediate gratification for a smaller reward is predictive of both concurrent and prospective maladaptive behavior. Such findings tend to support the conclusion that immediate gratification behavior is often maladaptive and may be an expression of an impairment in the ego or executive function of inhibitory capacity. However, this conclusion may overlook the possibility that immediate gratification, as well as perhaps other apparently impulsive behaviors, may have different meanings and different adaptive significance in different contexts. In particular, questions have arisen regarding the adaptive significance of immediate gratification in a resource scarce environment.

Griskevicius et al. (2013) have argued that in an environment of relative scarcity (and, one might add, in an unpredictable environment), choice of immediate gain and gratification as well as a general valuing of the present over the future may be quite adaptive rather than necessarily indicate impairment in ego functioning. On this view, in certain contexts, choice of immediate over delayed gratification may not reflect, or may not only reflect, inadequacy of inhibitory control, but rather a strategy that is adaptive to a particular environment – a sort of take your gains and gratifications now or they will be gone. This hypothesis is supported by Kidd, Palmeri, and Aslin (2013) finding that delay of gratification is influenced by the child's beliefs about environmental reliability. They note that delay of gratification "may not only reflect differences in self-control abilities, but also beliefs about the stability of the world" (p. 109).

Also supporting the preceding formulation is Liu, Feng, Suo, Lee, and Li's (2012) finding that simply being exposed to poverty versus affluence pictures influenced choice of immediate versus delayed gratification. In addition, compared with participants who received a monetary bonus (which, according to the authors, induced feelings of affluence), participants who did not receive a monetary reward (which presumably induced feelings of poverty) were more likely to choose immediate gratification. Unfortunately, the experimenters did not appear to collect data on the participants' SES and, therefore, could not determine whether there was any interaction between SES and the effects of priming on immediate gratification behavior. It is entirely possible that the main effect findings obtained by Liu et al. (2012) are primarily due to the responses of subgroups who view themselves as poor. Also, we cannot easily assess the ecological validity of these findings. That exposure to poverty cues in an experimental setting for a short period of time influences the monetary behavior of university student participants is an interesting finding. However, this finding does not necessarily tell us much about the monetary behavior of individuals who live or have lived in a poverty environment for a long period of time.

Unlike Liu et al. (2012), Griskevicius et al. (2011) did include SES information on the participants in investigating the effects of the experimental prime of mortality cues on monetary risk-taking choice and immediate gratification behavior. (The mortality cues consisted of participants reading a fictional citation of a supposed *New York Times* web story entitled "Dangerous times ahead: Life and death in the 21st century", which described recent trends in violence and death in the USA.) They found that the effect of mortality cues on these behaviors interacted with perceived childhood SES, such that for participants who reported growing up poor, exposure to mortality cues led to risky and immediate gratification behavior. Contrastingly, for participants who reported growing up in a wealthy environment, exposure to mortality cues was associated with less risky and more delayed gratification behavior.

An especially interesting finding was that, whereas perceived childhood SES interacted with the prime in influencing delay behavior, the participants' *current/expected* SES did not interact significantly with the prime. As Griskevicius et al. (2011) note,

> it appears that the influence of mortality cues on life history strategies – and the risky decisions associated with such strategies – depends more on a person's relative childhood SES than on a person's current/expected future SES. Hence, although childhood and adult SES are related, individuals' adult life history strategies may be particularly sensitive to the availability of resources when the individual was growing up.
>
> (p. 1019)

What makes this finding especially significant from a psychoanalytic perspective is the evidence that early schemas and strategies adapted to childhood conditions continue to have great influence on certain behaviors in conditions in which these early schemas and strategies are no longer appropriate. An implication of such findings is that we need to extend the idea that early schemas and strategies continue to influence later behavior not only in the "hot" areas of intimate relationships and biological drives, but also in the seemingly "cold" area of monetary decisions – although from a psychoanalytic perspective, monetary decisions may not be "cold", but may symbolically represent "hot" meanings having to do with such matters as deprivation, security, power, self-esteem, and so on.

In a review of the "effects of poverty-related adversity on child development", Blair and Raver (2012, p. 309) write that caregiving behaviors "can be understood to shape the development of child behaviors in ways that are appropriate or beneficial for the [environmental] context in which that development is occurring" (p. 312). Thus, they suggest that caregiving behaviors in a resource scarce environment may encourage immediate gratification as adaptive insofar as it is appropriate and beneficial in the environment in which one has been raised and presumably also in the environments one is likely to encounter.[9]

Even if resource scarce environments generate strategies adapted to that environment, it would not follow that either the child's environment will remain the same or that the strategies generated will be adapted to the characteristics and demands of the new environment. The ways of coping that may have been adaptive for early adverse environments may be maladaptive in later environments that differ in important ways from earlier ones. This is particularly likely to occur in view of the fact that there is a strong tendency for early schemas and coping styles to persist even when environments change. Thus, although a strong tendency to opt for immediate gratification may have been adaptive at one time in a particular environment, as a consequence of a mismatch between this preexisting coping strategy and altered environmental characteristics and demands, it becomes functionally equivalent to an impairment in ego or executive functioning.

Although the argument that immediate gratification in a resource scarce environment is adaptive may be plausible, there is little direct empirical carlson evidence demonstrating that this is, in fact, the case. Indeed, there is some evidence that would lead one to question that formulation. Thus, Ayduk et al. (2000) found that in both an upper-middle class sample as well as in a sample of inner city, low SES, minority children, whereas low delay of gratification was a risk factor in its interaction with the effects of rejection sensitivity on psychological functioning, high delay of gratification was a protective factor. There was no evidence in either sample that low delay of gratification bestowed any adaptive benefits to general functioning. And even in the low SES environment, high delay of gratification was associated with positive functioning.

Even if immediate gratification were, in certain respects, adaptive in a resource scarce environment, it would be a mistake to overlook or minimize the destructive effects of early poverty environments on development, including on the development of ego functioning. There is ample evidence of the negative effects on basic aspects of childhood development, including on the development of ego functioning of adverse childhood conditions and experiences in poverty environments. As Blair and Raver (2012) note, that the behaviors shaped (e.g., immediate gratification) may be appropriate to a particular environment does not mean that they are

> necessarily optimal or desirable states of functioning. On the contrary, adaptation to low-resource environments involves short-term

"benefits" as well as long-term "costs" to the organism, both psy-chologically as well as physically, that are due to increased stress on organ systems resulting from alterations to stress and immune system functioning.

(p. 119)

For example, although chronic heightened vigilance may be adaptive in a dangerous environment it is often harmful in the long-run in a number of ways. Chronic vigilance and readiness to respond to threat may increase the likelihood, on the behavioral level, of negative interpersonal interactions in the form of wariness and aggressive cues with new teachers and peers (See Dodge, Price, Bachorowski, & Newman, 1990) and, on the physiological level, in the form of alterations in the HPA axis function and glucocorticoid receptor density, which, in turn, are associated with poorer executive function. The point here is that, even when the child copes with a resource scarce environment with a strategy that is adaptive in that environment, there are nevertheless likely to be significant costs exacted by that environment.

These adverse conditions and experiences include nutritional deficiencies, greater exposure to environmental toxins, stress, negative parenting, familial trauma, maltreatment. The consequences of these adverse experiences include poorer performance on executive function tasks (DePrince, Weinzierl, & Combs, 2009; Raver, Blair, & Willoughby, 2013); higher cortisol level (Blair, Raver, Granger, Mills-Koonce, & Hibel, 2011); lower volume of brain grey matter (Hanson et al., 2013); less volume of left hippocampus (Johnson, Riis, & Noble, 2016; Rao et al., 2010); less cortical thickness in the right anterior cingulated gyrus and left superior frontal gyrus (Lawson, Duda, Avants, Wu, & Farah, 2013); large amygdala responses and low activation in areas of the prefrontal cortex during an emotion-regulation task (Kim et al., 2013); and poorer health outcomes (Schury & Kolassa, 2012).

The preceding consequences of low SES environments appear to be direct causal effects of certain negative aspects of low SES environments. Although the child may develop *compensatory* strategies to cope with adverse environments, the direct harmful effects of these environments remain. For example, although a child may develop strategies to cope with, say, uncertainty of food availability, poor prenatal and postnatal nutrition will have certain direct effects, including on birth weight and brain development, as well as the behavioral expressions of these effects, which may include impairments in ego functioning, including in the ability to delay gratification. Hence, the coping strategies an individual develops is likely to reflect both the direct effects of adverse conditions and experiences as well as the meanings given to these conditions and experiences. Thus, the impact of not having enough food during one's childhood will not only reflect the effects of poor nutrition on brain development and the strategies developed to cope with nutritional conditions, but also the psychological meanings of hunger and deprivation as well as the strategies developed to cope with experiences of deprivation.

As noted previously, although chronic hypervigilance in a dangerous environment may be adaptive, it also entails potentially serious physiological and psychological costs in the long run. Blair and Raver (2012) also observe that

> early stress alters gene expression and induces structural changes as well as changes in connectivity in brain areas that underlie stress response physiology (Karssen et al., 2007; Liston et al., 2006; Patel, Katz, Karssen, & Lyons, 2008; Radley, Arias, & Sawchenko, 2006). In turn, alteration of stress response physiology influences activity in neural systems that underlie self-regulation abilities, including executive functions (Cerqueira, Mailliet, Almeida, Jay, & Sousa, 2007).
>
> (p. 311)

Buffering and protective factors

In the previous discussion, I have focused on the effects of SES environments on subsequent development. However, there is evidence that object relational factors, in particular, maternal behavior, may mediate the negative effects of low SES environments. For example, Chen, Kubzansky, and VanderWeele (2019) found that maternal warmth buffers the effects of low SES. Similarly, Brody et al. (2019) reported in a study on African-American youths living in poverty conditions that an intervention program that enhanced supportive parenting assesses at ages 11 to 13 and 16 to 18 had a positive effect on employment income and poverty status at age 25.

There is also a good deal of evidence that mother's capacity for a high level of self-reflection serves to buffer the adverse effects of high risk environments. For example, in an early study, (Fonagy, Steele, and Steele,

1991; Fonagy et al., 1995) found that single teen mothers in high risk environments who had a high level of reflective capacity were far more likely to have securely attached infants at 1 year of age than mothers with a low level of reflective capacity. Since that study, a number of reports have appeared with similar findings (e.g., Fonagy & Target, 2008; Stacks et al., 2014; Slade, 2005; Slade, Grienenberger, Bernbach, Levy, & Locker, 2005). There is also evidence suggesting that maternal reflective functioning may influence the infant's attachment pattern through its association with maternal sensitivity (Alvarez-Monjaras, McMahon, & Suchmenn, 2019; Alvarez-Monjaras, Rutherford, & Mayes, 2019).

In a large scale study of data from 1,009 children and families from the National Institute of Child Health and Development Study of Early Child Care (NICHD), Hackman, Gallop, Evans, and Farah (2015) investigated the relationship between socioeconomic status (SES) and the executive functions (EF) of planning and working memory through middle childhood. They reported that early family income-to-needs and maternal education predicted EF at 54 months of age. These effects appeared early in childhood and persisted over time. There were a number of factors that mediated this relationship, including early home enrichment and maternal sensitivity. An important finding that emerged is that changes in SES are associated with changes in EF, with decreases in SES predicting lower EF and increases in income predicting higher EF. One of the authors' conclusions is that "these results converge to suggest that both the provision of a stimulating environment and the parents' own investment of time, guidance, and support in navigating the environment are of importance for the relation between SES and EF" (p. 697). I would add that the preceding results tend to throw into question the formulation that poorer EF (e.g., lower delay of gratification) may constitute an adaptive response to a relatively harsh environment.

The relationship between exploratory activity (an ego function) and the availability of a secure base (an object relational variable) posited by attachment theory (Bowlby, 1973) can serve as a model for an optimal relationship between object relational factors and ego development. According to that hypothesis, mother's physical and affective availability enhances the range and comfort of the child's exploratory behavior. There is much supporting evidence for this formulation. Passman and Erck (1978) reported that compared to a condition in which a film of a stranger was present, toddlers played longer and engaged in more locomotor activity when accompanied by either mother or a silent motion picture of her. This was true even when the children *misidentified* the picture of the stranger as mother. Similar results were found when mother's voice versus stranger's voice was broadcast (Adams & Passman, 1979); a clear versus a blurred photograph of mother (Passman & Longeway, 1982). In one study, over and above physical availability, mother's emotional availability (i.e., reading versus not reading a newspaper) increased exploratory activity (Sorce & Emde, 1981). There is also evidence that secure attachment, which is facilitated by an object relational environment of maternal responsiveness, is associated with greater social and cognitive competence; and insecure attachment, which is generated by an object relational environment characterized by relative lack of maternal responsiveness, is associated with poorer social and cognitive competence (e.g., Eagle, 2013; Thompson, 2008)

Group membership and delay of gratification

Doebel and Munakata (2018) write that "self-control behavior does not simply reflect self-control ability, but is also influenced by social contextual factors" (p. 24). We have seen evidence for the validity of this observation with regard to socio-economic factors in the previous section. There are, however, other social contextual factors that also influence self-control. Among the "social-contextual factors" that influence the ego function of delay of gratification is peer group membership. Doebel and Munakata (2018) reported that 5-year-old children showed greater ability to delay (in a one versus two marshmallow reward situation) when they believed that their in-group delayed and the out-group did not. They also "valued delayed gratification more if their in-group waited and the out-group did not" (p. 12). Interestingly, "group behavior influenced children to wait longer, but did not influence children to wait less" (p. 12), suggesting that whereas group membership influenced delay behavior, it did not change the children's "thinking about whether or not delaying gratification is generally a good thing" (p. 12).[10]

Trust and delay of gratification

Another social-contextual factor that influences delay of gratification is degree of trust. Studies on delay of gratification with children involve interpersonal interactions in which an implicit or explicit promise is made by an adult (i.e., the experimenter) to the effect that the child's delay will result in a larger reward. Hence, it is possible, perhaps likely, that the child's degree of trust will influence delay of gratification behavior. And, indeed, as we have seen in Chapter 1, there is evidence that children's delay of gratification is influenced by both trust in the individual promising the reward and generalized trust, that is, the degree to which they view others as trustworthy (Ma et al., 2018). These findings suggest that not only, as Ma et al. (2018) put it, "there is more to delay of gratification than cognitive capacity" (p. 118), but that the additional factors that influence delay of gratification include social-interpersonal influences. Although I do not know of any studies addressing this issue, it is possible, perhaps likely, that being gently touched enhances trust that a greater reward will be forthcoming if one delays gratification. Another possible factor involved in the relationship between touch and greater delay is the direct rewarding effect of a gentle touch. There is evidence that a pleasant touch activates the orbitofrontal and cingulated cortices, areas that are part of the brain reward center (Rolls, Kringelbach, & de Araujo, 2003; Rolls, O'Doherty et al., 2003).

Although not explicitly addressed, the issue of trust is also implicated in the relationship between resource scarce environments and delay of gratification discussed in the preceding section. That is, when one states that an individual in a resource scarce environment opts for immediate gratification because s/he is skeptical that delay will result in a larger reward, one is, in effect saying that the individual does not *trust* that the environment (as well as the individuals in it) will yield larger rewards if one delays gratification.

The issue of trust is also implicated in the exercise of another ego function, namely, exploratory behavior. In accord with attachment theory, and supported by a great deal of evidence, the child is more likely to engage in exploratory behavior when s/he is confident in the availability of the attachment figure (Bowlby, 1973). In effect, the relationship between exploratory behavior and confident expectation in the availability of the attachment figure is essentially a statement of the relationship between the exercise of an ego function (exploration) and interpersonal trust.

Peer relationships and psychological development

Beyond the concept of sibling rivalry (and with the exception of Sullivan's (1953) reference to the "juvenile era"), psychoanalytic theory has virtually nothing to say about the influence of peer relationships and interactions on psychological development and functioning. As Vivona (2010) observes, "the parent-child relationship has taken center stage in most subsequent [i.e., post-Freudian] theorizing, with siblings pushed to the periphery" (p. 9). Despite the explicit neglect of peer relations in Freudian theory, implicit in the Freudian formulation of the resolution of the Oedipus complex is the importance of peer relations for normal development. According to that formulation, adequate resolution of the Oedipus complex requires that the boy relinquish his libidinal ties to mother and invest in, as Freud (1912) puts it, an "extraneous object" outside the family. (Although Freud also includes a discussion of the girl's Oedipus complex, it is arbitrary and unconvincing; it is clear that his formulation refers mainly to the boy.) However, this idea is not elaborated further to include a discussion of peer relations.

Freud's main focus in his discussion of resolution of the Oedipus complex is on the *child's* relinquishment of libidinal ties to mother, in particular, as a consequence of his fear of punishment at the hands of the father (castration anxiety). Virtually nothing is said about the *mother's* role in discouraging such ties including through encouraging ties to peers. Other psychoanalytic theorists, however, Loewald and Mahler, for example, have recognized the importance of the child's increasing psychological separation from mother, quite apart from issues of libidinal incestuous ties. Indeed, Loewald (1979) reinterprets the Oedipus complex metaphorically in terms of the child's conflict between desire for unity with mother and the movement toward separation from the maternal matrix. This formulation is quite similar to Mahler's (1968), Mahler, Pine, and Bergman's (1970), and Mahler, Bergman, and Pine's (1975) positing of a universal developmental process involving tension between symbiotic ties to mother and the normal developmental aims of separation-individuation. Unlike Freud, Mahler does, indeed, recognize the mother's role in this process (See, for example, Mahler et al., 1970). However, neither Mahler nor Loewald discuss the role of peer interactions and relationships in negotiating the process of separation and individuation. Nor do they discuss the importance of peer interactions in the development of social skills and competence.

Indeed, the topic of social competence is hardly represented in the psychoanalytic literature. One of the few psychoanalytic theorists who has written about the development of social competence is Fonagy et al. (1991, 1995). He has hypothesized that a core adaptive function served by the child's prolonged helplessness and the infant-mother attachment bond is that they provide a milieu for the child's development of what he refers to as an Interpersonal Interpretive Mechanism (IIM), that is, a means of acquiring social skills and "rules" necessary to survive and thrive in a complex social world. However, note that Fonagy's focus on acquisition of skills is largely in the context of infant-mother interaction. There is no reference to the role of peer interactions in the process of becoming a socially competent individual. Although it also focuses on the parent-child relationship, implicit in attachment theory's account of the relationship between the availability of a secure base (i.e., the caregiver as attachment figure) and exploratory behavior is the caregiver's role in facilitating interactions and relationships outside the infant-mother attachment milieu (Bowlby, 1980). Thus, in facilitating and broadening the infant's and child's experiences beyond its relationship to the caregiver, the secure base enables the acquisition of knowledge and skills related to the physical and social worlds in a relatively safe way. Much exploratory activity among the young of a species necessary for the development of social skills and adaptation to the social world takes place in the form of interaction with peers. Thus, an important role of the attachment figure is not limited to the direct transmission of social skills, but also includes the provision of opportunities for the child to acquire these skills in the larger social world in a relatively safe way. The path for the attachment figure's encouragement of exploratory activity is facilitated by the inherent reward value that social interaction, particularly social play, has for a wide range of species. In a series of early studies, Mason et al. (Mason, Hollis, & Sharpe, 1992; Mason, Saxon, & Sharpe, 1963) demonstrated that the mere opportunity for social play serves as a reinforcer for young chimpanzees.

In short, implicit in attachment theory (as well as explicit in Harlow's [1959] formulations on the peer affectional system, and both of which are embedded in an evolutionary framework) is the idea that a good caregiver makes it possible, indeed encourages, her infant to move away from her toward peer relations, thus facilitating the acquisition of adaptive social skills and the development of ego functions related to social reality. Indeed, Harlow goes as far as to say, perhaps hyperbolically, that "mothers were not necessary for socialization, but merely facilitated the interaction of their infants with other infants" (as cited in Vicedo, 2009, p. 196).

As evidence in support of his conclusions, Harlow (1962) cites the finding that monkeys raised with peers and no mother develop greater social competence than monkeys raised with mother and no peers. Based on evidence of this kind, Harlow (1962) has argued that the peer affectional system is more critical for the development of social competence than the infant-mother affectional system. He writes (again, perhaps somewhat exaggeratedly):

> In the monkey, at least, it would thus appear that under favorable circumstances, real mothers can be bypassed but early peer experiences cannot. Thus, when playmates were denied, the infant monkeys were socially crippled, and when this variable was provided early, the infants survived both passive and brutal mothering and even no mothering at all.
>
> (p. 10)

As Vicedo (2009) observes, although Bowlby extensively cited Harlow's work on the vital importance of mother love, he never cited his work on the role of peers in personality development. Although not to the same extent, this is also true of Spitz.

One of the unexpected findings of Harlow's (1958) classic study in which monkeys were raised by surrogate wire and terry cloth mothers is that they developed into socially and sexually incompetent adults and incompetent mothers. This deviant development has generally been attributed to the absence of whatever inputs are provided by flesh and blood mothers as caregivers. However, as Vicedo (2010) points out, the infants raised by inanimate surrogate mothers were raised in separate cages and were deprived not only of flesh and blood mothers, but "were also deprived of fathers, siblings, friends, and all other members of a family and social group" (p. 196). The detrimental effects of being deprived of social interactions with peers is not limited to primates. Deprivation of opportunities to play during adolescence is associated with social and cognitive impairments in adulthood in rats (e.g., Trezza, Damsteegt, Achterberg, & Vanderschuren, 2011). There is also evidence that social play is rewarding and serves as an incentive for learning in rats (e.g., Trezza & Vanderschuren, 2008, Trezza, Baarendse, & Vanderschuren, 2009) as well as in certain strains of mice (e.g., Panksepp & Lahvis, 2007). It is worth noting that the most effective "therapeutic" intervention for the chimps who were raised by surrogate terry cloth and wire mothers was placing them in a normal peer group (Suomi & Harlow, 1972).

An important adaptive role played by mother is that, at a certain stage in the infant's development, she pushes the infant away from exclusive contact with her as a means of facilitating interaction with peers. Vicedo (2009) observes that were the infant to remain exclusively attached to mother, it would be handicapped in its social relations with other infants and later, with adult peers. As Harlow (1960) puts it: "An infant monkey cannot form adequate affectional patterns for other monkey infants unless it can break the contact bond which has been established between it and the mother" (p. 676).

There have been studies on the effect of rearing conditions on development, since Harlow's seminal work, that both support and also suggest some modifications of Harlow's conclusions. With regard to the former, Sackett, Ruppenthal, and Davis (2002) found no differences in survival, growth, neonatal deaths, disease, bite wounds, and pregnancy outcomes between that nursery-reared between nursery-reared and mother-reared pigtailed monkeys. They conclude: "We do not advocate rearing primates without mothers, but . . . these procedures are sufficient for producing physical health and adaptive juvenile and adult social skills in nursery-raised monkeys" (p. 165). However, Bastian, Sponberg, Suomi, and Higley (2002) reported that mother-reared rhesus monkeys outranked peer-reared monkeys as juveniles and adults. And Higley, Suomi, and Linnoila (1992) reported that, although both peer-reared and mother-reared monkeys exhibited less distress in a novel situation when they were with their most preferred peer, the peer-raised monkeys exhibited more distress than the mother-reared monkeys. Quite apart from peer- versus mother-reared conditions, it is interesting to observe that peers can serve as "primary attachment sources" (p. 1163).

An important caveat needs to be noted with regard to the studies discussed previously. They are all laboratory studies, which means that despite not being reared by mother, the peer-raised monkeys were nevertheless provided food and other necessities for survival by the experimenters. The conditions in the monkeys' natural environment is quite different. Although the laboratory studies may be important in their own right, the question of ecological validity certainly arises.

The Freud and Dann study

We do not know, of course, the extent to which Harlow's observations with monkeys would apply to human infants – although Harlow and Harlow

(1969) maintain that "[i]n primates – monkeys, apes, and man – socialization is essential to survival" (p. 36). Perhaps the closest we come to observing children raised with peers and without mother is A. Freud and Dann's (1951) description of the development of six German-Jewish children, whose parents were killed shortly after their birth, who arrived at the Terezin concentration camp at 6 to 12 months of age. According to Freud and Dann, the degree of adult caring they experienced was limited to meeting basic needs that enabled them to survive physically. After WW11 ended, they were brought to England when they were 3–4 years of age. Although their attitudes toward adults ranged from indifference to hostility, they were extremely caring and empathic toward each other and always wanted to be together. As an example of their empathic attitude toward each other, when one of the children, Paul, was taken for a ride in a pony cart – something he liked very much – he cried because the other children were not given the same experience. Freud and Dann write that there was a complete absence of rivalry and competition among the children.

In their Conclusion section, Freud and Dann write:

> They showed a heightened autoerotism and some of them the beginning of neurotic symptoms. *But they were neither deficient, delinquent nor psychotic* [my emphasis]. They had found an alternative placement for their libido and, on the strength of this, had mastered some of their anxieties, and developed social attitudes. That they were able to acquire a new language in the midst of their upheavals, bears witness to a basically unharmed contact with their environment.
>
> (p. 168)

It is not all clear that Freud and Dann's remarkable study has had much, if any, influence on psychoanalytic theorizing on the role of peer relationships on psychological development.

Peer relations and physical and psychological health

There is a great deal of evidence that peer relationships and interactions have a powerful influence on psychological development as well as health outcomes. It was more than 50 years ago that one of the first studies investigating the relationship between early experiences with peers and later development appeared (Roff, 1961). After that, a large number of studies investigating that relationship were carried out. A general finding from these studies is that early poor peer relations are associated with later negative outcomes, both concurrently and prospectively, in a number of areas of functioning. However, there are many complexities and variations on this theme. There are far too many studies to cover. I will summarize some representative and important findings. (For excellent reviews of research in this area, see Gustafsson, Janlert, Theorell, Westerlund, and Hammarström, 2012; Hay, Payne, and Chadwick, 2004; Prinstein et al., 2018.)

A number of studies have been published on the association between peer relations and physical health as well as psychological health. As an example of the former, in a 27-year longitudinal study of 881 school leavers, Gustafsson et al. (2012) reported a dose-response relationship between teachers' assessment of peer problems (i.e., social isolation and popularity) at age 16 and metabolic syndrome (defined in terms of waist circumference [for men], triglyceride level, blood pressure, HDL cholesterol, and fasting glucose) at age 43. Further, the association between peer problems and metabolic syndrome remained significant – only in women – after controlling for the following factors: health, health behaviors, school adjustment, and family circumstances at age 16, and for psychological distress, health behaviors, and social circumstances at age 43.

In another longitudinal study from birth to age 26 of 1,037 children, Caspi, Harrington, Moffitt, Milne, and Poulton (2006) reported that compared to non-isolated children, isolated children (operationalized by two items on the Rutter Child Scale: "is rather solitary" and "not much liked by other children") were at significant risk for poor adult health. As is the case in the Gustafsson et al. (2012) study, the relationship between poor peer relations and poor adult health remained significant after controlling for other risk factors: Low childhood IQ; childhood obesity; poor health behaviors, such as lack of exercise, smoking, alcohol misuse; and greater exposure to stressful life events. An additional important finding was "that chronic social isolation across multiple developmental periods had a cumulative dose-response relationship to poor adult health" (p. 805).

There is a good deal of evidence that peer status in childhood is a significant predictor of later adjustment and mental health problems. Roff and

Wirt (1984) reported that children with low peer status in grade school and high school showed two to three times greater risk for mental health treatment contact in young adulthood. Parker and Asher (1987) reported that a review of the literature showed that low acceptance and aggressiveness in childhood were significantly related to later life difficulties, including criminality. Olson and Lifgren (1988) found that negative peer nomination was significantly associated with measures of impulsivity and aggressive social problems. Ollendick, Weist, Borden, and Greene (1992) reported that children who were nominated as rejected and controversial by their peers showed poorer long-term adjustment than children nominated as popular, neglected, or average. (See Bullock, Ironsmith, and Poteat, 1988, for a review of sociometric techniques with young children). In a review of the literature on the relationship between peer difficulties and adjustment problems later in life, Parker and Asher (1987) found "general support for the hypothesis that children with poor peer adjustment are at greater risk for later life difficulties" (p. 357), particularly difficulties taking the form of dropping out and criminality.

A number of large-scale and relatively long-term longitudinal studies on the association between early peer relations and adult outcomes have been carried out during the last number of years. Analyzing the data on more than 10,000 men and women from the Swedish Birth Cohort Study, Modin, Ostberg, and Almquist (2010) reported that women's peer status in the sixth grade was predictive of hospitalization for anxiety and/or depression later in life. This relationship remained after "adjusting for family- and child-related family problem-load, . . . socioeconomic status, child's cognitive ability, ninth grade school grades, and continuance to upper secondary school" (p. 187). No significant relationship was found for men.

In another large study, Landstedt, Hammarström, and Winefield (2015) found that along with parental relationship, self-rated poor peer relations (i.e., social isolation) predicted adult internalizing symptoms and functional somatic symptoms. Bean, Pingel, Hallqvist, Berg, and Hammarström (2019) reported that for both men and women, poor peer relations at age 16 was significantly associated with depressive symptoms at age 43. In addition, poor social support at age 16 was associated with poor social support at age 30. This points to the cumulative effect of poor peer relations over time on later psychological health.

There are also studies on the concurrent relationship between peer relations and psychological problems. For example, Gorrese (2016) found significant relationships between peer attachment patterns and current symptoms. Secure peer attachment was associated with low anxiety and depression, whereas insecure peer attachment was associated with internalizing symptoms. The moderating effect of gender suggests that peer attachment was more strongly related to depression in girls. As another example, Oldfield, Humphrey, and Hebron (2015) found that secure peer attachment and school connectedness in 11- to 16-year-old children were associated with prosocial behavior.

It is important to note that the association between early peer relations and later physical and psychological outcomes does not necessarily indicate that early peer relations play a causal role in later outcomes. The relationship between the two is likely to be far more complex. Problematic early peer relations may point to dysfunctions that continue in the course of development into adolescence and adulthood. In this scenario, it is not poor early peer relations *per se* that constitute *the* causal factors in later outcomes; it is, rather, that a set of ongoing dysfunctions that is common to both early peer relations and poor later outcomes accounts for the association between the two.

The preceding is only one possibility. In another scenario, whatever the means by which it may have come about, poor peer relations may lead to poorer development of interpersonal and social skills. The relative lack of these skills may, in turn, have a continuing detrimental influence on later outcomes. In this scenario also, it is not poor peer relations *per se* that plays a significant causal role in later outcomes, but rather poor social skills that account for later outcomes. This possibility would generate the hypothesis that poor peer relations notwithstanding, were one able to help the child develop better social skills, one would expect more positive later outcomes.

Peer support in childhood and later psychopathology

The preceding findings on poor peer relations and later physical and psychological problems suggest that the obverse may also be true, that is, that supportive rather than poor peer relations would be likely to serve as protective factors in development. And, indeed, there is evidence supporting that implication. We have seen the protective role of peer relationships in the Freud and Dann (1951) study. There is a good deal of more recent evidence that early peer interactions influence not only psychological functioning but also long-term physical health. For example, with regard to the latter, Cundiff and Matthews (2018) found that "boys who were reported by their parents to be more socially integrated with peers during childhood evidenced lower blood pressure and body mass index in adulthood" (p. 1). (See also Allen, Uchino, and Hafen, 2015).

The Freud and Dann (1951) study points to the peer support as a protective factor in modulating the effects of harsh environments. A number of studies have investigated the role of peer support as a factor mitigating the effects of environmental adversity and early trauma. Yearwood, Vliegen, Chau, Corveleyn, and Luyten (2019) report on 644 adolescents who grew up in severely disadvantaged environments. Self-report measures were obtained on peer support, environmental adversity (defined as exposure to violence in the community), school, and media; complex trauma (defined as emotional abuse), emotional neglect, physical abuse, sexual abuse, exposure to violence in the home, parental conflict, and family dysfunction. As expected, adverse experiences were associated with increases in psychopathology (the participants in the study were followed for one year).

The most important findings were that, although the moderating role of peer support on psychopathology was not significant for environmental adversity, peer support did play a significant moderating role in regard to the relationship between early complex trauma and psychopathology. Indeed, for the subgroup with the highest level of peer support, complex trauma was not associated with psychopathology. Yearwood et al. (2019) suggest that peer support did not moderate the effects of environmental adversity (EA) because "in their [i.e., the adolescents studied] community EA is so high that it overwrites any possibility of mitigation by social influences" (p. 20). Why is this not the case with regard to the relationship between peer support and complex trauma? Yearwood et al. (2019) do not directly address this question. One possible answer to this question, only hinted at by Yearwood et al. (2019), is that in contrast to the ongoing unrelenting nature of EA, the residues of early negative life experiences that comprise complex trauma may not be unremitting and are therefore susceptible to influence by peer support.

As Bagwell, Newcomb, and Bukowski (1998) observe, peer relations include not only one's standing in a group of peers, but also whether or not one has a close friend. In a 12-year follow up study, Bagwell et al. (1998) investigated the association between both preadolescent peer rejection and presence or absence of a close friend and adjustment 12 years later. They found that having a close friend during preadolescence was significantly associated with overall adjustment in young adulthood, including better family interactions, less difficulty with authorities, more positive self-views, greater sense of competence, and less depressive symptomatology. The protective effect of friendship is suggested by the finding that "the unique relation between depressive status and depressive symptomatology was maintained even peer rejection was included as a predictor of these symptoms" (p. 149).

Processes underlying link between early peer relations and later outcomes

What are the processes that account for the relationship between early peer relations and later adjustment? This question can be posed with regard to any aspect of the relation between early experiences and later development. As one would expect, the answer to that question is not a simple one. Of course, I cannot provide an adequate discussion of this very complex question. What I can do, however, is highlight some issues that are relevant to any developmental theory, including psychoanalytic developmental theory, of the influence of early experience on later development.

An axiomatic assumption in psychoanalytic theory is that early experiences play a critical role in later development. Most developmental psychoanalytic theories are characterized by oversimplified linear formulations that go directly from early experiences to adulthood, with little attention to intervening experiences and processes. Examples of this pattern include accounts of the influence of fixations at particular psychosexual stages on later development of character structure; the effect of the nature of one's resolution of the Oedipus complex on a variety of aspects of later development, including object choice, integration between love and desire, gender identity, superego development and the development of neurosis; effect of early lack of parental mirroring on adult self-defects; effect of early projection and introjections on adult personality; and from early experiences and internalization of objects to schizoid conditions. These oversimplified formulations cannot possibly adequately account for the complex nature of development.

With regard to the area I have been discussing, as Hay et al. (2004) observe, it is unlikely that there is a "simple pathway from problematic peer relations to disorder" (p. 84). The relationship between the two is likely to be far more complex. As Hay et al. (2004) put it, "there is a reciprocal relationship between children's problems with peers and their psychological problems from infancy to adolescence" (p. 84). Furthermore, whatever the direction of the pathway, difficulties in peer relations may interfere with the adequate development of social and cognitive skills and thereby deprive the child of social support from peers that plays a role in the development of affect regulation and other ego functions. A more general to put it is to say that early experiences with peers moderates the relationship between early risk factors and later adjustment (Bagwell et al., 1998).

Turning now to the relationship between peer relations and physical health, there is evidence that social ties have a marked effect on physiological processes and mortality (e.g., House, Robbins, and Metzner, 1982; Kaplan et al., 1994; Seeman, 1996). As Caspi et al. (2006) write: "The need to belong is a fundamental human motivation that, when thwarted, compromises physical health" (p. 805). Hence, relative absence of or difficulties with social ties may lead to a greater allostatic load, that is, chronic activation of physiological stress systems that are especially sensitive to problems in that areas (Gustafsson, Janlert, Theorell, Westerlund, & Hammarström, 2012; Seeman & McEwen, 1996).

It could be argued that, as is likely the case in the relationship between peer relations and psychological distress that the association between poor peer relations and adult physical health is accounted for by poor childhood health and childhood risk factors (e.g., childhood obesity). However, the significant association between poor peer relations and poor adult health survived the control of childhood risk factors. Shedding light on this issue is the finding of the dose-response relationship between isolation from peers in childhood and adult health outcomes. For example, Bean et al. (2019) reported that poor social support at age 16 was associated with poor social support at age 30. That is, social isolation during *multiple developmental periods* (i.e., in childhood, adolescence, and adulthood) increases the likelihood of poor adult health outcomes. This suggests that *cumulative wear and tear* (allostatic load) is an important factor in accounting for poor adult health outcome. These findings, in Caspi et al.'s (2006) words, "under-score the usefulness of a life-course approach to health research" (p. 805). Although many competent psychotherapists informally adopt a life-course approach in which they examine cumulative and interactive influences from different developmental periods in the patient's life, this approach has not been integrated into psychoanalytic theories of psychological development.

Sibling relations as a special kind of peer relationships

In most mammalian species characterized by the birth of multiple off-spring, the earliest peer relations are generally with siblings. Although simultaneous birth of multiple offspring are relatively rare in humans, the earliest peer relations are sibling relationships. Although psychoanalytic theories tend to ignore the influence of peer relationships in psychologi-cal development, attention is given, certainly by Freud, to sibling rela-tionships (See Sherwin-White, 2007), with the primary focus on sibling rivalry and incestuous impulses. However, concern with any other role of sibling relationships has been pushed to the periphery.

Although there is some treatment of sibling relations in the psychoana-lytic literature that takes account of the potential positive impact of the sibling bond (e.g., Edward, 2003; Rustin, 2007), for the most part, even when sibling relations are discussed in the contemporary psychoanalytic literature, the focus generally remains on some form of sibling rivalry. For example, in her discussion of sibling relationships, Mitchell (2000, 2003) puts near exclusive emphasis on what Vivona (2010) describes as the "child's original crisis of nonuniqueness, the trauma of sibling dis-placement" (p. 9). Vivona (2010) continues:

> Feeling displaced by siblings, the child seeks to reclaim a unique posi-tion in the world, especially within the world of the family, and simul-taneously to avert recurrence of the original displacement by fending off potential rivals for that place in the center . . . to regain the sense of being the parents' one and only.
>
> (Vivona, 2010, p. 9)

Although Vivona (2010) does discuss other matters, such as sibling iden-tification and closeness, the discussion remains in the context of sibling rivalry. Thus, she refers to "identification with the sibling rival [as mollifying] competition with an agreement to be like the rival rather than to defeat the rival" (p. 13). In short, little attention is given in the psychoanalytic literature to the role of the sibling bond in providing critical psychological support in the face of problematic relations with parents and, more important in the present context, in developing social skills, including enhancement of interpersonal understanding.

Emphasis on ego control over instinctual impulses as measure of maturity and ego strength

Another area that needs revisions and corrections is the overemphasis of ego psychology on control of instinctual impulses as a primary measure of ego strength and mature functioning. As noted in Chapter 3, given the presumed "primary antagonism" (A. Freud, 1936, p. 172) and the threat to the ego that id impulses represent, adaptive functioning is understood in terms of enhanced ego control over dangerous impulses. This is the standard view of the id-ego model. However, as Apfelbaum (1966) has observed, (See also Eagle, 1984, 2018a), Freud presents a very different view of the relationship between the id in some of his writings. At one point, he writes "there is no natural opposition between ego and id; they belong together, and under healthy conditions, cannot in practice be distinguished from each other" (Freud, 1926b, p. 201). At another point, Freud (1915c) suggests that it is not the case that instinctual impulses are repressed because they are *inherently* dangerous, but rather that due to repression, they are endowed with increased power in the individual's fantasy life and therefore come to be subjectively experienced as dangerous As Freud (1915c) puts it, the

> repressed instinct-presentation . . . develops in a more unchecked and luxuriant fashion. It ramifies like a fungus, so to speak, in the dark and takes on extreme forms of expression [that are anxiety-provoking] due to the ways in which they reflect an extraordinary strength of instinct. This illusory strength of instinct is the result of an inhibited development of it in fantasy and of the damming-up consequent on lack of real satisfaction.
>
> (p. 149)

And finally, Freud writes that "if the ego remains bound up with the id and indistinguishable from it, then, it displays its strength" (as cited in Apfelbaum, 1966, p. 460). I take this to mean that ego strength is expressed, not in control over the id, but in integration of id material (See Loewald, 1960, 1975). Were these comments elaborated and their implication assimilated and integrated into psychoanalytic theory, the id-ego model would require substantial revamping. However, as it currently understood, the id-ego model, in its description of the ego largely in terms of control over id impulses, as a mechanical apparatus, and its failure to recognize the enlivening influence of impulses and desires on ego functioning, paints a picture that is more a depiction of obsessive rather than healthy and enlivened functioning.

Regression in the service of the ego

Partly in response to the criticism that ego psychology places excessive emphasis on ego control over id impulses, Kris (1952) introduced the concept of "regression in the service of the ego" (p. 177). (And as we have seen, Bellak et al. [1973] included "adaptive regression in the service of the ego" (ARISE) as an ego function.) According to Kris, adaptive regression is characterized by passive receptivity "to id and impulses and drive derivatives" (Knafo, 2002, p. 26) and to a primary process mode of experience. Although introduced in the context of writing about the nature of creativity and wit, regression in the service of the ego has also been invoked in regard to behaviors and experiences that, although entailing lessening of ego controls, access to primary process thinking, and primitive modes of experience, are nevertheless adaptive rather than pathological. Hartmann (1939 [1964]) writes in an essay entitled "Psychoanalysis and the concept of health" that "the mobility or plasticity of the ego is certainly a prerequisite of mental health, whereas a rigid ego may interfere with the process of adaptation" (p. 11). He then goes on to discuss the adaptive importance of the capacity to give up ego control.

Despite the unfortunate use of the term "regression", implicit in the concept of regression in the service of ego is an emphasis on *ego flexibility* rather that either over-control or under-control as a marker of ego strength. I say "unfortunate" because, as has been noted by others (e.g., Ehrenzweig, 1967; Gedo, 1983), the term "regression" is connotatively associated with pathology. Further, whatever else the term regression might mean, it refers to a return to an earlier state or to an earlier level of functioning. However, openness to earlier modes of experience and "ability to maintain contact with early body and self states and with early forms of object relationships, as well as with different modes of thinking" (Knafo, 2002, p. 29) are not regressive insofar as they involve an adult having experiential access to earlier states and modes *from his or her position of current level of functioning*. The individual does not return to an earlier state or earlier functioning in which he or she experiences and functions in precisely the way that s/he did as a child. In short, the access to earlier experiences and modes reflect *adaptive flexibility* of ego functioning rather than adaptive regression. Furthermore, the loosening of ego controls evident in ego flexibility is not limited to experiential access to early modes of thinking. It is also manifested in a variety of behaviors, such as humor, spontaneity, and creativity, that have little to do with earlier states and earlier modes of functioning. Indeed, with regard to the latter, the assumption that there are intimate links between creativity and some form of regression is a questionable one for which there is little evidence. This assumption is especially questionable when access to the unconscious processes recruited in creativity is viewed as equivalent to access to repressed infantile mental contents. It is clear that it is Hartmann's emphasis on ego flexibility – which, itself, has little to with regression, including adaptive regression – that should be at the forefront of healthy functioning.

Notes

1 However, as I have argued elsewhere (Eagle, 1984), the gratification of sexual and aggressive motives require "the fitting in of other persons" as much as the gratification of object relational motives do. Indeed, as we have seen, Freud defined the object as "the thing in regard to which the instinct achieves its aim" (Freud, 1905, p. 122). That is, if the instinct is to achieve its aim, the object must "fit in".

2 This does not mean that object relations are not biologically grounded. Rather, as reflected in attachment theory, for example, it means that the biological basis for (as well as the motivational organization of) object relations does not lie in the vicissitudes of sex and aggression or in hunger reduction, but in an autonomous instinctual system.

3 It should be noted that according to Guntrip, it is not only early object relations that influence ego functioning, but object relations throughout one's life. The same point is made by Bowlby (1980) when he writes that attachment bonds are a critical aspect of psychological life "from the cradle to the grave" (p. 442).

4 Bergmann (2000), too, suggests that an object relations perspective is incompatible with ego psychology. He writes that "Loewald's (1960) paper [with its ideas that 'were supported by the object relations theorists – Winnicott and Balint'] signaled the passing of the Hartmann era" (p. 61).

5 Given the assumption of an inborn and autonomous tendency to seek and relate to objects, the notion of a stage in psychological life that is pre-object or pre-object-relational or, from Mahler's (1968) perspective, a stage in which the infant is in an "autistic shell", is untenable (See Stern, 1985). Equally untenable from this perspective is the hypothesis that the infant turns to objects primarily because they are necessary for drive gratification. However, despite the positing of an early "autistic shell", Mahler was one of the early psychoanalytic theorists who recognized the importance of the early infant-mother matrix for the development of ego functions necessary for the achievement of separation-individuation.

6 For the purposes of this discussion, I am not distinguishing between the psychoanalytic concepts of object and object relations and Kohut's neologistic term "selfobject". They can be used interchangeably in the present context insofar as they both refer to a relational or interactional milieu for the development of vital functions. (See Eagle, 2018b, for a discussion of the important differences between object relations and self-selfobject relations.)

7 Kohut (1984) is undoubtedly correct in his critique of the Freudian account of agoraphobia, which is based mainly on oedipal dynamics or unacceptable instinctual wishes. I have described different psychoanalytic accounts of agoraphobia, including sexualization of locomotion (Abraham, 1913); street-walking or prostitution fantasies (Freud, 1926 [1925]); temptation to masturbate when alone (Freud, 1926 [1925]); the impulse to kill the trusted companion (Deutsch, 1929), all of which are dictated by the theorists' theoretical assumptions (which are often one form or another of drive theory), rather than by reference to the patient's experiences (Eagle, 2009).

8 We have been taught that certain behaviors mature at a particular set pace independently of learning. For example, in his classic experiment, Carmichael (1926, 1927) demonstrated that, compared to eels who were given swimming learning experiences, eels who were not given such opportunities caught up quite quickly in swimming proficiency and showed no long-term swimming differences from eels who had learning experiences. Thus, the learning versus no learning environments made no differences in acquisition of swimming proficiency. However, this does not mean that *any environment whatsoever* would not interfere with acquisition of swimming. Thus, if the no learning environment were outside a certain range (i.e., were traumatic in a particular way), it is not at all clear that that the eels in this environment would have caught up in their swimming proficiency.

9 A similar argument has been made to the effect that maternal behavior that generates an insecure attachment pattern (say, avoidant-dismissive attachment) can be understood to shape the child's behavior in ways appropriate to the context in which development is occurring as well as future environments the developing child is likely to encounter. (See Simpson & Belsky, 2008).

10 It should be noted that in the family of 97% of the participants, at least one parent had a four-year college degree or higher. This suggests that the children were generally socialized as to the value of delay of gratification.

5

An expansion of ego psychology

Interpersonal reality-testing

This chapter is devoted to the question of how different psychoanalytic theories deal with the issue of interpersonal understanding. The following chapter will address findings and formulations that need to be integrated into an adequate psychoanalytic theory of interpersonal understanding.

Psychoanalytic formulations of interpersonal understanding

When psychoanalytic theory does address the question of how one understands another, it is generally in the context of the treatment situation and is limited to the analyst's understanding of the patient's *unconscious mental states*. This is not only the case in classical theory, but also in other psychoanalytic *schools*. According to most, if not all, psychoanalytic theories, a potent factor that makes understanding of another difficult is the ubiquitousness of transference, particularly in emotionally laden relationships. To the extent that one responds to another as a stand-in for an early parental figure and tends to attribute characteristics and mental states of that early figure to a current other, to that degree will one's understanding of the other necessarily be compromised. Thus, from a psychoanalytic perspective, transference is a powerful force in limiting our ability to understand another.[1] Given the primacy of the concept of transference shared by different psychoanalytic schools, the focus is on our failure to understand another. The overriding concern is with the difficulty of understanding unconscious mental states rather than with the ordinary quotidian understanding of another's conscious intentions, actions, feelings, and thoughts that is critical in everyday interactions with others. In short, despite other theoretical differences, different psychoanalytic theories share a neglect of the phenomenon of ordinary interpersonal understanding.

The failure of psychoanalytic theories to systematically address ordinary interpersonal understanding is a striking lacuna for any theory that aims to examine how the mind works. It is a particularly striking gap for ego psychology, given its ambition of developing a general theory of mind. As we will see, there is a large research and theoretical literature on the processes involved in ordinary conscious interpersonal understanding as well as on individual differences in the adequacy of such understanding, which can be assimilated into an expanded ego psychology theory. Before turning to that literature, let me review how some major psychoanalytic theorists have dealt with the issue of interpersonal understanding.

As noted earlier, in view of the fact that we are social creatures, the capacity for interpersonal and social understanding is a vital ego function. And yet, no psychoanalytic theory adequately addresses the question of how we routinely understand each other's intentions, actions, feelings, thoughts, and communications in everyday interpersonal interactions. Although Hartmann (1939) writes that we must adapt to our social structure, he did not include among its adaptive functions the ego function of capacity for interpersonal understanding. If ego psychology is to serve as a foundation for such a theory, it needs to include findings and formulations on the basic ego function of interpersonal understanding.

In order for one to understand another, one must first have a conception of the other as a separate center of existence, not just an instrumentality to meet one's needs. Although the presence of this capacity does not guarantee that one will understand another, that is, it is not sufficient, it is a necessary condition for such understanding. As we will see, with a few exceptions, psychoanalytic theories have little to say regarding this capacity to have a sense of the other as a separate center of existence, with his or her own needs, desires, and added goals, rather than primarily a means to an end (See Eagle, 2018b).

As reflected in the concept of transference (the centrality of which, according to Wallerstein, 1990, is the "common ground" among different psychoanalytic theories despite other theoretical differences), as well as the assumption of its ubiquitousness, the primary focus of psychoanalytic theories is on *failure* to understand another. Also, the overriding concern of these theories is the understanding, largely in the clinical context, of the patient's *unconscious* mental states rather than quotidian understanding in ordinary interpersonal interactions. In short, despite other theoretical differences, different psychoanalytic theories share a neglect of the phenomenon of ordinary interpersonal understanding.

However, the fact is that from very early in life, just as we develop a consensually validated picture of the external physical world, most individuals successfully understand and communicate with each other in ordinary social interaction.[2] We have a pretty good idea of at least some of the processes involved in veridical perception of the external world. We also have some idea of the processes involved in the kind of interpersonal understanding that allow thousands of adequate interactions in a given day. Any adequate theory of mind needs to address the nature of these processes.

Freud on interpersonal understanding

From the perspective of Freudian theory and ego psychology, socialization consists primarily in increasing control over drive impulses, which, if permitted uncontrolled expression, would be inimical to society. Virtually nothing is said regarding socialization as a process characterized by enhanced capacity for interpersonal understanding and the acquisition of social "rules" and social skills. As we will see, this is the case not only with regard to Freudian theory and ego psychology but also with regard to other psychoanalytic theories.

Recall Freud's (1900) speculation that early in life the infant hallucinates the breast when hungry and learns that an actual object in external reality (i.e., the breast) is necessary for hunger reduction only after experiencing the failure of hallucinatory wish fulfillment to assuage hunger. Although not made explicit by Freud, the idea that the infant recognizes that s/he must turn to an actual object if his or her hunger is to be assuaged essentially points to the early emergence of an important aspect of interpersonal reality-testing, namely, the recognition that one must be in some kind of means-ends interaction with the object if one's needs and desires are to be gratified.[3] Failing this developmental achievement, the issue of interpersonal understanding does not even arise. Without the conception of an object separate from oneself, there is no entity to be understood.

Recognition that the actual breast in external reality is necessary for gratification can serve as a template for further learning about the nature of objects. According to A. Freud (1951), over time, the infant's development enables the experience of not only a partial object (i.e., the breast), but of an individual. However, from the perspective of Freudian theory and ego psychology, the individual remains mainly an instrumentality for need gratification. What is omitted from this account is recognition that, in normal development, the infant learns not only that the other is separate from oneself, but also that the other is the center of a *separate existence with her own needs, feelings, desires, thoughts, intentions, and so on, independent of one's own needs, wishes, and desires*. That is, the infant slowly comes to experience this object as a *subject* like oneself. This new development is a revolutionary one in that it marks the introduction of *intersubjectivity* into psychological life, as R. Eagle (2007) puts it, "the capacity to recognize and understand another's inner experiences" (p. 1). In the language of Buber's (1923) writings, one's conception of and interaction with objects are no longer limited to I-It, but now include I-Thou relationships (See also Benjamin, 1988).

This aspect of the development of interpersonal reality-testing is neither pursued nor developed by Freud or other psychoanalytic theorists. For Freud as well as for post-Freudian psychoanalytic theorists, the object continues to be viewed mainly in a transactional way (e.g., necessary for drive gratification, necessary for the enhancement of self-cohesiveness, for security, and so on) (See Eagle, unpublished manuscript for a further discussion of this issue). The task of addressing the question of how the child comes to experience the object as a *subject* is left to later theorists (e.g., Benjamin, 1988).

Recognition that objects are necessary in order for one's needs to be met may well constitute a developmental achievement and the beginning of reality-testing. However, such recognition may crystallize and remain at the level of an implicit conviction that objects exist only for one's gratification. If one's object relational world is to include the reality of the separateness and independent subjectivity of the other, that conviction needs to be modified. One must now come to terms with the enlarged recognition that there is a class of objects in the world comprised of subjects, who, like oneself, have needs, desires, and aims of their own, independently of one's own needs and desires. This means that one's very conception of objects can no longer be limited, to paraphrase Freud (1905), to the thing in regard to which one meets one's needs. One is now faced with the challenge of needing to understand the other if one is to survive and thrive in an interpersonal-social world. There is little or no discussion of how this challenge is met in psychoanalytic theories. As noted, the primary focus of psychoanalytic theories is on the factors involved in the *failure* to meet this challenge.

Freud on identification

If one were to look anywhere for a Freudian account of how one routinely understands another's mental states (i.e., actions, intentions, feelings, etc.), one would think that it would reside in the concept of identification. And yet, with the exception of a sentence or two in a footnote, this is not the case. One exception is Freud's (1921) linking of identification with empathy. He writes: "A path leads from identification by way of imitation to empathy, that is, to the comprehension of the mechanism by means of which we are enabled to take up any attitude at all toward another mental life" (p. 110).

Virtually all of Freud's limited number of comments about empathy are made in the context of one's reaction to jokes, a situation in which one compares oneself to the other telling the joke (Freud, 1905). (I must confess that I do not understand the role of empathy in this account.) The other references to empathy (*Einfühlung*) are made in relation to a fictional character (Freud, 1907 [1906]) and in the context of group psychology (Freud, 1921). Oddly, Freud (1921, p. 108), writes:

> Another suspicion may tell us that we are far away from having exhausted the problem of identification, and that we are faced by the process which psychology calls "empathy [*Einfühlung*]" and which plays the largest part in our understanding of *what is inherently foreign to our ego in other people*. [my emphasis]

For one thing, the conception of empathy as enabling us to understand "what is inherently *foreign* to our ego in other people" is certainly not in accord with the general understanding of empathy. Secondly, it is difficult to reconcile this conception of empathy with Freud's definition of empathy two pages later as "the mechanism by means of which we are enabled to take up any attitude at all towards another mental life".

All of Freud's other references to the concept of identification have little to do with empathy or with the general question of how we understand another's mental state. The concept of identification is given other work to do by Freud and is discussed in contexts not directly related to the question of how one understands another. Oddly enough, the one context in which Freud (1933 [1964], 1932) devotes much attention to the issue of how one gains access to another's mental states is in his discussion of telepathy and thought-transference. He writes: "I must urge you to have kindlier thoughts on the objective possibility of thought-transference and at the same time as telepathy as well" (p. 54). He also speculates that telepathy may have been an "archaic method of communication between individuals and that in the course of psychogenetic evolution it has been replaced by the better method of giving information with the help of signals which are picked up by the sense organs" (p. 55). It should be clear from this last passage that the "archaic method of communication between individuals" to which Freud refers is no ordinary one that requires information from the sense organs. Rather it entails "telepathic phenomenon [defined as] the reception of a mental process by one person from another by means *other than sensory perception*" (Freud, 1925 [1961], p. 136) (my emphasis).

In a strikingly prescient passage, Freud (1933 [1964], 1932) comes close to anticipating contemporary findings on mirror neurons and related processes that appear to play a central role in our routine and seemingly automatic ability to understand each other's actions and intentions (to be discussed later in the chapter). He writes,

> the telepathic process is supposed to consist in a mental act in one person instigating the same mental act in another person. What lies between these two mental acts may easily be a physical process into which the mental one is transformed at one end and which is transformed back once more into the same mental one at the other end . . . And only think if one could get hold of this physical equivalent of the psychic.
>
> (p. 55)

Somewhat peculiarly, by referring to a "telepathic process" and by extolling the virtue of accustoming oneself to the idea of telepathy, Freud appears to overlook the obvious implication that "if one could get hold of this physical equivalent of the psychical act" and if one did understand the "physical process" that "lies between these two mental acts", there would no longer be any need to invoke the process of telepathy, which, as we have seen, Freud defines as enabling thought-transference "by means other than sensory perception". Further, one need not be limited only to a "physical process" to dispense with telepathy in accounting for the quite ordinary and routine phenomenon of "a mental act in which one person instigates the same mental act in another person". For there are many ordinary psychological processes, for example, imitation, identification, and modeling that would account for a similar phenomenon.

We can see from the foregoing discussion, one, that apart from one or two comments on empathy, the concept of identification, as understood by Freud, does not shed much light on the questions of how we routinely understand another's mental state; and two, that Freud's reliance on telepathy and thought-transference as the basis for such understanding is woefully inadequate. One must conclude that, except for the prescient comments anticipating the mirror neuron discovery, classical psychoanalytic theory has no adequate account of what I refer to as interpersonal understanding, that is, the routine understanding of another's mental state.

Post-Freudian conceptions of interpersonal understanding

Klein on interpersonal understanding

Do we fare any better regarding the nature of interpersonal understanding with post-Freudian psychoanalytic theories? I begin with Kleinian theory. According to Klein, our understanding, indeed, our very experience of the external world, including the mental states of others, is largely the product of identification, projection, and projective identification. As the following passage makes clear, Klein (1975) assumes that projection is the basis for empathy:

> The process which underlies the feeling of identification with other people, because one has attributed qualities and attitudes of one's own to them, was generally taken for granted . . . for instance, the projective mechanism underlying empathy is familiar in everyday life.
>
> (pp. 142–143)

But projecting one's own qualities and attitudes onto another person is quite the opposite of empathy or of adequate insofar as one experiences what one has projected, not what the other person is feeling and experiencing.

In another reference to empathy, Klein (1975) writes: "where persecutory anxiety is less strong, and projection, mainly attributing to others good feelings, thereby becomes the basis of empathy, the response from the outer world is very different" (p. 258). (The sentence is difficult to follow.) But once again, one should note, projection of good feelings (or any set of feelings) is not the basis of empathy. In an important sense, it is the opposite of empathy. If I am not experiencing good feelings and you project them on to me, you are not being empathic or understanding of me. You are not expressing a capacity to understand or feel what I feel, but rather, you are egocentrically assuming that I feel what you feel. Instead of putting yourself in my shoes, you are putting me in your shoes.

It is worth noting that in the preceding context, Klein does not seem to think of projection as serving a defensive function, that is, as an attempt to rid oneself of a mental content by attributing it to someone else. Rather, she views it as a "normal" process by which one constructs and understands the external world. Thus, if I have a harsh superego and attribute to you attitudes that are similar to my self-critical attitudes, it is not necessarily motivated by my wish to rid myself of these attitudes. Indeed, such attitudes are often ego-syntonic. Rather, implicit in Klein's formulation is the idea that my experience of you having the same attitudes that I have is due to the fact that projection is the fundamental process through which I understand you. It would be more accurate to say, however, that it is the fundamental process through which I am likely to *fail* to understand you.

Insofar as Klein assumes that projection is the primary means of understanding (more accurately, *constructing*) the external world, including other people, there is no adequate Kleinian account of how one accurately understands another or, for that matter, of how one is able to get an accurate picture of any aspect of the external world. Rather, given its strong emphasis on projection, Kleinian theory, in effect, rules out the possibility of empathy or more broadly, of accurately understanding others.

In short, the possibility of truly understanding another seems to be precluded in Kleinian theory because projection of aspects of oneself on to the external world is not a contingency brought about by traumatic experiences. Rather, it is the primary, perhaps sole, means by which one experiences an external world at all. Also, what is projected in the construction of that external world are not contingent introjects that are the product of particular experiences, but inherent products of our fundamental drives. Given their rootedness in our biological structure, these are not aspects of oneself that can be "exorcised", as in Fairbairnian theory. That is, according to Klein, one can project either love or hate on to the other. But, in either case, one is not *understanding* the other as a separate being but is *creating* another through one's projections.

An implication of Klein's view is that one's experience of empathy or of understanding another is essentially an illusion; it is the product of projection of one's own "qualities or attitudes" to the other. What one experiences as "finding" in the other are only projected aspects of oneself. It is not clear from this formulation how it would even be possible to understand another's actions, intentions, and feelings.

Fairbairn on interpersonal understanding

Similar to Kleinian theory, according to the logic of Fairbairnian theory, it would seem exceedingly difficult for one person to understand another. According to Fairbairn (1952), under the impact of rejection and deprivation, the child internalizes the object, with the consequence that an *internal object* comes to constitute an element in his or her personality structure. As spelled out in Fairbairn's theory of the endopsychic structure of the personality, internal objects and ego structures enter into *internal object relations*. Most important in the present context, from Fairbairn's perspective, as a result of internalization one relates to another not in terms of who that other actually is but as a *stand-in* for an internal object; one's relationship to the other consists in a playing out of internal object relations. Thus, in presumably relating to an external other, one is actually engaged in an internal object relation. Further, insofar as an internal object is a structural element of one's personality, one part of oneself is relating to another part of oneself. Thus, one is trapped in a solipsistic dynamic rather than in an object relationship with an actual external other. Translating Fairbairn's language of internal objects into ordinary discourse, one can say that one attributes to the other (e.g., the analyst) attitudes and qualities of early figures that one has internalized as part of oneself and then experiences the other as having these attitudes and qualities.

Note the similarities between Klein's account in which one projects "qualities and attitudes of one's own" on to the other and Fairbairn's formulation that one projects on to the other attitudes and qualities of early parental figures *that one has internalized*. The difference between them lies in the fact that, whereas at the core of Kleinian theory is the assumption of inborn drives (i.e., love and hate), Fairbairn rejects drive theory. Thus, for Klein, the main sources of one's own qualities and attitudes that one projects onto others is linked to drive-related wishes and fantasies, whereas, according to Fairbairn, the main source of aspects of oneself that one projects onto others are parental qualities and attitudes that one has internalized and, in an important sense, have become part of oneself.

The idea that one projects characteristics of parental figures on to another is a relatively straightforward description of transference.[4] However, the important point to note is that insofar as one has internalized parental attitudes and rendered them part of one's personality structure, one is attributing to the other, not simply parental attributes and attitudes, but aspects of oneself, including attitudes one has toward oneself. In ordinary discourse this is equivalent to saying that one attributes to the other parental attitudes that have been internalized as part of oneself.[5]

The dynamic that Fairbairn describes would appear to preclude the possibility of adequately understanding another. However, Fairbairn hints at, but does not make explicit, a possible route to achieving some degree of understanding of another. As we have seen, in Fairbairn's (1952) theory of the endopsychic structure of the personality internal objects are viewed as structures or components of one's personality. However, they are not fully assimilated components; rather they are experienced as introjects. That is, they are at one and the same time experienced both as part of oneself as well as a foreign body that has been internalized, but not fully part of oneself. The origin of internal objects in Fairbairn's scheme lies in traumatic experiences (i.e., rejection and deprivation) that have not been fully metabolized or assimilated. The idiomatic expression of something "sticking in one's craw" – inside oneself, but not digestible – captures the phenomenology of internal objects (Eagle, 2017, p. 71). This metaphor of "sticking in one's craw" suggests that one means by which one can relate to another as an actual other rather than as a stand-in for an internal object is through "dissolving" the internal "bad" object (Fairbairn, 1952, p. 165). In effect, Fairbairn is saying that by ridding oneself of internalized negative parental attitudes, one can alter the psychological lens through which one perceives and relates to the other. However, Fairbairn is short on details regarding how one is able to "exorcise" the internalized object and has nothing to say regarding the processes involved in understanding another once the impediments to understanding are ameliorated.

Relational psychoanalysis and interpersonal understanding

In considering the perspective of relational psychoanalysis on the issue of interpersonal understanding, I will focus on Mitchell's writings insofar as they constitute the clearest, most sustained, and most articulate discussion of that issue, particularly in his 1998 paper on "The analyst's knowledge and authority". Given the emphasis on the *relational* aspects of psychological life, one might expect that relational psychoanalysis would address the issue of interpersonal understanding. However, according to Mitchell (1998), the psychoanalytic claim that one can gain "knowledge about what is going on in the mind" and "to the extent that it implies that there is something to be found there that is inert and simply discernible, starts us off on the wrong foot" (p. 17). According to Mitchell (1998)

> there are no clearly discernable processes corresponding to the phrase 'in the patient's mind' for either the patient or the analyst to be right or wrong about (p. 17). The kinds of mental processes which analysts are most interested in, both conscious and unconscious, are generally enormously complex and lend themselves to multiple interpretations. There is no singularly correct interpretation nor singularly correct best conjecture (p. 16).

Mitchell (1998) goes on to say: "In this way of thinking, mind is understood only through a process of interpretive construction" which, according to him, "is equally true for the first person who *is* the mind in question as well as for someone in the third person position who is trying to understand the mind of another" (p. 16). In light of the preceding passages, the general conclusion one comes to is that, according to Mitchell, one does not so much *understand another's mind, but rather constructs or co-constructs it* (at least in the analytic situation).

In Mitchell's (2000) reply to Silverman's (2000) critique of his 1998 paper, he writes:

> There is no place in my writings in which I argue against the idea that the patient has a mind with preexisting properties before ever encountering the analyst or that there are no continuities among the versions of ourselves that emerge with different people. This would, of course, be preposterous. But I think a problem with preconstructivist thinking is the assumption that there is a static organization to mind that manifest itself whole cloth across experiences. A very good description of the way I think about mind as preexisting but not preorganized is to be found in Ogden (1997).
>
> (p. 155)

The passage from Ogden reads as follows:

> The internal object relationship . . . is not a fixed entity; it is a fluid set of thoughts, feelings, and sensations that is continually in movement and is always susceptible to being shaped and restructured as it is *newly* experienced in the context of each new unconscious intersubjective relationship.
>
> (p. 190)

Mitchell does not clarify matters much with the distinction he makes between "preexisting" and "preorganized". How can mind be preexisting and not preorganized? Even if one grants Odgen's claim that mental organization is not fixed and can be influenced by "each new conscious intersubjective relationship", it would not follow that mind is not preorganized in some way. As Meissner (1997) comments,

> It seems odd . . . that one would think of the patient as he enters the consulting room for the first time, as without a history entirely of his own, without a developmental background, without a psychology and personality that he has acquired and developed in the course of a lifetime, all accomplished before he had any contact with the analyst.
>
> (p. 422)

Obviously, as Mitchell (2000) notes, to deny that the patient "has a mind with preexisting properties before ever encountering the analyst . . . is preposterous". However, the attempt to escape from this "preposterous" implication through the vague and untenable distinction between preexisting and preorganized does not work. The question that arises is: Why is it so important to reject the notion of a preorganized mind? The answer, I believe, ultimately lies in the embeddedness of Mitchell's views in the Sullivanian conception of an interactional field and his claim that the notion of an individual personality is an illusion (See Sullivan, 1950) – hence, the foundational assumption that mind is not so much a separate preorganized entity, but is rather constituted through ongoing social interaction. Thus, although for a different set of reasons, similar to other psychoanalytic theories, relational psychoanalysis does not include a theory of how we routinely understand another's mental states. Indeed, given the logic of relational theory, the question of how one understands another as a separate entity does not come to the forefront.

In this regard, although the specific contents vary, the situation is quite similar to the one encountered in Kleinian theory. In Kleinian theory, insofar as projection of our inner world is the primary means of creating the external world, it is meaningless to talk about understanding aspects of that world independent of our projections. Similarly, insofar as we "interpretively construct" another's mind, it is meaningless to talk about understanding another's mind whose organization is independent of our construction.[6]

There is a great deal more one can say about Mitchell's formulations (see Eagle, Wolitzky, and Wakefield, 2001 for a critique of Mitchell's views). However, in the present context, the point I want to emphasize is that despite its self-definition as a "two-person" psychology, in common with other psychoanalytic theories, relational psychoanalysis does not really have a theory about how one person routinely understands another's mental states. Indeed, and quite ironically, by virtue of its emphasis on "interpretive construction", from a relational psychoanalysis perspective, one person does not understand an independent another as a separate center of existence, with his or her own wishes, desires, needs, traits, etc. Rather, one constructs or co-constructs another in the course of interpersonal interaction.

Kohut on empathic understanding

Given the centrality of empathic understanding in self psychology, one would expect that, more than any other psychoanalytic theory, it would include a relatively delineated and robust account of interpersonal understanding. However, that is not the case. Kohut's (1984) comments on the nature of interpersonal understanding are pretty much limited to the claim that the analyst's main tool for understanding the patient is "vicarious introspection", that is, "the capacity to think and feel oneself into the life of another person" (p. 82). Indeed, he writes that "empathy defines the field of psychoanalysis" (p. 174), by which he appears to mean that the phenomena with which psychoanalysis is mainly concerned can only be investigated and understood via empathy or, as he refers to it, "vicarious introspection". There is no elaborated discussion of either the processes that underlie, interfere with, or facilitate empathy and interpersonal understanding.

It becomes clear in reading Kohut's writings that beyond the reference to "vicarious introspection" in the clinical situation, his primary interest is not in an examination of the nature of interpersonal understanding, but in the role of *feeling empathically understood* by the *selfobject* in the facilitation and maintenance of self-cohesiveness, both in the developmental and therapeutic contexts. Kohut's central concept of selfobject is critical here. According to self psychology theory, the selfobject is neither part of oneself nor a separate object. Rather, it refers to the narcissistic function, that is, the function of enhancing self-cohesiveness performed by a relationship (Wolf, 1988).

Kohut (1984) writes that in a successful psychoanalytic treatment the analysand will be able "to reactivate, in a selfobject transference, the needs of a self that had been thwarted in childhood". Through "optimal frustration" in the analytic situation, the patient slowly becomes able

> to sustain his self with the aid of the selfobject resources available in his adult surroundings. According to self psychology, then, the essence of the psychoanalytic cure resides in a patient's newly acquired ability to identify and seek out appropriate selfobjects – both mirroring and idealizable – as they present themselves in his realistic surroundings and to be sustained by them.
>
> (p. 77)

For example, Kohut (1984) writes that due to the strengthening of the patient' self-cohesiveness, he or she will be able to benefit from ordinary selfobject experiences, such as a friend placing a comforting arm on his or her shoulder. However – and this is a critical point – *the friend remains a selfobject*, even if a more mature and realistic one. That is, the friend continues to be experienced and related to in terms of the narcissistic function served by the relationship rather than as a separate person with needs, feelings, thoughts, and desires that can be understood and appreciated by the patient.

There is little in Kohut's writings that identify as a central goal of treatment or as a developmental achievement-enhanced capacity not only for object love – Kohut's *bête noir* – but also for understanding and appreciating the other as a separate subject, with his or her own thoughts, feelings, needs, and desires independently of one's own. That is, one finds little in Kohut's writings that refers to relating to another as a subject or what Rycroft (1972) calls a whole object, that is, "an object whom the subject recognizes as being a person with similar rights, feelings, needs, etc. as himself" (p. 102). Rather, Kohut's conception of object relations appears to be limited to self-selfobject relationships. As Bacal and Newman (1990), themselves self psychologists, point out, "In focusing on the experience of the selfobject function . . . self psychology has lost sight of the object that provides the function" (p. 230). One can sum up by saying that from a self psychology perspective, what is of primary importance is not understanding another, but *feeling understood*.

It appears that the importance of understanding another, not simply feeling understood, in self psychology is limited to the analyst's understanding of the patient (and the parents' understanding of their child). The only relationships described by Kohut that appear to go beyond self-selfobject interactions are the analyst's relationship to the patient and the parent's relationship to the child. In both contexts, the analyst in one case and the parent in the other, one person is in a caregiving relationship to another person. And in both contexts, the primary role of the caregiving person is to serve as a selfobject, that is, to offer empathic understanding and thereby enhance the self-cohesiveness, of another person (i.e., analysand or child). The questions that present themselves are the following ones: If, as Kohut suggests, self-selfobject relationships constitute the primary form of object relations, how does one understand the therapist's and parent's roles, which are characterized by one person (i.e., the therapist and the parent) relating to another (i.e., the patient and the child) not as a selfobject, but as a separate person to be understood?[7] How do the therapist and the parent escape the limits (when they do) of self-selfobject interactions that presumably characterize all other relationships?

One must conclude that insofar as self psychology limits its conception of the object and of object relations to their selfobject function of enhancing self-cohesiveness and does not include the capacity to experience and understand the other as a separate subject – as well as provide an adequate account of interpersonal understanding, including reciprocal understanding, in ordinary interactions – it cannot possibly constitute an adequate theoretical account of the nature of the mind.[8] In short, one cannot look to self psychology to shed much light on the fundamental question of the nature of interpersonal understanding. From a revised and expanded ego psychological perspective, in which interpersonal understanding is a vital ego function, the capacity for relationships that are limited mainly to self-selfobject interactions would be seen as a sign of a ego defect rather than an expression of normative functioning. This would apply to mature narcissism as well as to archaic narcissism.

Countertransference as the privileged route to understanding the patient

Although psychoanalytic theories do not have an adequate account of ordinary interpersonal understanding, they do have a specialized account of the analyst's understanding of the patient's unconscious mental states. As is well known, under the impact of early influential papers by Heimann (1950), Little (1951), Racker (1953), and others, the term countertransference was reconceptualized "totalistically" (Kernberg, 1965) "to cover all the feelings which the analyst experiences toward his patient" (Heimann, 1950, p. 88). Most important in the present context, countertransference, now totalistically reconceptualized, was no longer viewed as an impediment to treatment but as an indispensable tool to understand the patient's unconscious mental states. Indeed, in 1995, Gabbard wrote that agreement on this proposition constituted the "common ground" among psychoanalysts despite other theoretical differences. In a striking assertion of the importance of countertransference as a vital tool in understanding the patient, Racker (1968) wrote that the "thoughts and feelings which emerge [in the analyst] will be, precisely, those which did not emerge in the patient, i.e., the repressed and the unconscious" (p. 17). Even more so than when Gabbard (1995) made his "common ground" comment, there appears to be a widespread consensus among analysts that the analyst's countertransference reactions are the main tool for identifying and understanding the patient's unconscious mental states. So, if one were to ask: What is the contemporary psychoanalytic view on the question of how one person understands another, at least in the clinical situation? The short answer would be: through examining one's own thoughts, feelings, etc. in relation to the person with whom one is interacting and trying to understand.

Although not noted explicitly, this answer appears to be mainly intended to apply to the clinical situation in which the analyst is trying to understand the patient, particularly his or her unconscious mental states. According to Heimann (1950), what enables the analyst to rely so completely on his or her countertransference reactions is that s/he does not experience "violent emotions of any kind, love or hate. . . [that] impels towards action rather than towards contemplation" (p. 82) and that s/he "in his own analysis has worked through his infantile conflicts and anxieties (paranoid and depressive), so that he can easily establish contact with his own unconscious, he will not impute to his patient what belongs to the patient" (Heimann, p. 83); and as a variation of the preceding, because the analyst is less repressed than the patient, he or she has access to unconscious material that the patient does not have (Racker, 1968).

One must conclude that, while psychoanalysis may have a "specialized" theory regarding a certain kind of interpersonal understanding in a particular context (i.e., the therapist's understanding of the patient's unconscious mental states in the clinical situation), its various theories do not have a general theory of what makes ordinary interpersonal understanding possible. Furthermore, there is little evidence to support the theories it does have. In the next chapter, I will address theoretical formulations and research findings that need to be integrated if psychoanalysis is to have an adequate theory of the nature of interpersonal understanding.

Recognition that ego functions include the mediation of social reality and capacities that are involved in understanding and interacting with others opens the door to an expanded ego psychology framework that is able to encompass phenomena of central concern to different psychoanalytic *schools*. A rationale for the formulation of new psychoanalytic *schools*, for example, object relations theory, is the argument that certain important phenomena are not adequately accounted for by existing theory. Recognition that ego functions include the mediation of social reality and capacities that are involved in understanding and interacting with others opens the door to an expanded ego psychology framework that, through its ability to encompass phenomena of central concern to intersubjective and relational psychoanalysis, can contribute to a unified psychoanalytic theory.

Notes

1 Gill (1994) has argued that that the patient's experience of the analyst is largely a plausible construction based on cues emitted by the analyst. It is not clear what is being transferred in this construal of transference (See Eagle, 2018b; Wolitzky, 2000).
2 This is not to say that such understanding cannot be disrupted or impaired. It can be and often is.
3 In an important sense, this also constitutes the emergence of the earliest ego function. One can understand this development as an early expression of ego autonomy in the seemingly paradoxical sense that although reality-testing may be in the service of meeting one's needs, it must function relatively autonomously if one's needs are to be met.
4 Of course, we do not know the parents' actual characteristics, only the patients' reports.
5 To the extent that the patient mainly projects internal objects on to the other, it follows from Fairbairn's perspective that, to an important extent, transference is a superego phenomenon. This implication is strengthened by Fairbairn's view that it is mainly "bad" objects that are internalized and his reference to the internalized rejecting object as an "internal saboteur". This conception of transference is also congruent with Strachey's (1934) claim that softening the harshness of the patient's superego (a harshness projected on to the analyst) is a primary goal of psychoanalytic treatment.
6 Although the advent of relational psychoanalysis has presumably ushered in a "two-person" rather than a "one-person" psychology, the focus has been on how one person *influences* or has an impact on another rather than on a systematic investigation of the processes that enable one person to understand another.
7 From a revised ego psychology perspective that includes interpersonal understanding as a basic ego function, the experience of the other entirely as a selfobject would be viewed not as an aspect of normal development, but as an impairment in an ego function.
8 Although this may be an odd thing to say, I cannot help but view the overriding emphasis on the concept of selfobject and of self-selfobject relationships, not merely as a *description* of narcissism (archaic or mature), but as a narcissistic theory itself, that is, as a view of human nature and human relationships in which the only (or at least, the dominant) form of relationship possible is one in which one person mainly relates to another not as a separate other but in terms of the narcissistic function served by the relationship.

6

Research and theory on interpersonal understanding

As noted in the previous chapters, interpersonal understanding is a basic ego function, the absence or impairment of which would make everyday social and interpersonal interaction impossible. And yet, it is not discussed in psychoanalytic theories. Nor is it identified as a fundamental ego function in ego psychology. No psychoanalytic theory of the mind can be viewed as adequate without systematic attention to and systematic investigation of this basic ego function. Just as the infant and child learn about the nature of the physical world and acquire skills regarding how to function in that world, so similarly, the infant and child learn about the nature of the interpersonal-social world and acquire skills regarding how to function in that world. In both cases, early fundamental behaviors and capacities, either innate or emerging early in life, constitute the foundation for the acquisition of knowledge and skills. In the case of the physical world, for example, there is evidence that, very early in life, infants seem to have a conception of causality (Spelke, 1990). And in the case of the interpersonal-social world, very early in life, infants seem to have a capacity for affective communication (See R. Eagle, 2007, for a comprehensive review of this literature). These early conceptions and capacities serve as scaffolding for the development of further knowledge and skills.

There is a great deal of research and theory in cognitive and social psychology as well as cognitive and social neuroscience on interpersonal understanding that would need to be integrated into an adequate psychoanalytic theory of the nature of the mind. Let me turn to some representative research and theory in this area. Broadly speaking, two systems have been identified that underlie our capacity for interpersonal understanding. One system is immediate, automatic, implicit, and reflexive; and the other deliberative, explicit, effortful, and reflective. These two different systems have been variously referred to by such terms as "reactive" and "effortful control" (Posner & Rothbart, 2000); "System 1" and "System 2" or "fast" and "slow" thinking (Kahneman, 2011); "Type 1" and "Type 2" or "rapid autonomous" and "higher order reasoning" processes (Evans & Stanovich, 2013); subsymbolic and symbolic codes (Bucci, 2002; Epstein, 1994); and "automatic-reflexive" and "controlled-reflective mentalization" (Luyten & Fonagy, 2015).

Automatic and implicit processes involved in interpersonal understanding: Mirror neurons: self-other mapping and implicit imitation of motor actions

In the 1990s, neuroscientists at the University of Parma discovered a class of premotor neurons that were activated not only when macaque monkeys executed a goal-related action (e.g., grasping an object) but also when they observed another monkey carrying out these actions. These neurons were referred to as *mirror neurons* (Rizzolatti, Fadiga, Gallese, and Fogassi, 1996; Gallese, Fadiga, Fogassi, and Rizzolatti, 1996). A number of studies have demonstrated a similar system in humans in an homologous area of the brain (e.g., Grafton, Arbib, Fadiga, and Rizzolatti, 1996; Rizzolatti, Fogassi, and Gallese, 2001). Thus, when an individual observes an action being carried out by someone, a set of motor neurons that is activated in the one carrying out the action is also activated in the observer of the action.[1]

One of the properties that is striking about the mirror neuron system is that neural activation occurs in relation to the *goal* of the action (e.g., grasping an object) despite variations in the specific movements carried out to achieve the goal. For example, mirror neurons are activated both when the monkey used "normal pliers" (hand has to be closed to grasp an object) as well as "reverse pliers" (hand has to be opened to grasp an item). Thus, despite the opposite specific movements employed in the grasping action, the same brain areas are activated (Umilta et al., 2008). Rochat et al. (2010) found that in monkeys who were trained to grasp food with pliers, hand-grasping mirror neurons were activated when monkeys observed the experimenter spearing objects with a stick, an action never performed by the monkey. As Rochat et al. (2010) note, "Thus, what counts in triggering grasping mirror neurons is the identity of the goal (e.g., taking possession of an object) even when achieved with different effectors" (p. 614).

A similar result was found in humans. Cattaneo, Caruana., Jezzini, and Rizzolatti (2009) reported that the amplitude of the motor evoked potentials (MEP's) from the *opponens pollicis* muscle was determined by the goal of the motor act rather than the movements of the act (i.e., opened versus closed hand in reverse versus normal pliers). Gallese (e.g. 2006) refers to this phenomenon of responding to the goal and intention of the motor act as "intentional attunement", that is, attunement between the observed individual's action and the observer's understanding of the action.

Self-other mapping of emotional expression

A similar process takes place not only when one observes another's actions, but also when one observes another's emotional facial expressions. Observation of happy faces evokes increased zygomatic major muscle activity in the observer, while observation of angry faces evokes increased corrugators supercilii muscle activity, the same muscle areas activated in, respectively, happy and angry facial expressions (Dimburg, 1982; Dimburg & Thunberg, 1998; Dimberg, Thunberg, & Elmehed, 2000; Lundqvist & Dimberg, 1995). Congruent with these findings, Ekman, Levenson, and Friesen (1983) reported that when facial expressions associated with positive and negative emotions are constructed through facial muscle manipulations, autonomic activity differentiated between positive and negative emotions. There is also evidence that participants reported feeling an emotion consistent with the facial expression constructed (Ekman, 1984, 1992; Levenson, Ekman, & Friesen, 1990). Simply hearing an expression of anger increases activation of the muscles used to express anger (Hurley & Chater, 2005). There is also evidence that observation of sad faces automatically activates the amygdala (Posner & Rothbart, 2000), suggesting that the observer experiences a small dose of sadness. Interestingly, Edgar Allen Poe (1965, pp. 216–216) described his technique of trying to understand another by imitating the other's facial expression and then reflecting on "what thoughts and sentiments arise in my mind and heart" (p. 100).

Wicker et al. (2003) found that the area of the brain that is activated when one experiences disgust in reaction to an unpleasant odor is also activated when one views someone expressing disgust. This was also the case with regard to overlap between experiencing unpleasant tastes and observing facial expressions of disgust in response to such tastes. (Jabbi, Swart, and Keysers, 2007). Similar to findings on observation of actions and emotional expressions, there is also a good deal of evidence that the neural networks activated when one is experiencing pain are also activated when observing another in pain (e.g., Avenanti, Bueti, Galati, and Aglioti, 2005; Armstrong, 2018; Jackson, Meltzoff, and Decety, 2005; Lamm, Decety, and Singer, 2011; Morrison, Llloyd, di Pelligrino, and Roberts, 2004; Singer et al., 2004).

The preceding findings have been taken to support the formulation that perception of motor acts and emotional facial expressions leads to a form of automatic rudimentary *imitation* of the motor acts and facial expressions observed. These automatic imitative tendencies that form the basis for interpersonal understanding are present early in infancy and should be viewed as inborn apparatuses as fully as the inborn apparatuses identified by Hartmann. There is evidence that young infants are able to perceive "various movements of the head, the mouth, the hand, and more general body movements as meaningful, goal-directed movements" (Gallagher, 2008, p. 539).

A question that has been raised is why the presumed imitation is only rudimentary and not full-fledged imitation of a motor act or an emotional facial expression. One answer given in the literature is that in the course of development, one develops mechanisms that inhibit overt imitation. An implication of this account is that were these inhibitory mechanisms not present – as is the case in infancy – or impaired, one would observe not rudimentary, but overt imitation. The evidence for this hypothesis comes from two sources: the presence of automatic overt imitation in infancy, presumably prior to the development of inhibitory mechanisms; and the presence of overt and automatic imitation in adults with frontal lobe damage.

Mirror neurons and imitation in infancy

Although not definitively established, there is a good deal of evidence that the mirror neuron system (MNS) is present shortly after birth, or very early in infancy. Shimada and Hiraki (2006) found that the motor cortical areas that were activated when 6- to 7-month-old infants performed hand actions were also activated when observing someone performing a hand action. Nyström (2008) obtained EEG responses of both adults and 6-month-old infants while viewing goal-directed and non-goal-directed movements. He reported significant mu desynchronization (which has been shown to be a marker for the activation of the mirror neuron system) in adults viewing the goal-directed movements and significantly higher Evoked Response Potential (ERP) activation for both adults and infants when observing the goal-directed action. Nyström (2008) concludes that "this study demonstrates that infants as young as six months display mirror neuron activity" (p. 334). After reviewing the preceding plus other evidence, Lepage and Theoret (2007) conclude that "converging data strongly favor models that acknowledge the existence of an infant MNS in some form or other" (p. 520) (See also Bertenthal & Longo, 2007, who reach a similar conclusion).

Newborn infants are very susceptible to emotional contagion (Hoffman, 1982). For example, if one newborn in the nursery cries, the other infants are also likely to cry. According to Meltzoff and Moore (1977), infants shortly after birth imitate (e.g., tongue protrusion movements). They have also reported imitation of head movements in newborn infants (Meltzoff and Moore, 1989), as well as imitation of "both static facial postures and dynamic facial gestures in 6 week and 2 to 3 month old infants" (Meltzoff & Moore, 1983, 1992). Nagy et al. (2005) reported that neonates between 3 and 96 hours after birth made more finger movements after observing human movement than during a baseline period. Infants between 24 hours and 7 days after birth made significantly more mouth clutching movements during listening to "m" vocalizations and significantly more open mouth movements during listening to "a" vocalizations (Chen, Striano, & Rakoczy, 2004). And finally, Field, Woodson, Greenberg, and Cohen (1982) reported that observers could guess with greater than chance accuracy what facial expressions (happy, sad, and surprised) 3-day-old infants had seen by observing their facial expressions. The assumption is that imitation in infancy is at least partly attributable to the fact that neural mechanisms present in adulthood that inhibit overt imitation are not fully developed (See also Meltzoff, 1995).

There is far from universal agreement on the proposition that imitation is present in infancy. Whereas, as we have seen previously, some investigators have reported evidence for imitation in infancy, other investigators have failed to find such evidence. Anisfeld et al. (1979) re-analyzed Meltzoff and Moore's (1977) data and concluded that there was no solid evidence for their conclusions. Anisfeld (1996) also reviewed 17 studies and concluded that there was no reliable evidence that infants imitate head movements (HM) and mouth open (MO) movements. Although there was some evidence for imitation of tongue protrusion (TP) movements,

Anisfeld concludes: "Because matching behavior found is restricted to a single gesture [TP], it is best explained as a specific, directly elicited response, rather than imitation" (p. 149). Jones (2006) found that music "affected 4-week-old infants' rates of tongue protruding – evidence that tongue protruding is a general response to interesting distal stimuli" (p. 126). This conclusion is consistent with Anisfeld et al.'s (2001) suggestion that the infant's increased tongue protrusion in response to the experimenter's tongue protrusion is an arousal rather than an imitation response.

Before leaving the topic of infant imitation, I want to note an important limitation of research in this area. As we have seen, the focus of research is the infant's imitation of adult actions. However, outside the experimental situation, in many parent-infant exchanges, the interaction includes the parent imitating the infant's expressions and actions, which often institutes a back and forth series of imitational interactions. I recently observed the following interaction between father and a 2- to 3-month-old infant. Father approaches baby in the carriage, who upon seeing father, excitedly opens mouth and coos. Father responds by imitating baby's open mouth and cooing. Baby continues the interaction by even more excited mouth opening and cooing in response to father. This continues back and forth until father picks baby up and cuddles him.

As an observer, it seems to me that what is happening is that the infant's initial mouth opening and cooing are excited and pleasurable arousal responses to seeing father. However, when father imitates the baby's mouth opening and cooing and initiates a series of back and forth interactions, the baby's mouth opening and cooing are now not only arousal responses but become entrained into a series of interactive imitative behaviors. This phenomenon cannot be observed in the experimental condition limited to the infant's response to an adult action (e.g., tongue protrusion; mouth opening). Hence, we may be seeing infant matching behavior under relatively restricted conditions, which may limit the degree to which infant social imitative behavior can be observed.

It is worth noting that were the infant's initial behavior a negative emotional expression or simply crying, the interaction between baby and father would take a different course. Father would not imitate the baby's behavior. Rather, father would react with comforting behavior quite different from crying. This does not constitute a mirroring, but rather a complementary response to the baby's expression and behavior. Although upon perceiving baby's distress, matching neural areas might be activated in father, at the behavioral level, father's behavior is not one of mirroring, but of com-plementary comforting behavior. The notions of mirroring and mirroring transference (Kohut, 1984) have always seemed misleading. Understand-ing another is not normally expressed in mirroring their experiences and behavior, but rather in providing complementary appropriate responses.

Automatic imitation in frontal lobe patients

That the tendency to imitate remains rudimentary and does not normally result in full-fledged imitation of the actions and facial expressions we observe suggests the operation of a mechanism normally available to inhibit indiscriminate imitation. In support of this hypothesis, Luria (1966) observed that patients with frontal lobe damage automatically imitated every action they observed, a condition he referred to as "echopraxia". And Lhermitte (1986) reported that patients with frontal lobe damage showed "obstinate imitative behavior", that is, an urge to imitate every observed action. Darwin (1965) had already described people with certain brain diseases as showing "echo signs" (p. 355), that is, imitating everything they perceive.

My former teacher, Kurt Goldstein (1959) reported that whereas frontal lobe patients could not *pretend* to drink or comb their hair without holding, respectively, a glass or a comb (a phenomenon he referred to as the loss of the abstract attitude), if given a comb or glass, they could not refrain from respectively, combing their hair or drinking (a phenomenon Goldstein referred to as stimulus-boundedness). Thus, whereas in intact individuals, the perception of a glass or comb would trigger only a rudimentary motor response, in these brain-damaged individuals the motor response is a full-fledged imitative action. In other words, there is a failure of inhibition (See Craighero, Fadiga, Umilta, and Rizzolatti, 1996). Lhermitte, Pillon, and Serdaru (1986) report similar behavior that they refer to as "utilization behavior". According to Bien, Roebroeck, Goebel, and Sack (2009), the middle frontal cortex serves general inhibition and the frontoparietal area serves to inhibit "planned" imitation.

Is the automatic "imitative" behavior seen in infancy and frontal lobe patients imitation?

As we have seen, there is debate as to whether the automatic matching behavior seen in infants is imitation in the sense that we normally use the term. Rather, as noted by Kinsbourne (2002), perception of an action or facial expression triggers automatic execution of the action. Similarly, Lepage and Theoret (2007) essentially propose that the matching behavior seen in infants is essentially the product of what they refer to as "uninhibited perception". As they put it, "the newborn *performs* his perception" (p. 520). They write that the "MNS development may be best viewed as a process by which the child learns to refrain from acting out the automatic mechanism that links perception to execution" (p. 520). They go on to speculate that imitation in early infancy

> mediated by a rudimentary MNS comes down to *motor-matching behavior as uninhibited perception*. On this view, the reason why neonates perform imitative responses would be that they cannot yet actively suppress the motoric representation with the heard sound or gesture and mere perception would be the sole *necessary* condition to imitate.
>
> (p. 520)

The term "uninhibited perception" (p. 520) employed by Lepage and Theoret (2007) suggests that the automatic imitative behavior described previously is not so much imitation (it is certainly not intentional imitation) as the consequence of a relatively direct and automatic pathway from "perception to execution" of an action with no mediating inhibitory process between the perception and the action.[2]

As R. Eagle (2007) suggests, the early "reflexive vision-motor loop" becomes "increasingly involved in intentional behavior" as the infant matures (p. 219). In other words, the early direct link between perception and execution (of action) may be the foundation for its later integration into intentional behavior. R. Eagle (2007) writes: "True imitation, however, may still require the early innate matching capacity, except that at this later point, it must connect with intentionality" (p. 219). From a psychoanalytic perspective, one can say that "uninhibited perception", although perhaps remaining as a rudimentary tendency, is gradually replaced by the emergence of an inhibitory ego function necessary for true imitation to occur and to play a role in interpersonal understanding.

One can draw an analogy between the reflexive pathway from perception to execution and the pathway from need or impulse to immediate gratification. In both cases, there is a relative absence of a inhibitory process that intervenes between in the one case, the perception of an external stimulus and execution of action, and in the other case, between perception of an internal stimulus (experienced as need) and execution of action. This mediating inhibitory process that is absent in both cases is a basic ego function that entails the delay necessary for planning and assessment of the consequences of one's actions. From the perspective of Freud's (1950) *Project*, the automatic pathway from perception to action can be understood as immediate discharge or unbound rather than bound cathexis. And the processes that intervene between perception (or image) and action are ego functions.

The same issue of a direct link between perception and action is present with regard to frontal lobe patients. In contrast to normal functioning, for Luria's (1966) "echopraxia" patients, who repeat actions they perceive, and Goldstein's (1959) frontal lobe patients, who cannot refrain from combing their hair when given a comb, there are no mediating inhibitory processes between perception and execution. In the case of Goldstein's frontal lobe patients, there is no imitation – no person or object is being imitated. Rather, there is a relatively direct path from "perception to execution" (Lepage & Theoret, 2007), that is from perceiving the object to executing an action associated with that object. This "uninhibited perception" seems similar, in important respects, to the infant's imitative behavior as well as the "obstinate imitative behavior" described by Lhermitte (1986).

The question of whether imitation is an accurate description is even more germane in the case of MNS phenomena. It is not clear why the mirror neuron phenomena are viewed as imitation insofar as the "imitation" occurs only at the level of neural and muscle (electromyographic) activation rather than overt behavioral imitation. Also, there is evidence that when perceiving an object associated with a particular motor act (e.g., a hammer), canonical neurons that are activated are also activated when carrying out that act or observing someone else carrying out that act. In other words, the perception of a hammer activates the neural areas involved in actions associated with a hammer. As Hurley and Chater (2005) note, canonical neurons "fire when action is performed, but also triggered by perception of objects that afford such actions" (p. 3). There is no imitation here. Rather, perception of a hammer entails a rudimentary motor tendency. In normal perception, this motor tendency remains rudimentary. That is, unlike infants or frontal lobe patients, there is no direct reflexive pathway from perception to execution. Rather, congruent with <u>Freud's</u>

(1950 [1895]) description of the function of the ego structure, there are inhibitory mediating processes inserted between perception and execution. The point I want to make here is that many MNS phenomena, particularly the original discoveries regarding motor acts, do not require the invoking of imitation, but can be understood in terms of the links between perception and the activation of motor areas. A similar point can be made with regard to the finding that, compared to abstract verbs, merely listening to action verbs (e.g., "touch"; "take") activates brain areas that are activated in action execution (Di Cesare, Errante, Marchi, and Cuccio, 2017).

Although there may be evidence of an inhibitory mechanism that serves to keep a rudimentary tendency toward imitation rudimentary, there are additional factors that may account for the fact that a rudimentary tendency does not become full-fledged overt action. Gedo (1983) notes that "on average the motor discharge exhibited during action execution is significantly higher than that evoked by the observation of a similar action performed by others" (p. 582). It may be the case that a threshold for motor discharge must be met before overt action can take place, which would serve to keep a rudimentary tendency toward imitative action rudimentary. In short, "while it is certainly true that mirror neurons fire no matter whether the action is executed or perceived, it is always true that the *intensity of their response* is not the same in these two different situations" (p. 582).

As Gallese (2009) notes, a prior recognition of what he refers to as the "alterity" of the other guarantees that despite some neural overlap, "the cortical circuits at work when *we* act neither completely overlap nor show the same activation intensity as when *others* are the agents and we are the witnesses of their actions" (p. 582). An implication of Gallese's emphasis on the importance of recognition of the "alterity" of the other is that relative loss of boundaries between self and other should result in the reduced value of the mirror system in facilitating understanding of the other.

Gallese (2009) also notes that a similar process is at work with regard to sensations and emotions. He cites a study by Jabbi, Bastiaansen, and Keysers (2008) that shows

> experiences as different as being subjectively disgusted, imagining oneself as being disgusted and seeing disgust portrayed in the facial expression of others not only encompass the activation of the same network of brain areas (the anterior insula and the anterior cingulated

cortex), but also the activation of different brain areas according to the specific modality in which disgust is experienced (*my* disgust, my imagined disgust, your disgust).

(p. 582)

To return to the main issue of the chapter, namely, the processes involved in one's capacity to understand another. The functional role of the mirror system is to allow one to understand, not inferentially, but more directly and from the inside the intentions of motor actions and the sensations and emotions experienced by another through partial overlap of brain areas activated in the observer and the observed. As Rizzolatti, Semi, and Fabbri-Destro (2014) write:

> We maintain that in order both to act coherently and have a basic, first person, understanding of the behavior of others, it is necessary to posit the existence of a neuropsychological "motor" ego similar to the "rider" of the Freudian metaphor. [Rizollatti et al., 2014are referring to Freud's [1923] metaphor of the id as horse and the ego as rider.]
>
> (p. 143)

This by no means rules out the role of other factors, such as the inferential processes in Theory of Mind (TOM) in understanding another.

Distinction between self and other

Although the mirror neuron system involves a shared neural circuit between observer and observed, some findings suggest that its activation rests on the observer's ability to distinguish between self and other.[3] There is evidence that it is only the observation of what is experienced as another's action rather than one's own action that triggers motor responses. Schutz-Bosbach, Mancini, Aglioti, and Haggard (2006) have shown that, whereas observation of an experimenter's index-finger movement facilitated motor evoked potentials (MEP's) in the observer, MEP's were suppressed when, through the use of a variation of the rubber-hand illusion (Botvinick & Cohen, 1998; Tsakiris & Haggard, 2005), the observer experienced the experimenter's finger movement as his or her own finger moving. (Watching a rubber hand being stroked while feeling one's own unseen hand being stroked creates the illusion of the rubber hand being part of one's own body.) In other words, whereas observing an action that is attributed to another activates the observer's motor system, observing an action that is attributed to oneself suppresses motor cortical excitability. Schutz-Bosbach et al. (2006) comment that the "inhibitory network that suppresses a natural tendency to imitate others . . . would seem even more important for preventing inappropriate perseveration or entrainment when viewing one's own actions" (p. 183).

It would seem that precisely the opposite would be the case for the following reason: Whereas an inhibitory mechanism may be necessary to suppress the natural rudimentary tendency to imitate others (as reflected in the activation of the premotor cortex when observing another's action), inhibition is not necessary given the fact that there is no evidence of an imitative tendency when observing one's own actions. Indeed, Schutz-Bosbach et al. (2006) report a *suppression* rather than an activation of motor cortical activity when observing one's own action.

How much does the mirror neuron system explain?

Gallese (2003) interprets various findings on mirror neurons as indicating that "the meaning of expression of affective behavior seems to be automatically understood without the necessity of any intervening complex cognitive mediation" (p. 519). There is a good deal of controversy and debate surrounding claims that the mirror neuron system, understood as implementing a form of "embodied simulation", constitutes a fundamental basis for an automatic, immediate, and unmediated understanding of the other's actions, intentions, and feelings; or that: "*This implicit, automatic, and unconscious* process of embodied simulation enables the observer . . . to penetrate the world of the other without the need of explicitly *theorizing* about it" (Gallese, original emphasis). Indeed, Hickok (2014) has published a book entitled *The myth of mirror neurons: The real science of communication and cognition*.

Although the mirror neuron concept may be given too much work to do, the evidence strongly suggests that it is far from being a myth. There is little doubt that there are a set of motor neurons in humans as well as monkeys that are activated "both when an individual executes a specific motor act and when they observe the same or similar act performed by another individual" (Kilner & Lemon, 2013, p. 1057). There is also little doubt that observation of emotional facial expression (e.g., happy and angry faces) triggers the same facial muscle activity in the observer as is activated in the one observed (Dimberg, 1982; Lundqvist & Dimberg, 1995; Dimberg et al., 2000). There is also evidence that certain neural areas are activated both when disgust is triggered by natural stimuli as well as by observation of a disgusted facial expression (Wicker et al., 2003), and evidence of overlap in brain areas activated both when one experiences pain oneself and when one observes another person in pain (e.g., Singer et al., 2004). And finally, as we have seen, there is accumulating evidence that the MNS is present at birth or shortly after birth.

Thus, it would be accurate to say that the mirror neuron system is implicated in a fundamental way in interpersonal understanding. The issue is the extent and nature of its role in interpersonal understanding. There is little doubt that the mirror neuron system plays a vital in understanding relatively simple actions, emotional facial expressions, and certain sensations, such as pain. However, a question arises with regard to the role of the mirror neuron system in understanding the more complex mental states of another, such as desires and intentions not directly linked to motor actions. Another related question that arises is the degree to which mirror neuron activation is influenced by higher-order factors, such as one's attitudes toward the one being observed, an issue I address subsequently.

With regard to the former question, Rizzolatti and Sinigaglia (2008) acknowledge that the immediate and automatic perception of the action intentions of the other made possible by mirror neurons "is based exclusively on the vocabulary of acts and the motor knowledge on which our capacity to act depends" and "is completely devoid of any reflexive [sic], conceptual and/or linguistic mediation" (p. 25). Rizzolatti and Sinigaglia (2008) suggest that the automatic understanding made possible by the mirror neuron system does not extend to mental states such as beliefs and desires or to complex intentions unrelated to motor acts.

Top-down influences on the mirror neuron system

There is evidence that the activation of the mirror neuron system is influenced by top-down factors such as one's evaluative attitude in relation to the one being observed. For example, the pattern of shared neural circuits that are activated when observing another in pain varies with one's perceived fairness of the person observed (Singer et al., 2006). Hein, Silani, Preuschoff, Batson, and Singer (2010) found that participants showed stronger empathy related neural responses when observing ingroup rather than outgroup members in pain. There is also evidence that even with regard to observing simple actions, the pattern of neural activation in the observer varies with the degree to which he or she likes the person carrying out the observed action.

Other top down influences on the MNS were reported by Hein et al. (2010). Participants were given three options with regard to pain infliction on ingroup and outgroup members: They could help the member by volunteering to receive half the pain themselves; the second option was to watch a soccer video while the member was receiving pain; and the third option was to watch the other person receiving pain. The findings included the following: activation of the left anterior insula (AI), which is associated with empathic responses, predicted the number of trials in which participants chose the helping option and correlated negatively with number of trials in which participants chose to watch the video of the person receiving pain. Left AI activation correlated significantly with the participants' score on the Empathic Concern Scale; and both predicted helping behavior. The more negative the impression of the outgroup member, the greater the activation of the right nucleus accumbens (NAcc) (which is associated with reward) when seeing that member in pain, suggesting that observing an outgroup member in pain "was processed in a reward-related manner" (p. 158). A negative correlation between NAcc activation and helping behavior was found. An especially interesting finding is that NAcc activation was a better predictor of helping behavior than a self-report of the participant's impression of the person receiving pain. The authors suggest that the automatic neural response may be a more valid account than self-report of the participants' reactions to the other person insofar as it not influenced by factors such as social desirability.

Hein, Lamm, Brodbeck, and Singer (2011) measured skin conductance responses (SCRs) in individuals who were either subjected to pain themselves or observed another person receiving pain (vicarious SCR's). In a subsequent session, the participants could prevent the infliction of pain on another person by choosing to receive the pain themselves. They found that the higher the match between SCR magnitudes during self pain and observation of another person in pain, the more likely the participants would engage in "costly helping", that is, choose to endure pain themselves in order to keep another from experiencing pain.

Demonstrating real world validity of measures of neural responses to observing someone in pain, as well as the importance of individual differences in these responses, Brethel-Haurwitz et al. (2018) obtained fMRI responses to experiencing pain and observing someone in pain from two groups; a group of extremely altruistic people, as indicated by a kidney donation, and a control group. Overlap in anterior insula responses to experiencing and observing pain was significantly greater for the altruistic participants than for the control group. There is evidence that the greater the match of SCRs between partners, the greater the accuracy in rating one's partner's affect (Levenson & Ruef, 1992). This suggests that the greater the overlap between self and other mapping, the greater the degree of interpersonal understanding.

The preceding findings suggest that self-other mapping is not quite as simple and as automatic as originally described, but rather is influenced by contextual factors, including one's attitude toward and relationship with the person being observed, as well as individual differences in altruism, for example. In view of the preceding evidence, a plausible conclusion is that although the mirror system plays an important role in understanding of another's actions, emotions, and sensations, it may not be as unmediated and automatic as is suggested by "embodied simulation" theory. Rather, as Vivona (2009) observes, "simulation and inference can operate simultaneously, interact complexly, and inform one another" (p. 544).

It may well be the case that, as Rizzolatti and Sinigaglia (2010) note,

> although there are several mechanisms through which one can understand the behavior of other individuals, the parieto-frontal mechanism is the only one that allows the individual to understand the action of others "from the inside" and gives the observer a first-person grasp of the motor goals and intentions of other individuals.
>
> (p. 264)

Thus, Rizzolatti and Sinigaglia (2010) argue that although there may be different ways of understanding another, the mirror neuron system enables understanding "from the inside". However, as they suggest, this may be limited to delineated motor actions, facial expressions, and sensations rather than complex mental states. This raises the question of the processes involved in understanding the latter.

An adequate account of how one understands another's intentions, emotions, and sensations will likely include different systems and may require an integration of embodied simulation theory and traditional simulation theory, which proposes that one understands another through explicitly putting oneself in the shoes of the other. That is, A observes B's behavior and then infers (implicitly) that if s/he were doing what B is doing, s/he would intend or feel in a particular way and then attributes that particular intention or feeling to B (e.g., Gordon & Cruz, 2004; Jung, 2003); and a "theory theory" conception, which proposes that one understands another through observation and inference based on an acquired folk psychology theory (e.g., Carruthers & Smith, 1996; Stich & Nichols, 1992). Rather than these views being mutually exclusive, they may point to different ways of understanding another as well as different contexts of understanding.[4]

Effortful and deliberate systems in self and interpersonal understanding

mentalization and reflective function

Mentalizing is defined as "the capacity to understand ourselves and others in terms of intentional states, such as feelings, drives, wishes, and attitudes" (Luyten & Fonagy, 2015, p. 366). It is the ability to take what Dennett (1987) refers to as "intentional stance" toward oneself and others, which, although taken for granted in ordinary social interaction, is fundamental to one person understanding another. What Dennett means by "intentional stance" is one's ability to view oneself and others as beings with mental states and intentions. From a psychoanalytic perspective, capacity for mentalization is an ego function that is critical for self-understanding and understanding of the other. As Luyten and Fonagy (2015) observe, "this [mentalizing] capacity is central in human development" and "temporary or stable disruption in this capacity are one characteristic of almost all forms of psychopathology" (p. 366).

As Fonagy and Bateman (2006) (See also Bateman & Fonagy, 2006) observe, the psychoanalytic concept of the observing function of the ego and the distinction between the experiencing and observing ego (Sterba, 1934) are precursors of the concepts of mentalization and reflective function. However, what distinguishes the earlier concept of the observing function of the ego from the concept of reflective function and capacity is the emphasis of the former on *self*-reflection. Little is said in the psychoanalytic literature regarding the capacity to reflect on another's mental states (another expression of the relative failure of both classical theory and ego psychology to deal with interpersonal reality-testing and interpersonal understanding). To some extent, one can think of the concepts of mentalization and reflective function as corrective extensions and elaborations of the concept of the observing function of the ego to include reflection on the mental states of others as well as one's own.[5]

Mead's (1934) formulation of the relationship between the "I" and the "Me" aspects of the personality can also be seen as precursors of the concepts of mentalization and reflective function. One of Mead's central ideas is that one part of the self, the "I", takes one's experience or mental state or action as an object of reflection, which now constitute the "Me". (Note the parallel between Sterba's (1934) distinction between the experiencing and observing functions of the ego and Mead's distinction between the "I" and the "Me"). As Mead observes, the agentic act of observing and reflecting can itself become an object for further observation and reflection. Mead's formulations are not limited to self-understanding, but also include understanding of the other, which requires the ability to put oneself in the shoes of the other. Although the concepts of mentalization and reflective capacity are often equated, they are not the same. Whereas mentalization, conceptualized as an intentional stance, refers to the capacity to understand one's own and the other's behavior in terms of mental states (i.e., motives and intentions), reflective function refers to the capacity to *reflect* on the mental states one has experienced or has attributed to the other. Although mentalization is a necessary, it is not a sufficient condition for reflection. Reflecting on one's own or the other's mental states is an additional step that already presupposes the capacity for an intentional stance.

That the MNS automatically responds to motor behavior (e.g., grasping) in terms of its goal and intention, that is, as action rather than as sheer movements, suggests an implicit intentional stance toward the object of observation. However, it does not necessarily imply reflection on what one has observed. Also, the evidence that the MNS is present early in life and that it operates in non-human species suggests that mentalization can be present without reflection insofar as no one believes that infants are capable of self-reflection. One way to put it is to distinguish between attributing mental states to another (either automatically or deliberatively), which requires a capacity for mentalization, and reflecting on the attributions one has made.

In effect, Luyten and Fonagy (2015) make this point by distinguishing between "automatic" mentalizing, which is characterized as "unconscious, parallel, fast processing of social information that is *reflexive*" (my emphasis) (p. 368), and "controlled" mentalization, which is characterized as "conscious, verbal, and *reflective* (my emphasis) processing" (p. 368). It is clear from this distinction that what Luyten and Fonagy refer to as "controlled" mentalization is equivalent to reflective activity, which is contrasted with an "automatic" and "reflexive" intentional stance. In short, one can mentalize, that is, assume an "intentional stance", without reflecting on what one has mentalized.

Mentalization and Projection

The distinction between mentalization and reflective capacity becomes clearer when one considers that one can take an intentional stance toward another in a manner that *impairs* rather than facilitates understanding of the other. An obvious instance is when one projects unacceptable mental contents – let us say, a hostile intention – onto another. In the sense that one attributes an intention to another one is mentalizing, that is, taking an intentional stance toward that other. However, in projection, one is not *reflecting* on the basis for one's attributions. Let me describe some other concrete examples.

Lieberman (1999) describes the case of a young, high-risk mother who let her 2-day-old infant cry for 30–40 minutes "until mother is finished eating" and then describes her baby as "greedy" as if baby were intentionally attempting to interfere with mother eating her meal. Mother's behavior in this case is not a consequence of her failure to take an intentional stance or to mentalize, that is, to construe her infant's behavior as motivated by inner mental states. Indeed, she is attributing *too much* intentionality to her 2-day-old infant rather than simply recognizing that baby's crying is due to her distress from being hungry. Further, mother's mentalization is not only utterly unrealistic and inaccurate, but it is generated by her anger *at* having her meal interrupted; and, as Lieberman suggests, is the product of *projecting* her own unacknowledged sense of greediness on to her infant. Thus, although mother mentalizes, what she does not appear to be able to do is *reflect* on her own attributions and mental states, the mental states she attributes to her infant, and the connection between the two.

The preceding example illustrates a kind of projection that goes on in many situations, but that does not easily fit the conception of projection as a defense in which one attempts to rid oneself of an unwanted wish or aspect of oneself by projecting it on to someone else. The projection in the preceding example takes the following if-then form: if, in our interaction, I am hurt or angry or irritated, then it is due to your *intending* to hurt, anger, or irritate me. The attributions to the other made in such instances justify one's feelings of hurt, anger, or irritation. We see that starkly in the preceding case described by Lieberman (1999): If mother is irritated and angry in reaction to her infant's interrupting her meal, then it follows that baby *intended* to do that by her incessant crying. Hence, from mother's perspective, her irritation is perfectly justified. In this example, mother's anger is not defensively kept from consciousness through its projection on to someone else – her anger is consciously experienced. Rather, mother's anger is *justified* through attributing angry and greedy intentions to her baby. Such attributions, often automatic, constitute serious barriers to interpersonal understanding.

A similar dynamic is seen in some cases of infant abuse in which a parent reacts with rage at the infant's incessant crying, as if the infant *intends* to harass the parent. It is also seen in adult interactions, particularly with borderline patients. Gabbard and Horowitz (2009) describe a borderline patient who, because she feels affronted by a sales clerk's refusal to accept her credit card, automatically assumes that the sales clerk *intends* to humiliate her. She reacts with rage and verbally attacks the sales clerk. The if-then formula in these instances is: If I feel hurt or angry in response to something you said or did, then you must have intended to hurt or anger me; and I am justified in feeling hurt or angry. The therapeutic goal for this patient would not appear to be an enhanced capacity for mentalization. In an important sense, the patient is engaged in too much mentalization or in a kind of mentalization that is fueled by sensitivity to feelings of rejection and humiliation. Although Bateman and Fonagy (2013) label their treatment approach "Mentalization Based Treatment" (MBT), in view of the previous discussion, it would be more accurate to refer to it as "Reflective Function Therapy".

In the previous instances, the problem is *not* that the individual is *failing* to mentalize or to take an intentional stance – indeed, in a certain sense, they are over-mentalizing. The problem is that quite frequently, attributing intentions to another only on the basis of one's automatic feelings and reactions, that is, without reflection, is likely to constitute inaccurate attributions and consequent affect dysregulation, particularly when one's attributions are experienced as absolute and unquestioned and therefore relatively unsusceptible to revision and correction. Individuals with borderline and narcissistic personality disorders tend to automatically construe the behaviors of others as rejecting, abandoning, and so on. They are certainly mentalizing in the obvious sense that they are attributing intentional states to another. The maladaptive nature of their mentalization lies in the consistent attribution of negative mental states to other, the absolute conviction that their attributions are justified, and the difficulty in stepping back and *reflecting* on the intentional states they have attributed to the other.

I cannot help commenting on some family resemblance between the preceding description of attributing mental states to others based on one's own feeling and the currently popular psychoanalytic assumption that the therapist's countertransference reactions constitute a reliable guide to the patient's mental states. Of course, an important difference is that the therapist is advised and presumably trained to reflect on his or her countertransference reactions. However, one sees too many instances in the psychoanalytic literature in which the thoughts and feelings that enter the analyst's mind are taken as guides to the patient's mental states, with little critical attention given to reflection on the possible sources of such thoughts and feelings. For example, consider Racker's (1968) statement that the thoughts and feelings of the analyst will be "precisely" those of the patient's repressed mental contents and Levine's (1997) suggestion that, as a general rule, the analyst's thoughts and preoccupations, including personal ones that seem to have little to do with the patient, should be thought of as being triggered by the patient. Such statements would appear to encourage uncritical justification for rather than reflection on one's attributions to the patient. The problem is further exacerbated by the current infatuation with the concept of projective identification, particularly when it is understood in terms of patients somehow putting mental contents *into* the analyst (See Eagle, 2018b).

Empathy and interpersonal understanding

There is a large body of literature on the role of empathy in interpersonal understanding. We have already been discussing that topic without referring to the term empathy. For example, when Rizzolatti and Sinigaglia

(2010) state that the mirror neuron system enables the observer to understand another's actions "from the inside", they are, in effect, making the claim that the mirror neuron system is the basis for at least certain forms of empathy. And when we learn that observing someone's smile activates the same facial muscles in the observer as are activated in the observed and that observing an emotional facial expression triggers a small dose of that emotion in the observer, we have, in effect, already begun to discuss empathy.

Relationship between automatic and deliberate systems in interpersonal understanding and empathy

A plausible hypothesis based on the research findings discussed previously is that, whereas the automatic reactive system (including embodied simulation) may play an important role in understanding certain observed behaviors (e.g., familiar motor actions; emotional expressions; pain sensations), an adequate understanding of more complex mental states may also require a capacity to reflect on the subtle experiential cues that are generated by the automatic simulation and reactive systems. Another way of putting this is to say that in many circumstances adequate understanding of another is likely to require both an immediate and automatic activation of affective and other experiential cues as well as cognitive reflection on these experiential cues.

Although the automatic, fast, and reflexive system may result in cognitive errors (Kahneman, 2011), as well as interpersonal misunderstanding and difficulties (as in, for example, borderline conditions), it serves the highly adaptive function of very fast appraisals of both physical and interpersonal danger. Indeed, the concept of signal anxiety in reaction to very quick appraisals of danger can be understood in terms of the operation of this system. Difficulties arise under a number of circumstances, including in cases where the assessment of danger is not justified by reality, or in the case of chronic vigilance in response to chronic expectations of danger, or in the case where the individual shows an overall impaired capacity to reflect on his or her appraisals of danger. Such an impairment contributes to dysfunction in affect regulation.

There is evidence that the deliberative effortful control system serves to modulate the experiences automatically generated by the automatic reactive system.[6] Posner and Rothbart (2000) report that perception of sad faces automatically activates the amygdala in the perceiver, suggesting an experience of a small dose of sadness. They also report that "as sadness increases, this activation is accompanied by activation of the anterior cingulate as part of the attention network" (Blair, Morris, Frith, Perrett, & Dolan, 1999, p. 436), suggesting the involvement of the effortful control system, which according to Posner and Rothbart (2000), serves a self-regulatory function. They write that "effortful control may support empathy by allowing the individual to attend to the thoughts and feelings of another without becoming overwhelmed by their own distress" (p. 435). In support of this idea, Eisenberg and Okun (1996) reported that attentional control is positively related to sympathy and perspective taking and negatively related to personal distress. Posner and Rothbart (2000) are, in effect, suggesting that there are different reactions to observing another in distress, one of which can be described, broadly speaking, as "I feel what you feel", which may be largely mediated by the automatic reactive system; and the other of which can be described as "I can imaginatively put myself in your shoes and understand what you feel", which may involve greater recruitment of the deliberative effortful control system. Distinguishing between these two reactions goes as far back as McDougall's (1908) distinction between "sympathetic pain" (i.e., personal distress) and "tender emotion" (i.e., empathy).

There is a good deal of research on the distinction between empathy, understood as concern for the other, and personal distress (e.g., Carrera et al., 2012; Decety, 2011; Decety & Lamm, 2009; López-Perez & Ambrona, 2015). Personal distress as the primary reaction to observing someone in need or in distress is associated with negative emotional valence, high arousal level, and self-orientation (López-Pérez, Carrera, Ambrona, & Oceja, 2014) as well as relatively low likelihood of helping behavior (Carrera et al., 2012). Eisenberg and Fabes (1990) reported that "other-oriented sympathetic responding" (p. 131) to someone in distress is positively related to helping behavior, whereas personal distress reactions are associated with low helping behavior and higher physiological arousal. Batson, Fultz, and Schoenrade (1987) found that personal distress reactions to perceiving someone in distress (characterized by endorsement of terms such as "alarmed, upset, worried, disturbed, distressed, troubled") "seems to evoke egoistic motivation to reduce one's own aversive arousal" (p. 38). Contrastingly, an empathic reaction (characterized by endorsement of such terms as "sympathetic, moved compassionate, tender, warm, softhearted") was associated with the motivation to reduce the other's need. In another study, Batson, O'Quinn, Fultz, Vanderplas, and Isen (1983) found that individuals who showed a predominance of personal distress engaged in less helping behavior when it was easy to avoid the situation without helping; whereas individuals who reported a predominance of empathy were likely to engage in helping behavior whether it was easy or difficult to escape the situation. An especially interesting finding was that when the helping behavior was very costly, even empathic participants were more likely to escape the situation when it was easy to do so. Presumably, empathy and helping behavior have their limits. In a study that is especially interesting in a psychoanalytic context, Joireman (2004) found that proneness to shame was associated with personal distress and self-rumination, whereas proneness to guilt was associated with empathic concern and perspective taking. One way of understanding these findings is that, whereas shame is more directed toward the self, as Klein (1975) suggested, guilt is more directed to reparation in relation to the other.

One of my students, D. Posner (unpublished dissertation, 1999) found that participants who were high on anxious attachment (characterized by enmeshment and fears of abandonment) were also high on an empathy scale that stresses the tendency to feel what others are feeling (Mehrabian & Epstein, 1972), whereas participants who showed secure attachment (characterized by confidence in the availability of the attachment figure) were high on an empathy scale that taps what one might call cognitive empathy, that is, "the cognitive or imaginative apprehension of another's condition or state of mind" (Hogan, 1969, p. 307). Interestingly, the two measures of empathy were not significantly correlated with each other. Given the anxiously attached individual's preoccupation with fear of abandonment, his or her high score on shared feelings can be interpreted as reflecting anxious monitoring of the other's feelings and susceptibility to a contagion effect entailed in the subtle loss of boundaries between self and other. Contrastingly, securely attached individuals' experience of empathy would seem to reflect a combination of experiencing a small dose of the emotion expressed by the other, along with a stepping back and cognitively understanding the other's emotional experience. It is likely that that there is no sharp dichotomy between the two forms of empathy and that the form of empathy experienced will vary not only with attachment patterns, but also with other factors, including the relationship between oneself and the individual toward whom one is experiencing empathy.

Empathy and narcissism

We have seen evidence that there are at least two reactions to perceiving someone in distress: personal distress in the form of I feel what you feel; and I understand what you feel and experience a small dose of what you feel. Whether the former is a form of empathy or a failure of empathy attendant upon relative loss of boundaries is open to debate. One can understand the reaction of personal distress in the form of I feel what you feel in terms of the activation of automatic bottom-up processing (System 1) without adequate cognitive modulation (System 2).

There appears to be, however, another reaction to perceiving another person in distress that is characteristic of individuals high in narcissism, which represents a clear failure of empathy. In a study on a non-clinical sample, Fan et al. (2011) reported that individuals high in narcissism showed relative deficits in empathy, along with decreased activation in the right anterior insula. Jankowiak-Siuda & Zajkowski (2013) also reported that individuals high in narcissism showed deficits in empathy associated mainly with relative failure in bottom-up processing as shown by dysfunction in the right anterior insula, but also in top-down cognitive processing, suggesting a "disorder of affective sharing and [in] an understanding of the emotions of others" (p. 937). They also report, perhaps surprisingly, that individuals high in narcissism showed more personal distress on a subscale "which measures self-oriented feelings of personal anxiety and unease in stressful interpersonal settings" (p. 937). In other words, they show self-focused affects.

One can speculate further regarding the distinction between personal distress in the form of I feel what you feel and the personal distress shown by individuals high in narcissism. The former reaction can be understood in terms of the relative failure of top-down processes to modulate the automatic sharing of affect, and in that sense, can be understood as a form of empathy. However, the latter form of personal distress, which takes more the form of observing your distress disturbs me, is less understandable as empathy. From an ego psychology perspective, the former can be seen in terms of a relative failure of top-down modulation, that is, as a relative failure of an affect regulating ego function. In contrast, in the case of individuals high in narcissism, the personal distress, a reaction of "anxiety and unease [in reaction to a] stressful interpersonal" situation, is not affect sharing, but rather takes the form of desire to avoid an anxiety provoking and stressful situation. One would predict that compared to personal distress in the form of I feel what you feel, the personal distress associated with a high level of narcissism would lead to avoidance and withdrawal. A factor that is not addressed in the research discussed previously on narcissism and empathy, but that needs to be taken into account is the different forms of narcissism: the thin-skinned versus the seemingly over-confident form of narcissism.

Neural correlates of empathy

The most useful summary of the role of different neural and psychological systems in empathy is stated by Decety (2011), who writes:

> while the capacity for two people to resonate with each other emotionally, prior to any cognitive understanding, is the basis for developing shared emotional meaning, it is not enough for mature empathic understanding and sympathetic concern. Such an understanding requires forming an explicit representation of the feelings of another person, an intentional agent, which necessitates additional computational mechanisms beyond the emotion-sharing level, as well as self-regulation to modulate negative arousal in the observer.
>
> (p. 104)

Along with others, Decety (2011) has proposed that reactions to observing another's distress generally includes both a bottom-up neural process involving the limbic system, which triggers immediate affective arousal and affective sharing, and a top-down process, which involves areas of the prefrontal cortex, which facilitates awareness and cognitive understanding of another's emotions. A more cognitive form of empathy would be characterized by a pattern of activation of the amygdala and other components of the limbic system (leading to the experience of a small dose of the emotion expressed by the other) combined with activation of areas of the prefrontal cortex, which would serve to modulate amygdala activation and facilitate awareness and understanding of, as well as ability to reflect on, the shared affect. Contrastingly, a form of empathy more in the direction of contagion – I feel what you feel – is likely to involve activation of the limbic system relatively unmodulated by prefrontal cortical areas.[7]

There also disturbances in empathy that are characterized by reduced amygdala activation as well as lack of connectivity between amygdale and prefrontal cortical areas (Stein, Simmons, Feinstein, Martin, & Paulus, 2007; Young et al., 2017). Marsh et al. (2008) reported reduced functional connectivity between the amygdala and the ventromedial prefrontal cortex (vmPFC) in children with psychopathic tendencies. This sort of evidence suggests that, as Blair (2008) puts it, "The reduced amygdala respond-ing . . . diminishes empathy-based learning following the witnessing of another's distress and leads to reduced empathy generally" (p. 2562). One can speculate that optimal empathy includes an integration and balancing of both bottom-up and top-down processes. An imbalance in the direction of bottom-up processes may merge into the experience of strong personal distress, which may generate non-empathic avoidance behavior or an ina-bility to be helpful.

I noted the automatic imitative tendency in reaction to observing anoth-er's action. There is evidence that this tendency is attenuated in individual high in narcissism (Hogeveen & Obhi, 2012; Obhi, Hogeveen, Giaco-min, & Jordan, 2014). There is also evidence that brain resting state func-tional connectivity "between and within limbic and prefrontal systems as well as their connectivity with other networks" is lower among individuals high in narcissism (Feng et al., 2018). Although individuals high in gran-diose narcissism do not report sensitivity to rejection, they show increased reactivity to brain areas associated with the pain of rejection (Cascio, Konrath, & Falk, 2015). In an interesting study, Chester, Lynam, Powell, and DeWall (2016) reported that individual high in grandiose narcissism showed "reduced white matter integrity between brain regions that, in con-cert subserve self-esteem" (p. 1038). They suggest that "narcissists seek external self-affirmation to compensate for their internal deficit in self-reward connectivity than non-narcissists" (p. 1038).

From an ego psychology perspective, one would say that, in contrast to top-down processes, the automatic and immediate bottom-up processes that are activated when observing someone in distress and that are associ-ated with immediate affective arousal entail a minimum of intermediary ego functions. As Decety (2011) observes, these bottom-up processes are "grounded in perception-action coupling" (p. 93). That is, just as with-out inhibitory processes, mere perception triggers imitative behavior, similarly, without modulating top-down processes, the mere perception of someone in distress triggers what can be viewed as a kind of "imitative" behavior in the form of affective sharing. These top-down modulating processes can be understood, in the psychoanalytic context, as intermediary ego processes that make possible empathic responses characterized by clear boundaries between self and other, inhibition of contagion effects, awareness and understanding of the other's emotions, and ability to reflect on the other's as well as one's own emotions.[8]

Posner and Rothbart (2000) write that when the reactive system fails, the effortful control system can be enlisted to understand another. However, in accord with Rizzolatti and Sinigaglia's (2010) suggestion that the automatic MNS permits understanding "from the inside", one can speculate that understanding of another that relies solely on the effortful control system may generate a qualitatively different subjective experience than understanding that involves both systems. One can hypothesize that understanding of others that is based solely or primarily on the effortful control system (i.e., based largely on observation and inference) is likely to have the kind of awkward and stilted, and perhaps, over-intellectualized, quality that is quite different from understanding "from the inside".

One sees the former sort of behavior in autistic or Asperger individuals (see Grandin, 1992, 1995) who have to call upon explicit inference in order to understand another.[9] As noted earlier, some support for the idea that the automatic reactive system may be impaired in autistic individuals is provided by Dapretto et al.'s (2006) finding that during observation and imitation of emotional facial expressions autistic children did not show activation in the frontal mirror neuron system. However, as we have seen, this is a far from settled issue. There is a good deal of controversy and mixed findings regarding the question of whether there is an impairment in the MNS in autism. A number of investigators have argued and have found evidence for a MNS impairment in autism (i.e., Bird, Leighton, Press, & Heyes, 2007; Iacoboni & Dapretto, 2006; Oberman et al., 2005; Ouellet-Martin1997; Ramachandran & Oberman, 2006; Williams, 2008; Williams, Whiten, Suddendorf, & Perrett, 2001), whereas other investigators have failed to find such evidence (e.g., Leighton, Bird, Charman, & Heyes, 2008; Press, Richardson, & Bird, 2010; Southgate & Hamilton, 2008; Fan, Decety, Yang, Liu, & Cahng, 2010) for a central role of MNS impairment (See Hamilton, 2013; Williams, 2008, for a comprehensive review).

Factors that are likely to obscure the issue include the questions of whether different investigators have employed the same criteria for the autism diagnosis; whether they have controlled for severity of autism; use of different behaviors as indices of MNS functioning; and different measures of MNS neural activity (e.g., fMRI, TMS, and mu wave suppression on EEG). It may be the case that, whereas MNS impairment is present in moderate to severe autism, it is not as apparent in mild autism. Some evidence for that hypothesis is provided by Iacoboni and Dapretto's (2006) finding that MNS activity is correlated with severity of autism. In short, much clarification is needed in this area. However, for the present, I find most plausible de C. Hamilton's (2013) proposal that it is primarily the failure of top-down control signals based on capacity to evaluate current context and social situation rather than a primary dysfunction of the MNS that leads to abnormal MNS responses.

Neural correlates of automatic and effortful control systems

There is evidence that different areas of the brain are activated in immediate and automatic processing versus slower and more effortful reflective processes. A number of investigators have reported that the prefrontal cortex (PFC) is especially involved in representing mental states in oneself and others (e.g., Frith & Frith, 1999; Modinos, Ormel, & Aleman, 2009). We have already noted Posner and Rothbart's (2000) finding regarding the operation of an immediate and automatic "reactive" system, which in response to negative stimuli activates the amygdala, as well as a slower and more deliberate system they refer to as the "effortful control system," the neural substrate of which is the anterior cingulate and the frontal cortex. They present a good deal of evidence that, whereas activation of the former brain areas is correlated with immediate experience of negative emotions, the activation of the latter brain areas is implicated in the regulation of negative affect. In support of this formulation, Davidson and Sutton (1995) reported that seeing frightening scenes produces strong activation of the amygdala, which can be modulated by frontal cortical activity. In another study, Blair et al. (1999) found that sad faces activate the amygdala, but as sadness increases, the anterior cingulate is also activated, suggesting an attempt to modulate the experienced sadness.

There is evidence that the anterior cingulate and the medial prefrontal cortex are also implicated in mentalization and empathy. Singer et al. (2004) found that observing one's partner in pain is associated with greater activation of the anterior cingulate, but not with the somatosensory component, which is activated when one experiences pain oneself.[10] Further, participants who scored higher on a measure of empathy showed greater activation of the anterior cingulate. It is important to note that activation of the anterior cingulate and the medial prefrontal cortex is associated with both mentalizing about the others and one's own mental states (Lieberman et al., 2007). Although it may be an odd way to put it, given the association of anterior cingulate and medial prefrontal cortex activation both with empathy for other's mental states as well as reflecting on one's own mental states, one can think of the latter as enabling a kind of empathy for one's own mental states. That is, one may not only have an immediate affective experience in relation to an aspect of self experience, but also through self-reflection understand the basis for one's experience, similar to how one might understand the basis for another person's affective reaction. In this regard, this distinction parallels the earlier noted distinction between perceptually detecting an affective valence in another and being able to reflect on and understand the context of that mental state, including in some instances one's role in triggering it.

Feeling empathically understood and empathically understanding another

In the clinical context, the issue of the patient *feeling* understood is of paramount importance. It is worth noting, however, that a patient can feel empathically understood even when the therapist does not empathically understand the patient. And conversely, the patient may *not* experience being empathically understood by the therapist even when it can be shown that he or she does in fact empathically understand the patient. One reason that these contingencies and disjunctions are possible is that one's feeling of being understood by another person is not simply a matter of the other person's inner experience of – that, in itself, may convey little – but is largely a matter of how and what that other person *communicates*. This is especially the case given the fact that there is no one-to-one correspondence between one's experience of understanding another and one's communication of that understanding. And by communicative expression,

I refer to verbal, paralinguistic, and nonverbal forms of communication. For example, it is possible that at least in some cases, the therapist's benevolent silence or nonverbal expressions may be more likely to elicit the patient's feeling of being understood than explicit verbalization of understanding, particularly if the latter is communicated in a manner that does not resonate with the patient.

Secure base script knowledge

The preceding studies have dealt with automatic and deliberative factors in understanding another. However, in the context of ongoing interpersonal interactions, interpersonal understanding is not limited to understanding another's mental state, but also involves a sense of how to react to the other. A specific expression of that capacity is the ability to recognize someone's distress as well as knowledge of social "rules", such as if someone is distressed one does such and such.

Tini, Corcoran, Rodrigues-Doolabh, and Waters (2003) and T. E. A. Waters and Rodrigues-Doolabh (2004) have developed an Attachment Script Assessment (ASA) method in which individuals are given a list of words and are asked to tell stories using that list. The words lend themselves to a "secure base script" narrative, that is, to stories that are characterized by the elements of someone in distress, a bid for help, help provided, and distress replaced by the hitherto distressed individual feeling comforted. The stories are scored for degree of "secure base script knowledge". The ASA is based on the assumption that individuals whose narratives reflect a high degree of secure base script knowledge have available to them a secure base schema or set of "rules" in which one recognizes another's distress and bid for help and responds with comforting behavior.

T. E. A. Waters, Brockmeyer, and Crowell (2013) have shown that 80% of the variance between coherence on the Adult Attachment Interview (AAI, See Main & Goldwyn, 1998) and adult couples' caregiving and care seeking in a laboratory situation reported by Crowell et al. (2002) is accounted for by secure base script knowledge. Tini et al. (2003) reported that mother's secure base script knowledge predicted with 76% accuracy infant's attachment status in the Strange Situation. A similar finding was reported by T.E.A. Waters, Raby, Ruiz, Martin, and Roisman (2018). (See T. E. A. Waters and Roisman [2019] for an overview of research in this area.)

Employing the ASA, Groh and Haydon (2017) found that compared to mothers whose narratives were high on secure base script knowledge (SBSK), mothers low on SBSK showed significantly larger amplitude in the P3b component of their EEG electrical response potential (ERP) in response to photos of their infant's distressed facial expressions (which the authors interpret as "indicative of greater resource allocation", p. 246). This was not the case with regard to infant's happy facial expressions. Also, mothers with lower SBSK scores had a greater total number of missed responses, that is, were less accurate in recognizing their infant's distress cues. Taken together, these results suggest that "mothers with limited access to a secure base script might respond less sensitively to infant distress because such cues overwhelm their cognitive resources, undermining their ability to organize sensitive behavioral responses" (p. 251).

Further research is needed on the relationship among interpersonal understanding, construed in terms of accurate identification of another's mental states, one's knowledge of social "rules" such as how one is supposed to behave in response to such understanding, and one's ability to actually behave in the real world in accord with both one's understanding of the other and one's knowledge of social rules.

Summary

What are some of the implications of the discussed findings for a revised and expanded ego psychology?

(1) Along with other ego functions identified and accorded ego autonomy by Hartmann, a revised and expanded ego psychology needs to include the capacity for interpersonal understanding as a core ego function that develops in an average expectable environment.

(2) The capacity for interpersonal understanding appears to entail two systems: an automatic reactive system that includes the components of the social smile, affective attunement, imitation and intentional attunement as aspects of the MNS; and a deliberative system, the components of which include the capacity for a theory of mind, for taking the perspective of the other, and for reflecting on one's own and others' mental states.

(3) The automatic and deliberative systems are underlain by different neural networks. There is evidence that in adaptive functioning the two

systems operate smoothly together, with the deliberative system serving to modulate the activation of the automatic system.

(4) As revealed in the literature, empathy is a complex concept which can range from one extreme of reactions akin to contagion (i.e., I feel as distressed as you do) to the other extreme of understanding based primarily on observation and inference. The "optimal" form of empathy in many situations (i.e., the therapeutic situation) would appear to include an experience of a moderate dose of what the other is experiencing combined with a cognitively oriented understanding.

(5) Interpersonal understanding includes not only understanding of another's mental contents, but also a sense of how to act in various interpersonal situations.

Notes

1 Anticipating the discovery of the mirror neuron discovery, the Gestalt psychologists Köhler (1958) and Koffka (1935) also argued that understanding of another person's actions, etc. is automatic and attributed such immediate understanding to "isomorphism", that is, to activation of shared brain patterns in the observer and the observed.

2 There are historical precursors to the concept of "uninhibited perception" and indeed, to the mirror neuron embodied simulation hypothesis. As Stock and Stock (2004) write, some form of an ideo-motor hypothesis was formulated as far back as 1816 by Herbart, in 1845 by Laycock, and 1852 by Carpenter, the latter two invoking cerebral reflex actions. Lotze (1852) and in 1861 by Harless, who viewed the ideo-motor process as a fundamental mechanism for all intentional behavior. The various views on the ideo-motor principled were consolidated by James (1890), who wrote that "We may then lay it down for certain that every representation of a movement awakens in some degree the actual movement which is its object" (as cited in Stock & Stock). Herbart (1825) wrote that even the idea or image of an action can activate nerves and muscles involved in that action.

3 To avoid confusion, it is important to distinguish between activation (or excitation) and inhibition at the neural and the behavioral levels. The inhibition of a behavior requires activation of a particular neural area.

4 In his description of Lipps' theory of empathy and aesthetic experience, Zweig (1967) writes that "the object contemplated is the resultant of two components: the sensorially given and the subject's activity of apperception" (p. 486). Zweig suggests here that in Lipps' theory, empathy includes two components: the immediate sensory data as well as cognitive processing.

5 In a recent interview in the *New York Times Book Review*, the author being interviewed, Yu (2020) refers to a definition of emotional intelligence as "seeing yourself from the outside and seeing others from the inside" (p. 6).

6 In a very different context, one is reminded of Schlick's (1918) philosophical distinction between experience (*erleben*), which is fleeting and immediate, and knowledge (*erkennen*), which goes beyond the immediately given and entails concepts and judgments and understanding the relations among experiences. The relevance of Schlick's distinction in the present context is that knowledge and understanding of oneself as well as of others is the product of reflective activity in relation to immediate experience.

7 There is some dispute as to whether this reaction to the observation of another's distress should be viewed as a form of empathy or rather the relative absence of empathy, that is, the replacement of empathy by personal distress.

8 What has not been discussed here are the issues involved in the question of one's relationship to the one being observed.

9 In a recent review of a memoir by Oliver Sacks' longtime partner (Oliver Hayes), the reviewer refers to Sack's difficulty with bringing himself to "emotional life" as similar to "a shyness so deep it resembled a form of Asperger's syndrome". He goes on to say that Sacks' ability to connect with his patients was linked to "an intense intellectual curiosity in place of empathy to put himself in their minds" (Bram, 2017, p. 13)

10 This is somewhat of a controversial area. There is evidence that whether or not one detects a somatosensory component associated with observing another in pain is at least partly a function of the measurement technique employed (e.g., fMRI or TMS).

7

Ego functions, aims and motives

Freudian theory and ego aims

The assumption of Freudian theory that all behavior, directly or indirectly, is motivated by the need to discharge drive excitation is expressed in a number of overlapping ways: the constancy principle (Freud, 1893 [1962]); the conception of the mind as a discharge apparatus (Freud, 1950 [1895]); the assertion that only a wish can set the mind in motion (Freud, 1900 [1953], 1901); and the axiomatic claim that all behavior is governed by the pleasure principle, with unpleasure defined as the build-up of excitation and pleasure defined as the discharge of excitation (Freud, 1900 [1953]). With the advent of drive theory, this fundamental assumption can be stated as the claim that all behavior, directly or indirectly, is in the service of drive gratification, that is, discharge of drive tensions.

As we have seen in Chapter 1, according to Freudian metapsychological theory, early in life, the infant is governed by the tendency of blind discharge of drive tensions reflected, for example, in hallucination of the breast in regard to the hunger drive. The development of an ego structure and ego functions, including reality-testing, delay, and thinking is necessary if actual drive reduction is to be possible. Thus, from early in Freud's writings, the ego is defined, in large part, in terms of its function of finding ways to effect drive gratification in the real world in a realistic way.[1] No distinctive motives associated with the ego and its functions that have the same motivational force as drive motives are posited.

The more experience-near clinical material presented by Freud (1893–1895) in *Studies on hysteria* does not quite jibe with the preceding metapsychological picture. In virtually all the early clinical cases discussed by Freud, the mental content that is "incompatible" with the ego and therefore repressed is a wish, desire, or fantasy that violates the women's moral sense and self-image. Therefore, to become aware of the mental content, let alone act on it, would elicit strong negative affects. Hence, one can refer not only to the ego *function* of repression, but also add that the *motive* for triggering that function is the avoidance of negative affect. In a broader context, one can say that in these cases, both the function of and the motive for repression is a form of self-protection or self-preservation.

And, indeed, at one point in his writings, Freud (1916–1917) posited the existence of both ego instincts and sexual instincts. However, these two instincts were not given equal motivational status. Whereas, according to Freud, the sexual instincts are energized by libido and driven by libidinal aims, the quasi-aims of the ego instincts are referred to as "interests" (*interesse*) rather than full-fledged aims and motives. Freud (1916–1917) writes: "We termed the cathexis of energy which the ego directs toward the objects of its sexual desires 'libido'; all the others which are sent out by the self-preservative instincts, we termed 'interest'" (p. 414). It seems clear that in defining ego instincts as self-preservative instincts, Freud was essentially stating that the ultimate function of the ego is to enhance survival through its role as a structure necessary for gratification of basic needs in a realistic and safe way. Freud never acknowledged the possibility that self-preservative instincts can generate personal aims, motives, and desires in the way that the sexual instincts generate proximal sexual desires, motives, aims, and fantasies.

The result was, as noted earlier, that, although Freud toyed with the idea of motives and aims specifically related to the ego and ego functioning, he never granted full motivational properties to behaviors associated with ego functioning. Such properties were limited to the instinctual drives. The end result was that no independent ego motives were posited, only ego *functions*, which ultimately remained in the service of drive gratification. Further, as Strachey (1915) writes: although "'Ego-interest' or simply 'interest' is regularly contrasted [by Freud] with 'libido', the exact nature of these non-libidinal instincts are obscure" (p. 115). What is clear is that Freud was reluctant to open the door to viewing non-libidinal aims as full blown motives and aims. His compromise is to refer to such aims as "interests".

After a bewildering and utterly confusing series of discussions on the relationship between ego instincts (or equivalently, self-preservative instincts) and sexual instincts, Freud eventually abandoned his dual model of ego instincts and sexual or libidinal instincts in favor of conceptualizing the ego instincts themselves as sexual. He refers at one point to "the self-preservative sexual instincts" (Freud, 1920, p. 55) and writes that "the instincts of self-preservation were also of a libidinal nature: they were sexual instincts, which instead of external objects, had taken the subject's own ego as an object" (Freud, 1923 [1961], 1922).[2] Freud's altered view of ego instincts as libidinal enabled Freud to avoid a theoretical position which allowed the positing of non-libidinal instincts as the ultimate source of all motives. This position was also occasioned by his need to refute Jung's positing of a non-libidinal "life-force" (See Strachey, 1914, p. 70) rather than by the primacy of libido.

At one point, Freud (1923 [1961], 1922) aligns the ego instincts with the aggressive drive and, at another point, with the death instinct. With regard to the latter, he writes that the function of ego instincts is "to assure that the organism follows its own path to death" (p. 39). In short, Freud does not seem to know what to do with the idea that we might have aims and strivings the source and goals of which are non-libidinal. In the course of Freud's writings, we are presented with a bewildering array of dualities: ego-libido versus object-libido; narcissistic libido versus object libido; and life versus death instincts. In these writings, Freud is at his most speculative, most unmoored from any real life phenomena, and largely concerned with arcane metapsychological issues.

When we get to Freud's late (1940 [1938]) work, *An outline of psychoanalysis*, the demise of the concept of ego instincts is essentially complete, along with the possibility of recognizing distinctive ego motives. The ego is now conceptualized as a structure with various functions, including voluntary movement, perception, memory, response to danger, learning, and adaptation. Freud (1940 [1938]) writes that the functions and tasks of the ego are "gaining control over the demands of the instincts" (p. 146) and "discover[ing] the most favorable and least perilous method of obtaining satisfaction, taking the external world into account" (p. 148).

Thus, according to this id-ego model, the instinctual drives (id) provide the energy for mental functioning – only a wish can set the mind in motion (Freud, 1950 [1895]) – and are the source of our motives and desires, whereas the ego controls and channels these motives and desires. (Recall Freud's [1923 (1961)] horse and rider metaphor). In this model, the ego is essentially equated with mental functioning, which serves biologically based drives that generate inner stimuli that activate and make demands on the mind. It is then the primary function of the mind (a central aspect of which is ego structure) to find ways in reality to discharge the tensions associated with drives – in psychological terms, to gratify needs, wishes, and desires. There is no room in this model for distinctive ego motives and desires, that is, motives and desires linked to ego functioning. If one harbors any doubt as to Freud's views regarding the fundamental source of our aims and motives, to dispel these doubts, one need only turn to his comment late in his writings that "the power of the id expresses the true purpose of the individual's or organism's life" (Freud, 1940 [1938], p. 148), with the overriding task of the ego residing in the carrying out the id's purpose in a reality-oriented way. As G.S. Klein (1976) has observed, when ego functions are referred to by Freud, function is understood "in an entirely *non-motivational* sense" (p. 153) (emphasis in the original). Although Freud toyed with the idea of motives and aims specifically linked to the ego and ego functions, they were never granted full motivational properties. Rather, behaviors linked to ego functions were accorded the status of "interests" (*interesse*).

Ego aims and motives in ego psychology

The emphasis on the autonomy of ego functions in ego psychology does not contradict their primary role in drive gratification, but, indeed, is *required* for realistic drive gratification to be possible. Nor does it alter Freud's formulation that the id is the source of our fundamental purposes and aims and that the ego is the structure that controls and channels these purposes and aims. Indeed, in her writings on ego psychology, Anna Freud (1945) writes that the ego needs to function as "[reliably] as a mechanical apparatus" (p. 144). Insofar as the ego is viewed as an "apparatus", it cannot be attributed motives and aims. An apparatus does not have aims; rather, it functions in the service of fulfilling aims that have been set elsewhere, in the case of Freudian theory, by the drives. In short, given their general theoretical framework and their particular conception of the ego as an "apparatus", ego psychologists could not entertain the possibility that aims and motives could be associated with ego functions themselves.

To recognize the existence of ego motives and aims not identical to or derived from presumed primary drives of sex and aggression is to assert not only the autonomy of ego *functions* from these drives, but also the autonomy of *a set of desires, motives, and aims*, and even other instinctual systems (e.g., the attachment system) from these primary drives. To take that step is to challenge the very fabric of the id-ego model and other aspects of Freudian theory. This step was too radical for the ego psychologists to take. Although the concept of secondary autonomy seems to allow for ego motives, to an important extent, these motives are derivatives of instinctual drives and require "neutralized" energy from id sources.

Despite its significant revisions of classical psychoanalytic theory, in important respects, including the positing of primary and secondary autonomy of ego functions, the ego psychology of Hartmann retained an id-ego model that did not clearly assign full motivational status to ego functions. Hartmann (1950) writes that although at one point,

> Freud identified the self-preservative tendencies with 'ego drives' . . . however, today we no longer speak of 'drives of the ego' in the strict sense, since it was realized that all the drives are part of the system id.
>
> (p. 135)

In other words, whatever else they are, what were referred to as "ego drives" do not have the kind of motivational status that instinctual drives have.

In various of his writings, Hartmann does refer to ego aims. For example, at one point, he refers to "the substitution of ego aims for instinctual aims" (Hartmann, 1954 [1964], 1964, p. 213). He also writes that "[a] systematic study of ego functions would have to describe them in regard to their aims" (Hartmann, 1950, 1939 [1964], p. 134). And as a final example, in the context of providing an example of secondary autonomy, Hartmann (1947 [1964], 1964) writes that

> in the case of intelligence, we see that a function that has (partly) developed as defense against the instincts may become an independent aim of the ego . . . We must indeed realize that a great many of the ego's aims originate in such a way.
>
> (p. 44)

Despite the previous references to ego aims, they are not accorded the same motivational status as are given to drive motives and aims. Nor are Hartmann's references to ego aims elaborated or developed in a way that that they can be readily integrated into a revised id-ego model. Rather, they are referred to here and there in a relatively non-systematic way, which gives them a marginal status relative to accounts of drive aims and motives. In addition, at least in some of the references, ego aims are derivative in one way or another. For example, in his brief comment on substituting ego aims for instinctual aims, Hartmann (1954 [1964], 1964) suggests that ego aims require energy that is a product of the "neutralization" of instinctual energy. He also refers to the use of neutralized aggressive energy in the ego function of defense. Implicit in Hartmann's concept of "neutralized energy" is the assumption that because the ego has no source of energy of its own, in order to carry out even its autonomous functions, it relies on neutralized energy derived from the drives. The irony here is that although Hartmann's intention is to establish the possibility of ego autonomy from drives, ego functions continue to rely on libidinal energy that is neutralized (whatever that means).

As Greenberg and Mitchell (1983) point out, in some of his writings, Hartmann (1955) introduces the ideas that the ego can have sources of energy independent of drive. He writes: "part of mental energy – how much or how little we can hardly estimate – is not primarily drive energy but belongs to the very first to the ego" (p. 236). It is difficult to reconcile these different views. Equally important, it is difficult to resist viewing the entire discussion of neutralized or deaggressified or delibidinized energy at the disposal of the ego versus the ego's own energy as a scholastic debate, having little to do with phenomena in the real world.

Hartmann (1950) introduces the concept of "ego interests" (*Ich interesse*) as a sort of watered-down version of basic motives that include the desire for wealth, for success, and for social status. He writes, however, that these ego interests are not of primary interest to psychoanalysis because "they play no essential part in the etiology of neurosis" (p. 135) and that they "follow not the laws of the id but of the ego" (p. 135). Hartmann (1950) goes on to say that their "relevance . . . becomes clear the moment we turn to viewing them from the angle of general psychology" (p. 135). Hartmann's confident assertion that ego interests play no part in the etiology of neurosis is based not clinical observation, but rather on the theoretical assumption that phenomena that follow the laws of the ego rather than those of the id play little or no role in psychopathology. Also, as Greenberg and Mitchell (1983) observe, one of the axiomatic assumptions of psychoanalytic theory is that there is a continuum from mental health to pathology rather than a sharp dichotomy. Hence, it is odd to assert that ego interests play an important role in the general functioning of the mind, but do not play any role in the etiology of the neuroses.

Hartmann (1955) writes that the ego has its own set of motives related to adaptation, including ego interests and moral imperatives and refers to independent moral motivations. He writes that "there are moral motivations which have the full dynamic significance of independent forces in the mental economy" (Hartmann, 1960, p. 40) and also refers to ego gratification and moral gratification alongside instinctual gratification (Hartmann, 1960, p. 36). He also writes the "the development of ego psychology . . . broadened our views on the hierarchy of motivations" (Hartmann, 1960, pp. 59–60). However, Hartmann does not go on to discuss the implications of this position for the understanding of motivation in Freudian theory and for the entire theoretical structure regarding the relationship between the id and the ego.

Along with most analysts, and perhaps many theorists of other theoretical persuasions, Hartmann assumes that our moral values and ego interests are strongly influenced by our early experiences within the family. However, it does not follow from this assumption that the early experiences that have a special influence on our later moral values and interests – and indeed, on our character and personality formation – have specifically to do with instinctual drives, including psychosexual factors. It is highly likely that the early experiences that influence our adult self-image, interests, values, competence, character, ego and personality functioning are in areas having to do with such matters as separation-individuation, the nature of parental discipline (rewards and punishments), the availability of a secure base for exploration, maternal sensitivity and responsivity, being affirmed, valued, and understood, implicit values suffusing family interactions and one's subculture, modeling and identification, and so on. These are factors that are hardly well represented in Hartmann's ego psychology.

The special importance given to instinctual drive factors is seen not only in terms of the influence of early experiences on later behavior, but also in regard to the influence of current factors on behavior. Consider Waelder's (1936 [1930]) principle of multiple function, which Hartmann refers to approvingly on a number of occasions in his writings. Waelder's basic idea is that any given behavior fulfills a number of functions. However, the functions that the behavior fulfills are limited to drive, ego, and superego. Thus, the assumption is made that for all individuals and for any piece of significant behavior, the most important determinants of that behavior are limited to these factors. However, this is an a priori formulation based not on observation but on axiomatic theoretical assumptions.

I bring up Waelder's multiple function principle for a number of reasons. One reason is to demonstrate Hartmann's approving references to it suggest that, despite charting new territory, Hartmann remains faithful to classical drive theory. Another reason is to reinforce the point that, although the principle of multiple function may be valid in noting the multiple determinants of a given slice of behavior, it may not possess equal validity in identifying the particular determinants for that behavior. And finally, the third reason is to make the observation that the overt conscious determinant of the behavior cannot be reduced to the covert "hidden" one (e.g., unresolved early oedipal conflicts) nor can the "hidden" determinant be given primary importance except in cases where the particular behavior is problematic and irrational.

Other critiques of Freud's and Hartmann's dichotomy between ego functions and motives

A number of cogent critiques of the preceding formulation of the relationship between motives and ego functions appeared in the psychoanalytic literature. White (1959, 1960) and Hendrick (1942, 1943) rejected the dichotomy between ego functions and motives and proposed that the pursuit of competence and mastery are autonomous motives associated with ego functions and are relatively independent of their role in gratification of the dual drives of sex and aggression. Indeed, Hendrick (1943) posited a separate "instinct to master" (p. 561)[3]; and White (1959) referred to an "intrinsic" need to deal with the environment and a "feeling of efficacy" when one interacts with the environment in a competent manner. At the center of White's and Hendrick's posits is the implication that the conception of the ego should not be limited to a set of controlling functions, but should also include distinctive motives, desires, and aims, the pursuit and fulfillment of which are adaptive, pleasurable, and contribute to feelings of well-being and the non-fulfillment of which can be maladaptive, unpleasurable and contribute to feelings of ill-being, even if the pleasure and unpleasure experienced do not fit the Freudian quantitative conception of pleasure and unpleasure.

White (1963) referred to "neurogenic" motives associated with ego functioning, which in contrast to the "viscerogenic" motives emphasized by Freudian theory, cannot easily be assimilated into a discharge or drive reduction model of motivation. What White means by "viscerogenic" motives are those involving reduction of excitation through consummatory activities (e.g., hunger); and what he means by "neorogenic" are those motives that do not involve drive reduction and indeed, involve further stimulation. White's positing of "neurogenic" motives was a radical departure from the classical and ego psychology division of the mind into a realm that generates wishes, desires, motives, aims, fantasies, etc. (the id) and a structural realm that is comprised of a set of functions that serve to control, defend against, gratify, modulate, sublimate, etc. one's wishes, desires, motives, etc. (the ego). It is also a radical departure from the model of both classical psychoanalytic theory and ego psychology, in which all of one's wishes and desires are essentially id derivatives that are dealt with in a variety of ways by a structure – the ego – with a set of functions, but with no wishes, motives, or desires of its own. More recently, Greenberg (2001) has posited "safety" and "effectance" as superordinate motives for a wide range of behavior. These clearly can be understood as ego motives.

In his contrast between the id as "directed exclusively to obtaining pleasure" and the ego as governed by "considerations of safety", Freud (1926) suggests that the pleasure principle operates primarily in regard to drive gratification, whereas the reality-principle, as expressed, for example, in "considerations of safety", operates primarily in regard to ego functioning. What enables Freud to limit the pleasure principle to the id is the metapsychological conception of pleasure in terms of the build-up and discharge of excitation emanating from drives rather than in terms of negative and positive affective feelings. The result is a conceptual dissociation between the pleasure principle and the subjective experience of affect. After all, feeling unsafe is a negative affect one is motivated to avoid experiencing, and feeling safe is a positive affect one is motivated to maintain. In short, when pleasure is understood in terms of its ordinary qualitative meaning, behaviors linked to "considerations of safety" are as fully in accord with the pleasure principle as drive-related behavior.[4] And yet, Freud never spoke of motives and desire linked to feeling safe. In a forceful and cogent critique of ego psychology's exclusively structural conception of the ego, Apfelbaum (1966) addressed the problems inherent in a dichotomy between desires and aims, on the one hand, and controlling ego structure, on the other. One such problem is that it leads to the odd conclusion reached by Rapaport (1960) that the effectance, mastery, and competence behaviors and feelings associated with ego functioning should be viewed as *caused* rather than *motivated*, based on the assumption that in order for a behavior to be viewed as motivated it must be characterized by buildup of tension and excitation and pleasure accompanying the discharge of excitation and tension and must possess appetitive and consummatory properties, that is, arousal and discharge.[5] This is a conception modeled after the sexual orgasm (or, as Holt (1976) observes, after the urge to urinate and pleasure accompanying urination). However, as Hendricks and White and many others have argued, many motivated phenomena do not conform to this model. Apfelbaum (1966) suggests that the obvious way out of this untenable position is to abandon the structure-motive dichotomy and view the ego, as well as the id and superego, as *aim-organizations*. As he puts it: "The organization and enduring patterns of these aims constitutes the ego-id-superego differentiation" (p. 469).[6]

Cognitive motives and drive-reduction learning theories

Freudian theory was not alone in its axiomatic assumption that reduction of drive tensions is the central motivational factor in virtually all learned behavior. A similar assumption also constitutes the foundation for drive-reduction Hullian theory (e.g., Hull, 1943). Hull employs similar reasoning to Freud's in accounting for a wide range of behaviors that are presumably indirectly linked (i.e., through secondary reinforcement) to reduction of primary drives (e.g., hunger). Thus, according to the logic of Hullian theory, cognitive behaviors, such as curiosity or exploration, do not have motivational properties of their own but, so to speak, achieve derived motivational properties through their association with reduction of primary drives (e.g., hunger), that is, through their achievement of secondary reinforcement properties. Thus, on this view, one can say that these behaviors are engaged in due to their indirect association with drive reduction. One way to put it is to say that curiosity and exploration behaviors are acquired due to the fact that engaging in such behaviors increases the probability of leading to reduction of primary drives (i.e., they increase the probability of finding food or finding a mate) and then get reinforced. In other words, curiosity and exploration behavior have no intrinsic reward value of their own but have acquired reward value only due to their association with reduction of primary drives.

At approximately the same period of time that the critiques of Hendricks and White appeared in the psychoanalytic literature, a number of important experimental studies were published in psychology journals, the main theme of which was an attempt to demonstrate the reward value of cognitive behaviors and motives in animals and humans that were independent of reduction of primary drive reductions, that is, that could not be easily accounted for through their association with reduction of primary drives. These studies showed that cognitive behaviors, including curiosity, manipulation, exploration, responses to novelty, sensory change, and activity, have motivational reinforcing properties of their own. That is, animals and humans will learn and work when the opportunity to manipulate objects, explore, satisfy curiosity, or experience a novel stimulus constitute the sole rewards, that is, where the learning and work are "not dependent upon, nor derived from, internal drives such as hunger or thirst or their incentive systems" (Harlow, Blazer, & McClearn, 1956, p. 444).

Indeed, certain cognitive motives may have drive-like properties, as seen in Butler's (1957) finding that rats deprived of visual experience for a short period show increased responsiveness to visual stimuli and visual exploration. Further, the motivational properties of these cognitive behaviors are triggered by external stimuli rather than by internal drive demands. Environmental change itself can serve as a reinforcer (Kish & Barnes, 1961; Barnes, Kish, & Wood, 1959; Robinson, 1959). As Harlow (1953) puts it: "The key for human learning is motivation aroused by external stimulation" (p. 23). And as Berlyne (1950) writes: "Novelty [figures] prominently among the qualities that can give stimuli the power to attract attention" (p. 68). In one of the few studies on children rather than animals, Terrell (1959) reported that kindergarten and elementary school children who were allowed to engage in manual manipulations during a problem-solving task learned more quickly than a group who were shown a light flash when making a correct response as well as a group of children who were promised a bag of candy.

To sum up, the studies carried out during this period were intended to refute the claim of Hullian theory that a wide range of behaviors not directly in the service of drive reduction were acquired due to their secondary reinforcement properties, that is, to their association with drive reduction. The findings of these studies demonstrated that, contrary to drive-reduction theory, a range of cognitive behaviors had motivational properties independent of their association with reduction of so-called primary drives.

Although ego psychology and the cognitive theorists I have referred to converged on the idea that certain behaviors were autonomous of drive-reduction, a critical difference between them is that, whereas ego psychologists posited the autonomy of ego *functions* from drives, the non-psychoanalytic researchers and theorists whose work I have described focused on the autonomy of cognitive *motives*, that is, motives that were not secondary derivatives of so-called primary drives. From the ego psychology perspective formulated by Hartmann and Rapaport, behaviors such as curiosity, manipulation, and exploration are viewed as derivatives of and energized (through "neutralization") by instinctual drives rather than as behaviors that have their own motivational source. Unlike the ego psychologists however, the researchers on cognitive motives were not theoretically encumbered by one, the dichotomy between ego functions and ego motives; and two, the need to restrict the conception of drives and drive-like properties to fit the discharge model of psychoanalytic instinct theory. Hence, they could view behaviors such as curiosity and exploration – which from an ego psychology perspective would be classified as ego functions – as having motivational and even drive-like properties.

However, despite the cogency of the contributions of such critics as Hendricks (1943), White (1959, 1960), and Apfelbaum (1966), they did not lead to the systematic theoretical changes in ego psychology required to allow for, so to speak, full blown ego motives (not only ego functions) that are autonomous of the dual drives of Freudian theory, and the satisfaction of which were independent of the gratification of these drives. A revised and expanded ego psychology clearly needs to correct this theoretical state of affairs.

Ego functioning and social motives

I have been arguing that ego functions are accompanied by a distinctive set of desires and motives, including a desire for competence and mastery and pleasure in activities such as curiosity, manipulation, and exploration. However, insofar as we are social creatures, the adaptations served by ego functions also include social and interpersonal skills and behaviors, such as interpersonal understanding, which are also accompanied by a distinctive set of desires and motives. From a psychoanalytic perspective, such motives and desires are described as object relational in nature and are referred to by Fairbairn (1952) as "object seeking" (p. 82).

In the research on cognitive motives, behaviors such as exploration, manipulation, and curiosity are most frequently investigated under experimental conditions in which a single animal is tested one at a time and which, therefore, provide little opportunity for the observation of social factors. However, anyone who has observed animals and humans in their natural habitat or pet kittens and puppies can attest to the degree to which *social play* is a ubiquitous feature of the behavior of young animals and children. As we have seen in Chapter 6, social motives, such as the mere opportunity for social play serves as a reinforcer for young chimpanzees. Indeed, under certain circumstances, the opportunity for play was a more potent reward than food. Social play is a highly rewarding activity not only for chimps, but also for rat pups and for certain strains of mice (e.g., Thiel, Okun, & Neisewander, 2008; Thiel, Sanabria, & Neisewander, 2009; Panksepp & Lahvis, 2007).

Further, the opportunity for play can serve as a powerful motive. In a series of early studies, Mason et al. (Mason, Hollis, & Sharpe, 1962; Mason et al., 1963) demonstrated that the mere opportunity for social play serves as a reinforcer for young chimpanzees. Mason and his colleagues used an apparatus in which a retractable window in a cage could be opened by pressing a lever. They found that the opportunity for social play was an incentive for pressing the lever. They also reported the following findings: Not surprisingly, sated chimps chose to open the window more often when play rather than food was the reward. Also not surprisingly, food-deprived chimps pushed the lever more often when food rather than play was the reward. However, the food-deprived chimps chose play almost 50% of the time and chose play more than 80% of the time when low-preferred food was the reward.

Social motives, such as the desire to play, not only serve as powerful reinforcers but also play a critical role in psychological development. As noted in Chapter 6, deprivation of opportunities to play during adolescence in rats results in cognitive and social impairments in adulthood (Trezza et al., 2011). Also noted in Chapter 6 is the intriguing finding that the most effective "therapeutic" intervention for the Harlow monkeys raised by surrogate mothers was contact with normal monkeys. One plausible interpretation of the findings discussed previously is that experience of social contact, which can be broadly understood as an ego motive independent of drive gratification, is a vital ego need, the deprivation of which interferes with psychological development.

The ubiquitousness of social play points to the importance of social motives in behavior; and represents still another instance of a set of behaviors that is "not dependent upon, nor derived from internal drives such as hunger or thirst or their incentive systems" (Harlow et al., 1956, p. 444). In this regard, it is interesting to observe the trajectory of Harlow's research from attempts to demonstrate the inadequacy of drive reduction theory in regard to cognitive motives to attempts to demonstrate its inadequacy in regard to the social bond between infant and mother. In both cases, neither drive reduction nor secondary reinforcement adequately account for these phenomena.

As we have seen in Chapter 6, the existence and importance of social motives are perhaps most clearly seen in the influence of peer relations on development, particularly social development. Although Harlow's research on the infant-mother bond is most well-known, his research on the peer affectional system (Harlow, 1960) serves equally compelling evidence against drive reduction theory, particularly its emphasis on secondary reinforcement as the basis for a wide range of behaviors. As Vicedo (2010) observes, in the near exclusive focus on Harlow's research on the infant-mother bond, his work on the importance of the peer affectional system tends to be underemphasized. Harlow (1962) found that compared to monkeys raised with mother and no peers, monkeys raised with peers and no mother were more socially competent as adults. Insofar as mother is the means through which reduction of the hunger drive occurs, a plausible case could be made that the infant's attachment to mother is based on her drive reduction role. However, insofar as peers are not the agent for hunger drive reduction, there is no similar plausible case to be made that the peer affectional system is a product of drive reduction or secondary reinforcement. To sum up, in a broadened conception of ego functions, one that includes social-interpersonal skills, the pleasures associated with play and social interaction with peers can be viewed as critical ego motives.

As is the case with other ego functions, motives, desires, and aims are associated with interpersonal understanding and reality-testing. Further, the motives and aims associated with these ego functions are not simply derivatives of instinctual sexual and aggressive drives, but rather constitute an autonomous system. For example, motives and aims associated with the experience of security are linked to the attachment system rather than derivatives of sex and aggression. As another example, motives and aims linked to object-seeking are not necessarily byproducts of the object's role in drive gratification – "the thing in regard to which the instinct achieves its aim" (Freud, 1915b, p. 122) – when the instinct is understood as the sexual drive. Rather, as Fairbairn (1952) has argued, the motives for object seeking and connection to the object are autonomous of drive gratification. Further, according to Fairbairn (1952), the motivational force associated with object seeking is related to its role in adequate ego functioning (See Jones' Preface to Fairbairn's 1952 book). One sees a similar conception of the relationship between the object and ego functioning in Bowlby's (1988) formulation of the relationship between a secure base and exploratory activity.

Modell (1975) asserts that "[i]t is this new dimension of object relations that has yet to be integrated within Freud's model of *The Ego and the Id*" (p. 58) and suggests that if psychoanalysis is to remain a viable theory of human nature, this integration must take place. One of the ways Modell suggests that this can be accomplished is to allow for two classes of instincts: one, the sexual instinct characterized by tension-reduction and impulses seeking discharge; and the other class of "quieter" (p. 189) behaviors that are related to safety and relatedness (Modell, 1990). Experiences of safety and object relations are inextricably linked insofar as, from early in life on, safety is associated with the availability of the other. This is recognized not only by Bowlby, but also by Freud (1926) in his linking of signal anxiety to the "danger situations" that include loss of the object and of the object's love.

Modell (1990) writes that somewhat confusedly, Freud viewed the self-preservative instincts – as "both an ego function and an instinct" which he placed under the heading of *Eros* (p. 189). The confusion is somewhat resolved when one assumes, as Freud (1940, p. 199) did, that "considerations of safety" is a central ego function and that a set of social and object relational aims and motives are associated with that ego function. Finally, Modell (1990) writes: "Object relations theory has successfully challenged Freud's theory of instincts, but has not as yet provided a fully realized alternative. I see this as our 'next assignment'" (p. 195).

Intrinsic motivation: Conflation of proximal motives and distal functions

As suggested by White's proposal, to the extent that one has an intrinsic need for competence and efficacy, one can say that the cognitive behaviors discussed previously are *intrinsically* motivated in the sense that, rather than having reward value solely as a means to an end (e.g., finding food), engaging in these behaviors is rewarding in its own right. In one respect, this is another way of saying that these cognitive motives are autonomous of primary drive reduction. However, this is not to say that being effective and competent may not have rewarding consequences, for example, enhancing one's self-esteem. The point, however, is that one does not necessarily seek to be effective and competent solely or primarily *as a means of experiencing self-esteem*. That is, the experience of self-esteem is not necessarily the motive for effectance and competence, but frequently a *byproduct* of effective and competent behavior. Thus, being competent and effective may be rewarding in itself and not solely because it brings a reward extrinsic to the carrying out of effective and competent behavior.

This is also the case for behaviors such as curiosity, exploration, and novelty-seeking. That cognitive behaviors such as curiosity and manipulation are intrinsically rewarding does not mean that they may not serve adaptive survival functions. For example, exploration may increase the probability of finding food, thus contributing to the gratification of a primary drive. However, this does not mean that the primary motive for exploration is finding food or that the individual has learned to engage in exploratory activity solely or primarily on the basis of its association with hunger reduction. Rather exploration carries its own reward; it is pleasurable even if not in the sense of tension reduction.

Animals who tended to explore and who found exploratory activity interesting and pleasurable may have found greater success in, among other things, finding food and finding a mate, thus were more likely to survive and transmit their genes to future generations. In this way, the tendency to explore may have been selected for in the course of evolution. According to this account, the animal initially engages in exploratory activity as an inborn propensity as well as, later in life, as a pleasurable activity. As we have seen, the mere opportunity to carry out ego functions has motivational properties and can serve as a reinforcer for various behaviors.

One needs to distinguish here between proximal motives and distal functions. That is, the proximal motive for exploratory activity is that it is inherently pleasurable and rewarding. Because engaging in exploratory activity is likely to increase the probability of finding food, it may come to be associated with and motivated by the aim of finding food. But this does not mean that exploratory activity is not intrinsically motivated independent of primary drive reduction. That is, it does not mean that exploratory activity is engaged in due to its secondary reinforcing properties, that is, due to its association with primary drive reduction.

A similar point can be made with regard to the pursuit of one's interests. In a paper entitled "Interests as object relations", I proposed that, because similar to object relations, genuine and abiding interests may provide a cognitive-affective connection to something outside oneself, they can enhance ego functioning (Eagle, 1981). From this perspective, an important functional *consequence or outcome* of abiding and deep interests is enhancement of ego functioning. However, this is very different than saying that genuine interests are *motivated* by the desire to enhance one's ego functioning. Indeed, the direct pursuit of ego enhancement as a primary aim is likely to interfere with the ability to develop deep interests. When viewed solely as a means to an end, interests become an *instrumentality* in the pursuit of a goal extrinsic to the interests. However, it is in the very nature of authentic and deep interests that they are, to a significant extent, at least, *intrinsically* motivated, that is, pursued for their own sake. I am not suggesting that motives, desires, and fantasies extrinsic to one's interests are not present in authentic interests. They undoubtedly are present. However, to the degree that extrinsic motives play the overriding role in one's pursuits, one is no longer dealing with truly authentic and intrinsic interests. In short, it is the very nature of authentic interests that outcomes such as ego enhancement are a *byproduct* rather than the primary motivation for pursuing them.

There is evidence that an extrinsic reward, particularly one not substantively related to the individual's activity, tends to undermine children's intrinsic motivation and interest. For example, Lepper, Greene, and Nisbett (1973) reported that compared to no-reward or unexpected-reward conditions, 3- to 5-year-old children showed less intrinsic interest in a target activity when they engaged in the activity in order to obtain an expected extrinsic reward. And Marinak and Gambrell (2008) found that third grade students who either received no reward or were given a book as a reward showed more enhanced reading motivation than children who were given a token extrinsic reward.

The importance of making this distinction between the motive for and the byproduct consequence of behavior is seen in a number of important areas in life, from the mundane situation of falling asleep to the grander aim of pursuing happiness (Farber, 1966). With regard to the former, directly *trying* to fall asleep is often counterproductive. It is generally far more effective to place oneself in circumstances that facilitate falling asleep. As for the latter, rather than pursuing happiness directly (how would that be done?), which is likely to be futile, the experience of happiness is generally the byproduct of other meaningful activities and aims.

Proximal motives and distal evolutionary functions

Just as one can conflate motives for behavior and its consequences in the context of intrinsic motivation, one can also conflate proximal motives and distal evolutionary functions. (See Mayr [1961] who refers to "ultimate causes".) The distal function of a behavior does not necessarily reveal its proximal motives. For example, whereas the distal functions of sex include propagation of one's genes, the proximal motives include desire, sexual pleasure, intimacy, and so on. As another example, although an obvious distal function of eating is survival, one eats for a variety of motives including pleasure, social motives, and so forth. That distal function and proximal motive can be dissociated from each other is seen in such conditions as anorexia nervosa, obesity, and diabetes.[7]

Consider the distinction between proximal motives and distal functions in regard to such behaviors as curiosity, manipulation, and exploration. Although the distal evolutionary function of these behaviors may include increasing the probability of finding food, finding a mate, and acquiring social and physical skills – all of which enhance the probability of individual survival and propagation of one's genes – the proximal motives for engaging in these behaviors may have little to do with these outcomes. Evolution works and accomplishes its distal function by making curiosity, manipulation, and exploration pleasurable in themselves.

Conflation of motives for and consequences of behavior

The tendency to conflate motives for behaviors with their consequences is perhaps most apparent in regard to behaviors that have harmful self-destructive consequences. An obvious example is smoking, which is obviously harmful and self-destructive. However, this does not mean that the primary *motive* for smoking is self-destruction. Even a behavior as

obviously self-harmful and self-destructive as self-cutting is often motivated, not primarily by the desire to harm or destroy oneself, but by a self-
regulating desire to escape numbness and distressing affect. Perhaps the
most striking and tragic example of dissociation between motive and consequence is suicide that is not primarily motivated by the desire to destroy
oneself, but by such fantasies as revenge or of being rescued.

An egregious example of conflation of motive and consequence in the
psychoanalytic context is the positing of a death instinct. There are many
behaviors that people engage in that have self-destructive consequences.
Although in some cases, the motives for these behaviors may include the
desire to destroy oneself, in many instances, the primary motive is not
self-destruction, but other motives. To define all these behaviors under
the rubric of death instinct renders that concept relatively meaningless
(although it may also be meaningless for other reasons as well). It also cuts
off the investigation and understanding of the individual's idiosyncratic
motives for his or her behavior.

I am reminded of Sechehaye's (1951) description of her schizophrenic
patient, Renee, in *Symbolic Realization*. Renee refuses to eat and would,
indeed, die, if left on her own. However, one learns that Renee is terri-
fied at the thought of eating because persecutory voices tell her that she
must not eat and will be destroyed by them if she does eat. From an outside perspective, Renee is destroying herself by not eating. From Renee's
inner motivational perspective, however, she is not eating, not in order to
destroy herself, but to *save her life* and protect herself from the persecutory demons.

Ego functions as aim organizations

A number of theorists have suggested that we think of ego functions not
simply as functions, but as aim organizations (e.g., Apfelbaum, 1966; Klein,
1976). Consider the impulse to express or act upon angry feelings and one's
reaction to the impulse. In the context of both psychoanalysis and the cognitive psychology of executive functions the primary emphasis is on ways
to modulate and control the anger and the impulse. Little attention is given
to the possible role of desires and aims that Frankfurt (1971) refers to as
"second-order desires" that may serve to modulate and inhibit expressions
of anger that are fueled by "first-order desires". For example, the impulse
to act on feelings of anger may be influenced by a second-order desire to

not be self-destructive or to not harm someone or to preserve an important relationship. These are as much desires as the angry desire to harm and hurt.

Frankfurt (1971) writes that whereas both animals and humans have the capacity for first-order desires, that is, desires to do or not do something, only humans are capable of second-order desires and volitions, which entail an evaluative assessment of first-order desires. The relationship between first-order and second-order desires can be one of conflict or one of congruence and endorsement of first-order desires. That is, actions generated by one's first-order desires can be experienced as violating what one wants to want or as being in conformity with what one wants to want and desire. From Frankfurt's perspective, one may think of impairment of ego functioning not only in terms of failure of control over first-order impulses but also in terms of failure to develop second-order desires. This way of looking at things would be congruent with Apfelbaum's (1966) suggestion that both ego and should be conceptualized as "aim organizations" rather than in terms of aims and wishes versus controlling structure.

In certain respects, but only in certain respects, Frankfurt's distinction between first-order and second-order desires bears a family resemblance to the distinction between id and ego. Insofar as a second-order desire entails an evaluative reflection on first-order desires, it can be understood as akin to an ego function that serves to modulate first-order impulses and actions. Indeed, the parallel between id-ego and first-order and second-order desires goes further. For the extent to which an individual is incapable of forming second-order desires, his or her first-order desires are likely to go unchecked and unmodulated. In the psychoanalytic context, this state of affairs characterized by the absence of second-order desires would be understood in terms of an impairment in ego functioning. The critical difference, however, between Frankfurt's formulation and the id-ego model is that whereas in psychoanalytic theory the modulation of id impulses and desires is entirely a matter of a controlling structure (the ego), for Frankfurt, modulation of first-order desires is not simply a matter of a controlling structure, it entails second-order desires that interact with and are in some kind of dynamic relationship with first-order desires. Thus, one reason that first-order desires would go unmodulated and unchecked is that there are no counteracting second-order desires. If one were to combine Frankfurt's perspective with a revised id-ego model, one would say that an important aspect of ego functioning lies in the degree to which the individual has second-order desires.

Consider the behavior of smoking. Let us say that one (Person A) has the impulse to smoke and tries to resist acting on that impulse through the exercise of one's willpower. The term willpower suggests a capacity of which one possesses less or more. In the standard account embedded in the context of a dichotomy between impulse and controlling function, control of the impulse to smoke reflects the successful operation of one's ego or executive function of inhibiting action. Both the psychoanalytic and executive function accounts of this phenomenon take the form of an interaction between an impulse or desire, on the one hand, and a controlling function, on the other (or perhaps more accurately, a structure [i.e., the ego or the executive] with controlling functions).

Contrast this scenario with another person (Person B) who also has a first-order desire to smoke, but, in addition, a strong second-order desire to not smoke, which is as much a motivated act as the desire to smoke. The desire to not smoke would be reflected not simply in the exercise of willpower but in certain actions, such as not keeping cigarettes around and other actions that at least offer the possibility that might ultimately result in not having the desire to smoke. One way of putting this is to say that whereas for Person A, the desire to smoke is more of an ego-syntonic act, and it is the exercise of willpower that is likely to be experienced as an ego-alien force, for Person B, the desire to smoke is more likely to be experienced as ego-alien and the desire to not smoke more as ego-syntonic.

It may be the case, as Frankfurt suggests, that wanting to smoke and wanting to not smoke may be instances of different classes of desires. That is, wanting to smoke may be experienced as peremptory and urgent, whereas wanting to not smoke may be experienced less as peremptory and more in the context of one's long-term goal. However, wanting to smoke and wanting to stop smoking are, nevertheless, both desires. This is obscured by a theoretical framework in which wanting to smoke is understood as a desire and not acting on that desire is entirely understood as attributable to controlling functions.[8]

This seems mistaken. According to this view, whereas the impulse to smoke is understood in the motivational terms of the desire of an agent, control of that desire is attributed not to the agent's motives and desires, but to the efficiency of a set of functions separate from motivation and desire. Insofar as motivation implies agency in the sense that one has motives and reasons for what one does and does not do, the implication is that, whereas wanting to smoke is the desire or motive of an agent, refraining from smoking is attributable to a less agentic controlling function, which is weaker or stronger, more effective or less effective. But the urge to smoke is often subjectively experienced non-agentically, that is, as peremptory and urgent, beyond one's control, whereas refraining from smoking is often experienced agentically, that is, more clearly reflecting the agent's reasons and motives. In short, it is not clear why the peremptory urge to smoke is granted agency, whereas the second order desire to refrain from smoking is categorized largely as a controlling function.

To the extent that one thinks only in terms of impulse versus controlling function, the only adaptive option, particularly in regard to an undesirable impulse such as wanting to smoke, appears to be enhancement or strengthening of the controlling function. But this overlooks one, the possibility that dealing with undesirable peremptory impulses may entail not only the exertion of control, but also the development and enhancement of a particular set of desires; and two, the possibility that the intensity of the desire to smoke can itself be altered and that wanting to not smoke can be transformed into not wanting to smoke, that is, in not having a peremptory desire to smoke.[9] The individual who has a desire to smoke but refrains from smoking through exerting control retains the identity of a smoker who is resisting smoking. Contrastingly, in relation to the individual whose second order desire has prevailed and no longer has the desire to smoke, his or her identity is that of a non-smoker.

Notes

1 One can understand Freud's reasoning here as the conceptual origin of Hartmann's (1939) formulation regarding the need for the emergence of an "organ of adaptation".

2 However, in contradiction of this resolution, Freud continued to distinguish between ego instincts and sexual instincts.

3 Hendricks (1943) argued not only for the importance of mastery as a motive that is independent of the sexual instinct, but also posits an *instinct* for mastery. One wonders whether Hendricks believed that he had to accord mastery the status of an instinct if it were to have a motivational status equal to behaviors linked to sex and aggression; In his *Three essays on sexuality*, Freud (1905) refers to the instinct of mastery a number of times. However, the context for these references is a discussion of pregenital sexual organization, in particular, the "sadistic-anal organization" (p. 198). There is no positing of an instinctual system independent of sexuality.

4 Indeed, in an important sense, this is the case even when the pleasure principle is understood in the metapsychological terms of build-up and diminution of excitation. After all, feeling unsafe is associated with the build-up of excitation in the form of anxiety, and feeling safe is associated with the diminution of such excitation.

5 According to this logic, many object relational behaviors and motives such as security, for example, could also not be thought of as motivated.

6 It is interesting to observe that many years later, Brenner (2002) essentially takes a similar position in his call for the abandonment of the structural model of the mind and for its replacement with the simple idea that all we can ascertain is the presence of conflicting aims and compromises among these aims. A problem with Brenner's position, however, is that he does not address the question of the processes involved in the effecting of compromises among aims. Addressing this question suggests the idea that some sort of structure would appear to be necessary for such compromises to take place.

7 Diabetes is a particularly clear example of the possible dissociation between proximal motive and distal function. In the environment of "evolutionary adaptedness" (Bowlby, 1973, p. 145), the dislike of bitter foods and the preference for sweet foods was highly adaptive insofar as bitter foods were more likely to be poisonous. However, the congruence between proximal motives (preference for sweet foods) and distal function (enhancement of probability of survival) can be disrupted in particular environmental contexts in which the normally adaptive preference becomes maladaptive.

8 As we have seen, this is precisely the assumption that leads Rapaport (1960) to maintain that the attribution of motives is applicable only to drive related wishes and desires and not to ego functions.

9 This is essentially the point that Apfelbaum (1966) makes when he states that aims themselves may change.

8

Psychoanalytic theories of affect and affect regulation

Freudian theory of affect

Implicit in his early writings in which he introduces "defense hysteria" and the "cornerstone" concept of repression as reactions to an incompatibility between an idea and the ego, Freud (1894) implicitly references affect regulation as an ego function. However, as we will see in the following, it was not until the midpoint of his writings that Freud (1926 [1925]) viewed the experience of affects as a central aspect of ego functioning.

Rapaport (1953) identified three phases in the Freudian theory of affect: In Phase 1, affect is equated with sum of excitation. In Phase 2, in which the center of interest are id phenomena, affects are understood as equivalent to motor and drive discharge. And in Phase 3, in which Freud shows an increasing interest in the ego and its functions in the specific context of discussing anxiety as an affect, Freud (1916–1917) writes:

> By 'anxiety' we usually understand the subjective state into which we are put by perceiving 'the generation of anxiety' and we call this affect . . . An affect includes in the first place particular motor innervations or discharges and secondly certain feelings; the latter are of two kinds-perceptions of the motor actions that have occurred and direct feelings of pleasure and unpleasure, which, as we say, give the affect its keynote.
>
> (p. 395)[1]

With the advent of drive theory (in Rapaport's [1953] terms, Phase 2 of the Freudian theory of affects), in which affect is viewed as a product of drive discharge, the earlier concept of "quota of affect" is essentially replaced by an emphasis on the build-up of excitation due to accumulation of drive tensions, which plays the same functional role as "strangulated affect". That is, the failure to discharge excitation remains as a critical pathogen. However, failure to discharge excitation is now equivalent to failure of drive gratification. Or, to put it more precisely, failure to gratify drives now replaces "strangulated affect" as a pathogen.

The appraisal function of affect

Phase 3 of Freud's theory of affects introduces two important components of Freud's theory of affects: one, affects as subjective feelings; and two, the appraisal function of affects. In his 1917 essay, Freud refers, although only in passing, to anxiety as "a signal". That is, the affect of anxiety is given an appraisal function. He writes:

> The more the generation of anxiety is limited to a mere abortive begin-
> ning – to a signal – the more will preparedness for anxiety transform
> itself without disturbance into action and the more expedient will be
> the shape taken by the whole course of events.
>
> (p. 395)

It is in *Inhibitions, symptoms and anxiety* that Freud (1926 [1925]) more fully develops the concept of anxiety as a signal of danger. The important point to be noted here is Freud's recognition of the *appraisal* aspect of affect (at least of the affect of anxiety) and in doing so, clearly suggesting that affect and its regulation are ego functions. As Freud (1940 [1938]) writes,

> Just as the id is directed exclusively to obtaining pleasure, so the ego
> is governed by considerations of safety . . . It [the ego] makes use of
> the sensations of anxiety as a signal to give a warning of dangers that
> threaten its integrity.
>
> (p. 199)

The appraisal function is well described by Smith (1970) who writes:

> To understand affect as ego response and as a continuing process of
> response is to conceive of it as our primary way of 'listening' to our
> inner impulses, our conscience, our store of knowledge and experience,

and our anticipation of the future as these messages combine in an immediate situation.

(p. 558)

This conception of affect in Phase 3 is congruent with contemporary views of affect and emotion in the following respects: one, a key component of the emotion system is the experience of subjective affective feelings; two, subjective affective feelings, which can be pleasurable or unpleasurable, are understood essentially as perceptions of certain bodily states; and three, and especially important in the present context, emotional reactions and feelings serve an *appraisal* function, particularly appraisals of danger and safety. Freud's view here is quite similar to Damasio's (2003). Both use the term "affect" to include three components: one, subjective feelings; two, physiological and neural processes, which Damasio refers to as "emotions"; and three, overt behavior. All three components are part of the emotional system. Also similar to Damasio, Freud views subjective affective feelings as implicit appraisals of both one's inner world of bodily states as well as external environmental stimuli. And both Freud and Damasio note that the physiological and overt behavior components of the emotional system can be present without the experience of subjective affective feelings.

In the ego's appraisal function, the dangers to which it is sensitive are those originating in the "danger situations" of childhood: loss of the object, loss of the object's love, castration, and superego condemnation. These dangers are associated with parental reactions to drive-related wishes and impulses (e.g., incestuous wishes) expressed in childhood. From that point on, when these wishes threaten to reach conscious experience, they trigger "signal anxiety". Through generating a small dose of anxiety, the ego signals that there is danger ahead, namely, that signal anxiety will become traumatic anxiety if the forbidden wishes are permitted to reach conscious experience.

Does psychoanalysis have an adequate theory of affects?

Despite the increasing adequacy of the Freudian theory of affects from Phase 1 to Phase 3, nevertheless, as Rapaport (1953) wrote: "We do not possess a systematic statement of the psychoanalytic theory of affects"

(p. 476). This view has been echoed many years later by Rosenblatt (1985), who writes that "[n]either cognitive psychology nor psychoanalysis has developed a comprehensive theory of affects" (p. 85), as well as by Sandler (1991), who writes that

> Freud's theories of affects in which affects were seen as derivatives of instinctual drives have proved to be inadequate, yet the different theories on the role and nature of affect put forward by psychoanalysis have been proved equally unsatisfactory so far.
>
> (Foreword to Stein, 1991)[2]

This is true not only of Freudian theory, but also of post-Freudian psychoanalytic schools, as well as ego psychology.

One reason identified by Stein (1991) for the unsatisfactory status of psychoanalytic theories of affect is that because, particularly in his later writings, affects were viewed by Freud as conscious experiences, they were of relatively little interest to psychoanalysts, whose main concerns were unconscious processes and phenomena. As Stein (1991) puts it, because affects were seen as necessarily conscious, they "lost their proper psychodynamic status to a phenomenological explanation that could not encompass unconscious levels and hence belong to the psychoanalytic domain" (p. 170).

Another important reason for the failure to develop a more adequate theory of affects of Freudian theory lies in its metapsychological conception of unpleasure and pleasure – a fundamental dimension of affects – in terms of build-up and discharge of excitation. This conception of pleasure and unpleasure is grounded in the fundamental assumptions of the constancy principle, of the mind as a discharge apparatus, and of build-up and discharge of instinctual drive tensions as the main conditions for unpleasure and pleasure. Although reduction of drive tensions can be pleasurable and saturated with affects, it is clear that there are pleasures that have little to do with drive reduction. The result is that the pleasure principle, as conceptualized by Freud, does not serve well as a theoretical foundation for an adequate conception of the nature of pleasure and unpleasure as well as of affects.[3]

To borrow from the title of a book by Gillick and Bone (1990), there are many "pleasure(s) beyond the pleasure principle", pleasures associated with feelings of connectedness, self-affirmation, a sense of security and safety, feelings of appreciation, a sense of competence and mastery, carrying out a function and skill, upholding one's values, a sense of meaning, and so on. And there are unpleasures and a sense of disquiet and distress associated with feelings of isolation, of incompetence, of a sense of insecurity and danger, inability to carry out a function and skill, betraying one's values, loss of a sense of meaning, and so on. These "quieter" pleasures and unpleasures, which are not directly linked to appetitive drives or consummatory behaviors, are associated with feelings of well-being, contentment, and meaning versus disquiet, distress, and dissatisfaction. To try to reduce all these sources and forms of pleasure and unpleasure and affect to expressions of the constancy principle or to derivatives of dual instinctual drives is to deform the phenomena being investigated beyond recognition.

For example, as Modell (1990) suggests, affects associated with object relational motives and behaviors cannot be adequately understood in terms of "impulses seeking discharge" (p. 189). I recall seeing a video recently of a mother and infant laughing together joyously. This sort of pleasure simply cannot be understood in terms of discharge of excitation or of the mind as a discharge apparatus. Freud (1924) himself was aware that the *subjective experience* of pleasure often does not match the metapsychological conception of pleasure in terms of discharge of excitation. He writes that "it cannot be doubted that there are pleasurable tensions and unpleasurable relaxations of tensions" (p. 160) and notes that "the state of sexual excitation is the most striking example" of the former (p. 160). "Pleasure and unpleasure, therefore, cannot be referred to an increase or decrease of a quantity (which we describe as "tension due to stimulus"), although they obviously have a great deal to do with that factor. It appears that they depend, not on this quantitative factor, but on some characteristic of it which we can only describe as a qualitative one. If we were able to say what this qualitative characteristic is, we should be much further advanced in psychology" (p. 160). However, Freud does not pursue this issue further, nor does his recognition of the qualitative aspect of pleasure lead to a significant modification of the pleasure principle that is formulated solely in quantitative terms.

Affect regulation in Freudian theory

In Phase 1 of his view of affects, Freud observes (1893 [1888–1893]) that a "quota of affect" accompanies every experience. He writes: "Every event, every psychical impression is provided with a certain quota of affect (*Affektbetrag*) of which the ego divests itself by means of a motor reaction or by associative psychical activity" (pp. 171–172). Viewing affects as equivalent to "a sum of excitation" (Freud, 1893 [1888–1893], p. 172), Freud also wrote that every quota of affect needs to be adequately discharged. When adequate discharge is not possible due to circumstances or to a traumatic event, which, by definition, entails a large quantity of affect, the result is pathogenic "strangulated affect". One method of dealing with strangulated affect is abreaction, which enables a discharge of excitation.[4] Thus, during this phase of Freud's formulation of affect, one means of affect regulation – which is equivalent to excitation regulation – consists in finding a way to adequately discharge excitation. As can be seen, this is essentially an hydraulic model of affect and its regulation. To be noted here is the importance of Freud's observation that every experience is accompanied by some degree of affect.[5]

As for regulating affect through "associative psychical activity", Freud does not elaborate further at this point. However, he returns to this issue in *Preliminary communications* (Breuer & Freud, 1893). He writes:

> Abreaction, however, is not the only method of dealing with the situation that is open to a normal person who has experienced a psychical trauma. A memory of such a trauma, even if it has not been abreacted, enters the great complex of associations, it comes alongside other experiences, which may contradict it, and is subject to rectification by other ideas.
>
> (p. 9)

Freud's description here of "associative psychical activity" is essentially similar to what in the contemporary psychological literature would be referred to as *reappraisal*.

Defense as affect regulation

The concepts of defense and repression occupy a central place in the history of psychoanalysis. Freud's (1894) introduction of the concept of "defense hysteria" as well as of repression – which he viewed as the "cornerstone" of psychoanalysis – marks the birth of psychoanalysis. Insofar as the core function of repression (as well as of other defenses) is understood as a means of banning from conscious experience unacceptable mental contents that would trigger anxiety were they to be consciously experienced, one can say that defenses serve as affect regulators. Thus, the importance of regulation of negative affects has been recognized from the very beginnings of psychoanalysis.

Notwithstanding Freud's (1893–1895) early claim that the mental contents defended against were invariably of a sexual nature, it is clear in the early cases presented by Freud that the mental contents that were "incompatible" with the ego and therefore needed to be defended against, had to do with wishes, desires, thoughts, and feelings that violated the patient's self-image and moral standards, and therefore were associated with negative affects, including guilt and shame. Thus, the clinical case material in Freud's own writings, in *Studies on hysteria*, for example, make it clear that *any* mental content that triggers negative affect is subject to defense.[6]

From a Freudian metapsychological perspective, including the assumptions of the constancy principle and a conception of the mind as a discharge apparatus, the greatest danger to the "mental apparatus" is that of being overwhelmed by excessive excitation. Further, given the conception of drives in terms of build-up of excitation, they constitute the greatest source of undischarged excitations and therefore the greatest threat to the integrity of the ego. Freud (1937) writes in the context of his discussion of the "danger situations" "that . . . in the last analysis, all anxiety is fear of experiencing a traumatic state, of the possibility that the organization of the ego may be overwhelmed by excitation". He continues:

> However, after the ego is developed enough to control instinctual actions and to bring about gratification, the instinctual impulses ought not to be frightening anymore. If they still are, it is due to the fact that fears over loss of love or castration have induced the ego to block the normal course of its excitements, thus creating an insufficiency of discharge.
>
> (Freud, 1937)[7]

As late as 1940 Freud writes "that an excessive strength of instinct can damage the ego" (p. 111). He also writes that the danger in the "danger situations" of loss of the object, loss of the object's love, and castration threats lies in the fact that these dangers leave the individual helpless in the face of "an unpleasurable tension due to instinctual need" (p. 139).

A. Freud (1936) refers to anxiety in terms of "fear of strength of instincts" (p. 172) and proposes that strength of instinct can precipitate a breakdown in ego functioning, including psychosis. And even Modell (1975), who attempted to revise the id-ego model, nevertheless refers to the danger of "affects associated with anger (aggression) and love (sex) are experienced with such intensity as to induce a sense of annihilation" (p. 61). In short, according to the id-ego model, the greatest danger to the integrity of the ego lies in the build-up of undischarged drive excitation.

In common with undischarged drive tensions, anxiety also entails the build-up of excitation. Indeed, in his first theory of anxiety, Freud (1887–1902) proposed that anxiety was the direct product of undischarged libido. Hence, the category of "actual neurosis", which was viewed as a form of pathology, not due to psychological conflict, but largely to unhealthy sexual practices such as *coitus interruptus*. In his second theory, Freud (1926) viewed anxiety as an affect linked to anticipation of danger, ultimately, the danger of being left helpless at the mercy of ego damaging undischarged drive tensions. According to this formulation, "signal anxiety" operates as a warning that if defensive steps are not taken, the danger will not be averted; signal anxiety will develop into traumatic anxiety. The primary step that needs to be taken to avert traumatic anxiety is to ban from conscious experience the mental contents that, due to their association with danger (e.g., loss of the object's love, fantasized castration threats), triggered the signal anxiety. In short, the step that needs to be taken is to institute the defense of repression.

Let us say that defense is not effective and that signal anxiety develops into traumatic anxiety. (As Strachey [1926] notes: "The traumatic situation itself is clearly the direct descendent of accumulation and undischarged tension in Freud's earliest writings on anxiety. Some of the accounts given here [i.e., in Freud's later theory of anxiety] might be quotations from 1894 or 1895" [p. 81].) Thus, in the case of failure of defense and consequent return of the repressed, it is not excessive excitation associated with undischarged tensions from drive that constitute the danger to the ego. Rather, it is the sheer traumatic intensity of anxiety itself, that is, the sheer degree of excitation, that constitutes an inherent quantitative threat to the ego. (Recall that long before the development of his drive theory, Freud (1894) equated a "quota of affect" with sum of excitation).

It was the advent of drive theory that allowed Freud to locate the primary source of excitation in drive tensions and that led him to attribute the primary source of danger to the ego to undischarged drive excitations. This obscures the central idea that defenses defend against the experience of subjective negative affects rather than undischarged drive tensions, which may constitute only one source of negative affects. Further, the primary affect defended against in Freudian theory is a high level of anxiety, an affect that entails excessive arousal and excitation. This characteristic of anxiety allowed Freud to conflate the quantitative threat to the ego from the sheer intensity of arousal and excitation associated with anxiety and the presumed quantitative threat associated with undischarged drive excitation.[8]

Indeed, at one point, Freud (1915c) himself questions whether drive derivatives are inherently threatening and suggests that they are repressed not because they are inherently threatening, but rather that they are experienced as threatening *due to* repression. He writes that the "repressed instinct-presentation . . . develops in a more unchecked and luxuriant fashion . . . It ramifies, like a fungus, so to speak, in the dark and takes on extreme forms of expression" that are alien to and terrify the individual because of "the way in which they reflect an extraordinary strength of instinct. *This illusory strength of instinct* [my emphasis] is the result of an uninhibited development of it in phantasy and of the damming-up consequent on lack of real satisfaction" (Freud, 1915c, p. 149). Although Freud continues to maintain that dammed-up excitation from drive is a threat, he appears to relinquish the idea that the strength of drive itself is a threat to the individual. This isolated passage is especially interesting because it is one of the few occasions in which Freud suggests that the experienced "strength of instinct" may be illusory, the result of a fantasy that is generated by frustration and remains unchecked because, due to anxiety, it is not exposed to the light of reality through repression. However, Freud does not further develop the implications of this isolated passage for the "standard" conception of the id-ego model.

There are other conceptual difficulties with regard to Freud's formulation regarding the relationship between defense and the danger of undischarged drive excitations. It is not clear how a defense such as repression, for example, is capable of reducing the strength of instinct and thereby reducing the danger of dammed-up undischarged excitations. How does banning a wish from conscious experience reduce excessive excitation or protect one against the "strength of instinct"? Indeed, it would seem that, insofar as defense inhibits experience and action in regard to an instinctual impulse, it would *increase* the quantity of excitation. The only way that a defense such as repression could reduce the danger of excessive excitation is not through lessening the intensity of drive excitation, but through reduction of the degree of anxiety associated with the wish. Further, defense would operate to reduce anxiety triggered by *any* anxiety-laden contents, not just specifically anxiety-laden drive derivatives. In short, defense reduces the danger of excessive excitation through preventing or modulating the intensity of negative affect, in particular, the affect of anxiety. The "standard" classical model should be renamed from drive-defense to negative affect-defense.

It is not uncommon for individuals who feel psychologically fragile or who have recovered from an acute psychotic episode to report that, for them to remain psychologically stable, they need to avoid over-stimulation from any source. For such individuals, who are already struggling to cope with a high level of anxiety, additional stimulation or excitation can be experienced as destabilizing. Thus, Freud's intuition that sheer intensity of excitation may constitute a threat to psychological stability may be valid. However, there is no evidence that the primary source of sheer quantitative intensity of excitation is specifically linked to drive impulses. Rather, the intensity of excitation to be avoided can *come from any source.*

If one dispenses with Freud's limiting of defense to drive-related mental contents, what remains is the core idea that the regulatory function of defense is to protect the individual from the conscious experience of negative affect that is generated by threats to one's self-image, self-esteem, and identity as well as to the integrity of the ego when the negative affect is especially intense. This concept of defense in terms of its affect-regulating function, unencumbered by drive theory, can be more readily integrated with current research and theory on defense, as well as with conceptions of defense in contemporary ego psychology, self psychology, and object relations theory.

Are defenses "mechanisms" or actions of an agent?

Too often, references to defenses banning unacceptable mental contents from conscious experience, are thought of as subpersonal forces that influence and shape our experiences and actions. The term "*mechanism*" captures the connotation that defensive processes are impersonal, automatic, and unconscious in the way that unconscious computational processes are unconscious. However, this simply seems wrong. Unconscious computational processes, such as those involved in, say, size constancy, are not motivated and are inaccessible to consciousness under any and all circumstances. Further, it would be meaningless to say, in regard to these processes, that when certain barriers are lifted and when attention is drawn to them, we can become conscious of them. Contrastingly, at the core of the psychoanalytic concept of defense are the assumptions, one, that it is motivated by the desire to avoid the experience of negative affect; two, that the barriers to conscious experience of their use can be lifted (analysis of defense would be meaningless without this assumption); three, that when these barriers are lifted, it is possible to become aware of the hitherto unconscious mental contents that one is motivated to avoid fully experiencing. None of these assumptions applies to subpersonal mechanisms.

Thus, despite the reference to mechanism, when one states that an individual is engaging in a defensive process, one is not referring to a subpersonal process, but to a process or action (e.g., repression) carried out by an agent acting on certain motives. In that sense, one is placing defensive processes in the same general conceptual domain as an agent thinking, wishing, and desiring. And when we say that individuals are engaged in defensive processes, what we find is that they do ordinary things and engage in a variety of ordinary strategies, such as distracting themselves, turning their attention away from a disturbing mental content, mislabeling the mental content, failing to make connections (Klein, 1976), failing to spell out or articulate certain thoughts and feelings as well as the intentional project in which they are engaged (Fingarette, 1963, Sartre, 1956), failing to formulate further relatively unformulated mental contents (Stern, 2003), and actively suppressing certain mental contents – all in the service of avoiding the experience of negative affect (See Singer & Sincoff, 1990).

Perhaps because defensive processes can become habitual and virtually automatic, they may be viewed as subpersonal. For example, Freud's account of signal anxiety can be understood in the following way: Because of their past association with the "danger situations" certain mental contents that are about to reach full consciousness may automatically elicit a vague sense of anxiety (i.e., signal anxiety). That is, because the experience of certain mental contents, even if at the periphery of consciousness, is associated with expectation of disapproval and punishment in some form, it triggers the conditioned response of a mild form of negative affect. This negative affect then triggers defensive processes that prevent the mental contents from being fully consciously experienced. As noted previously, this can be carried out in a number of ways, including not formulating further the relatively unformed mental content (Stern, 2003); similar to Stern, not spelling out or articulating one's motivations (Fingarette, 1963); and distraction, that is, deploying one's attention away from the mental contents. That these strategies are carried out in a seemingly automatic way, at the fringe of consciousness, that is, preconscious, makes it appear that they are subpersonal. However, it is important to recognize that conscious-unconscious is a continuum rather than a dichotomy and that states of consciousness can be dissociated from each other. These features of consciousness make possible such phenomena as self-deception and defense, which despite disavowal, are the actions of an agent rather than the product of subpersonal processes.

Post-Freudian theories of affect and affect regulation

For the most part, although affects are referred to in discussions of clinical material and theoretical issues in post-Freudian theories, the nature of affects is not addressed as a separate topic, certainly not in a systematic way. As for affect regulation, that is not a term one finds very often in the psychoanalytic literature. Rather, the issue of affect regulation appears in discussions of such concepts as defense, holding, containment, mirroring, projection and introjections, and projective identification. (See Pedersen, Poulsen, & Lunn, 2014 for a discussion of these concepts in the context of affect regulation.) Affect regulation is a large topic. In the discussion that follows of affect and affect regulation in post-Freudian theories, I comment only briefly on the role of affect and affect regulation in these theories.

Ego psychology and affects

The ego psychology of Hartmann and others, although recognizing certain aspects of affects overlooked by Freud, does not fare much better in developing an adequate theory of affects. Possibly the greatest challenge confronting the project of viewing ego psychology as the foundation for a unified psychoanalytic theory is its inadequacy in dealing with affect and, more generally, with subjective feelings and experience. As Stein (1991) points out,

> although Hartmann undoubtedly realized the profound importance of feelings in the clinic [and one should add, in one's ongoing life] . . . his general conception of what a theory ought to look like . . . compelled him to exclude the subjective aspect from theory.
>
> (p. 52)

Stein (1991) notes that although Hartmann (1927 [1964]) viewed subjective experience as "the very nucleus of the personality", he nevertheless concluded that it is "inaccessible to explanation" (p. 375). From the perspective of Hartmann's ego psychology, which retains the primacy of drive gratification, to the extent that affect is included at all, the ego's affect regulating function remains the enablement of drive gratification in a way that does not threaten to bring about traumatic anxiety or other consequences that would trigger negative affects (e.g., guilt). In short, the ego psychology approach to affect and affect regulation is not essentially different from the perspective formulated in Freud's later writings.

Affect regulation in Kleinian theory

Stein (1991) writes that insofar as Kleinian theory deals with the conflict and interplay of love and hate and employs the conceptual language of feelings, it "can be profitably regarded as a kind of affect theory" (p. 500). According to Kleinian theory, the conflict between life and death instincts or love and hate is present from the beginning of life and is dealt with by various maneuvers, including splitting, idealizing expulsion (of negative affects), projecting and introjecting, and projective identification. It is important to note, however, that despite employing affective terms, they do not refer to subjective feelings, but to complex and byzantine unconscious fantasies attributed to young infants, replete with references to oral and anal sadism, fear of persecution and retaliation by bad objects, fear of destruction of good objects, and so on that are far removed from recognizable aspects of the emotional system, including subjective feelings. Hence, contrary to Stein, Kleinian theory is not a theory of affects when that is understood as a theory of subjective feelings.

Consider the following passage that is representative of Klein's discussions of emotions and affect:

> A little child, which believes, when its mother disappears, that it has eaten her up and destroyed her (whether from motives of love or hate) is tormented by anxiety both for her and the good mother which it has absorbed into itself.
>
> (Klein, 1935, p. 266)

Other than commenting on the child's anxiety, there is little reference to the child's subjective feelings. The love and hate referred to have little to do with feelings of love and hate, but rather are constructs embedded in theoretical formulations regarding unconscious fantasies. The formulation regarding the child's anxiety that she has eaten her mother up has little to do with the child's subjective feelings; rather, it is derived from theoretical assumption regarding unconscious fantasies.

Fairbairn on affect and affect regulation

A core assumption of Fairbairn's object relations theory is that "libido is not primarily pleasure-seeking, but object-seeking" (Fairbairn, 1952, p. 137). The critical importance of the object for psychological functioning is, as Jones (1952) notes in his Preface to Fairbairn's 1952 book, is that "at the center of the personality, the ego . . . strives to reach an object where it may find support" (p. V). In other words, the ego cannot function without a connection to the object. As Fairbairn (1952) puts it: "Any theory of ego development that is to be satisfactory must be conceived in terms of relationships with objects and in particular relationships with objects that have been internalized during early life under the pressure of deprivation and frustration" (p. 162). And "the integrity of the ego depends upon object relationships" (Fairbairn, 1952, p. 51).

Given the centrality of object relations for the development and functioning of the ego, it follows for Fairbairn that virtually all significant affects – love, hate, despair, futility, depression anxiety, sexual feelings, guilt, and so on – are generated in the context of the vicissitudes of the relationship between the ego and its objects, both external and internal. Of all the affects one can experience, from the perspective of Fairbairn's object relations theory, the most consequential negative affects one can feel are those associated with threats to a libidinal connection between the ego and objects. Hence, because the ego cannot function without object-relationships, such threats represent the possibility of the loss of the ego, which Fairbairn (1952) refers to as "the ultimate psychopathological disaster" (p. 52), that is feelings "as if there was nothing of him, or as if he had lost his identity, or as if he were dead, or as if he had ceased to exist" (p. 52). Fairbairn (1952) also refers to feelings of futility, depression, anxiety, and "an affective experience which is singularly devastating" (p. 113) in reaction to loss of connection to the object. It is worth noting that Fairbairn does not seem to have a concept of the nature of pleasure. Nor relatedly, is there much reference in his writings to positive affects.

As for affect regulation, like Freud, Fairbairn places much emphasis on the role of defense. As is the case in Freudian theory and ego psychology, in Fairbairn's object relations theory, the primary function of defense is to protect the ego. However, whereas in Freudian theory, the primary threat to the integrity of the ego is the danger of excessive excitation, in Fairbairn's object relations theory, the primary threat to the ego is to be without libidinal connection to objects, both internal and external. The ego cannot function or survive psychologically without such connections. And, Fairbairn (1952) makes clear, the "loss of the ego is the ultimate psychopathological disaster" (p. 52). Hence, patients defensively cling to "internal 'bad' objects as preferable to an empty inner world devoid of object relations" (Eagle, 2017, p. 78).

According to Fairbairn, defenses are erected not against the danger of the emergence of drive derivatives, but rather against the experience of one's infantile dependence, of the release of bad objects and bad object experiences from the unconscious, and above all, of the experience of depressive affect and schizoid states, the latter characterized by "a pronounced sense of futility" (Fairbairn, 1952, p. 131) and a sense of inner emptiness. Fairbairn also discusses the defense of viewing oneself as bad as a means of keeping alive the hope of earning the object's love.

An important contribution that Fairbairn makes to an understanding of affects lies in his description of the serious affective consequences of one's sense of loss of connection to one's external and internal objects. One can observe that dynamic at work in seriously dysfunctional relationships. For a number of years, my colleagues and I worked with women who were subjected to domestic violence. The following scenario was not uncommon: When one of the women was finally able to leave her abusive partner, she would become seriously dysregulated, fall in a total state of despair and inability to function. Only when she returned to her partner would her regulation be restored. We were struck by the degree to which this pattern fit the model of an addiction in which the absence of the addictive "substance" led to dysregulation and the provision of the addictive substance restored some level of regulation.

Kohut on affect and affect regulation

Given its emphasis on experience-near phenomena, one would expect that of the different psychoanalytic schools, self psychology would be, as Stein (1991) puts it, "marked . . . by sensitivity to feeling states of the self and between the self and the self object" (p. 181). However, somewhat surprisingly, Kohut's 1984 book has no index entries for "affects" or "emotions". Rather than a direct discussion of these topics, references to them are embedded in other issues. Affects are discussed by Kohut (1984) in the following contexts: the patient's rage and despair, as well as "disintegration anxiety" (p. 16) in reaction to his or her experience of traumatic empathic failure.

With regard to affect regulation, according to Kohut (1984), the "operative principle" with regard to defense is "the primacy of self-preservation" (p. 143). Thus, the "primary anxiety" the individual can experience is in relation to threats to the preservation of the self, what Kohut (1984) refers to as "disintegration anxiety" (p. 16). He also writes that "the so-called resistances serve the basic ends of the self; they never have to overcome" (p. 148). This is so because, from a self psychology perspective, "the so-called defense-resistances are neither defenses nor resistances. Rather, they constitute valuable moves to safeguard the self. . . [and to] protect the defective self" (p. 141). As we will see in Chapter 11, the idea that defenses and resistances need not be overcome in treatment is identical to Gray's (1994) ego psychological approach to treatment. The difference is that Gray maintains that it is important for the patient to become more aware of his or her defenses and more flexible in their use.

If the patient employs "so-called" defenses to "safeguard" and "protect" the self, why the reluctance to refer to them as defenses? Is not such safeguarding and protection the essence of defense? The reason for Kohut's reluctance appears to be that he rejects what he views as a "morally tinged theory about the therapeutic certainty of truth-facing" (p. 141) that he believes characterizes the attitude toward defense and defense analysis of classical and ego psychology psychoanalysts. However, it is entirely possible to view defenses as an adaptive means of affect regulation in response to experienced threats to the self or the ego rather than in a "morality tinged" righteous insistence on the patient facing the truth. There is little of a "morality tinged" insistence on the truth in the approach to the analysis of defense in the work of ego psychologists, such as Gray (1994) or Sugarman (2006, 2007). In addition, the early ego psychologists, including Hartmann, viewed defense as normal aspects of ego development and hardly expressed a "morality tinged" attitude their use. (See Cramer, 2001, for a review of research and theory on defense.)

For Kohut, the primary means of regulation of negative affect is the individual's experience of being empathically understood by the selfobject. However, this seemingly simple account is not without its complexities. One complicating factor, according to Kohut, is that, due to early traumatic failures in experiencing adequate empathic understanding, the individual struggling with self-defects demands perfect mirroring. Because this demand cannot be met, one can expect expressions of rage and despair in reaction to experienced failures of empathic understanding. In the treatment context, the regulation of these intense negative affects consists in the analyst's acknowledgement of his or her empathic failures, communication of empathic understanding of the patient's reactions, including a linking of the patient's reaction to his or her experience of the analyst's empathic failure. Over time, according to Kohut, the patient learns to avail himself or herself of what one might call good enough empathic understanding.

Kohut also discusses pleasure and positive affect. However, his conception of pleasure is quite different from Freud's. He writes that attempting to fulfill one's nuclear ambition in accord with one's basic talents, skills, and basic ideals "makes possible a creative-productive, fulfilling life" (Kohut, 1984, p. 5). As an expression of his differences with Freud, Kohut (1984) writes that

> the claim in question is that human beings may have the experience that they are leading – or, toward the end of their lives, that they have led – joyful, fulfilling lives despite the absence of pleasure and despite the presence of physical and psychological (including psychoneurotic) suffering.

(p, 211, fn. 1)

Kohut is referring here to experiences that, although not generally included under the rubric of affects, nevertheless strongly influence the affective tone of how one experiences one's life. These experiences include a sense of *meaning* and a sense that one is living and has lived one's life in accord with one's values and ideals and in a way that has realized one's talents and skills. It seems to me that Kohut's recognition of the importance of realizing one's talents and skills in accord with one's values and ideals expands one's understanding of affects to include subtle affective and quasi-affective factors that strongly influence one's sense of how one is living one's life. (I will have more to say about that topic in the next section.)

Some points of convergence

Despite significant theoretical differences, there is convergence among Freudian theory, Fairbairn's object relations theory, and self psychology on the central idea that the ultimate threat of affect dysregulation is breakdown of ego functioning. For Freud, the threat is the ego being overwhelmed with excessive excitation; for Fairbairn, the danger is the "ultimate psychopathological disaster" of the loss of the ego; and for Kohut, it is "disintegration anxiety" and self fragmentation (I include self fragmentation as a form of breakdown of ego functioning). Although understood in different ways, there is also convergence, despite other theoretical differences, on the central idea that the primary trigger of affect dysregulation that threatens the integrity of the ego is loss of connection to the object. For Freud, it is loss of the object and the object's love; for Fairbairn, it is loss of ego support; and for Kohut, it is traumatic lack of empathic mirroring from the selfobject.

Affect and affect regulation in relational psychoanalysis

As for relational psychoanalysis, virtually all the references to affect in Greenberg and Mitchell's (1983) *Object relations and psychoanalytic theory* have to do with how affect is dealt with in other psychoanalytic theories rather than with an account of affects specific to relational psychoanalysis. Further, there are no references to either "affect" or "emotion" in the index of Mitchell's (1988) *Relational concepts in psychoanalysis* or *Hope and dread in psychoanalysis* (Mitchell, 1993). However, despite the lack of explicit attention to affect, implicit in the two-person perspective of relational psychoanalysis is the centrality of the interpersonal nature of affect and affect regulation. In referring to the work of interpersonal psychoanalysts (i.e., Sullivan, Fromm, & Horney), Greenberg and Mitchell (1983) write that "the content of . . . passions and conflicts . . . is not understood to derive from drive pressure and regulation, but from shifting and competing configurations composed between self and others, real and imagined" (p. 80). Mitchell makes clear in his writings that his view of affect regulation is quite close to that of Fairbairn's. That is, affects are not only generated in the context of object relations but are also regulated in that context.

As is recognized in relational psychoanalysis, a central deficiency of both Freudian theory and ego psychology lies in their failure to adequately recognize object relations as a central source of affects as well as affect regulation. Indeed, as expressed in the preceding passage from Greenberg and Mitchell (1983), our most intense affects, both positive and negative, are experienced in our interactions with others. This is such an obvious reality that it tends to be taken for granted and overlooked or minimized in some theoretical accounts. As Sandler (1976) observes, even presumably drive related wishes and fantasies that are undoubtedly accompanied by strong affects, always entail oneself in a particular role interacting with another in a complementary role. For example, an exhibitionistic wish entails one exhibiting oneself to another who observes one's exhibitionistic behavior. It follows that the affect associated with the wish is embedded in an object relational context. To some extent, the primacy of object relations as an affect motivating factor is true not only of human behavior, but also of the behavior of other mammals. For example, in a recent study, when given a choice to receive a dose of heroin or methamphetamine or spend time with a peer, rats consistently chose social interaction (*Nature Neuroscience* – referred to in *Monitor on Psychology*, February 2019, p. 19). Any adequate psychoanalytic theory needs to integrate this obvious reality of psychological life.

The interpersonal nature of defense as affect regulation

Although defense becomes internalized as an intrapsychic ego function, its origins lie in early interpersonal interactions characterized by the "danger situations". In that sense, the need for defense is the consequence of the internalization of parental disapproval and punishment of certain wishes, desires, and fantasies. However, it is not only the origins of defense that are embedded in interpersonal interactions, but also its overall functioning. As I have argued elsewhere (Eagle, 2018a) defenses are also likely to be triggered by implicit assessments of how people important in one's current life, particularly people who are redolent of parental figures, would react to one's experience and expression of certain feeling, thoughts, wishes, desires, and fantasies. (See also Stern, 2003.) In that sense, defenses are not simply intrapsychic events, but also interpersonal interactional processes. More specifically, appraisals of danger that trigger defense are not limited to reactions to intrapsychic cues, but also include reactions to interpersonal cues, that is, cues emanating from the other with whom one is interacting. Thus, the appraisal function of the ego includes appraisals of social-interpersonal interactions. This conclusion accords with the argument that social-interpersonal understanding is a vital ego function.[9]

Subjective feelings of well-being and sense of meaning

Kohut (1977) makes the important point that some people manage to lead "worthwhile lives and are blessed with a sense of fulfillment and joy" despite some degree of pathology (pp. 281–282). This is very likely the case. As Kohut (1984) suggests, subtle affects and feelings, which cannot easily be equated with pleasure and unpleasure, are associated with having lived a meaningful life in accord with one's values and passionate interests (Eagle, 1981). I am reminded of the account in a biography of Wittgenstein – who was in many ways a tortured soul – that his dying words were that he had lived a fulfilling life. I have been impressed in my own clinical experience that despite showing a similar degree of psychopathology, the individual with abiding interests, values, and a sense of purpose generally has a better prognosis.

There is a good deal of research indicating that the experience of meaning in life, the components of which include having a purpose, goals, an overarching aim, and a set of values and coherent identity, is associated with positive affect and a sense of well-being (King, Hicks, Krull, & Del Gaiso, 2006; Steger, Oishi, & Kashdan, 2009), and serves as a protective factor against depression (Mascaro & Rosen, 2005). Because the relationship between meaning and the affect of well-being is correlational, it is difficult to assign a causal direction. King et al. (2006) attempted to address this issue by demonstrating that induction of a positive mood influenced responses to a meaning of life scale. However, because this study is wanting with regard to ecological validity, its findings should not be given much weight.

In a recent study, Jebb, Morrison, Tay, and Diener (2020) reported on four predictors (marriage, employment, prosociality, and life meaning) of subjective well-being using a representative cross-section of more than 1.7 million respondents ranging from 15 to 99 years of age from 166 nations. The subjective well-being construct includes three different measures: life satisfaction, positive affect, and negative affect. Marital status (married versus unmarried) had a statistically significant, but very small effect on well-being. Findings for prosociality were trivial. Being employed versus being unemployed showed a moderate relationship with well-being. The most robust relationship was between *life meaning* and all three measures of subjective well-being in every region of the world and across the life span.

These are very important findings. Virtually all psychoanalytic theories ignore the often critical role of experiencing one's life as having meaning and purpose in maintaining a sense of well-being – the exceptions include self psychology and existentially oriented theories (e.g., Frankl, 1959). I have argued (Eagle, 1981) that abiding interests and value systems serve object relational functions in the sense that they entail "cognitive and affective involvement with an object [and] modulated pleasure" (p. 528), and thereby contribute to intact ego functioning, particularly in extreme circumstances. I also point to evidence that individuals with a robust sense of values (either spiritual or moral-political) are most able to remain intact and cope with extreme situations (Cohen, 1953).

Much work in this area, including Frankl's, has been characterized as humanistic and existentialist, and for the most part, has been cited infrequently, if at all, in the psychoanalytic literature. However, the category under which this work has been placed should not deter one from recognizing the role of a sense of meaning in contributing to feelings of well-being and to maintaining and enhancing psychological functioning. Rather, the experience of a sense of meaning and purpose can be viewed as a superordinate organizing ego function; and the experience of a lack of meaning can be viewed as an impairment in this organizing function. Findings and formulations having to do with affectively tinged affective states such as feelings of well-being and a sense of meaning need to be integrated into a revised and expanded ego psychology.

Hartmann is certainly concerned with issues of values and meaning in his writing, as indicated by his reference to moral motivations independent of drives. He also writes that the healthy person must be *"able to must"* (original emphasis) (Hartmann, 1939, p. 94). As an example of this capacity, Hartmann cites Martin Luther's "Here I stand – I cannot do otherwise". In taking this stand, Luther is stating that he is willing to suffer and even to risk his life in the service of his values. In other words, Luther is "compelled", not in the way that drives compel behavior but in the agentic sense of an extraordinary commitment to his value system. Hartmann is telling us that this feeling of being compelled reflects not a weak ego driven by forces beyond its control, but a strong ego that is willing to sacrifice life itself in order to stand fast for the values that are at its core. Hartmann offers many astute observations and ideas that are cogent and important in themselves. However, it is not at all clear that these observations and ideas are integrated into ego psychology theory.

The motivational primacy of affects

The motivational primacy Freud accords to drive gratification leads him to cite approvingly Groddeck's (1923) assertion that we are "lived by our id" and that "what we call our ego behaves essentially passively in life, and that, as he expresses it, we are 'lived' by unknown and uncontrollable forces" (Freud, 1923, p. 23), namely, the id. It is undoubtedly the case that bodily forces of which we are unaware influence our thoughts, feelings, desires, goals, decisions, behaviors, and so on. In that sense, one may be justified in saying that we are powerfully *influenced* by our id. However, our everyday lived experience is normally one of being motivated by our affects, intentions, and goals. Hence, it is more accurate to say that we are lived by our ego, when ego is understood as the seat of subjective experiences, feelings, perceptions, and thoughts. The account of experience in terms of being buffeted about by "unknown and uncontrollable forces" is more a description of serious psychopathology than of everyday perceiving, thinking, feeling, acting, and carrying out our intentions. The claim that we are lived by our id is one version of the general argument that agency and free will are illusions. However, the philosophical issue is not the point here. From a psychoanalytic and – more generally, from a psychological – perspective, the issue is the degree to which one *experiences* oneself as an agent who desires, acts, makes decisions, and so on, versus as an entity being buffeted apart by uncontrollable forces or as an automaton robotically carrying out a pre-set program.

The idea that hidden forces, including instinctual drives, *directly* influence behavior, without reference to the mediating role of personal desires, feelings, and motives does away altogether with the role of subjective experience in behavior.[10] This perspective is appropriate to a programmed automaton rather than to a human being or, for that matter, to any living organism beyond a certain level of complexity. (See Davis & Panskepp, 2018.) Bodily states, including physiological conditions, generally do not influence behavior directly, the way a program directs the behavior of an automaton. Rather, they influence behavior by having a causal influence on what the individual *wants* to do, that is, his/her affects, motives, desires, preferences, and so on. These subjective states can be thought of as a sort of motivational funnel that reflect the influence of various factors of which we are unaware. It is important to distinguish between the defensible proposition that our subjective feelings and motives are influenced by factors and processes of which we are unaware and the questionable proposition that these factors and processes directly motivate our behavior.

Another way of making this point is to note that an adequate explanatory account of our subjective feelings, an understanding of their provenance and etiology (Black, 1967), requires reference to factors and processes that go beyond subjective feelings. However, that this is the case does not mean that these factors and processes constitute the "real" motives for our behavior. Indeed, they are not necessarily motives at all. Rather, they causally *influence* the motives and subjective feelings we have.

Complicating matters is the fact that in a psychoanalytic context, the "hidden" factors that are identified as influencing our subjective feelings are of the same order as the subjective feelings themselves, namely, desires and motives, save for the fact that they are unconscious. They are then viewed as the "real" motives and desires that underlie our behavior – similar to the latent meanings that underlie the manifest content of dreams. Thus, unconscious motives and desires are not understood simply as aspects of an *explanatory* account of subjective feelings, which have their own reality and importance, but rather as an account of what is *really going on*. A consequence of this is that the motivational role of subjective feelings is minimized or they are viewed as essentially dissimulating (See Ricoeur, 1970), that is, a manifest disguise for underlying latent meaning.

Although the preceding way of thinking may work with regard to unconscious motives, thought, wishes, and desires, it does not work for affects. This is so because, as Freud (1915a, 1923) noted, affects are, by definition, conscious. As Freud recognized, they are a quintessential instance of conscious subjective feelings. He writes: that although we have come to speak of 'unconscious feelings', that is "not entirely correct" nor "altogether justifiable" (Freud, 1923, p. 22). This is so because "it is surely of the essence of an emotion that we should be aware of it, i.e., that it should become known to consciousness" (Freud, 1915a, p. 177). (See Wakefield, 1991 for a clarifying discussion of this issue.) Whereas unconscious factors may influence conscious affects, it would make little sense to say that underlying conscious affects are unconscious affects. In short, whatever the influences on them, affects constitute a primary motivational factor in themselves.

The motivational primacy of affects is recognized by Sandler (1981), who maintains that the emphasis on gratification of instinctual drives needs to be replaced with the recognition that affects constitute the primary motivational factor in behavior. As Sandler (1981) puts it: "A psychoanalytic psychology of motivation related to the control of feeling states should, I believe, replace a psychology based on the idea of an instinctual drive discharge" (p. 188). (See also Lichtenberg, 1989.) Insofar as feeling states are the province of the ego, Sandler is, in effect, proposing an ego psychology perspective for a psychoanalytic theory of affects. A. Freud (1954) wrote that the ego defends itself not only against instinctual aims, but also against the affects associated with these aims. As another example, for Brenner (1982) it is the pleasurable and unpleasurable affective accompaniments of wishes for drive gratification that trigger either attempts at gratification or defenses against unpleasurable affects associated with drive gratification. As Fenichel (1945) puts it in his exposition of classical theory: "Thus, in the last analysis, any defense is a defense against *affects*. 'I do not want to feel any painful sensation' is the first and final motive of defense" (p. 161).

Despite the recognition that it is affects that motivate behavior – indeed, this is implicit in the pleasure principle – Freud and other ego psychologists consistently link affects to drive gratification. When one frees the pleasure principle from its metapsychological framework in which it is synonymous with drive discharge, it becomes clear that it is essentially a statement of the motivational role of affects in psychological functioning. More specifically, it states that, generally speaking, one tends to avoid the experience of negative affects and seek the experience of positive affects. Indeed, one may think of subjective feelings and their regulation as processes that "coordinate" the relationship between distal evolutionary survival functions and proximal motives (i.e., subjective feelings of positive and negative affects). That is, generally speaking, distal evolutionary functions are "served" by the proximal motive of seeking pleasurable experiences and avoiding unpleasurable experiences (probabilistically associated with adaptive outcomes).

Notes

1 Note Freud's reluctance to relinquish the idea of affects as primarily discharge phenomena. Also, although the idea that affects can be understood as perceptions of bodily states is plausible (See Damasio, 2003), it is not clear why "motor innervations" are what is perceived as affects; Freud (1916–1917) then confuses matters by writing that the experience of affects "could only be a very early impression of a very general nature, placed not in the prehistory of the individual but of the species. To make myself more intelligible – an affective state – would be constructed in the same way as an hysterical attack and like it, would be the precipitate of a reminiscence. An hysterical attack may thus be likened to a freshly constructed individual affect, and a normal affect to the expression of a general hysteria that has become a heritage" (p. 396). It is difficult to know what to make of this passage.
2 For an excellent survey and critical discussion of psychoanalytic theories of affect, see Stein (1991) (See also Spezzano, 1993).
3 To argue, however, as Fairbairn (1952) does, that libido is object seeking *rather than* pleasure seeking, or to deal with the desire for sexual pleasure mainly as a "disintegration product", as Kohut (1984) appears to do, leaves little room for recognition of the obvious fact that the desire for sexual pleasure – whatever other motives may be involved in sexual activity – is an important motive in that cannot be reduced to other motives.
4 Janov's (1970) primal scream therapy continues to view unexpressed affect as the main cause of psychopathology and abreaction of affect as a primary treatment approach.
5 The observation that some degree and form of affect is part of every experience is also made by Damasio (2003).
6 What threats to one's self-image and self-esteem share in common with anxiety, guilt, and shame is the experience of negative affect.
7 Despite the obvious logical implications of highlighting the role of the "danger situations", Freud (1926 [1925]) retains the idea that the danger inherent in the "danger situation" is "that of a non-satisfaction, of a *growing tension due to need* [original emphasis] against which [the infant is helpless" (p. 137). Although the non-satisfaction of the infant's and child's basic biological needs would, indeed, be dangerous – to the point of threatening survival – what Freud seems to overlook is that even under conditions in which the child's basic needs are met, parental disapproval and rejection remain "dangerous" and elicit anxiety. One way of putting it is to say that as noted in attachment and object relational theories, the need for mother's approval, love and

attachment is as much a biological need as the tension-linked needs emphasized by Freud.

8 It also resulted in his primary focus on anxiety and the relative de-emphasis of other negative affects, such as depressive feelings, shame, humiliation, and envy that did not easily lend themselves to be understood in terms of intensity of arousal and excitation.

9 I have not discussed other formulations of affect regulation, including the concept of holding associated with the work of Winnicott nor the concepts of containment and alpha function associated with the work of Bion (e.g., 1962). Despite the evocative power of these concepts, in order for them to be adequately understood, they need to be delineated and elaborated further – a project not directly related to the main purpose of this book; For important further discussions of affect and affect regulation in a psychoanalytic context, see Jurist (2005) and Silverman (1998). Also, for a presentation of the early roots of affect regulation in the caregiver's regulation of the infant's physiological regulation, see the work of Hofer (e.g., 2003, 2006).

10 The linking of drive and drive reduction directly to behavior, without reference to intervening states is a perspective that characterizes "black box" theories, such as Hullian drive-reduction theory, in which increases and decreases in drive-tension directly influence behavior, with no reference to intervening feelings, desires, and motives.

9

Research on affect regulation

There is a large research literature on affect regulation, far too large for any chapter to cover. Indeed, thick handbooks are periodically published to cover this literature (e.g., Gross, 2013). If one includes defense as an affect regulator, the literature is even more voluminous. Hence, my discussion will be limited to some representative examples of research on affect regulation in four areas:

(1) Defense as affect regulation: "Repressive style"
(2) Attachment patterns as affect regulation
(3) Interpersonal aspects of affect regulation: Caregiving and social support
(4) Reappraisal and reflective function as affect regulation

Defense as affect regulation

Perhaps more than any other psychoanalytic concept, defense has been assimilated into non-psychoanalytic theory and research. As we have seen in the previous chapter, defense is a central ego function, the primary function of which is avoidance of conscious experience of negative affect. In the *Project*, Freud (1950 [1895], pp. 323–324) assigns the ego the function of distribution of attention; and in his later work he conceptualizes repressive defenses in terms of deployment of attention away from anxiety-provoking stimuli, primarily inner stimuli. (See Rapaport, 1959 [1967].)

There is a good deal of evidence supporting the hypothesis that at least one way repressive defenses operate is through deployment of attention away from both inner mental contents as well as external stimuli that are likely to trigger negative affect. As an example of the latter, Luborsky,

Crits-Cristoph, and Alexander (1990) reported that, compared to non-repressors, repressors tended not to look at a part of a photograph that showed a woman's breast. They also showed greater restriction of attention as measured by scatter of eye fixations. As another example, in a study of concept formation, Szalai and Eagle (1992) found that compared to participants who employed non-repressive defenses, repressors made more errors and required more trials in acquiring an aggressive concept. This was not the case in regard to a neutral concept (numerosity). Most important in the present context, repressors tended to focus their attention on the non-aggressive aspects of the pictorial stimuli presented to them. A similar finding of directing eye movements away from threatening stimuli was reported by Broomfield and Turpin (2005).

Repressive style

The most extensive research on repression is concerned with "repressive style", which describes a group of individuals who despite reporting low anxiety on an anxiety scale, show behavioral and physiological indices of anxiety (e.g., GSR, heart rate, forehead muscle tension as measured by EMG) and score high on the Marlow-Crowne Scale of Social Desirability (Weinberger, Schwartz, & Davidson, 1979). Despite reporting low anxiety, repressors were rated as more anxious than low anxious individuals by independent judges during public delivery of a talk (Derakshan & Eysenck, 1997). Compared to their own self ratings, repressors are also rated significantly higher in anxiety by individuals who know them very well (Eysenck & Dearkshan, 1999). These findings indicate dissociation among the three components of the emotional system. That is, there is a disjunction between subjective feelings on the one hand, and autonomic and behavioral components of the emotional system on the other hand (Davidson, 1983).

Repressors tend to show the following characteristics: they tend to deny having unpleasant or anti-social thoughts; sixth-grade repressors tend to be described by their class mates as showing high restraint, high self-control, and being less prone to misconduct (Weinberger, 1990, p. 370); as young adults, are low in use of alcohol and drug use and are significantly more tolerant of pain (Weinberger, 1990); poorer immediate recall for self-relevant threatening stimuli (Alson et al., 2013; Fujiwara, Levine, & Anderson, 2008. See Eagle, 1998, 2000, 2018a); relatively low levels of reported daily unpleasant affects and low recall of unpleasant events (Cutler, Larsen, & Bunce, 1996); recall of fewer negative childhood memories (Davis & Schwartz, 1986; Myers & Brewin, 1994); later age of recalled childhood memories (Luborsky et al., 1990; Myers & Brewin, 1994); poorer retrieval of words related to anger and fear (Davis, 1990); greater conventionality (Bonanno & Singer, 1990); greater ability on a dichotic listening task to shut out information from the non-shadowed ear (Bonanno & Singer, 1990); ratings of negative words as less self-descriptive (Codd & Myers, 2009); in an elderly population, fewer number of falls reported despite contradictory objective information (Hauer et al., 2009); low levels of daily unpleasant affect as recorded in a diary as well as low-ered delayed recall of unpleasant affect related to an unpleasant experience (Cutler, Larsen, & Bunce, 1996). Tomarken and Davidson (1994) describe the repressor in the following way:

> a self-serving attributional style, . . . a hindsight bias, . . . impaired memory for negative self-relevant feedback . . . and for negatively toned autobiographical events . . . attentional avoidance of threatening cues . . . a relative inability to consciously perceive negative affective stimuli under specific conditions.
>
> (p. 240)

Employing a thought suppression paradigm, Geraerts, Merkelbach, Jelicic, and Smeets (2006) asked participants to suppress positive and anxious autobiographical thoughts. The results were that regardless of suppression instructions, compared to other groups (i.e., low anxious; high anxious; and defensive high anxious), repressors were reported as being better able to suppress their most anxious thoughts during the experiment. However, over a seven-day period, repressors showed the highest number of intrusive anxious thoughts. They conclude that "our results demonstrate that repressive coping might be adaptive in the short run, but counterproductive in the long run" (p. 1451).[1] Compared to sensitizers, repressors showed greater neural activation in certain brain regions in response to threatening as well as happy faces. "There was no brain region in which sensitizers showed increased activation to emotional expressions compared to repressors" (p. 989). The authors conclude that in accordance with vigilance-avoidance theory, "repression is associated with immediate hypersensitivity and subsequent avoidance".

Derakshan, Eysenck, and Myers (2007) propose that repressive coping involves both an initial rapid vigilant response, which triggers physiological responses to self-relevant threatening stimuli, as well as a subsequent avoidance stage characterized by avoidant cognitive operations, including deployment of attention, poorer memory due to shallow processing or barriers to retrieval. They refer to this as a vigilance-avoidance theory of repression. There is some evidence for at least the vigilance component of this formulation. In an fMRI study, Paul et al. (2012) briefly presented fearful, angry, happy, and neutral faces masked by supraliminal neutral faces. They found that repressive coping "is associated with hypersensitivity in the automatic processing of threatening as well as positive stimuli" (p. 986). The authors account for the hypersensitivity to the happy faces by suggesting that repressors may not perceive happy faces as unambiguously positive. I would suggest the perhaps more plausible hypothesis that vigilance to the possibility of threat requires repressors to be hypersensitive to emotional valence in order to distinguish threatening from non-threatening stimuli.

Although repressive coping is characterized by poorer recall of self-threatening material, there is evidence that the defended against threatening material is not altogether lost. Fujiwara et al. (2008) reported that although repressors showed poorer recall of negative self-relevant trait words, their implicit memory for this material, as indicated in a lexical decision task, was not significantly different than other groups. Green, Sedikides, and Gregg (2008) found that, although after experiencing ego deflation, participants showed poorer *recall* for self-threatening material, they did not show poorer *recognition* for such material. In other words, despite failure of recall, the material remained psychologically available in some form.

What are the implications of the preceding findings for one's understanding of the concept of repression as an affect regulator? In important respects, these results are congruent with the psychoanalytic account of repression as entailing two stages: one an initial rapid signal of danger (signal anxiety) followed by avoidance through deployment of attention away from threatening material. There are, however, a number of questions that arise: One, are the processes involved in both stages unconscious, as is claimed in classical psychoanalytic theory?[2] Two, what is the ecological validity of the preceding findings on repressive coping?

With regard to the first question, although not addressed explicitly, the suggestion in vigilance-avoidance theory appears to be that whereas the processes in stage one are automatic and unconscious, the processes in stage two entail top-down motivated cognitive strategies (deployment of attention; shallower processing; barriers to retrieval) that are preconscious habitual patterns that may be accessible to awareness when attention is focused on them. The finding that repressors do not show poorer implicit memory or poorer recognition of self-threatening material suggests that repressed material may not be as "deeply buried" and inaccessible to ordinary means of retrieval as is assumed in the psychoanalytic concept of repression. Repression may be more a matter of such preconscious processes as not articulating, not spelling out (Fingarette, 1963), not formulating or encoding further (Stern, 2003), attention deployment (Rapaport, 1959), and cognitive biases.[3] As for the question of ecological validity, despite the contrived experimental situations of the preceding studies, there would appear to be a great deal of ecological validity, as reflected in the fact that repressive style is predictive of significant real life behaviors and outcomes, such as health status, susceptibility to certain somatic illnesses, trajectory of recovery from myocardial infarction, protection against certain expressions of psychopathology, and autobiographical memory, degree of social conformity and conventionality, and self-image. Overall then, one can say that the repressive coping investigated in the previously discussed (and other) studies, at the very least, bears a strong family resemblance to the concept of repression as it is understood in the psychoanalytic context.

"Repressive style": Costs and benefits

Despite the tendency to view defenses as pathogenic in the psychoanalytic literature, from the very beginning of his writings, in which he introduced the "cornerstone" concept of repression, Freud (Breuer & Freud, 1893–1895) pointed to its benefits as well as its costs, its adaptive as well as its maladaptive aspects and consequences. Also, Hartmann (1939 [1964]) writes that "we first became familiar with the mechanisms of defense in their pathogenic aspect, and it is only now that we are gradually coming to recognize the part they play in normal development" (p. 12). With regard to its benefits, the core function of repression (as well as other defenses) is to protect the individual from consciously experiencing excessive psychic pain. In one of his early papers, Freud (1894) writes that

> an incompatible idea [i.e., a mental content about which one is conflicted] is rendered innocuous by 'its sum of excitation being transformed into something somatic' [emphasis in the original] . . . By this means the ego succeeds in freeing itself from its contradiction with which it is confronted.
>
> (p. 49)

In other words, there is an affect-regulating trade-off: conscious psychic pain is avoided, at the cost however, of somatic symptoms. As we will see in the following, there is a good deal of research demonstrating both the benefits as well as costs associated with the use of repressive defenses, including, as Freud reported, evidence of a trade-off between less conscious experience of negative affects and greater susceptibility to certain somatic illnesses.

Freud also makes it clear that although the use of repression may have pathogenic consequences, it is *the failure of repression and the consequent return of the repressed* that generate neurotic symptoms. Freud makes this point repeatedly, as early as 1896 in both letters to Fliess and in his paper, *Further remarks on the neuro-psychoses of defense*, and as late as 1937 in *Constructions in analysis*. Perhaps the clearest expression of this formulation is seen in the following passages:

> it is not the repression itself that produces substitutive formations and symptoms, but . . . these latter are indications of a *return of the repressed*. [emphasis in the original]
>
> (Freud, 1915a, p. 154)

> There is nothing new in our characterization of neurosis as the result of a repression that has failed.
>
> (Freud, 1924, p. 183)

Thus, it is not conflict *per se*, but the failure of the ego function of defense that precipitates neurotic symptoms.

Benefits of repressive style

An obvious benefit of repression noted in Freud's (1894) early writings is that it is associated with less conscious experience of distressing affects. This capacity to reduce the conscious experience of negative affects appears to play an adaptive role in coping with various illnesses, including life-threatening ones. Reported findings in this area include relatively high levels of repression and relatively low levels of anxiety in children with cancer (Phipps & Srivastava, 1997; Phipps & Steele, 2002; Phipps & Steele, 2002). Compared to other groups, lung cancer patients who were repressors reported significantly lower scores for pain quality, pain catastrophizing, and depression (Prasertsri, Holden, Keefe, & Wilkie, 2011). Ward, Leventhal, and Love (1988) reported fewer and less severe side effects of treatment in repressor cancer patients. Jurbergs, Long, Hudson, and Phipps (2007) found that children with cancer who were identified as repressors reported the highest level of health-related quality of life. Interestingly, the children's ratings were higher than their parents' ratings. Ginzburg, Solomon, and Bleich (2002) reported that repressive coping was associated with less self-reported acute stress disorder and PTSD in myocardial infarction patients both within a week of their cardiac episode as well as seven months later. Although repressors with erectile dysfunction did not differ from nonrepressors with regard to reports of sexual function, they described themselves as less depressed, as experiencing fewer physical complaints, and rated the quality of their relationship as higher (Wiltink, Subic-Wrana, Tuin, Weidner, & Beutel, 2010). Myers, Davies, Evans, and Stygall (2005) reported that among patients with diabetes, repressors showed significantly better metabolic control than nonrepressors. They also found that repressors showed better dental self-care behaviors (i.e., brushing their teeth more frequently) than non-repressors. They note that repressors appear to engage in more adaptive behaviors when they experience being in control.

The benefits of repressive style are also seen in a comparison of the memory patterns of repressors versus sensitizers in coping with threatening material. Unlike repressors, who seem to show a pattern of early vigilance and later cognitive avoidance, sensitizers tend to deal with threatening material with high vigilance and low cognitive avoidance. That is, they engage in "sensitive maintenance" (Peters, Hock, & Krohne,

2012, p. 201). According to Peters et al. (2012), the continued "focus [of] attention on the threat" (p. 201) by sensitizers is motivated by their "concern . . . to reduce uncertainty and the likelihood of being negatively surprised" (p. 201).

In support of their hypothesis, Peters et al. (2012) reported that in an *old* versus *new* recognition task involving threatening pictures and words, recognition following a 40-minute delay, sensitizers showed significantly less forgetting of threatening material than repressors as well as any other groups (i.e., low anxious and high anxious); this was not the case for non-threatening material. Under high cognitive load, there were no significant differences in forgetting between sensitizers and repressors. According to Peters et al. (2012), these findings are attributable to the fact that sensitizers were able to engage in their strategy of "sensitive maintenance" under low cognitive load because under that condition cognitive resources (i.e., repeated rehearsal and elaborative processes) were available; under high cognitive load, such resources were not similarly available. Peters et al. (2012) suggest that, although, in part, "sensitive maintenance" is adaptive in that it protects the sensitizer against negative surprise, it is maladaptive in its similarity to rumination, worry, and intrusive thoughts. And herein lie the comparative benefits of repressive coping when it is effective, namely, in the avoidance of such negative experiences as worry, rumination, and intrusive thoughts.

Costs of repressive style

In discussing "defense hysteria", Freud (1894) observed that although repression accorded the benefit of minimizing conscious experience of negative affect, it exacted the cost of producing somatic symptoms. There is a good deal of evidence of a positive association between repressive style and somatic dysfunction. Some representative findings include the following: Despite reporting low anxiety, repressors show higher heart rate and facial anxiety during a stressful task (Asendorf & Scherer, 1983). Compared to non-repressors, repressors had a fewer number of circulating T-helper cells, lower HDL, higher total HDL/cholesterol ratio, higher fasting insulin level, and an attenuated increase in number of natural killer cells during a stressful task (Stroop Conflict Test) (Berger et al., 2006). In a rather dramatic finding, Denollet et al. (2008) followed 731 patients with coronary heart disease for periods of five and ten years and, compared to other groups, found a two-fold risk for death from myocardial infarction for repressors. Frasure-Smith et al. (2002) reported a similar finding of reduced survival rate in a five-year follow up of male and female patients among repressors who had suffered a myocardial infarction. Based on a meta-analysis of 22 studies, Mund and Mitte (2012) reported "a significant association between repressive coping, cancer, and cardiovascular diseases, especially hypertension" (p. 640). However, particularly with regard to cancer, the association may be due to the use of repression as a way of *coping* with the diagnosis of cancer rather than as a risk factor for cancer. However, in a longitudinal study on women with metastatic breast cancer, Sephton, Sapolsky, Kraemer, and Spiegel (2000) reported poorer survival of repressors. Given the findings that a relatively flat diurnal cortical slope was found to be associated with early mortality and that repressors with metastatic breast cancer had a relatively diurnal cortical slope (Giess-Davis, Sephton, Abercrombie, Durian, & Spiegel, 2004), Myers (2010) suggests that there is a hormonal link to the poorer survival of the repressors. Oskis, Loveday, Hucklebridge, Thorn, and Clow (2009) reported lower cortical reactivity in a psychosocial stress situation among repressors, which they interpret as indicating blunting of the hypothalamic-pituitary-adrenal (HPA) response to stress. Cooke, Myers, and Derakshan (2003) found that despite reporting significantly higher adherence, asthmatic repressors had significantly worse lung function than other groups. However, Myers et al. (2005) reported opposite results regarding lung function among repressors. It is not easy to account for these discrepant findings.

There are other seemingly inconsistent findings with regard to repressive style. For example, congruent with findings on repressive style, Cousineau and Shedler (2006) reported that individuals who show a dissociation between explicit self-report and implicit measures of well-being and distress, which bears a family resemblance to repressive style, made a significantly greater number of visits to the university health center and had a significantly greater number of illnesses as verified by attending nurses. However, Coifman, Bonanno, Ray, and Gross (2007) reported that repressive coping in both a bereaved and non-bereaved sample was associated with fewer somatic complaints, and in the bereaved sample, with fewer symptoms of psychopathology. They conclude that contrary to the (presumed] Freudian claim that defensive avoidance of negative affect is maladaptive, . . . "repressive coping may serve as a protective buffer from

emotional disorders, particularly in the context of adverse life events"
(p. 755).[4]

Given what we know about self-report of repressors, the ecological
validity of Coifman et al.'s (2007) use of a self-report check list to measure somatic complaints is likely to be compromised. Contrastingly, health
status in the Cousineau and Shedler (2006) study was objectively assessed
through independent records maintained by the campus health center.
Also, because many of the health measures used in the preceding studies, such as blood pressure, immune response, cardiac episodes, etc. do
not depend on the individual's self report, they are likely to be more valid
indicators of health status than self-report.

Processes underlying susceptibility to somatic costs of repressive style

As we have seen, there is a good deal of evidence that repressive style (and
to some extent, avoidant attachment) are associated with greater susceptibility to certain somatic illnesses. What are the mechanisms or processes
that may account for this association? Freud's (1915a) early answer to
this question is found in his statement that repression requires "a constant
expenditure of force" (p. 151), which suggests that maintaining repression entails excessive wear and tear on various physiological systems.
Indeed, the very definition of repressive style includes the component
of a high level of autonomic arousal despite self-report of low anxiety.
Esterling, Antoni, Kumar, and Schneiderman (1990) hypothesize "that to
inhibit ongoing behavior, thoughts, and feelings, physiological work must
be performed" and that "the work of inhibition may serve as a low level
chronic stressor which has the potential of long-term cumulative damage"
(p. 407). (See Diamond, Hicks, & Otter-Henderson, 2006, for physiological correlates of repressive coping.)

A number of specific processes have been identified that may play a role
in the relationship between repressive style and susceptibility to somatic
costs. They include a fewer number of circulating T-helper cells, lower
HDL, higher HDL/cholesterol ratio, higher fasting insulin level, and
an attenuated increase in number of natural killer cells during a stressful task among repressors (Berger et al., 2006); less vagal influence on
cardiac functioning among avoidantly attached adults (Maunder et al.,
2006); under-utilization of health resources among avoidantly attached

(Ciechanowski, Walker, Katon, & Russo, 2002); higher vagal withdrawal and higher adrenocortical and sympathetic adrenomedullary activity in the Strange Situation among avoidant infants (Hill-Soderland et al., 2008); less ability among avoidantly attached women to avail themselves of social support, which serves to modulate physiological activity (Feeney & Kirkpatrick, 1996; Simpson, Rholes, & Nelligan, 1992).

There are other possible factors that may mediate the relationship between repressive style and somatic costs. Lieberman et al. (2007) reported that labeling a negative affect reduces amygdala activity. Insofar as repression prevents the conscious experience and, therefore, the labeling of affect, repressors are likely to be subjected to heightened amygdala and associated physiological activity. Brody et al. (2000) found that among firefighters under age 45, those who were high on social desirability on the Marlow-Crowne (Crowne & Marlowe, 1964), a component of repressive style, had a higher morning salivary cortisol level. It is possible that the firefighters over age 45 did not show this effect due to cortisol blunting, a consequence of sustained stress.

Are defenses necessarily unconscious?

The assumption made both in psychoanalytic theory and non-psychoanalytic theories is that in order for defenses to be effective in regulating negative affect, they must operate unconsciously (e.g., Baumeister & Newman, 1994; Cramer, 2001; Sherman, Bunyan, Creswell, & Jaremka, 2009). The reasoning behind this assumption is that if one consciously knows that one is engaging in a defense, it will not work – the jig will be up. This is similar to the reasoning that if one consciously knows that one is being self-deceptive, one can no longer continue to deceive oneself. On this view, there is a categorical or qualitative distinction between conscious suppression and unconscious repression. However, there may be no sharp dichotomy between the two. In a recent review, Rosenzweig (2016) found little evidence supporting the assumption that defenses need to be unconscious in order to be effective; and, indeed, found much evidence that being aware of employing defensive strategies does not necessarily affect their effectiveness. As Rosenzweig (2016) notes, one can be aware of one's defensive bias and yet fail to be aware of how that influences one's assessments, including self-assessments. Rosenzweig also notes that in reconstruing an emotional event in order to reduce its negative emotional impact, one's awareness of one's re-appraisal does not necessarily inter-fere with its effect.

Consider also Freud's (Breuer & Freud, 1893–1895) own description of the case of Lucy R. that presumably instantiates the use of repression. Freud interprets to Lucy R: "I believe that you are really in love with your employer, the Director, though perhaps without being aware of it yourself" (p. 117). Lucy R. responds: "Yes, I think that's true". Freud replies: "But if you knew you loved your employer, why didn't you tell me?" Lucy R. answers: "I didn't know – or rather I didn't want to know. I wanted to drive it out of my head and not think of it again; and I believe latterly I have succeeded". And she adds the comment: "People would laugh at me if they had any idea of it" (p. 117). Lucy R.s description of how she dealt with unwelcome thoughts and feelings hardly serves as an example of the unconscious status of repression. Rather, as we will see in Chap-ter 11, this clinical vignette is quite congruent with Gray's (1994) assump-tion that because defensive activities take place just below the surface of consciousness, they can be accessed by bringing the patient's attention to them.

Attachment patterns as affect regulation strategies

An important normative function of the attachment system is to regulate negative affect (e.g., fear) by seeking proximity to the attachment figure, as well as by accessing internal representations of the attachment figure. In optimal development, which is characterized by a high level of maternal responsiveness, the child develops a pattern of secure attachment, that is, confident expectation in the availability of the attachment figure, particu-larly when the child is distressed and needs comforting (e.g., in encounter-ing the unexpected during exploratory behavior). Thus, one would expect that secure attachment would be associated with adequate affect regulation. And, indeed, there is evidence supporting this hypothesis (e.g., Borelli, Compare, Snavely, & Decio, 2015). It should be noted that, according to Masterson (1981), mother's availability only when child is distressed and not when the child is engaged in exploration is an etiological factor in the development of borderline personality disorder.

Disruptions in the normative pattern are reflected in the development of insecure attachment patterns, which are often understood as forms of defense against negative affect triggered by inadequate parental responses to the child's attempts to have his or her attachment needs met.[5] For example, in describing avoidant attachment as entailing "defensive exclusion" (p. 45), Bowlby (1980) clearly viewed it as a defensive strategy. Lyons-Ruth (2003), too, writes that insecure attachment patterns can be understood as "defensive adaptation to caregivers' refusals or failures to provide the needed soothing responses to infant fear or distress" (p. 108). As she also observes, quite remarkably, "the early appearance and systematic use of defensive strategies" (p. 108) is already present in infants by one year of age. However, as we will see, whereas avoidant attachment can be readily understood as a defensive strategy, it is far less evident in regard to anxious attachment.

There is evidence that avoidant attachment is associated with the use of repressive defenses. For example, Vetere and Myers (2002) reported that compared to nonrepressors, repressors show higher levels of avoidant attachment. Edelstein and Gillath (2007) found that avoidant attachment participants are better able to divert attention away from attachment-related words in a Stroop task, which they refer to as an "avoidant defensive strategy" (p. 179). There is also evidence that similar to repressive style, avoidantly attached individuals tend to show dissociation between subjective report and physiological responses during discussion of attachment-related issues. There is evidence that this is also true in childhood. Sroufe and Waters (1977) reported that avoidant children in the Strange Situation show increased heart rate rather than the usual decelerated heart rate during exploratory play, which suggests that the play activity is defensive and anxiety-laden rather than comfortable and enjoyable.

Costs and benefits of attachment patterns

Avoidant attachment: Benefits

Although constituting an insecure pattern, on a number of measures avoidantly attached individuals' responses are more similar to the responses of securely attached individuals than to anxiously attached individuals. For example, compared to the anxiously attached, both securely and avoidantly attached individuals report a higher level of well-being. Also in contrast to anxiously attached and similar to securely attached, avoidantly attached report a higher level of use of reappraisal in dealing with stressful situations (Karreman & Vingerhoets, 2012). Compared to anxiously attached, avoidantly attached showed less body image dysfunction and less anxiety around social evaluation (Cash, Thériault, & Milkewicz Annis, 2004).

Adam, Sheldon-Keller, and West (1996) reported that in a group of outpatient and inpatient male adolescent patients, whereas an anxious/ preoccupied attachment pattern combined with Unresolved on the Adult Attachment Interview (AAI) was a risk factor for suicidal ideation and behavior, a dismissive/avoidant attachment pattern combined with absence of Unresolved serves as a protective factor for suicidal ideation and behavior. With no history of suicidal ideation and behavior, the predominant attachment pattern was avoidant/dismissive, without the presence of Unresolved features on the AAI. Adam et al. (1996) also reported that there were no significant differences between patients with and without suicidal ideation and behavior in the *incidence* of attachment related trauma (e.g., parental loss, family disruption, and physical and sexual abuse). The critical factor was whether or not the patients were *unresolved* with regard to trauma. That is, presence or absence of suicidal ideation and behavior appears to be a function not simply of the *occurrence* of trauma, but how the individual *copes with the trauma*, more specifically, how adaptively or maladaptively the individual is able to regulate the negative affect generated by the trauma as well as of the effects of the consequences of the trauma on his or her functioning. This suggests that the avoidantly attached patients were not subjected to less trauma, but rather dealt with the trauma more effectively, at least with regard to suicidal ideation and behavior.

Avoidant attachment: Costs

As is the case for repressive style, avoidantly attached individuals also tend not only to show greater dissociation between self-report of subjective distress and physiological activation (e.g., Sroufe & Waters, 1977; Zelenko et al., 2005), but also appear to pay a physiological cost. For example, Ciechanowski, Katon, Russo, and Walker (2001) reported that whereas 34% of securely attached diabetic individuals had mean HbA1c levels equal to or greater than 8%, this was the case for 62% of avoidantly attached diabetic patients. Maunder et al. (2006) reported evidence of less vagal influence on cardiac function among avoidantly attached individuals during a stressful task, a phenomenon linked to greater mortality risk.

There is evidence of reduced activation in brain areas linked to dopamin-
ergic and reward in response to positive social signals among avoidantly
attached individuals (Vrtička, Andersson, Grandjean, Sander, & Vuilleumier, 2008). Avoidant infants showed significantly higher vagal withdrawal
and salivary alpha amylase (which is a biomarker of hypothalamic-
pituitary-adrenal (HPA) axis and sympathetic adrenomedullary (SAM)
activity in the Strange Situation (Hill-Soderland et al., 2008). Ciechanowski, Walker, Katon, and Russo (2002) report that whereas health resources
are over-utilized by anxiously attached, they are under-utilized by avoidantly attached (as well as fearful attached). Combined with the fact that
avoidant attachment is associated with somatization, under-utilization of
health resources may be a significant health risk factor. Mikulincer, Florian, and Weller (1993) found that during the Gulf War, whereas anxiously
attached Israeli students reported more distress, avoidantly attached students showed more somatization, distancing, and hostility.

There is a good deal of evidence that there are "clear reductions in physiological activity to [a] stressful task in the presence of a close, supportive
(but non-evaluative friend, relative to the stranger and alone conditions"
(Feeney & Kirkpatrick, 1996, p. 256). Simpson et al. (1992) reported that,
compared to securely attached women who sought support from their partner in an anxiety-provoking situation, avoidantly attached women were
less likely to seek support. Herein lies another cost of avoidant attachment, namely, lessened ability to turn to the attachment figure for support.
This relative inability may be a factor in the somatic costs associated with
avoidant attachment.

Anxious attachment: Benefits

There few benefits associated with anxious attachment. There is evidence
that the anxious/ambivalent attachment classification in the Strange Situation is associated with a history of caregiver unpredictability with regard
to the child's attachment needs. Hence, the development of a pattern of
persistent demands on the part of the child would appear to be an adaptive
strategy for having his or her attachment needs met insofar as this pattern
increases the probability that at least on some occasions, the attachment
figure will come through. One can understand this pattern of persistent
demands as a sort of intermittent reinforcement. A similar pattern is present in adult anxious and enmeshed/preoccupied attachment, which is

characterized by a persistent fear of abandonment as well as persistent needs for reassurance.

Perhaps one benefit associated with anxious attachment is that, unlike the avoidantly attached pattern, the anxiously attached individual continues to strive and to be motivated to seek an intimate affective connection. This may make the anxiously attached individual more ready to seek therapeutic change. However, the degree to which this can be viewed as a benefit rather than still another cost is likely to be a function of the intensity and rigidity of the anxiously attached individual's ambivalence, how susceptible it is to change, and how realistic and open to change his or her attachment needs and demands are.

Anxious attachment: Costs

I think it is accurate to say that there are mainly costs and few benefits associated with anxious and enmeshed/preoccupied attachment. The downside of this pattern include the likelihood that the child's persistent demands will anger the caregiver and thus decrease the probability that the child's attachment needs will be met. Also, as seen in the child's behavior pattern in the Strange Situation, s/he may develop a strong ambivalence toward the attachment figure, with the consequence that s/he cannot be easily soothed or comforted even when the attachment figure is available (hence, the classification "anxious/ambivalent" that is often used).

Indeed, insofar as anxious or enmeshed/preoccupied attachment is characterized by a relatively high level of conscious anxiety, chronic conscious fear of abandonment, and intrusion of disturbing thoughts into cognitions, it would seem more accurate to view this pattern as reflecting not only a particular strategy, but also a relative *failure of defense* rather than an effective defensive means of affect regulation. Viewing it this way is consistent with the relatively closer association between anxious attachment and serious psychopathology, such as borderline personality disorder (Barone, 2003; Fonagy et al., 1996; Patrick, Hobson, Castle, Howard, & Maughan, 1994) as well as greater suicidal ideation in an adolescent clinical sample (Adam et al., 1996; Lessard & Moretti, 1998), and Livesley (1991) that anxious attachment is associated with the "emotional dysregulation" component of borderline personality disorder. After reviewing 13 studies, Agrawal, Gunderson, Holmes, and Lyons-Ruth (2004) conclude that despite different measures, "the types of attachment found to be most

characteristic of BPD subjects are *unresolved, preoccupied, and fearful*"
(p. 94).

Similar to the situation in childhood, these behaviors may serve to alien-
ate one's attachment figure. Also similar to the anxious/ambivalent child,
the anxiously attached adult is likely to harbor ambivalent feelings (i.e.,
neediness combined with anger), which result in the individual being less
able to adequately avail himself or herself of what the attachment figure
is able to provide. If one adds to this picture the tendency to select a partner based on the template of the parental figure (See Heffernan & Fraley,
2013), one sees a recipe of chronically unstable affect regulation associated with anxious and enmeshed/preoccupied attachment.

There is a good deal of additional evidence that indeed, anxious attachment is associated with a variety of costs. For example, as noted, anxious
attachment is associated with a variety of negative experiences, including depression, social anxiety, and lower life satisfaction (Eng, Heimberg,
Hart, Schneier, & Liebowitz, 2002) as well as relatively low levels of
well-being (Karreman & Vingerhoets, 2012). Brumariu and Kerns (2008)
reported that children classified as anxious/ambivalent in grades 3 and
5 were higher in social anxiety in grade 5. Quirin, Pruessner, and Kuhl
(2008) found that attachment anxiety was positively correlated with cortisol level in response to stress and negatively correlated with cortisol on
awakening, which is a measure of adrenocortical activity. As discussed
previously, Adam et al. (1996) reported that among 133 adolescents con-
secutively admitted for inpatient and outpatient psychiatric treatment, a
history of suicidal ideation and behavior was significantly associated with
enmeshed/preoccupied attachment classification combined with Unresolved in regard to trauma on the AAI.[6]

Interpersonal aspects of affect regulation: Caregiving and social support

Affect regulation begins at birth and is a vital function of the caregiving system. As the work of Hofer and his colleagues demonstrates, the
caregiver's ministrations serve as a complex and multidimensional regulator of the young infant's vital physiological processes. Hofer and his
colleagues (e.g., Hofer, 2006; Polan & Hofer, 2008) have shown that the
rat dam provides a complex set of regulations for her pups. For example,
mother's warmth regulates the pup's activity level; mother's milk regulates

heart rate; mother's tactile stimulation regulates infant's production of the growth hormone ornithine decarboxylase (see Schanberg & Kuhn, 1980), and so on.[7]

Mother's various inputs not only regulate the pups' physiological processes, but also undoubtedly generate associated feelings of well-being; and loss of these inputs through maternal separation not only result in dysregulation of physiological processes that are normally regulated by mother's inputs, but also generate associated feelings of distress – as evidenced, for example, by distress vocalizations and other behavioral signs. In short, early in the life of the rat pup, mother's ministrations serve to regulate physiological processes and accompanying affects.

Processes similar to those described previously are undoubtedly also present in primate, including human, infant-mother interaction. What Winnicott (1956) refers to as "primary maternal preoccupation" during a period following the birth of a child seems designed to facilitate the physiological regulation of infant processes similar to the regulation described by Hofer and his colleagues in rat pups. Indeed, Hofer (2003, 2006) proposes that for a wide range of mammalian species, including humans, the mother's role in physiological regulation, as well as feelings of well-being and distress accompanying such regulation, constitutes the early basis – a sort of pre-attachment attachment – for the later psychological attachment bond between infant and caregiver. Interestingly, Hofer (2006) states that early pre-attachment attachment can be usefully described in terms of an addiction model in the sense that, similar to the action of an opiate, mothers' inputs facilitate homeostasis and well-being, while absence of these inputs result in dysregulation and distress.

Franchi (2011) writes that "the homeostatic system's search for equilibrium maps to Freud's 'principle of constancy'" (p. 235). This is a charitable view of the constancy principle.[8] It is more accurate to view it as a misguided interpretation of homeostasis. If homeostasis is to map to the constancy principle, the latter would require at least the following interrelated revisions: one, insofar as a low as well as a high level of excitation can constitute a deviation from homeostasis, the constancy principle cannot be formulated in terms of discharge of excitation; two, homeostasis cannot be understood simply in quantitative terms; and, three, homeostatic states are accompanied by subjective feelings. As Damasio (2018) writes: "feelings are the mental expressions of homeostasis" (p. 6) and tell the mind what is going on in the body. These feelings have both a negative (subjective distress) valence, which can be a marker for emotional dysregulation, and a positive (subjective well-being) valence, a marker for homeostatic regulation. In the course of development, mother's external regulation becomes increasingly internalized in the form of self-regulation. Another way to put it is to say that self-regulation becomes increasingly autonomous of mother's inputs. For example, as the child gets older, psychical growth becomes increasingly autonomous of mother's tactile stimulation. Or, as another example, it is likely that heart rate and activity level become increasingly independent of direct maternal input of, respectively, milk and warmth.

This shift toward self-regulation takes place not only in regard to physiological regulations, but also in regard to regulation of affects: the child gradually develops internal regulating structures and processes that are less and less immediately tied to the caregiver's physical presence and inputs. The use of the transitional object (e.g., the "blanky" or teddy bear) for comforting and soothing during separation from the caregiver is a good example of an affect regulating process that is transitional in the sense that it lies somewhere between total reliance on the actual caregiver and reliance on an internal structure. Although, like the caregiver, the transitional object is an external object, the capacity of the transitional object to provide comforting and soothing is made possible by the symbolic meaning given to it by the child himself or herself. That is, in an important sense and as Winnicott (1953) suggests, the transitional object is the child's own creation. Further, unlike the relationship with mother, the transitional object is portable and always available.

In the course of development, symbolic representations of mother can also serve affect regulation. For example, as discussed earlier, there is evidence that the presence of a photograph of mother is associated with less anxiety and a greater range of exploratory behavior in toddlers (Passman & Longeway, 1982). Thus, as is the case in using the "blanky" or teddy bear during separation, the child can make use of a concrete object as a symbolic stand-in for mother for comforting purposes (Winnicott, 1953).

As a further step in the course of development, the use of a concrete object for comforting is replaced, or at least supplemented, by internal representations and structures in the form of an internal working model (IWM). In optimal development, the IWM is characterized by a confident expectation in the availability of the attachment figure (Bowlby, 1980) as a safe haven in times of distress and as a secure base for exploration. That is, an internal representation of the attachment figure, as well as the expectation that she will be available if needed reduces the need for the actual physical presence of the attachment figure.[9] From this perspective, one can understand secure attachment as an effective means of affect regulation.

Coregulation of affect

As we have discussed previously, in the course of development, the child transitions from coregulation to varying degrees of self-regulation (Fonagy, Gergely, Jurist, & Target, 2002). However, as a good deal of recent research has shown, interpersonal regulation continues into adulthood and exists alongside self-regulation. With regard to the latter, we continue to be regulated by our partners in close relationships, as evidenced by the physiological and affective dysregulating consequences of disruption in long-term intimate relationships (e.g., Hofer, 1984). Indeed, Hofer (2006) has suggested that there is a continuum between the effects on the infant of maternal separation and parallel dysregulating effects of loss of one's attachment figure in adult relationships.

Much of the work on coregulation is presented in the context of Social Baseline Theory (SBT). According to Hughes, Crowell, Uyeji, and Coan (2012), "Social baseline theory proposes that healthy human functioning is dependent upon adequate social support and that, at baseline, biological systems are adapted to operate interdependently rather than independently" (p. 21). Nowhere is this more apparent than in the early infant-caregiver interactions described by Hofer and his colleagues as well as by attachment theory. As Coan (2010) notes, we "are hardwired to assume close proximity as a baseline affect regulation strategy" (p. 213). According to Beckes and Coan (2011): "Social proximity and interaction attenuate cardiovascular arousal, facilitate the development of nonanxious temperament, inhibit the release of stress hormones, reduce threat-related neural activation, and generally promote health and longevity" (p. 81).

Feeney and Kirkpatrick (1996) carried out a complex study in which they investigated the effects of absence or presence of romantic partner on physiological responses (i.e., heart rate [HR], systolic blood pressure [SBP], and diastolic blood pressure [DBP]) to stress, as a function of individual differences in attachment pattern (which were defined categorically rather than dimensionally). Among their findings, I want to note the following: Whereas HR of secure and avoidant participants was similar in partner-present condition, it was significantly higher for avoidant participants in the partner-absent condition. A similar pattern approaching significance was found for DBP.

There was also an interesting and meaningful order effect. When partner was present in Phase 1 of the experiment, there were no significant differences in HR between the avoidant and secure women, which continued in Phase 2, that is, even when partner returned to the laboratory. However, when partner was absent in Phase 1, compared to secure women, the HR of avoidant women was significantly higher, and remained higher throughout the experiment. The authors account for this finding in the following way: "it seems that we may have inadvertently manipulated separation anxiety and created an adult version of Ainsworth, Blehar, Waters, and Wall (1978) Strange Situation procedure in our experimental design" (p. 268). They note that in partner-absent condition, the partner is escorted out of the room similar to mother leaving the room in the Strange Situation, and the participant is left alone in a stressful situation, similar to the child being left alone when mother leaves the room. Hence, according to the authors, separation anxiety is aroused in both the anxious and avoidantly attached participants and continues throughout the experiment. The authors account for the latter by suggesting that once the situation is appraised as stressful, it remains so throughout the experiment. For the secure and non-anxious participants, the partner-absent condition is less stressful and triggers less separation anxiety because, in contrast to the anxious and avoidant participants, the physical presence of the partner is not required in order for him to be experienced as a secure base, that is, to serve as an affect regulating figure.

There is a good deal of evidence that generally, there are "clear reductions in physiological activity to [a] stressful task in the presence of a close, supportive (but non-evaluative) friend, relative to the stranger and alone conditions" (Feeney & Kirkpatrick, 1996, p. 256). Ferrer and Helm (2013) reported covariation in heart rate and respiration among couples performing laboratory tasks. Helm, Sbarra, and Ferrer (2014) found covariation of respiratory sinus arrhythmia (RSA) during laboratory tasks among romantic couples. Further, the covariation was higher for couples with higher relationship satisfaction.

Other evidence for social baseline theory include the finding that loss of a close relationship through divorce or death of a spouse is associated with a range of negative health outcomes. As Sbarra and Hazan (2008) observe, "The loss of coregulation can portend a state of biobehavioral dysregulation, ranging from diffuse psychophysiological arousal and disorganization to a full-blown (and highly organized) stress response" (p. 141).

SBT shares much with attachment theory and would concur with Bowlby's (1980, p. 442) statement that

> Intimate attachments to other human beings are the hub around which a person's life revolves, not only when he is an infant or a toddler or a schoolchild but throughout his adolescence and his years of maturity as well, and on into old age.
>
> (Bowlby, 1980, p. 442)

Both theories posit an inborn tendency to seek proximity to others; and both theories focus on the interpersonal regulation of affect. However, Hughes et al. (2012) write that "most attachment researchers propose a developmental trajectory of increased behavioral control such that, by adulthood, nearly all self-regulation is independent" (p. 21). They contrast this position with their proposal that early adequate caretaking is related to later adaptive outcomes "via healthy expectations of continued co-regulation in adulthood" (p. 21). I think Hughes et al. (2012) are mistaken in their in their characterization of "most attachment researchers" (and theorists) Indeed, their proposal that early adequate caretaking is related to later outcomes "via healthy expectations of continued co-regulation" can serve as a definition of secure attachment.

It also seems to me that Hughes et al. (2012) draw too sharp a dichotomy between what they refer to as "independent" self-regulation and co-regulation. For after all, although strongly influenced by early and ongoing interpersonal experiences, healthy expectations and trust that one's partner will be available – or the lack of such expectations and trust – represent internalization of interpersonal experiences and are characteristics of the individual, although such representations can be enhanced or attenuated by ongoing interpersonal interactions and experiences.

Indeed, there is a good deal of evidence that it is *perceived* rather than actually received social support that plays a primary role in regulation of distress and is more predictive of well-being and psychological and physical health (e.g., Priel & Shamai, 1995; Vaux, 1992). Further, there is only a modest association between the two. Based on the review of 23 studies, Haber, Cohen, Lucas, and Baltes (2007) found an average correlation of r=.35 between received and perceived social support, which accounts for about 12% of the variance.

The situation is even more complex. Thus, if mistrust in one's partner availability is very rigid and deeply engrained, one may be relatively unresponsive to partner's behaviors, rendering co-regulation exceedingly difficult.[10] Thus, individual characteristics and "independent" forms of self-regulation have an important impact on the possibility of co-regulation. Also, there are situations in life in which one's partner may not be available and in which, therefore, one may need to rely on "independent" self-regulation. There is likely a dynamic and circular causal relationship between "independent" and co-regulation. Thus, individual differences in expectation and perception of social support, along with the emitted cues associated with these expectations and perceptions, are likely to influence the availability of interpersonal social support. And conversely, differences in the history of the availability of social support are likely to influence "independent" self-regulation.

The preceding comments notwithstanding, the important contribution that the concept of co-regulation makes is that all regulation, both independent and co-regulation, takes place in an interpersonal and social milieu and are influenced and maintained by others in that milieu, particularly in long-term relationships. Striking support for this proposition is provided by evidence of the dysregulating physiological and psychological effects – including serious illness and death – of the loss of one's partner in long-term relationships. Such evidence suggests that "silent" co-regulation (Coan, 2008) has been going on during the duration of the relationship.

Reappraisal as an affect regulating strategy

There is a large body of research on affect regulating strategies other than repressive style and attachment pattern – far too large a body to cover. In the ensuing pages, I briefly summarize some findings on reappraisal, not only because it a much researched affect regulating strategy, but also because it is a clear expression of the role of an ego function in regulating negative affect. The essence of reappraisal, as the term suggests, is re-assessing and often altering one's perspective in relation to an emotion eliciting situation and thereby regulating one's affective reactions.

The results on the use of reappraisal in coping with negative affect are quite complex and vary as a function of a number of factors, including, for example, cultural factors and overall level of anxiety. However, there are a number of findings that, compared to other strategies (e.g., behavioral suppression), the use of reappraisal is more effective in modulating negative affect. There is also evidence that whereas reappraisal is associated with increased activation of regions in the prefrontal cortex (PFC) and decreased activation in the amygdale (Kober et al., 2010), suppression of behavioral expression of emotion is associated with increased activation of both the amygdala and PFC regions of the brain (Goldin, McRae, Ramel, & Gross, 2008; Ochsner & Gross, 2005). There is also evidence that the habitual use of reappraisal to deal with negative emotions is associated with a range of positive outcomes, including higher positive affect and well-being, lower levels of negative affect, better interpersonal functioning, and fewer symptoms of anxiety (e.g., Memedovic, Grisham, Denson, & Moulds, 2010; Wang, Shi, & Li, 2009).

There is a family resemblance between reappraisal and reflective function (RF). In some circumstances, in order for one to reappraise one's emotional reaction to a situation, one needs to reflect on one's initial, often automatic construal that is associated with negative affect, and alter one's initial construal and perspective. Both reappraisal and RF entail the recruitment of top-down processes (i.e., higher level ego functions) as a means of influencing one's more immediate and reflexive negative affective reactions. I discuss reflective function further in Chapter 11.

Notes

1 Given that Geraerts et al. are reporting group results, it is very likely that not all repressors report intrusive thoughts during the seven-day period. That is, there may be individual differences among repressors; and what we might be seeing is differences in effectiveness of ability to repress and suppress negative material.

2 Erdelyi (2006) has correctly argued that in his early writings, Freud viewed repression as conscious. However, in his later writings, he referred to repression as an unconscious process. Indeed, Freud's introduction of the structural theory was based on his belief that certain ego processes such as defense, are unconscious.

3 Indeed, as we will see in Chapter 11, the ego psychological approach to treatment of Gray (1994) suggests that defenses are carried out just below the surface of consciousness and can be accessed by bring the patient's attention to them.

4 Coifman et al.'s (2007) rendering of Freud as stating that the defensive avoidance of negative affect is maladaptive is over-simplified to the point of constituting somewhat of a distortion.

5 There is also evidence that genetic factors play a significant role in the development of attachment patterns.

6 The Unresolved aspect of the AAI merits further discussion. It refers to the AAI scorer's judgment that, as reflected in the AAI narrative, the narrator is Unresolved and often cognitively disorganized in regard to attachment-related trauma. It is viewed as the adult analogue of the infant's disorganized/disoriented pattern in the Strange Situation (Main & Hesse, 1990) and is a pattern that is most strongly associated with psychopathology (e.g., Moss & Rousseau, 1998). In adults, preoccupied attachment is more frequently associated with Unresolved than avoidant/dismissive, which at least partly accounts for the former's greater association with psychopathology. This is not surprising insofar as the very term "preoccupied" suggests a continuing and an ongoing struggle with trauma in the life of the individual.

7 There is evidence that massage therapy for preterm newborns leads to greater weight gain compared with standard treatment (Field, 2001). (See also Field, Diego, & Hernandez, 2010, for a review of the effects of touch on various behaviors).

8 By viewing the pleasure principle in terms of excitation reduction and aligning it too closely to the principle of constancy, Freud (1920) finds himself in the somewhat odd position of concluding that the pleasure principle is ultimately equivalent to the death instinct – insofar as both ultimately entail a zero level of excitation, which, of course, is death. The simple step of understanding the pleasure principle as equivalent to homeostasis does away with this metapsychological *reductio ad absurdum*.

9 Something akin to this occurs in the context of psychotherapy. Geller and Farber (1993) report that following termination of therapy, former patients tend to invoke representations of the therapist when distressing affects are experienced, and that this tendency is associated with greater number of therapeutic sessions and positive therapeutic outcome. Such evocations of the therapist suggest the former patients' capacity for "libidinal object constancy", that is, the ability to retain a sense of connection with the other despite physical absence.

10 Such rigid expectations and perceptions can be understood as a relative failure of interpersonal reality-testing. (See Chapter 5).

10

Ego psychology and psychopathology

Introduction

The birth of psychoanalysis is marked by the attribution of psychopathology, specifically, hysterical neurosis, to both the presence of inner conflict and the particular means of dealing with it, namely, repression. Freud (1894) writes that hysterical patients had "enjoyed good mental health up to the moment at which *an occurrence of incompatibility took place in their ideational life*" (original emphasis) (p. 47) – that is, until confronted with inner conflict. The mere presence of inner conflict, however, is not sufficient to account for the outbreak of hysterical symptoms. What needs to be also present is the use of repression of the incompatible idea as a means of dealing with the intense "distressing affect" (p. 47) that is aroused by the incompatible idea. As Freud (1893) writes, "before hysteria can be acquired for the first time, one essential condition must be fulfilled: an idea must be *intentionally repressed from consciousness* [Freud's emphasis] and excluded from associative modification" (p. 116).

The preceding descriptions are formulated early in Freud's writings, prior to the introduction of drive theory. Nevertheless, they capture a central feature of the psychoanalytic conception of neurosis as essentially a state of affairs characterized by an inadequate means of coping with a psychological situation in which what the individual desires and feelings are experienced as ego-alien and inimical to his or her sense of who s/he is, as if they were forces outside oneself.[1] With the introduction of drive theory and the formulation of psychosexual stages of development, including the stage of the Oedipus complex, Freud (1905) also included *fixation* (p. 123) at different stages and, above all, failure to resolve oedipal conflicts as core aspects of his etiological theory of neurosis. An assumption often made by Freudian theorists was that the earlier the psychosexual stage at which fixation occurred the more severe the psychopathology. For example, Freud (1911) links schizophrenia to regression to early fixation at the stage of auto-erotism (p. 77), whereas neurosis was associated with fixations at later psychosexual stages, in particular, with the stage of the Oedipus complex.

An ego psychology perspective on the nature of psychopathology

Although not much noted, the identification of impaired ego functioning as a critical factor in psychopathology was already present in Freud's early writings. He writes that "intentional forgetting" of "things of this kind" (Freud, 1984, p. 48) does not always lead to pathology. Many people, Freud continues, who employ "intentional forgetting . . . under the same psychical influences remain healthy. I only know that this kind of 'forgetting' did not succeed with the patients I analyzed, but led to various pathological reactions" (p. 48). For these people, Freud suggests, it is the bringing about a state, which is "bound up with a splitting of consciousness. . . [which] is to be regarded as the manifestation of a pathological disposition, although such a disposition is not necessarily identical with individual or hereditary 'degeneracy'" (p. 48). The pathological disposition expressed in the form of splitting of consciousness can be understood as a problem with *integrative capacity*.

One would expect that an ego psychology perspective on the nature of psychopathology would be relatively straightforward in highlighting failures and impairments in ego functioning in one form or another. And yet and perhaps surprisingly, Hartmann has relatively little to say of a direct and specific nature regarding psychopathology. Rather, he provides an indirect conception of the nature of psychopathology in the context of formulating a psychoanalytic concept of the nature of mental health. Unsurprisingly, according to Hartmann (1939 [1958]), from an ego psychology perspective, "what we designate as health or illness is intimately bound up with the individual's adaptation to reality" (p. 318) and constitutes "an 'evolutionary' concept of health" (p. 320).

Thus, for Hartmann, the essence of psychopathology consists in a relative failure to adapt to the demands of reality. However, Hartmann includes more subtle considerations, including the fact that "the processes of adaptation are always appropriate only to a limited range

of environmental conditions" (p. 319) (which reflects Hartmann's recognition of the fact that from an evolutionary point of view, adaptation is always to a particular environmental niche); that ego flexibility
contributes to adaptation, whereas ego rigidity interferes with it, and
that the synthetic and regulatory functions of the ego are essential to
adaptation.

Hartmann also makes it clear that in his view psychopathology is less
a matter of the content of one's conflicts and unacceptable wishes and
impulses *per se* and more a matter of how adaptively or maladaptively one
copes with these conflicts, wishes, and impulses. Or to put it another way,
from an ego psychology perspective, common to all psychopathology is
some kind and degree of impairment in ego functioning. Hartmann also
recognizes that what is seen "from without" (p. 320) as adequate versus
disturbed adaptation, when viewed "from within" (p. 320) presents itself
as "mental harmony" versus subjective distress.

Ironically, a more apparent ego psychological perspective on psychopathology is present in the formulations of theorists who are critical of ego
psychology. For example, despite his sharp critique of ego psychology,
Guntrip (1969) identifies "ego weakness" due to early environmental failure as at the core of psychopathology. This is also the case with regard to
Balint's (1968) concept of the "basic fault", and the centrality of splits in
the ego also due to environmental failure in Fairbairn's (1952) formulation
of psychopathology.

Fairbairn (1952) writes that splits in the ego due to maternal rejection
and deprivation are at the core of all psychopathology and that the usu-
ally identified neuroses (e.g., phobias, obsessional phenomena) are not
distinctive forms of psychopathology, but primarily "transitional" means
of coping with the underlying core schizoid "psychopathological disaster"
of ego disintegration and living in an inner world devoid of connections to
objects. What is striking here is Fairbairn's claim that ego impairments are
viewed as at the core of psychopathology.

An ego psychology on the nature of psychopathology is especially
apparent in self psychology theory, in particular, in Kohut's (1984) central idea that self-defects due to traumatic lack of empathic mirroring. As
Kohut (1977) puts it, "self psychology considers the structural and functional deficiencies of the patient's self as the primary disorder and focuses
its attention on them, whereas traditional analysis saw the content of conflicts as the primary disorder and focused on it" (p. 29). A shift from a

focus on content to functional deficiencies is a quintessential ego psychology perspective.

Surely, structural and functional deficiencies of self as well as deficiency in calming structure (i.e., in affect regulation) should be viewed as ego impairments. Thus, his rejection of ego psychology notwithstanding, Kohut (along with the other theorists noted previously) essentially identifies defects in ego functioning as constituting the core of psychopathology. In effect, Kohut, as well as the other theorists, essentially understands and conceptualizes psychopathology in terms of relative impairment of ego functions, including affect regulation, regulation of self-esteem, a coherent sense of identity, self-defects, and a sense of competence. Indeed, in contrast to conflict theory, virtually any version of psychopathology in terms of defects and deficits is essentially a theory of failure in ego functioning.

It has been argued that the form of psychopathology at the core of which are developmental defects and arrests needs to be distinguished from the less severe neuroses, which are characterized by inner conflict, with however, relative intactness of ego functioning (e.g., Eissler, 1953; Gray, 1994; Stolorow & Lachmann, 1980; Sugarman, 2007). For example, Eissler (1953) distinguishes between the psychoneuroses and more severe forms of psychopathology that require the use of "parameters" in treatment. As another example, in his earlier writings, Kohut (1971, 1977) distinguished between "structural conflicts" and self-defects and suggested that each configuration of psychopathology required different kinds of therapeutic interventions.[2]

Throughout his 1984 book, Kohut's description of the characteristics, etiology, and treatment of self disorders are described in terms that are entirely compatible with an ego psychology perspective. Indeed, at times, Kohut's (1984) formulations read as if he were writing from an ego psychology structural perspective translated into a self psychology language. For example, he makes repeated references to "structural deficiency" (as opposed to "the content of conflicts") (Kohut, 1984, p. 29) and "faulty structures" (Kohut, 1984, p. 86) as constituting the core of psychopathology. And he writes that "psychoanalysis cures by the laying down of psychological structure" (p. 98) and via "the accretion of psychic structure" (Kohut, 1984, p. 108). Kohut (1984) himself acknowledges the affinities between ego psychology and self psychology. For example, he writes that "with reference to the issue of cure, the continuity between ego psychology and self psychology is most palpable" (Kohut, 1984, p. 95). He also writes that

> a sensitive and intelligent analyst will up to a point will be able to employ the concepts of the tripartite model of the psyche in a reasonably satisfactory way, by emphasizing *synthetic function of the ego* [my emphasis] and construing it as roughly parallel to the conceptualization of self psychology.
>
> (Kohut, 1984, p. 65)

Despite these acknowledgements, Kohut (1984) faults ego psychology on a number of grounds: one, that it does not provide "an experience-near understanding . . . of the inner life of the analysand" (p. 95); and two, as cited earlier, ego psychology

> does not allow us to formulate in a satisfactory way those crucial attributes of the psyche as it moves toward health: the capacity for self-soothing, the sense of continuity of the self in time, and the crucial role of the self object in providing the opportunity for the acquisition of these attributes.
>
> (p. 65)

Kohut (1984) also writes that the theoretical formulations of ego psychology are "based on the erroneous theoretical conception of the adult personality as an autonomous organization – an organization that had relinquished ties to selfobjects, that had overcome the need for a nurturing self object milieu" (p. 218, fn. 2). Kohut (1984) concludes that "an unforced theoretical conceptualization of these psychic states and processes is, to my mind, not possible with the armamentarium of even the most sophisticated ego psychology; it requires the complementary framework of the psychology of the self" (p. 65). It is not at all clear on what basis Kohut argues that ego psychology does not allow us to formulate in a satisfactory way both the capacity for self-soothing, which can be readily understood as an expression of the quintessential ego function of affect regulation, as well as the continuity of the self in time, which Kohut himself appears to recognize as a synthetic function of the ego.

Kohut's distinction between structural conflicts and self-defects, present in his 1971 and 1977 books, gave way in his 1984 book to the claim that at the core of *all* psychopathology are particular forms and perhaps degree of self-deficits and defects. Consider, for example, Kohut's (1984) clinical vignette in which he describes a woman whose mother

> was apparently not able to provide a calming selfobject milieu for the little girl which . . . would have been transmuted into self-soothing structures capable of preventing the spread of anxiety. It is this structural deficit, the deficiency in calming structures . . . that necessitates the presence of a companion . . . who temporarily replaces the missing structure and its functions.
>
> (p. 30)

Kohut is essentially describing here an impairment in the development of affect regulation due to early object relational failure.[3]

Has the nature of psychopathology changed?

One of the questions that arises is to what degree the emphasis on ego defects is a product of the "widening scope" of patients seen in psychoanalytic treatment and to what degree the psychopathology presented by patients is viewed from a different clinical-theoretical lens. As far back as 1950, Gitelson was already commenting that the psychopathology of patients being seen in psychoanalytic treatment could no longer be viewed in terms of repression as defense against dealing with inner conflict. And it was in 1952 that Knight's classic paper on borderline conditions appeared. There seems to be widespread sense in the psychoanalytic community that the modal patient seen in psychodynamic or psychoanalytic treatment presents a configuration quite different from the presumed typical neurotic patient. For example, we see more and more references to trauma and dissociation than to inner conflict, more diagnoses of personality disorders, and more references to deficits and defects. In this regard, we see clinical formulations that are more redolent of Janet (e.g., 1907) than of classical Freudian theory. Considerations of adequacy of ego functioning become more central to understanding psychopathology and to guiding the nature of treatment.

As noted in Chapter 2, a good deal of early research was carried out on the relationship between adequacy of ego functions and psychopathology. For example, Bellak et al. (1973) assessed 12 ego functions in schizophrenic, neurotic, and normal samples. Barron (1953) investigated the relationship between ego strength and response to psychotherapy. Roessler et al. (1963) studied the relationship between ego strength and physiological responsivity. And Watson and Clark (1984) argued that ego strength scales essentially measure the degree of "negative affectivity" experienced "at all times and across situations, even in the absence of overt stress" and the tendency "to dwell on the negative side of themselves and the world" (p. 465). Much of this kind of research is now carried out outside the psychoanalytic context.

Conceptions of psychopathology: Evidence of a general factor

In the last few years, a number of papers have appeared which propose that, instead of viewing psychopathology in terms of distinct diagnostic categories, a good deal of evidence provides support for the idea that underlying a wide range of psychopathology is a general dimension – labelled the "p factor" – a concept analogous to the g factor in assessments of intelligence (Caspi & Moffitt, 2018). The evidence for a "p factor" includes high comorbidity among different psychiatric disorders, relatively high correlations among the domain of internalizing, externalizing, and psychotic experiences, which hover around 0.5 (Wright et al., 2013), longitudinal data indicating that a mental disorder at one time is as likely to predict a different disorder as a similar disorder at a later time (Costello, Mustillo, Alaattin, Keeler, & Angold, 2003; Lahey et al., 2015; Moffitt et al., 2007), and the fact that although parental psychopathology is strongly associated with offspring psychiatric disorders, there is very little specificity between the two.

What makes the proposal of a "p factor" especially relevant in the present context is its parallel to what, from a psychoanalytic perspective, could be viewed as a general dimension of ego impairment that is expressed in different domains (i.e., different ego functions) and that underlie different specific expressions of psychopathology. Indeed, Caspi and Moffitt (2018) note that the idea of a general factor of psychopathology was anticipated by Ernest Jones in his 1946 valedictory address to the British Psychoanalytical Society. Jones writes that

> there may well be an innate factor akin to the General Intelligence G, the nature of which is still remains to elucidate, but which may be of

cardinal importance in the final endeavour to master the deepest infantile anxieties, to tolerate painful ego-dystonic impulses or affects and
so to attain the balanced mentality that is our ideal.

(p. 10)

Jones further describes the G factor as "the capacity to endure the non-
gratification of a wish, . . . to retain the stimulating affects of an afferent
impulse without immediate discharging them in an efferent direction"
(p. 10).[4] Jones is obviously referring here to a central ego function of
inhibitory capacity and more specifically, to a capacity for delay of
gratification.

As Caspi and Moffitt (2018) observe, Jones is suggesting that "poor
impulse control over affects", which they note, "subsumes a variety of
deficits in response inhibition" is a core factor in a wide range of psychopathology. And as they also note, "support for this hypothesis comes from
longitudinal research that shows that poor childhood self-control, reflecting emotional dysregulation and executive deficits, cuts across all disorder
liabilities and is a salient early developmental predictor of the p factor"
(p. 835). In short, from a psychoanalytic perspective, one can translate
Caspi and Moffitt's formulations as stating that deficits in ego functioning,
in particular, emotional dysregulation and deficits in response inhibition,
are at the core of a wide range of psychopathology.[5]

Support for the hypothesis of a general factor underlying psychopathology comes from a large-scale genetic study using National Regis-
ter data from more than three million siblings, which suggests the role
of a general genetic factor in a wide range of psychopathology, including depression, anxiety, ADHD, alcoholism, drug abuse, violent crime,
schizophrenia, and schizoaffective disorder (Petterson, Larsson, &
Lichtenstein, 2016).

Negative emotionality has also been identified as a general factor underlying a wide range of psychopathology. Based on data from a sample of
1,569 twin pairs, Tackett et al. (2013) found evidence for the prediction
that "variance in a general psychopathology bifactor overlaps substan-
tially – at both phenotypic and genetic levels – with the dispositional trait
of negative emotionality" (p. 1142). Donahue, Goranson, McClure, and
Van Male (2014) found that emotional dysregulation mediated the relationship between negative affect and impulsive behaviour in the form of
physical aggression.

These findings are in accord with the psychoanalytic formulation on the relationship between impairment in ego function and a disposition to experience negative affect. For example, insofar as the primary function of ego defense is to prevent the experience of negative affect (e.g., anxiety), it would follow that an impairment in that function would increase the likelihood of the chronic experience of negative affect. From the perspective of ego psychology, the chronic tendency to experience negative affect as well as the relative incapacity to tolerate it without engaging in maladaptive behavior are core aspects of impairments in ego functioning implicated in a wide range of psychopathology.

There is also neural evidence in support of the hypothesis of a general psychopathology factor. Gray matter volume is reduced and activation is altered in the brain regions of the dorsal cingulate cortex and the left and right anterior insula across a wide range of psychopathology. (Goodkind et al., 2015; McTeague et al., 2017). According to Caspi and Moffitt (2018), "this collection of regions is thought to be part of a network that is involved in attention and cognition control", which suggests "that cognitive control impairments are shared by all the disorders analyzed" (p. 838). This is equivalent to stating, in the language of psychoanalytic theory, that impairment in particular ego functions is shared by a wide range of psychopathology.

Perhaps the clearest example of the experience of chronic and intense negative affect is seen in individuals receiving the diagnosis of borderline personality disorder. Such individuals are characterized by a high level of rejection sensitivity and susceptibility to feeling denigrated and disrespected, and respond to such experiences with intense negative affect, including rage and despair (Lieb, Zanarini, Schmahl, Linehan, & Bohus, 2004; Gunderson, 2008). Additional characteristics of borderline personality disorder include the attribution of rejection and other negative intentions to the other, which is experienced as unquestioned and absolute. That is, they feel there is no other way to experience the other's behavior and, therefore, are convinced that their intense negative reactions are fully justified. In short, they seem relatively incapable of regulating their intense negative affects through reflecting on their automatic construal of negative intentions to the other and the intense negative affects these construals generate. (Further, the chronic attributions of negative intentions to the other can be seen as a failure in interpersonal reality-testing.) (See Chapters 5 and 6.)

The combination of easily triggered feelings of rejection and hurt and a relative failure to reflect on these feelings leads to a vicious circle in which the experience of rejection triggers intense negative affect; the arousal of intense negative affect interferes with the individual's capacity to reflect (Bateman & Fonagy, 2008); failure to reflect keeps the negative affect going; and the intensity and chronicity of negative affect tends to trigger rejection by the other and contributes to instability of relationships; this, then, triggers the entire cycle of rejection, intense negative affect, relative failure to reflect, instability of relationships, and so on. With regard to this last point, Clifton, Pilkonis, and McCarty (2007) have reported that patients diagnosed with borderline personality disorder (BPD) are six times more likely to break up with current partners than non-BPD patients. A vicious cycle ensues in which the break-up of relationships triggers feelings of rejection etc., which, in turn, arouses negative affect, and so on.

Kohut (1984) describes a similar dynamic for narcissistic personality disorders in which the patient often reacts with rage and despair to any response from the other that is experienced as less than being perfectly understood. As is the case with the borderline patient, in this state of high affective arousal, reflecting on one's affective reactions, which could serve to regulate negative affect, is extremely difficult, with the consequence that the negative affect remains unregulated and that threats to the relationship are intensified. Despite these obvious descriptions of failure in ego functioning, Kohut does not explicitly refer to impairments in ego functions of affect regulation and reflective function. Indeed, as cited earlier he argues that "the armamentarium of even the most sophisticated ego psychology" (p. 65) cannot account for these clinical phenomena. However, the capacities to which Kohut refers (affect regulation; continuity of identity) are quintessential ego functions.

Mentalization, reflective function, and psychopathology

Let me describe a clinical vignette that is illustrative of the affect regulating role of reflective function. My patient came to a session expressing feelings of rage and rejection in response to her father's suggestion that, rather than pick her up and interrupt his dinner, she take a taxi. Her father's suggestion constituted unshakeable evidence to my patient of his total rejection of her. These sorts of interactions with her father (as well as others) would repeatedly trigger the following pattern: An emotional conviction that her father does not care for her, followed by rage and resolve never to see him again ("I'll show him. I don't need him"). The resolve cannot be sustained, which is then followed by self-contempt ("I'm weak and needy"), depression, and suicidal thoughts.

There were, of course, early roots to my patient's repetitive pattern. However, failing the ability to reflect on her automatic construal of her father's behavior and her consequent affective reactions, this pattern repeatedly recurred. After much work, on the occasion that I am describing, my patient was able to wonder aloud whether she was "overreacting", which suggested an opening to the possibility of another way to construe the interaction with her father. She was also able to actually have some empathic sense of her father not wanting to interrupt his meal when a short taxi ride was an easily available alternative. What was striking about all this was the affect regulating effect her reflective thoughts had on the pattern of her hitherto explosive affect and on the subsequent depressive pattern. My patient referred to this new budding ability as her "new tool" and was able to employ it in other situations.

Gabbard and Horowitz (2009) describe a clinical vignette in which a borderline patient reacts with rage in response to a sales clerk refusing to accept her credit card. She creates an embarrassing scene in which she feels humiliated. In describing the event, she seems to feel certain that the sales clerk intended to humiliate her. One way of conceptualizing both the case presented by Gabbard and Horowitz as well as my patient is in terms of failure of an effortful control process (reflective function) to modulate the reactive system (implicit and automatic affective reactivity). In short, in the context of ego psychology, one can say that insofar as affect regulation is an ego function, the failure to modulate the reactive system, through reflective function, for example, constitutes the relative failure of an ego function. It would follow that a central therapeutic aim would be strengthening of the ego function of reflective capacity. (This issue will be discussed further in Chapter 11.)

In addition to clinical evidence, there is also much research evidence indicating that the effortful control system is able to modulate negative affect. For example, Torre and Lieberman (2018) reported that as relatively a simple a response as verbal labeling of an negative affect stimulus is accompanied by decreased amygdala activity along with increased activation of the prefrontal cortex. And we have seen, Posner and Rothbart

(2007) report not only that seeing sad faces activates the amygdala in the perceiver, but also that as sadness increases, the anterior cingulate also gets activated, which suggest an effort at modulating the sadness. Other representative examples of the affect regulating function of the effortful control system includes the finding that highly anxious individuals show deficits in cortical dampening of amygdala (Young et al., 2017); and Viviani, Dommes, Bosch, Stingl, and Beschoner's (2008) finding of a significant positive relationship between increased emotional reactivity and diminished attentional control in individuals diagnosed with borderline personality disorder (BPD).

Borderline personality disorder, affect regulation, and empathy

Miano, Dziobek, and Roepke (2017) reported that whereas there were no significant differences between BPD patients and healthy controls (HC) in measures of "empathic accuracy" in neutral and personal threat situations, compared to HC, female BPD patients showed greater empathic accuracy in the context of relationship threat. Understanding these findings requires some background information. Reduced empathic accuracy, described as "motivated inaccuracy", refers to "a defense mechanism that protects couples from the potentially negative effect of correctly understanding any relationship-threatening thoughts or feelings of their partners" (Miano, Dziobek, & Roepke, 2017, p. 356). Thus, the reasoning goes, in the context of relationship threat, less rather than more empathic accuracy (i.e., greater empathic inaccuracy) is adaptive insofar as it protects the relationship and the individual against experiencing rejection and fear of abandonment.

Empathic accuracy in Miano et al. (2017) and other studies is operationally defined as the degree of match between the participants' ratings of the affective valence of the person with whom he or she has interacted and the other's self rating of his or her own affective valence. It is questionable, however, whether such accuracy should be viewed as empathy defined as putting oneself in the shoes of the other or taking the perspective of the other or even feeling what the other person feels. None of these elements of what we ordinarily mean by empathy is necessarily present in the sheer accurate identification of another's affects. Indeed, given their rejection sensitivity (Foxhall, Hamilton-Giachritis, & Button, 2019) and fear of abandonment, the BPD patients' accuracy in identifying affects related to these fears, particularly in situations of relationship threats, is more meaningfully understood not as an expression of empathy, but rather of *vigilance* in relation to feared dangers and lowered threshold for detecting these dangers (See Rosenbach & Renneberg, 2014; Staebler, Helbing, Rosenbach, & Renneberg, 2011 for studies on rejection sensitivity and borderline conditions).

Consider the likely experience of a BPD individual of a relationship threatening interaction. S/he is likely to be exquisitely sensitive to cues of rejection, which, along with other cues, are not infrequently present in fraught interactions. Hence, the individual will find these cues in the other's behavior, that is, will be likely to be accurate in his or her identification of the other's affect. But this accuracy is not the product of empathy. The borderline patient is neither experiencing what the other is experiencing – the BPD individual is feeling *rejected*, whereas the other is feeling *rejecting* – nor cognitively understanding what the other is experiencing, that is, is not taking the perspective of the other, which if s/he could, might include an understanding of why the other feels rejecting. Rather, the BPD individual's only concern, which overwhelms other concerns, is the danger of rejection and abandonment. Thus it would be more accurate to refer to *perceptual* accuracy rather than empathic accuracy.[6] Miano et al. (2017) write that their results "partially" contradict the assumption made by Fonagy and Bateman (2008) and others "that drawing mind inferences is disturbed in emotional arousal in BPD . . . More specifically, our data do not support the assumption of the mentalization model that mentalization is decreased in BPD individuals in emotional arousing relationship contexts" (p. 363).

Miano et al.'s (2017) conclusions are misguided on a number of grounds. Their data neither support nor refute the claims that mentalization is decreased in BPD individuals in situations of emotional arousal or that "drawing mind inferences" is or is not disturbed by emotional arousal in BPD. This is so for a number of reasons. One, and perhaps the most basic reason, is that the Miano et al. (2017) study did not investigate either mentalization or drawing mind inferences, the latter requiring reflective capacity. Rather, they investigated the ability of BPD patients to accurately identify another's affective valence. Miano et al. (2017) themselves recognize the limitations of their findings. As they acknowledge:

The present study has implied that BPD patients have at least comparable accuracy for detecting changes in their partners' affect in

threatening and nonthreatening situations. However, they are unaware of the consequences on drawn inferences and assumptions. BPD
patients might be able to recognize how their partner feels, but be
unable to infer the correct cause. Simultaneous assessment of accuracy in understanding thoughts and feelings and the interpretation of
these inferences (e.g., to test the mentalization hypothesis) is required.

(p. 363)

To make my points more forcefully regarding the distinction between
accurate perceptions of emotional valence and understanding or empathy,
consider the common clinical observation that paranoid individuals not
only frequently attribute hostility to others, but are frequently able to accurately detect it in others. However, such accuracy, for one thing, is highly
selective, the product of an exquisite hypersensitivity to detection of negative cues. Most important in the present context, one would hardly refer to
the paranoid individual's accuracy as *empathic* accuracy insofar as there is
no evidence of an ability to take the role or perspective of the other or to
understand the other. There is also certainly no evidence that the paranoid
individual is capable of reflecting on his or her own mental states or on the
hostility that he or she detects in the other.

With regard to the last point, quite often the hostility accurately detected
in the other by the paranoid individual at least in part, is elicited by his or
her own behavioral cues of which he may not be aware. This is important
because it highlights the fact that one can *accurately perceive* another's
affective valence and yet not understand the basis for it. It also highlights
the frequent inextricable link between understanding the mental states of
others and understanding one's own mental states and behaviors.

In assessing the adaptive or maladaptive significance of behavior, one
needs to take account of the context in which it occurs. A given behavior
such as immediate gratification or, say, aggressive behavior, may not only
have different etiologies, but also different psychological significance in
different contexts. I am reminded of my experiences at my first clinical
job, at a community center, Henry Street Settlement, in New York City
with a group of inner city children, who at the tender age of 8, were sus-
pended from the public school system due to their aggressive impulsive
behavior. Although they all exhibited such behavior, the nature and significance of the aggressive behavior differed among the children. For
example, in the case of one child (M.R.), the aggressive behavior was

triggered by vigilance in relation to perceived threat, was self-protective, and seemed adapted to the dangerous environment in which he grew up and lived. Contrastingly, in the case of another child (H.E.), the aggressive behavior was unpredictable, random, explosive, carried out in a dissociated state, and not directed toward a specific threat. I recall how helpful it was in my attempt to understand these children to recognize the differences in the nature of their ego organization and ego functioning. Whereas M.R. showed relatively intact ego functioning in many areas, H.E. showed pervasive difficulties in ego functioning.

In both cases the aggressive behavior was maladaptive, as evidenced by the fact that it led to expulsion from the public school system. However, the specific nature and the psychological significance of the maladaptive behavior was very different for the two children. As noted, for M.R., the aggressive behavior, which developed in adaptation to his early environment was relatively organized and purposive and was present in a child whose overall ego functioning was relatively intact. Contrastingly, H.E.'s aggressive behavior, which was dissociated and non-purposive, occurred in a child with pervasive impairments in ego functioning. Hence, the psychological significance of the aggressive behavior was quite different in the two children (as were the prognosis and the needed interventions).

These differences would call for different kinds of interventions. For M.R., the context for the maladaptive behavior suggests that the problem is as much the persistence of early schemas that had been adaptive to the early environment as it is failure of inhibitory control. If this is so, the challenge here would be to find ways to alter these early schemas or modulate their influence. H.E. presents quite different challenges having to do with how to deal with pervasive impairments in ego functioning.

Reflective function as a protective factor in risk for psychopathology

There is evidence that the caregiver's maternal responsiveness plays an important role in the infant's security of attachment. However, maternal responsiveness is made possible and facilitated by mother's capacity to understand her infant's and her own mental states, which in turn, is facilitated by mother's capacity for reflective functioning (RF). There is a good deal of evidence that mother's high level of reflective is associated with secure attachment in her infant. This is especially so in the case of high risk mothers (i.e., conditions of poverty, single, parenting, overcrowding). For example, Fonagy et al. (1995) found that a high level of RF in high risk mothers served as a protective factor in regard to their infant's attachment status. They reported that 16 out of 17 high risk and high RF mothers had securely attached infants, whereas only 1 of 17 high risk and low RF mothers had a securely attached infant. Even in a sample of substance-dependent mothers, level of RF is positively correlated with maternal sensitivity, which is likely to serve as a protective factor for the children of these mothers (Alvarez-Monjaras, McMahon, & Suchman, 2019). In a study on reflective function in the offspring rather than mother, Borelli et al. (2015) reported that high RF served as a protective factor in adolescents with regard to the effects of early parental neglect on security of attachment.

Notes

1 Despite the traditional historical account that the birth of psychoanalysis is marked by Freud's rejection of Janet's claim that constitutional weakness is a core factor in the development of hysteria, the strong family resemblance between Freud's invocation of a "pathological disposition" (p. 48) and Janet's emphasis on constitutional weakness in their accounts of hysteria is striking. Freud is obviously aware of this resemblance. He writes that "such a disposition is not necessarily identical with hereditary degeneracy" (Freud, 1894, p. 48). Although the "pathological disposition" Freud refers to may not be equivalent to Janet's appeal to constitutional weakness, the differences between them is one of degree rather than constituting the sharp dichotomy depicted in most historical accounts.

2 According to Mitchell (1995), different forms of psychopathology had to be found in order to justify departures from the classic approach to psychoanalytic treatment.

3 From the joint perspective of attachment theory and ego psychology, one can say that because mother was not available as a comforting safe haven and secure base, the little girl was not able to adequately develop the ego competencies necessary for affect regulation and exploration.

4 I am not suggesting, nor are Caspi and Moffitt (2018) as I understand them, that the 'p factor' is an entirely innate factor.

5 Once again, we see the importance of Freud's (1950 [1895]) emphasis on capacity for response inhibition as at the core of ego functioning.

6 Although BPD patients may be able to accurately (and selectively) identify the other's affect valence, they appear to be relatively unable to reflect on and understand the other's experiences and perspectives that generate the affect.

11

Ego psychology and psychoanalytic treatment

If some form of ego impairment is a common factor in psychopathology, it would seem to follow that it would be the focus of treatment. Greenberg and Mitchell (1983) write that "the essential goal of psychoanalysis remains for Hartmann, as it was for Freud, 'capturing the repressed' (Hartmann and Kris, 1945)" (p. 264). However, this understates Hartmann's view of the nature of successful psychoanalytic treatment. He writes that in successful treatment, "the ego is strengthened, and a synthesis of the task set by itself, by the instinctual drives, by the claims of moral conscience, and by reality is made possible; the individual learns to coordinate his aims" (Hartmann, 1947 [1964], p. 67). In the context of citing Freud's "Where id was, there shall ego be", Hartmann (1947 [1964]) also refers to "the successful integration of [other] functions into the ego [which] presupposes ego strength, relative freedom from anxiety, and intactness of the organizing function" (p. 67). It is clear that for Hartmann, as one would, indeed, expect from an ego psychology perspective, ego integration and strengthening are the primary goals of psychoanalytic treatment.

In the psychoanalytic context of a drive-defense model, the most obvious expression of an ego psychology perspective is the shift in focus from analysis of the id to analysis of the ego. What this has come to mean is essentially a shift from an emphasis on uncovering represses id impulses to a focus on analysis of defense, that is, identifying and bringing defensive processes to awareness. As Sugarman (2007) puts it, "the focus of analysis remains on expanding awareness into the intricacies of mental functioning more than becoming aware of any particular repressed content(s)" (p. 424).

Gray and the analysis of defense

Nowhere is this shift from a focus on contents to an examination of process clearer than in the work of Gray (e.g., 1994) (as well as Sugarman, e.g., 2006; and Busch, e.g., 2009). Gray's focus in his analysis of defense approach is on helping patients understand how their mind works and thereby use their mind more adaptively rather than on uncovering repressed mental contents.[1] Gray (1994) writes that the aim of treatment is to bring to conscious awareness "those familiar ego activities that, in spite of being near at hand, have remained estranged from the patient since oedipal childhood" (p. 154), that is, "making the unconscious ego conscious" (p. 154).[2] In the context of Gray's writings, "making the unconscious ego conscious" can be paraphrased as "where mindless and reflexive use of defensive activities were, there shall mindful, reflective, and flexible use of defenses be". In both cases Gray is referring to an *agent* who is doing something: in one case, reflexively deploying attention away from certain mental contents; and in the other case, directing attention and reflecting on one's reflexive tendency to deploy attention in a particular way. This is in contrast to the classical goal of "where id was, there shall ego be", when that is understood in terms of essentially non-agentic instinctual impulses blindly seeking discharge becoming increasingly subject to greater ego control. Also, there is no talk in Gray's formulations of the ego's "progressive conquest of the id" (Freud, 1923, p. 56) or "appropria[tion] of portions of the id" (Freud, 1933 [1964], 1932, p. 80).

In Gray's therapeutic approach, the aim of analysis of defense is not to *overcome* defense or resistance, but rather to render it more flexible and bring it under more conscious control. This aim is in accord with the previously noted evidence that defensive activities are associated with benefits as well as costs. In short, from Gray's perspective, analysis of defense does not mean undoing defenses, but helping patients become more aware of their defensive activities, thus bringing them under conscious control. More generally, the overriding goal of psychoanalytic treatment is "a fuller development of autonomous faculties" (p. 71) and an enhancement of the observing function of the ego (See Sterba, 1934). Although Gray refers to "autonomous faculties", his exclusive focus appears to be on the ego function of defense, an approach he refers to as "close process attention" (Rao, 1998). The close process attention approach is directed toward defensive processes that are just below the surface of conscious awareness and that can be readily brought to conscious awareness by directing the attention of patients to "clearly documented examples of their resisting minds at work" (p. 70). Gray continues: "With repeated experiences, patients gradually learn that they can bring these activities more and more under conscious management" (p. 70). According to Gray (1994), it is primarily, if not exclusively, the threat of anxiety-laden drive derivatives being consciously experienced that triggers defensive activities. Gray's near exclusive focus on analysis of defense reflects his view that the essence of neurosis is the implicit use of defensive activities as a reaction to conflict and anxiety triggered by drive derivatives.

In contrast to the emphasis in Freudian theory on enhanced self-knowledge in the form of increased awareness of one's repressed desires, wishes and impulses, from the perspective of Gray and his colleagues, the kind of self-knowledge that is to be achieved in treatment is in the form of better understanding of how one's mind works, particularly, what one does when one feels threatened. Further, on Gray's view, when the observing capacity of the ego is strengthened, and the patient gains more flexible control over defenses, the experience of desires, wishes, and impulses will, so to speak, take their natural course. Gray (1994) notes that drive derivatives would naturally reach conscious experience were there no defensive barriers. The analyst's "focus of attention" needs to be "on points of change in the flow of material" (p. 176) rather than on identifying the nature of the drive derivatives. The drive derivatives will, so to speak, "take care of themselves" once they are not subject to defense. As Gray (1994) puts it: "The instinctually derived material incrementally move more freely into consciousness as the surface-accessible conflict and the ego's defensive solutions are analyzed" (p. 177).

The role of the therapeutic relationship

In Gray's approach to treatment, the analyst's role is limited to that of a neutral and objective observer – a sort of mentor – who directs the patient's attention to certain, largely defensive, patterns, with the aim of the patient herself or himself acquiring and strengthening this "skill". Gray refers approvingly to Hartmann's description of the analytic situation – as cited in Lowenstein (1982, p. 220) – as a shared "scientific investigation" (p. 71). There is little room for any role of the analyst beyond that of a co-investigator. Any expanded role of the analyst would run the risk of "nonanalytic influence" (p. 133) which, although it may bring about "relief from conflict" and an image of the analyst "as an affectionate, approving, and protective [parental] authority" (p. 133), would not help the patient achieve what is for Gary the central goal of treatment: development and strengthening of a self-observing and self-analytic function.

In Gray's (1994) view, the therapeutic relationship is unreliable as the agent of change insofar is it rests on the shaky ground of a "continued existence of a fantasy of object-relatedness with the analyst" (p. 143). Therapeutic benefits that are the product of a fantasy may be undone once the fantasy is dispelled. What Gray is aiming for is something that he believes is more useful and reliable, namely, the strengthening of self-observing and self-analytic "skills" and "tools" that the patient can carry with him or her beyond the duration of the treatment.[3]

Interpersonalizing of defense

Gray (1994) writes that the "danger situations" are re-activated in the analytic situation, as manifested in the patient's expectation and fear of the analyst's negative reactions to his or her expression of drive derivatives. I have referred to this dynamic earlier as the interpersonalizing of defense (Eagle, 2018a) in the sense that defense is triggered not only in reaction to an intrapsychic threat but also in reaction to an expected threat from the other. In the treatment context, an important motive for the patient's defense is his fear of the analyst's anticipated negative reaction. Gray (1994) writes that the anxiety associated with the mental contents defended against is "crucially heightened by a fantasy that to put into words what comes to mind in the presence of the analyst is to *create some kind of risk – some consequence which will arise from or within the analyst*" (p. 1086, my emphasis). As Gray also observes, this fantasy is nothing less than the transference-based fear that the early "danger situations" (Freud, 1926, p. 129) will be repeated in the treatment situation.

Consider the following clinical vignettes as instances of the interpersonalizing of defense:

Vignette 1

> *Patient:* "I am so angry with Betty. I could strangle her. . . [he elaborated for a while, then he became hesitant]. . . . On the other hand, she has many fine qualities, etc."

Analyst: "Now you are focused on her fine qualities, a moment before you were experiencing very different feelings, then your feelings shifted. Can you see what happened here?"

Patient: "I was afraid you would think I was a brute for feeling so angry at her." (my emphasis)

Vignette 2:

Patient: relates a dream in which his mother might be crushed in a crowd and he could not help her.

Analyst: In your description of the dream you seem to pick up on the problem you were up against just before you told me the dream.

Patient: [He appeared to be thinking for a moment.] It was something about my mother . . . the sheets.

Analyst: You sounded as if you were hesitating to speak critically about your mother, and then the memory of the dream interrupted.

Patient: Yes, I remember.

Analyst: Maybe it got unsafe to show me critical feeling toward your mother.

Patient: I don't want you to think I'm being unfair to her.

After the patient talks about becoming a Christ-like white-robed figure, analyst states: "I guess it suddenly got safer for you to have you see me as sort of Christ-like and on the receiving end of someone *else's* resentment, rather than my hearing your resentment toward your mother" (Davison, Pray, & Bristol, 1990, pp. 603–604).

It can be seen in both vignettes that the patient's expectation of a negative reaction from the analyst play a central role in the former's defensive activities.

Suitability for analysis

For a long period of time, the received wisdom was that psychoanalytic treatment was suitable primarily for individuals suffering from neurosis, which, as Waelder (1960) puts it, is "a circumscribed affliction in an otherwise normal person" (p. 35). Gray (1994) makes clear that he adopts this position, as expressed in his view that a close process attention approach is appropriate mainly for analyzable, neurotic patients, that is, patients who are capable of engaging in and sustaining an analysis of the ego. Gary has in mind patients who are capable of some significant degree of self-observing capacity, but who can benefit from strengthening and fuller use of such capacities, in contrast to more disturbed patients who need to "draw especially on preoedipal elements of maternal relatedness" (p. 141); who are characterized by a "threat to the integrity of the self" (p. 142); and who show a "ubiquitous clinical *need to preserve* safety-seeking aspects of transferences of defense" (p. 142) (emphasis in the original).

Critique of Gray's approach to treatment: Correctives and revisions

Exclusive focus on analysis of defense

Gray seems to view the unconscious use of defensive activities in reaction to conflict and anxiety-laden drive derivatives as constituting the essence of neurosis. However, this view seems to be at odds with evidence that intact defenses serve to prevent the conscious experience of anxiety, a hallmark of neurosis. As is implicit in the classical theory of neurosis, it is the *failure* of a defense and the consequent "return of the repressed" (Freud, 1896, p. 170) that is the precipitating factor in neurosis. In fairness to Gray's position, it should be noted that in his close process attention approach, the treatment goal of analysis is not the overcoming of defense, but greater flexibility and more conscious control over defense. This conception of the role of defense in psychological functioning is in accord with much research evidence regarding the adaptive as well as maladaptive functions of defense (See Chapter 9). There is evidence, for example, that in certain circumstances, when effective action is not possible, denial can be adaptive, even life-saving (Eagle, 2018a); that self-enhancing self-deception can protect against depression (e.g., Taylor, Kemeny, Reed, Bower, & Grunewald, 2000); and that a "repressive style" is associated with benefits as well as costs (e.g., Eagle, 2018a).[4]

It is unlikely that neurosis can be adequately understood from the single perspective of unconscious defense. Indeed, the idea that neurosis is entirely due to the unconscious status of defenses tends to give support to the claim that psychoanalysis is a form of treatment for the "worried well".

There are impairments in ego functions other than rigidity of defense that are implicated in neurosis, including the extremes of either excessive inhibition or relative inability to delay gratification, difficulties in affect regulation, subtle impairments in interpersonal reality-testing, and persistence of early maladaptive expectations, beliefs, and internal working models. An adequate formulation of neurosis and its treatment needs to include these components. Gray (1994) himself refers to the strengthening of "autonomous functions" and the observing function of the ego as overriding goals of psychoanalytic treatment that go beyond the exclusive focus is on the analysis of defense.

Drive derivatives and defense

In limiting his discussion of mental contents that trigger defense to drive derivatives, Gray (1994) suggests that it is only drive-related mental contents that are conflict and anxiety laden and therefore, require defensive activities. This *a priori* assumption appears to be based on adherence to Freudian drive theory rather than on clinical-empirical evidence. Thus, A. Freud (1936) writes that there is a "primary antagonism" (p. 172) between the id and the ego and that drives are inherently dangerous and therefore need to be defended against. And Freud (1940) [1938]) writes that "an excessive strength of instinct can damage the ego in a similar way to an "excessive stimulus from the external world" (p. 199).

However, Freud (1926) also writes that drives and drive derivatives are dangerous because they are associated with parental behaviors that comprise the "danger situations" of loss of the object, loss of the object's love, castration threats, and superego condemnation.[5] On this view, the danger to the ego from drive-related thoughts and impulses is not inherent, but rather *conditional* upon environmental circumstances, in particular, parental behaviors (e.g., disapproval, prohibitions, threats). An implication of this view is that were parental reactions to the child's expression of drive-related behavior more benevolent, these behaviors would not be experienced as dangerous. Freud could argue that, because as socialization agents parents will necessarily disapprove of certain behaviors of the child, the "danger situations" are inevitable. However, even if this were so, there would surely be individual variations in the nature, range, and intensity of parental prohibitive and punitive behaviors that comprise the "danger situations" and, therefore, in the child's experience of danger. However,

Freud universalizes the "danger situations" and devotes no attention to individual differences.

The therapeutic relationship

As we have seen, Gray (1994) is concerned that the use of the therapeutic relationship or any stance beyond that of strict analytic neutrality runs the risk of increasing the role of suggestion. However, and ironically, the a priori assumption that it is only or mainly drive derivatives that trigger defense also carries the risk of what one might call selective suggestion. That is, there is the risk that the analyst will selectively bring the patient's attention to material that involves drive derivatives.

One is reminded here of an analysis of a therapeutic session conducted by Rogers. Murray (1956) carried out a content analysis of eight tape-recorded psychotherapy sessions of a patient treated by Carl Rogers. At the beginning of the therapy the patient felt that his problems were primarily sexual in nature. Rogers appeared to believe that such problems were manifestations of issues having to do with the self and maturity. Over the eight hours, the patient's references to sex dropped markedly and his references to independence increased significantly. It is especially noteworthy that Rogers viewed his treatment as non-directive.

Truax (1966) analyzed another therapy case of Rogers. He found that Rogers' expressions of empathic understanding and unconditional positive regard varied with the patient's behavior; and that these behaviors increased over time. Another finding was that percentage of "uh huhs" or "Mmmms" versus silence varied with the patient's themes. There are other examples of similar phenomena. In a set of verbatim typescripts of psychoanalytic psychotherapy sessions, Gill and Hoffman (1982) reported that the analyst's interest in sexual themes enhances the "possibility of a subtle imposition of this preference on the patient" (pp. 77–78).

The preceding findings may not be especially problematic if one believes that a wide range of coherent and plausible narratives may be therapeutic to the extent that they elicit, in Freud's (1937) words, the patient's "assured conviction" (See Frank, 1981; Masling & Cohen, 1987; Wampold, 2015). There is a good deal of evidence supporting that hypothesis. Indeed, this may be an important finding central to a theory of psychotherapy. However, it does not follow that different coherent and plausible narratives have equal explanatory status or truth value. Explanatory adequacy or veridicality of an account may have only a weak association with its impact or persuasiveness (Eagle, 1980). It may be the case – and this would be an interesting finding not only in regard to psychotherapeutic effectiveness, but also as a general finding about the nature of the mind – that, as Schafer (1976) observes, finding "meaning and significance where none had been apparent" (p. 6) is ego enhancing and is associated with greater feelings of well being.

As we have seen, Gray's (1994) view of the appropriate stance of the analyst is that of a neutral, objective observer, and co-investigator. Any role of the analyst or of the therapeutic relationship that goes beyond this parameter would constitute "nonanalytic influence" (p. 133) and would stimulate the patient's fantasies of safety and of the analyst as "an affectionate, approving, and protective authority" (p. 133). Indeed, according to Gray, if left unanalyzed, these fantasies are likely to strengthen the patient's resistance to examining his or her defensive activities.

Gray (1994) writes that reliance on the unobjectionable transference can be seen as a means of eliciting the patient's compliance and readiness to accept the analyst's interpretations, amounts to *using* the transference rather than analyzing it, and is essentially equivalent to suggestion and subservience to authority. (See Brenner, 2002, who makes a similar argument.) As Gray (1994) observes, such presumed "cure" is based on the fantasy of being loved by the analyst. The question that Gray raises is: What kind of cure is it that depends on maintaining an illusion and a fantasy rather than analyzing them? This is especially important for Gray insofar as his interest "lies in identifying technical ways of reducing the irrational, that is, the use of suggestion, and increasing use of autonomous learning as early as the patient's characteristics permit" (Gray, 1994, p. 68).

I think Gray's arguments regarding the uses of the transference, in particular, of the "unobjectionable positive transference", are cogent and need to be addressed. However, there a number of problems with his formulations regarding the therapeutic relationship. For one thing, Gray seems to assume that a position of analytic neutrality somehow eliminates the influence of relationship factors. However, analytic neutrality, defined as not taking sides in the patient's conflicts, is not equivalent to eliminating the influence of the therapeutic relationship. Rather, it is *a particular kind of relationship*, indeed, one that may be precisely the kind of therapeutic relationship that many patients feel as safe. It may be the case that the patient's experience of safety is associated with the analyst's benevolently neutral stance characterized by continuing the analytic work rather than taking a more directive stance largely because it is experienced as non-intrusive, and as a situation in which a sincere effort is made by the analyst to keep the patient's aims and goals foremost and at the center of attention rather than the analyst's aims and goals.

A stance of analytic neutrality does not and probably cannot eliminate inadvertent cues emitted by the analyst regarding his or her attitudes, reactions, and personality. Thus, the patient's feelings of safety (or danger) may not be simply the product of fantasy, but may also entail plausible construals of these cues (See Gill, 1982, 1994; Portuges & Hollander, 2011). To overlook these considerations runs the risk of reverting to the "blank screen" conception of the role of the analyst, which, too often, was characterized by coldness, aloofness, long silences, and "deep" and presumably authoritative interpretations, all of which add up to influencing the patient through establishing a particular kind of therapeutic relationship rather than the absence of a relationship. It is important to add that the analytic stance of silence, aloofness, and emotional coldness has little or nothing to do with analytic neutrality when that concept is properly understood, not as an absence of caring, but rather as not taking sides in the patient's conflicts.

As we have seen in previous chapters, the focus of ego psychologists has been on the autonomy of ego functions from drives, with little attention given to the relationship between ego functions and object relations. One can see in Gray's conception of the role of the analyst the extension of this neglect of object relational factors to the analytic situation. Just as ego psychologists neglected the influence of the object relational milieu on ego functions in the developmental context, so similarly, Gray neglects the influence of object relational factors (beyond that of suggestion) in the therapeutic situation. Gray overlooks the constructive role that the therapeutic relationship can play in the treatment. Although the positive transference may be misused, it may play an important role in motivating the patient to begin the treatment and to engage in the process, including close process attention. Also, in his description of the patient's feelings of safety as essentially fantasy, Gray seems to exclude the possibility that the patient's feelings of safety and trust may be largely based not on fantasy, but on experiences in the therapeutic relationship (e.g., the experience of being empathically understood). As far back as 1937, Bibring wrote that the patient's sense of security linked to the therapeutic relationship is a precondition for psychoanalytic treatment. Further, it is not at all clear that the need to feel safe in the treatment is limited to more disturbed patients. It is likely to play a role for a wide range of patients.[6]

There are other ego psychology oriented approaches to treatment that include the role of the therapeutic relationship. I refer here to the work of Loewald, Control-Mastery theory, Mentalization Based Treatment (MBT), and, in certain respects, self psychology and attachment theory.

Loewald on role of the relationship in psychoanalytic treatment

In his emphasis on "structural change", Loewald's conception of the goals of psychoanalytic treatment is entirely in accord with an ego psychology perspective. However, it is an ego psychology perspective that recognizes the role of object relational factors in structural change. He writes: "If structural changes occur in the patient's personality, it must mean that ego development is resumed in the therapeutic process in psychoanalysis. And this resumption of ego development is contingent on the relationship with a new object, the analyst" (Loewald, 1980, p. 221). Note the degree to which this position is entirely in accord with the perspective of object relations theorists.

Control-Mastery Theory and the role of the therapeutic relationship in ego functioning

The emphasis in control-mastery theory on the ego's assessment of danger is obviously based on Freud's (1926) identification of safety and danger as a critical ego function. Indeed, Weiss (1998) writes that control-mastery theory is based on Freud's later writings, "which he developed into his ego psychology" (p. 413). Similarly, Sampson (1976) observes that the ideas that comprise control-mastery theory "carry forward the main line of development within psychoanalytic ego psychology regarding how therapy works and how it fails to work" (p. 255). And as Silberschatz writes, "control-mastery was originally presented as an extension of ego psychology" (p. 222).[7]

As Weiss & Sampson and their colleagues (1986) have shown, the patient's experience of safety in the therapeutic situation is not necessarily based on fantasy, or certainly not entirely on fantasy, but rather on his or her assessment of the therapist's behavior, in particular, whether the therapist's behavior carries the risk of retraumatization or constitutes the provision of conditions of safety. They have presented evidence that the vicissitudes of defensive activity, at least to a significant extent, is a function of the patient's assessment of the therapist's test-passing or test-failure. In short, control-mastery theory also represents an ego psychology approach to treatment that recognizes the important role of the therapeutic relationship. In an integration of Gray's approach and Control-Mastery theory, it would be interesting to determine to what extent therapist test-passing and consequent patient feelings of safety enhances the patient's ability to become aware of his or her defensive activities via close process attention. Although both Gray's close process attention approach and Control-Mastery theory view the flexible use rather than the overcoming of defense as a central therapeutic goal, they differ regarding how that is facilitated. For Gray, it is sufficient for the analyst to bring the patient's attention to instances of defensive activities. From a control-mastery perspective, the patient's expectation regarding how the therapist will react to the patient's expression of certain material strongly influences the latter's defensive. What a classical analyst is likely to view as resistance to awareness and expression of certain impulses, a control-mastery therapist is likely to see as the patient's fear of re-traumatization by the therapist. In short, according to control-mastery theory, defense and resistance are more likely to be instituted when danger is experienced and more likely to be relaxed under experienced conditions of safety.

It follows on this view that, similar to Gray's perspective, the goal of treatment is not overcoming of defense and resistance but rather increasing their flexibility and enhancing the patient's control over their use, that is, being better able to employ them when necessary and relinquish them when not necessary. As Silberschatz (2005) notes, such flexibility of defense allows the patient to bring previously warded-off thoughts and feelings as a function of his or appraisal of whether "it can be done safely" (p. 225). As Sampson, Weiss, Mlodnosky, and Hause (1972) put it, "the patient's capacity to regulate the warded-off mental contents makes it safe for him to experience it because he can control the experience, turning away from it at will if it becomes too painful or threatening" (p. 525). Note that on this view, increased flexibility of defense enables the patient himself or herself rather than the therapist's interpretations to titrate the emergence of threatening material.

Mentalization Based Treatment (MBT) and the role of the therapeutic relationship in ego functioning

MBT is another example of an ego psychological approach to treatment that includes a role for therapeutic relationship factors and that does not dilute the primary focus on enhancing ego functioning (i.e., reflective function) through suggestion or the patient's compliance. There is evidence that intense negative emotional arousal is incompatible with the exercise of reflective function (Bateman & Fonagy, 2009).[8] There is also clinical evidence not only that a decrease in the intensity of such arousal is a precondition for adequate reflective functioning, but also that the patient's experience of being empathically understood by the therapist serves to reduce the intensity of negative emotional arousal and thereby facilitate the exercise of reflective functioning. (It is interesting to observe that the analyst's activity in directing the patient's attention to his or her just below the surface of consciousness defense is likely to be experienced by the patient as being empathically understood.)

Attachment theory and the role of the therapeutic relationship in ego functioning

A core tenet of attachment theory is that in optimal development the attachment figure serves as a secure base from the child can safely explore the world and thereby acquire knowledge and skills necessary to function in a complex physical and social world. Although, of course, the situation is vastly different in adulthood, according to attachment theory, the need for an attachment figure as a secure base, particularly in times of distress continues into adulthood. Bowlby (1988) writes that from an attachment theory perspective, the therapist serves as a secure base from which the patient can feel safe to engage in often distressing self-exploration. (There is, indeed, evidence that the therapist is experienced as an attachment figure by the patient [e.g., Parish & Eagle, 2003].) In the present context, I want to highlight the interaction between the relationship factor, that is, the therapist as a secure base, and the facilitation of the ego function of self-exploration. In this formulation, the influence of therapeutic relationship is not necessarily based on fantasy. Nor does it operate through compliance and suggestion. Rather, it serves as a foundation for self-observation and exploration. Indeed – and this is an empirical question – it is likely that the patient's experience of the therapist, including the neutral therapist, as a secure base will facilitate the patient's readiness to engage in close process attention.

Bowlby (1988) seems to assume that the patient will somehow automatically experience the therapist as a secure base – just as Gray seems to assume that the patient will readily engage in close process monitoring relatively independently of the analyst's behavior so long as the analyst takes a stance of neutrality. However, there is evidence that, although the patient tends to experience the therapist as an attachment figure, the degree to which the therapist is experienced as a secure base will vary with his or her attachment pattern (Parish & Eagle, 2003). Thus, compared to securely attached individuals, dismissive/avoidant and enmeshed/preoccupied patients are less likely to experience the therapist as a secure base in a straightforward, simple way. Indeed, a good deal of the treatment, including the analysis of the transference, will likely deal with the barriers to the patient's ability to experience the therapist as a secure base. (Note the congruence between this view and the formulation in Control-Mastery theory regarding the relationship among therapist's test-passing versus test-failing, the patient's experience of conditions of safety, and the emergence of warded-off contents.)

Self psychology and the role of the therapeutic relationship in ego functioning[9]

The therapeutic relationship also plays a critical role in the self psychology approach to treatment. More specifically, according to Kohut (1984) and similar to MBT, the therapist's empathic understanding serves to diminish the patient's intense negative affect and to contribute to "accretion of psychological structure" (p. 98). Although he does not explicitly describe it this way, what Kohut means by "accretions in psychic structure" is essentially enhanced ego functioning, including more adaptive regulation of negative affect and of self-esteem. In short, Kohut's formulation is essentially a description of the facilitating interaction between a relationship factor – the therapist's empathic understanding – and the enhancement of ego functioning.

Revisiting the interpersonalizing of defense

Gray (1994) writes that, due to the resurrection of the "danger situations" of childhood in the analytic situation, the patient's motives for defending against the conscious experience and expression of certain mental contents are likely to include fear of the analyst's disapproval. Recognition that defense can include fear of another's reaction to expressions of one's mental contents entails what I refer to as the "interpersonalizing" of defense (Eagle, 2018a; See also Portuges & Hollander, 2011). As we have seen in the preceding Davison et al. (1990) clinical vignettes, the analyst directs the patient's attention to the latter's defensive activities in reaction to the expectation of the analyst's negative reaction. However, in these clinical vignettes (nor in clinical examples presented by Gray) does the analyst explore in any depth the relationship between the patient's specific fantasies in relation to the analyst and his or her construals of cues emitted by the analyst.

Thus, Gray's recognition of the interpersonal and interactional aspect of defense is a limited one insofar as he appear to assume that, given the analyst's neutrality, the patient's fear that the analyst will react negatively to his or her expression of drive derivatives is entirely the product of an intrapsychic process, namely, a superego projection. However, the analyst's neutral stance notwithstanding, it is inevitable that as is the case in any interpersonal interaction, it is also the case in the clinical situation that the analyst will emit cues, and that the patient's construals of these cues will influence the patient's experience of the analyst's attitudes toward his or her behavior. (See Gill, 1994; Portuges & Hollander, 2011.) Surprisingly, neither in his theoretical formulations nor in his clinical examples do we find evidence that carrying out close process attention includes directing the patient's attention to his or her construals of the analyst's behavior, including his or her attitudes. A fuller examination of the patient's expectations and attributions underlying defensive activities including the possible cues on which they are based, could enhance the ego function of what I have referred to as interpersonal reality-testing. Instead, Gray limits the enhancement of the observing function of the ego to observation of intrapsychic processes.

Control-Mastery theory and the interpersonalizing of defense

Control-Mastery theory places much emphasis on the ego function of assessment of safety and danger. According to control-mastery theory, the likelihood of the patient bringing forth defensively warded-off mental contents in treatment is a function of the patient's assessment of whether it is safe to do so. In order to make such an assessment, the patient unconsciously presents tests to the therapist, which the latter can pass or fail. The tests largely have to do with whether the therapist's behavior tends to disconfirm (which constitutes test-passing) or confirm (which constitutes test-failure) the patient's pathogenic beliefs. There is evidence that test-passing, which is an indication that conditions of safety obtain (Eagle, 1986), is reliably followed by the emergence of warded-off material and diminution of anxiety; and test-failing, which is an indication of danger, by an increase in defense (e.g., Weiss & Sampson, 1986; Silberschatz, 2005). Thus, control-mastery theory adds an interactional element to a primarily intrapsychic ego psychology perspective.

Mentalization Based Treatment and the interpersonalizing of reflective function

In contrast to the primary emphasis in classical theory on self-reflection, Mentalization Based Treatment (MBT) places equal emphasis on the capacity to reflect on the mental states of the other. Indeed, as one's own mental states are frequently reactions to the mental states (e.g., malevolent intentions) one has attributed to the other, self-reflection often necessarily entails reflection on the mental states of the other. In view of this reality, MBT refers to "reflective function" rather than self-reflection in order to make the point that reflective capacity refers both to self-reflection as well as the ability to reflection on the mental states one has attributed to the other.

It is not simply defense and reflective function that need to be understood from an interpersonal perspective, but also wishes and desires. As noted, Sandler (1976) and Sandler and Sandler (1998) write that a wish entails a desired role of the other. For example, an exhibitionistic wish implicitly includes a desired observer who will observe one's exhibition. If Sandler is correct, it follows that the reaction to one's wishes that one attributes to the other will play a role in one's affective reaction to one's own wish. It would seem to follow that reflection on one's wishes and accompanying affects very frequently – if not always – entails reflection on the mental states of the other, more specifically, the mental states one has attributed to the other. For example, let us say that one construes another's behavior as rejection or disapproval of one's wish or need. Let us also say that one reacts with rage and despair. Any reflection on one's affects of rage will necessarily entail reflection on how one has construed the other's behavior and on the intentions one has attributed to the other. In short, reflection on one's own wishes, desires, and defenses is often inextricably linked to reflection on the mental states one has attributed to the other.

Is defense limited to drive derivatives?

As noted previously, Gray's (1994) suggestion that defense is primar-ily triggered by drive derivatives is based on the assumption in classical theory that there is an inherent antagonism between the id and the ego and therefore that drive derivatives are associated with conflict and anxi-ety. However, despite taking this position throughout much of his body of work, Freud contradicts this "standard" view in at least two places: He writes that "there is no natural opposition between ego and id; they belong together, and under healthy conditions, cannot in practice be distinguished from each other" (Freud, 1926, p. 201). This suggests that the "standard" model of a necessary and inherent conflict between the id and the ego is more a description of psychopathology than of healthy functioning.

Freud further dilutes the claim of an inherent conflict between the id and the ego in his surprising and isolated observation that it is not that warded-off contents are repressed because they are inherently threatening, but rather that they are experienced as threatening and dangerous *due to* repression. He writes that the "repressed instinct-presentation . . . develops in a more unchecked and luxuriant fashion. . . . It ramifies, like a fungus, so to speak, in the dark and takes on extreme forms of expression" that are alien to and terrify the individual because of "the way in which they reflect an extraordinary strength of instinct. This illusory strength of instinct is the result of an uninhibited development of it in fantasy and of the damming-up consequent on lack of real satisfaction" (Freud, 1915c, p. 149).

Freud's (1915c) idea that certain mental contents are experienced as dangerous due to the uninhibited development of fantasy suggests a subtle failure in reality-testing brought about by repression, more specifically, a failure in the ego's realistic assessment of danger. It also suggests the treatment goal of helping the patient more realistically assess conditions of danger and safety. From a Freudian perspective, this would take the form, largely through analysis of transference and defense, of helping the patient recognize that in the context of current reality, his or her experience of certain wishes and impulses as dangerous (e.g., may lead to abandonment and castration) is based on fantasy. In effect, the emphasis is on enhancing interpersonal reality-testing in the sense that it entails examination and reflection on unwarranted attributions to the other.

If drives do not represent an inherent threat to the ego, there is no good theoretical (as well as clinical) reason to limit defensive activities to drive derivatives. Indeed, there is much every day evidence that it is not only the threat of consciously experiencing drive derivatives, but a wide range of other mental contents, including contents that are threatening to self-esteem, that trigger defensive activities. "Liberating" ego psychology from drive theory allows recognition of the wide range of human aims, motives, desires, and feelings that many individuals defend against consciously experiencing and acknowledging.

As is exemplified in Control-Mastery theory, defense may be erected against normal developmental strivings that have been rendered danger-ous by virtue of parental communications regarding these strivings. These strivings that met with parental disapproval are not necessarily asocial or anti-social ones that need to be socialized, but rather expressions of nor-mal desires for separation and individuation and success. Such strivings may be met by parental communications such as: "If you separate from me, you will be abandoning and harming me" or "If you outdo me, you will incur my wrath". In reaction to such communications, the child may form the pathogenic belief that his or her strivings for autonomy and suc-cess constitute a danger to one or another parent and/or will be met with parental hostility. Hence, normal strivings for autonomy and success trig-ger separation and survivor guilt, and anxiety, the reaction to which is to defensively inhibit such strivings. Hence, on this view, it is not only infantile and antisocial impulses, but normal strivings that are likely to trigger defense. One finds in clinical practice many instances of this kind of conflict – what one may call reverse oedipal conflict or generational. In short, a revised ego psychology needs to take account of a wide range of aims and desires that are likely to trigger defense.

Insofar as oedipal incestuous and hostile wishes are inherently anti-social and inherently inimical to normal development and adequate functioning, the treatment goal in the context of Freudian theory and ego psychology is ideally sublimation or, if that is not possible, renunciation and repudiation, of these wishes. However, if it is largely normal developmental strivings and wishes that have been met with parental disapproval, the treatment goal would obviously not be repudiation or renunciation, but rather enhanced freedom to pursue them. It would be not the wishes and strivings that are problematic, but rather the pathogenic beliefs based on parental communications in which they are embedded.

Suitability for analysis

According to Gray (1994), a close process attention approach (as well as other approaches that can be legitimately be viewed as psychoanalytic) are suitable primarily for neurotic patients with relatively intact ego function and who are analyzable "by more conventional conflict-and resistance-oriented analytic technique" (p. 144). Gray suggests that such patients have the capacity to become aware of their defensive activities, but need to be motivated and, so to speak, mentored to do so. This conventional analytic approach, however, is presumably not suitable for "wider scope" patients who "draw especially on preoedipal elements of maternal relatedness" (p. 141) and who, therefore, require "supportive, therapeutic *uses*" (p. 141) rather than analysis of the transference. Gray (1994) writes that supportive uses of the transference is "widely true of object-relations practitioners" (p. 141) and suggests that they do so even with "patients who demonstrably do not need such limitations" (p. 142), which "inadvertently detract from the possibility of effective analysis of the ego and superego activities" (p. 142).

There are a number of problems with this position. One problem is that there is evidence that, contrary to received psychoanalytic wisdom, patients who show lower object relational functioning benefit more from analysis of the transference than higher functioning patients (Hoglend et al., 2011). Another problem is that the kinds of patients deemed suitable for psychoanalysis by Gray are relatively scarce and appear to be becoming scarcer. They no longer appear to constitute the typical patient in psychoanalytic treatment and psychoanalytic psychotherapy (See Doidge et al., 2002). As Sugarman (2007) writes, "today, borderlines and narcissistic types of psychopathology continue to receive serious attention while nary a word is heard about neurosis" (p. 410). This is not an entirely new phenomenon. As far back as 1953, Gitleson wrote that the use of repression was no longer characteristic of many patients seen in analysis. During the same period, Eissler (1950, 1953) wrote about the use of "parameters" (i.e., variations of classical techniques) with more disturbed patients; and in a paper entitled "The widening scope of indications for psychoanalysis", Stone (1954) also discussed the issue of psychoanalytic treatment for more disturbed patients.

Sugarman's ego psychology approach to psychoanalytic treatment

Sugarman's (2006) contemporary ego psychology approach to psychoanalytic treatment represents a further development of Gray's (1994) close process attention. In distinguishing between insight and "insightfulness", Sugarman (2006) observes that insight has been traditionally understood in terms of conscious awareness and knowledge of one's repressed unconscious mental contents, whereas insightfulness refers to a capacity for abstract, symbolic functioning, which enables one to become aware of how one's mind works. For example, the capacity to become aware of one's defensive activities that is emphasized by Gray can be understood from Sugarman's perspective, as an expression of insightfulness. (Note that what Sugarman refers to as insightfulness is similar in meaning to the concept of reflective function.)

It appears that Sugarman and Gray have in mind patients who, although experiencing much distress, do not show any obvious or serious impairments in ego functioning and would not necessarily fit into any clear cut diagnostic category of serious psychopathology. Rather, for these patients, ego functions are not operating optimally. Sugarman (2006) writes that "an important, and not always appreciated, assumption implicit in the structural model is that psychopathology arises from mental functions not working optimally (Hartmann, 1955; Rapaport, 1967)" (p. 966) and that "all mental functions work better and facilitate self-regulation when they work in abstract, symbolic ways" (p. 965).

In Sugarman's and Gray's descriptions, although these patients do not necessarily show any marked impairments in ego functioning, they require therapeutic help in bringing to bear their already considerable ego capacities on how they deal with early maladaptive schemas, expectations, and beliefs. For Sugarman, therapeutic work would be directed toward "mental functions . . . working [more] optimally" (p. 965). For Gray, whose emphasis is on analysis of defense, more optimal functioning may be brought about primarily through directing the patient's attention to his or her defensive activities in a therapeutic environment. The point here, in regard to both Sugarman's and Gray's accounts, is that although there may be no obvious or gross *structural* impairment in ego functioning in the patients they describe, they can nevertheless benefit *functional* enhancement of ego functioning. This is surely what is implied in Sugarman's observation regarding mental functions not working optimally.

According to Sugarman (2006), psychopathology is characterized by the failure "to develop or losing the symbolic level of organization, either in circumscribed areas or more ubiquitously". He writes that "all mental functions work better and facilitate greater self-regulation when they work in abstract, symbolic ways" (Sugarman, 2006, p. 965). Accordingly, the central goal of psychoanalytic treatment is to help "the patient attain or regain the symbolic level in all mental functions" (p. 965). Sugarman (2006) also writes that the achievement of a "verbal, symbolic mind" (p. 965) and the subordination of other modes to the verbal, symbolic mode are essential goals of psychoanalytic treatment. Citing Wilson and Weinstein (1996) and Levenson (1998), (see also Gray, 1994), Sugarman (2006) writes that the acquisition or strengthening of insightfulness is more like learning a new skill than gaining knowledge of one's repressed mental contents (although the latter can be a byproduct of insightfulness).

Although the distinction between insight and insightfulness is an important one and although an argument can be made that a central goal of psychoanalytic treatment is enhanced insightfulness, it is not evident that "all mental functions work better and facilitate greater self-regulation when they work in abstract, symbolic ways" (p. 965). It is important to distinguish between the plausible assumption that the *ability* to reflect on the workings of one's mind is adaptive and the less than plausible assumption that reflection on the workings of one's mind is inherently adaptive or that all mental functions work better when they work in abstract, symbolic ways.

Sugarman (2006) also writes that analysis should help "patients become aware of, and integrate or *subordinate*" (my emphasis) procedural knowledge "to symbolic" knowledge (p. 975). There is an important difference between "integrate" and "subordinate". Whereas *integration* of procedural (or implicit) and symbolic knowledge is highly adaptive, it is not clear that becoming aware of or *subordinating* procedural knowledge to symbolic knowledge is necessarily adaptive. I think what Sugarman likely has in mind is the therapeutic value of becoming aware of problematic procedural knowledge. For example, it would be important for the patient to be able to reflect on his or her internal working model when it is characterized by an implicit expectation of rejection from significant figures. However, there is no adaptive purpose served by subordinating procedural or implicit knowledge to a symbolic mode when procedural knowledge is non-problematic. Indeed, such subordination can interfere with smoothly functioning, spontaneous experience and behavior. One does not need to know how one's mind works when it is working smoothly and adaptively. In some contexts, some mental functions operate more smoothly and adaptively when they are not the object of reflection and are carried out implicitly. Indeed, reflecting on them may interfere with their smooth functioning.

Sugarman's emphasis on the subordination of procedural knowledge to symbolic knowledge can be contrasted with Loewald's position that ego maturity consists in access to and integration of psychic material and modes from earlier levels of organization. He writes:

> Perhaps the fully developed, mature ego is not one that has become fixated at the presumably highest or latest stage of development, having left the others behind it, but it is an ego that integrates its reality in such a way that the earlier and deeper levels of ego-reality integration remain alive as sources of higher integration.
>
> (Loewald, 1951, p. 20)

He also writes that "the more alive people are (though not necessarily the more stable), the broader their range of ego-reality levels" (Loewald, 1951, p. 22).

It seems to me that Sugarman arrives at the conclusion that all mental functions work better when they work in abstract, symbolic ways through the following steps:

(1) Psychopathology is associated with the failure to develop or loss of the symbolic level of mental functioning.

(2) Hence, a central goal of treatment is to help patient "attain or regain the symbolic level" in all their mental functions.

(3) However, the claim that the ability to function symbolically is not equivalent to the claim that all mental functions work better when they are subordinated to the abstract, symbolic level.

Bucci (2002) has presented evidence that relative to the presence of abstract words in psychotherapy sessions, positive therapeutic outcome is associated with the presence of concrete words that elicit imagery and affect. This finding is not consistent with the claim that all psychological functions work better when they work in symbolic and abstract ways. If, as Sugarman writes, the development of the capacity for insightfulness and reflective function can be understood as the acquisition of skills, one would expect that they would become increasingly implicit and etched in the body rather than remain abstract and symbolic. It is the nature, not only of motor skills, but of psychological skills, that with practice, they become increasingly automatic and implicit.

The emphasis on *subordinating* procedural or implicit knowledge to abstract, symbolic knowledge is but one expression of an approach to psychoanalytic treatment that has been subject to the criticism of over intellectualization that goes back to Ferenczi & Rank's 1924 critique and that perhaps played a role in the waning influence of ego psychology. Ferenczi and Rank (1924 [1956]) wrote, as described by Makari (2008), "that psychoanalytic method had fossilized . . . and became an overly intellectualized process of educating patients about the contents of their unconscious" (Makari, 2008, p. 352). In his own writings, Rank "argued that healing did not take place through the simple acquisition of new knowledge". Rather, the patient needed "to relive their original libidinal situation" (Makari, 2008, p. 353). Criticism of the classical approach to treatment as overly intellectualized, overly focused on the acquisition of self-knowledge, and overly concerned with adaptation were common themes among object relations theorists. However, the position they adopted had difficulties of its own. For example, Balint (1968) maintained that a "basic fault" due to early environmental failure was at the core of psychopathology, and that confrontation with and experience of the "basic fault" are defended against through the erection of "sheltering structures" (Bonomi, 2003, p. 219). Given this conception of psychopathology, effective treatment is understood as requiring the undoing of these "sheltering structures" through the patient's regression in the safety of the therapeutic situation. Such regression facilitates the patient's subjective experience of his or her "basic fault", which in turn, allows the possibility of a new beginning.[10] Adaptation to the environment is at the cost of loss of one's authenticity and with in-touchness with vulnerable and vital aspects of oneself. For Ferenzci, insofar as ego maturity is a defensive response to trauma and adaptation to a mad environment, which entails a surrender of a vital part of the personality (Winnicott's [1965] "true self"), enhancement of ego maturity as a treatment goal is wrongheaded. Indeed, according to Ferenczi, insofar ego maturity is seen as the product of compliance or adaptation to social demands (i.e., constitutes a "false self") and is essentially a form of pseudo maturity, the maintenance of which entails a chronic strain in the individual.[11] In an important sense, a primary task of psychoanalytic treatment is to undo pseudo ego maturity – equated with "sheltering structures" – through therapeutic regression and, in effect, to provide a form of re-parenting, which will then allow the resumption of developmental growth. Although Ferenczi does not state this explicitly, presumably the resumption of developmental growth will entail a process in which ego maturity will develop not on a defensive basis, but on the basis of in-touchness with one's vulnerabilities and vital needs. For the most part, Ferenczi's and related views were met with hostility on the part of the more conservative members of the psychoanalytic community. For example, in his review of Ferenczi's *Final Contributions*, Bromley (1957) wrote – not sympathetically – that Ferenczi had "abandon[ed] psychoanalytic technique in favor of might be described as rapport therapy" (p. 113) (obviously a reference to an emphasis on the therapeutic relationship). And as Bonomi (2003) reminds us, Jones (1957), writing in a very ugly tone, "described Ferenczi as a dissenter wrecked by progressive mental deterioration" (Bonomi, 2003, p. 220) "that revealed themselves in, among other ways, a turning away from Freud and his doctrines" (Jones, 1957, p. 47).

Some version of Balint's central idea that the patient's "sheltering structures" need to be undone through regression in a safe therapeutic environment in order for the patient to experience and confront his or her "basic fault" is echoed in various ways in the writings of Guntrip, Winnicott, Laing, and to a certain extent, Fairbairn. Guntrip's (1969) concept of "ego weakness" obviously parallels Balint's concept of "basic fault". Further, like Balint, Guntrip (1969) believes that defenses that protect against the experience of ego weakness must be undone and that facilitation of the experience of ego weakness via regression must take place in order for the patient to confront the core of his or her pathology, which, in turn, will presumably allow "recuperation and rebirth" (p. 78) to proceed. As Guntrip (1969) writes: "The final aim of this therapy is to convert regression into rebirth" (p. 78).

Winnicott (1958), too, emphasizes "therapeutic regression aiming at the rebirth of the true self" (p. 249). He refers to a patient whose successful "classical analysis had somehow left the core of her illness unchanged" (p. 249). Winnicott's (1954) concepts of therapeutic regression and "holding environment" (Winnicott, 1963) as well as the very title of one of his books, *The maturational process and the facilitating environment* (Winnicott) reflect his view of psychopathology in terms of arrested development and the formation of a defensive "false self"; and his corresponding view of treatment in terms of the provision of a therapeutic environment that will facilitate in-touchness with one's core true self and resumption of developmental growth.

Although in a more subtle way, Fairbairn (1952) also includes therapeutic regression as a component of treatment in his emphasis the therapeutic importance of the patient re-experiencing the bad object and the original bad object situation in the safe condition of the therapist as a good object. Fairbairn (1952) writes: "the deepest source of resistance [in the treatment] is fear of release of bad objects from the unconscious" (p. 68). He goes on to say that

> the release of bad objects obtained in analytical treatment differs, however, from a spontaneous release of such objects in that it has a therapeutic aim – and ultimately, a therapeutic effect by virtue of the fact that it is a release controlled by the analyst and safeguarded by the security imparted by the transference situation,
>
> (p. 75)

that is, by the presence of the therapist as a good object.

According to Fairbairn, the internalization of the therapist as a good object should enable the patient to dissolve the patient's "devotion" and "obstinate attachment" to early objects. He suggests that this would lessen the likelihood that the patient will project attitudes and qualities associated with the "bad" internal object on to the other and will thereby increase the possibility of a understanding of the other as a separate other relatively unfettered by projections. In the present context, this can be understood as enhancing the patient's ego function of interpersonal reality-testing. Fairbairn (1952) also identifies as a central aim of treatment the amelioration of splits in the ego and strengthening the central ego through its re-appropriation and integration of psychic domains that have been split off from it.

Although there are also differences – for example, Kohut does not place much emphasis on therapeutic regression – there are common views shared by the preceding theorists and self psychology with regard to conceptions of psychopathology and treatment. Paralleling the claims that a "basic fault", "ego weakness", and splits in the ego due to environmental failure are at the core of psychopathology is Kohut's (1984) claim that self-defects are at the core of psychopathology. As for conceptions of treatment, there are clear parallels between the preceding views on ameliorating ego weakness and splits in the ego in treatment and Kohut's (1984) emphasis on "repair" of self-defects and accretion of psychic structure through the therapist's provision of empathic understanding, the need for which was not adequately met in the patient's early life. Thus, in common with the preceding views, Kohut's conception of treatment also focuses on repair of ego impairments generated by parental failure. Also, in his emphasis on enhancement of self-cohesiveness, Kohut is essentially saying that strengthening a central ego function is an important goal of treatment.

Laing (1967) extends some of the preceding views to the treatment of psychosis and schizophrenia. For example, he applies the central idea of undoing defensive structures and thereby repudiating one's "false self" via therapeutic regression and applies it to psychosis. (It is not surprising to learn that Winnicott was one of Laing's supervisors.) Appearing to take quite seriously ideas that therapeutic regression aims at "the rebirth of the self" (Winnicott, 1958, p. 249), and that the "final aim" of therapy is to convert regression into rebirth (Guntrip, 1969), Laing and some of his colleagues created the Philadelphia Association and started a psychiatric community at Kingsley Hall. In this presumably safe environment, patients were to go through their psychosis, shed their "false self", and at the end of this process, resume developmental growth, often described by Laing and his followers as a kind of rebirth.

Strikingly, their eschewal of structural theory and ego psychology notwithstanding, the preceding theorists essentially propose not only an ego psychology conception of psychopathology (i.e., characterized by an emphasis on ego weakness and impairments), but also a correspondingly ego psychology approach to treatment characterized by an emphasis on ameliorating ego weakness and strengthening ego functioning. I think, therefore, it is useful to read the critiques of ego psychology raised by the preceding object relations theorists, not as alternatives to ego psychology, but rather as a particular variation of an ego psychology approach with more severely disturbed patients, and I would add a variation of ego psychology that is hyperbolic regarding the nature and outcome of psychoanalytic treatment.

Hovering in the background of this discussion is the question of how Alexander and French's (1946) concept of corrective emotional experience fits into an ego psychology perspective on treatment. The different formulations of the role of the therapeutic relationship in psychoanalytic treatment – the facilitating environment, the good object, the provision of empathic understanding, the safe place for regression – can all be understood as a form of corrective emotional experiences. However, in contrast to the theorists I have discussed, Alexander and French (1946) make no reference to therapeutic regression and the resumption of developmental growth. Rather, their emphasis is on altering the patient's maladaptive interactional *expectations and schemas*, a goal that can be understood in terms of enhancing the patient's interpersonal reality-testing.

Where id was, there shall ego be

I leave for last arguably the clearest and most important expression of an ego psychological conception of the overriding goal of psychoanalytic treatment, namely, "where id was, there shall ego be" (Freud, 1933, p. 80). Given the view of the id as the natural enemy of the ego in Freudian theory, Freud's adage is often understood as strengthening ego control over id impulses, as well as facilitating renunciation of id impulses or ideally, achieving sublimation of these impulses. (For a cogent critique of this reading, see Apfelbaum (1966); see also Eagle, 1984.)

A different reading of "where id was, there shall ego be" emerges when one translates the original German "Wo es war, sol ich warden" literally as "where it was, there shall I become" (Brandt, 1966). Indeed, neither Freud nor Hartmann wrote about the ego, ego psychology, or ego functions. Rather, they wrote about "Das Ich", *Ich psychologie*, and *Ich functionen*, that is, respectively, to "the I", I psychology, and I functions. Thus, quite ironically, despite the austere and experience-distant language that Hartmann employs, he places "the I", that is, the "personal element", at the center of psychological functioning. Translated more freely, the literal translation can be rendered as "where impersonal it was, there shall personal I be (or become)", a translation that emphasizes the integration of the impersonal "it" into the personal "I".[12] It can also be even more freely translated as "where experience of drivenness was, there shall a sense of agency be".

None of these translations limits the impersonal "it" to id impulses. The "it" can include any set of mental contents or potential experiences which, because they are experienced as threatening the stability and integrity of the ego, remain as an ego-alien, impersonal "it" (See Eagle, 1984). For example, many people describe conscience as a not fully integrated introject, as a homunculus standing on their shoulder, telling them what to do and not do. Thus, one can just as plausibly say that where superego was, there shall I be as where id impulses were, there shall I be.

In the preceding translations, the goal of treatment is not primarily increased ego control, but rather an enhanced integration of the hitherto ego-alien "it" into the realm of the personal "I". Such integration should not only expand the range of one's experience and sense of agency but would also make it more likely that the experience of a personal "I" will represent one's vital needs and desires. Indeed, one can think of the evolutionary emergence of a personal "I" at the center of subjective experience as an adaptive development selected in the course of evolution that enhances the likelihood of one's vital needs being represented in experience and, therefore, more likely to be met.[13]

Our language reflects the use of I as an agent and as the center of experience and action, and self as representation and object of reflection. We do not say "myself is hungry" or "myself wishes and desires", but rather "I am hungry" or "I wish and desire". Consider also the concepts of self-esteem and self-image. When I say that I have low or high self-esteem, I am referring to myself as an object of evaluation. Similarly, when I refer to my self-image, I am referring to myself an object of reflection. Thus, when Kohut (1984) refers to regulation of self-esteem (as an aspect of self-cohesiveness), he is referring to such processes as how I feel about myself, how my feelings about myself vary with the presence or absence of external admiration and praise, and so on. Such processes entail an interaction between an agent or an I and an object of reflection, which is captured in

Meissner (1996) distinction between "self as subject" and "self as object". Although the preceding observations may seem to identify merely mundane linguistic usage, as Wittgenstein (1966) observed, the use of language reflects "forms of life" (p. 174).

A question that arises is the relations between the concepts of self and ego or I. It is important to recognize that whereas the German word for ego or I is *Ich*, the German word for self is *selbst*. And we know that Freud and Hartmann wrote about *Ich psychologie*, not *Selbst psychologie*. This distinction is also made by Fast (1990), who writes that one can view the self as a representation to the ego. The basic distinction between the "I" and the "me" can be traced back to Mead, who writes that the moment one thinks about oneself, one's experiences, actions, feelings, and thoughts, the me is an object of representation to the reflecting "I".

Ego as both "I" and set of functions

How does one understand the relation between the ego as "I" and the ego as a structure with a set of functions? G. S. Klein (1976) raises a variation of this question in his comment that "current ego psychology tries to straddle" (p. 157) the perspectives of concern with impersonal processes and personal aims, motives, and intentions. This specific question is but one instance of the general question of how to relate to each other Freud's language of mechanism and language of personal experience and meanings or what Rubinstein (1974) refers to as the different perspectives of viewing the individual as organism versus person. As Ricoeur (1970) has noted, the tension between meaning and mechanism or what he refers to as "energetics" and "meaning" is present throughout Freud's writings.

Although this is an extraordinarily complex issue, that cannot be adequately discussed here, one can say (1) that in order for ego functions to operate, there must be a subject, an "I", to carry them out; and (2) the "I" is the experiential aspect (e.g., sense of agency, sense of competence, feelings of well-being) of the carrying out of ego functions.

One can think of the I as a "waystation" through which various factors, including biological and psychological needs and unconscious processes, exert their influence on us. That is, they do so, not the way a computer program directs an automaton, but rather through exerting an influence on "the I", that is, on what I desire, I prefer, I attend to, I wish, and what I want and intend to do. Rather these influences are mediated by the intervening structure of "the I". As noted, the evolution of human subjectivity, of an I that carries out ego functions such as deployment of attention, delay and planning, affect regulation, and so on, enable one to survive and meet one's vital needs. Surely, this is something of what Hartmann (1939) had in mind in his conception of the ego as an "organ of adaptation" (p. 50) emerges in the course of evolution. From this perspective, the enhancement of ego functions serves to facilitate the representation and integration of impersonal "it" processes into I experiences. Note that we have returned to the core of Freud's (1950 [1895]) conception of the ego as an intervening inhibitory structure and to Hartmann's conception of the I as an "organ of adaptation" and to his surprising emphasis on the "personal element".

The capacity for intervening processes and functions such as planning, thinking, anticipating consequences, desiring, and so on already implies the emergence of an I at the center of subjective experience. Further, whatever the factors that influence them and whatever the underlying explanatory account, the fact is that it is one's lived experiences that make one's life meaningful. And it is these lived experiences that are the primary phenomena that need to be accounted for in any adequate theory of the mind. In that sense, contrary to Freud's (1923) endorsement of Groddeck's aphorism that we are lived by our id, although we may be influenced by our id, we are, indeed, lived by our ego.

Ego functions as skills

As noted, earlier, Gray (1994) and Sugarman (2006) view the strengthening of insightfulness and of the patient's ability to attend to his or her defensive activities as similar to the acquisition of a skill. If this analogy is an apt one, it would follow that, like any skill, ego functions such as reflective function would, over time, become increasingly implicit and take its place as an aspect of one's procedural knowledge rather than continue to occupy the center of one's attention. Consider the process of learning to ride a bicycle or learning to play the piano. These procedural skills became increasingly implicit; continued focal attention to the processes involved in the skill may disrupt performance – much like the fabled centipede trying to reflect on and understand how it can walk. Explicit and focal attention are likely to be productive only during the early stages of acquisition of a skill or when difficulties and disruptions arise and when new learning takes place. In the smooth performance of a skill, attention is directed not to one's movements but to the task. Thus, in riding a bicycle, one attends, not to one's movements, but to the external terrain on which one is cycling. And an accomplished pianist attends, not to his or her fingers, but to the music.

Too often, the product of analysis is excessive and explicit self-reflection on one's mental states rather than on the acquisition and internalization of a capacity which allows one the freedom to simply have an experience without reflecting on it. Excessive self-reflection is not equivalent to the *capacity* for reflection, but rather makes for stiltedness rather than a capacity for a normal and spontaneous flow of experiences. It is also literally, a form of *self-absorption* that is likely to interfere with cognitive and affective investment in the outer world as well as necessary action in the world. In that sense, excessive self-reflection can be understood as a form of narcissism.

In his essay On Narcissism, Freud (1914) writes that "in the last resort, one must love in order not to fall ill" (p. 85). It is clear from the context that what Freud means by love here is libidinal investment in some object – "person or thing" – in the world. The reason one must love in order not to fall ill, provided by Freud, is that if one does not libidinally cathect objects, the ego will be damaged due to inundation of excessive excitation. Translating this metapsychological formulation into ordinary discourse, Freud's adage can be read as stating that an intact ego requires cognitive-affective investments outside oneself, and that excessive self-absorption is inimical to adequate ego functioning. Hence, the imperative, for Freud, of the developmental progression from narcissism (i.e., self-absorption) to the capacity for object love.[14] One would hardly aim for excessive self-absorption as an outcome of treatment. However, excessive self- reflection – sometimes derisively described as 'navel-gazing – is too often an outcome of psychoanalytic treatment.[15]

From a perspective quite different from Freud's, Kohut (1984) also takes the position that excessive self-reflection is an indication of non-optimal functioning. He writes that positive treatment outcome results in the laying down of "regulatory structures which post-analytically function outside of awareness – that is, without the need to reinstate the functions of the selfobject analyst in the form of a conscious exercise of self-analysis" (p. 170). He also writes that although "the ability to employ a self-analytic function is to be welcomed, . . . in principle, it is an indication that the analysis has remained incomplete" (p. 217, fn. 1 for chapter 5). Unfortunately,

Kohut confuses matters by referring to the *ability* to employ a self-analytic function. Notwithstanding his reference to "ability", the logic of his argument suggests that it is not the *ability* to employ a self-analytic function that points to a less than ideal outcome, but rather the excessive and compulsive use of that function.

Ideally, self-reflection, like other ego functions, operates implicitly and becomes the explicit focus of attention mainly when something goes awry. For example, Freud (1914) writes that, because they turn libidinal cathexis inward, illness and pain interfere with one's capacity for cognitive-affective investment in "persons and things" in the external world. I would suggest that a similar relationship holds with regard to ego functions and affective investment in the external world. When ego functions, including reflective capacity are operating smoothly and implicitly, one need not devote explicit attention to them; one can, therefore, direct one's interest and attention to "persons and things" in the external world rather than to one's own mental contents. Thus, in an important sense, smooth operation of ego functions without excessive self-absorption can be perhaps viewed as a pre-condition for the capacity for object love.

I referred earlier to Fonagy's formulation of reflective function (RF) in terms of the capacity to reflect both on one's own mental states and the mental states of the other. Insofar as one's mental states are frequently generated by one's construals of the other's behavior and the intentions one has attributed to the other, as Fonagy and his colleagues (e.g., Luyten, Cambell, Allison, & Fonagy, 2020) note, optimally reflective function would not be limited to one's own mental states, but would also include reflection on the other's mental states, as well as the relationship between the two. That is, reflection would turn outward as well as inward.

It is useful to recall Brentano's (1874 [1973]) – one of Freud's most important teachers – conception of the mental in terms of the property of *aboutness*. That is, according to Brentano, mental contents – thoughts, desires, intentions, wishes, etc. – are always about something outside the mental content itself. For example, desire is about something desired; when I think, the thought is about something; an intention is to do something; a wish is for something to happen (which, as Sandler (Sandler, 1976, Sandler & Sandler, 1998) has noted, entails a role for the other). In short, the primary function of ego functioning is to help us make our way in the world, including the interpersonal world. Hartmann (1939) essentially makes this point when refers to the ego as an "organ of adaptation" (p. 50).

This is also implicit in Freud's reputed comment that psychological health is expressed in the capacity for love and work. When, however, explicit self-reflection becomes a general mode of functioning, there is the risk that the focus is on desiring, thinking, etc. themselves rather than on the objects of desire and thought.[16]

Does increased self-knowledge remain as a primary goal of psychoanalytic treatment?

As noted earlier, according to Gray and Sugarman, the kind of self-knowledge acquired in treatment is not primarily knowledge of one's repressed mental contents, but rather of how one's mind works. Further, this latter emphasis is on here-and-now just below the surface of experience. For example, the patient's blocks or breaks in free association are understood as defenses against expressing hostile feelings toward the analyst that are just below the surface of conscious experience. The emphasis in treatment is not on uncovering deeply repressed unconscious mental contents, but on helping the patient understand what s/he does when feeling conflicted or afraid of repercussions from the other or some other danger.[17]

In his later writings, Freud essentially diluted the aim of self-knowledge as well as of making the unconscious conscious as singular psychoanalytic aims. In one of his late papers, Freud (1937) acknowledges that because the ideal goal of bringing repressed memories and other mental contents to conscious awareness through interpretation is far from always achieved, one must settle for *constructions* that elicit an assured conviction in the patient. Thus, the emphasis on recovering the repressed gives way to an emphasis on a plausible and persuasive construction. Freud (1937) clearly assumed that the analyst's constructions, which elicited the patient's "assured convictions" were generally veridical. He did not seem to entertain the possible disjunction between veridicality and therapeutic effectiveness, that is, the possibility that coherent and persuasive narratives could be therapeutic despite their questionable veridicality. This was not a trivial issue for Freud. It went to the heart of his abiding concern with the criticism that it is *suggestion* rather than self-knowledge that is the primary factor in bringing about therapeutic change in psychoanalysis (Meehl, 1994). Indeed, he argued that only "interpretations that tally with what is real (in the patient)" would bring about therapeutic change. (Freud,

1917, p. 452). To assess this hypothesis requires assessments of veridicality independent of assessments of therapeutic change. I know of only one or two studies that have even attempted such an investigation. The dominant view in contemporary psychotherapy theory is that narrative coherence *per se* is a significant factor in therapeutic change (e.g., Frank, 1981; Wampold, 2015). However, I do not know of any study that has assessed the relative contributions of narrative coherence and narrative veridicality to therapeutic change.

The philosopher of mind, Moran (2001) has raised questions regarding the nature of knowledge of mind, in particular, the nature of the distinction between first-person and third-person knowledge. As I understand Moran, the essence of first-person knowledge is not solely a matter of epistemology, but also of acknowledgement and of a stance of standing behind one's commitments in good faith. That is, I understand Moran to be saying that, in contrast to third-person knowledge, first-person knowledge is not simply a matter of knowing oneself, but also of knowing oneself in a particular way, that is, not through observation and inference – the mode of third-person knowledge – but through direct experience, which makes more likely authentically committing oneself to a certain course. Hence, while self-reflection and mentalization may be important, they are mainly important to the extent that they facilitate acknowledgement and commitment to a particular life course. As Moran observes, self-reflection and self-knowledge can be as much employed in the service of evading one's commitments as mere commitment without self-reflection and self-knowledge.

Consider Sartre's (1956) example of the akratic gambler discussed by Moran. The gambler resolves to stop gambling. He knows and is able to reflect on the knowledge that he has made such resolutions in the past and has failed to stick to them. As Moran observes, the gambler can evade his resolution to stop gambling (and be in bad faith) in two contrasting ways: one, by viewing himself as an object and submerging himself in his history and facticity, something like "both you and I know my history and based on that history, the high probability that I will also break my resolution this time". An excessive immersion in this "empirical" perspective in relation to oneself can serve to weaken one's resolution and bring about backsliding in the form of "Given my history, I might as well not fight it and break my resolution now". Here, the gambler is reflecting on his past and making predictions about himself as an object, similar to reflecting and predicting about another person. The second way the gambler can be in bad faith is by *totally ignoring* his history and submerging himself in his current conviction without any reflection on the reality of his history.

In his discussion of how one expands one's personal perspective to include other perspectives, Nagel (1986) refers to the "new problem of reintegration" (p. 9), which, in certain respects, is related to the issue raised by Moran (2001) regarding the integration of first- and third-person self-knowledge. As Moran notes, in contrast to first-person self-knowledge, which is immediate and non-inferential, objective third-person self-knowledge is obtained through observation and reflection on one's own behavior and therefore not essentially different from knowledge about another person. In both Moran's and Nagel's accounts, an issue that arises is the conditions that enable third-person self-knowledge to become integrated into first-person self-knowledge, that is, to a sense and avowal of who one is and to a moral and psychological commitment to the self that is the product of the new reintegration. Stated more succinctly, the question is: how does the self-knowledge obtained from a third-person perspective become integrated into one's organic sense of oneself, including one's desires and aims?

This has been a question from the very beginning of psychoanalysis, as seen, for example, in Freud's relinquishment of hypnosis as a primary therapeutic intervention. Although the patient may have remembered and learned a great deal about himself or herself through hypnosis, to the extent that this knowledge was not *integrated* into the ego, its therapeutic effects were evanescent. Later in the history of psychoanalysis, a similar issue arose in the context of lack of therapeutic change in patients who seemed to have acquired a great deal of insight and self-knowledge. A common explanation was that these patients had acquired only intellectual insight rather than emotional insight. This explanation is largely circular insofar as no empirical evidence was presented indicating that intellectual and emotional insight, as independently assessed, was associated with therapeutic change. Rather, the absence of therapeutic change is attributed to lack of emotional insight; and evidence for lack of emotional insight is failure to change.

The "new problem of reintegration" identified by Nagel (1986) emerges in the clinical situation in the following way: let us say that as a response to interpretation and through the exercise of self-reflection, the patient is able to view aspects of himself or herself as objects of reflection. The "new problem of reintegration" (p. 9) that arises is how one

> incorporate[s] these results [i.e., of a detached observing perspective] into the life and self-knowledge of an ordinary human being. One has to *be* the creature whom one has subjected to detached examination, and one has in one's entirety to *live* in the world that has been revealed to an extremely distilled fraction of oneself.
>
> (Nagel, 1986, p. 9)

In the psychoanalytic context, "the new problem of reintegration" is how to integrate the results of the observing ego into the experiencing ego (Sterba, 1934). That is, how does one integrate what one has learned from a relatively "detached observing perspective" into one's sense of who one is and into one's ongoing life? The hyperbolic claims of rebirth notwithstanding, paraphrasing Nagel, one remains the creature whom one has subjected to examination. One is not reborn as a new person. Therefore, however incomplete or distorted one's prior perspective might have been, insofar as it spoke to an important aspect of one's experience, it needs to take its place as one aspect of oneself and as a viewpoint that needs to be understood and integrated into a more complete representation of oneself.

Freud's (1927 [1930]) emphasis on renunciation, repudiation, and sublimation of infantile instinctual impulses and desires will simply not do. It is based on the assumption that these wishes and desires are inherently antisocial and represent an inherent danger to the ego. However, when this assumption is relinquished, the rationale for repudiation and renunciation evaporates.[18] Rather, treatment is now directed toward helping the patient recognize that his wishes and desires are not inherently dangerous but are experienced as such due to parental reactions and to ego immaturity during childhood. The patient's recognition of these realities should, in turn, facilitate his or her capacity to integrate as part of oneself these mental contents that had been experienced as ego-alien. In short, a far more effective response provided by Freud to the "new problem of integration" lies in the aim of "where id was, there shall ego be" (Freud, 1933 [1964], p. 80). That is, the hitherto ego-alien aims and desires to which one has gained greater access through self-reflection can be acknowledged and experienced as part of oneself in the safety and immediacy of the therapeutic relationship.

Notes

1 In a similar vein, without referring to the work of Gray, Sugarman, or Busch, Ferro (2006) writes that "there is not an unconscious to be revealed, but a capacity for thinking to be developed, and . . . the development of the capacity for thinking allows closer and closer contact with previously non-negotiable areas" (p. 102).

2 Although Gray refers to unconscious defense, insofar as he views them as just below the surface of consciousness, they are more accurately described as preconscious.

3 Although classical analysts have argued that therapeutic improvement that is due mainly to relationship factors rather than to interpretation and insight is mainly a "transference cure" and is not lasting, there is little evidence that this is the case.

4 As noted earlier, Hartmann (1939) observed that defense can be an aspect of normal development and that flexibility of defense is adaptive. However, the implications of this view for analysis of defense in treatment was not articulated by either Freud or Hartmann.

5 As noted earlier, Freud's fealty to the view that excessive excitation represents the primary danger to the ego is seen in his formulation that, ultimately, the "danger situations" are dangerous due to the fact that they leave the child at the mercy of undischarged excitation.

6 Despite my criticism of Gray's relative neglect of the role of the therapeutic relationship in treatment, I have a good deal of appreciation for his general position. Although it may swing the pendulum too far in the opposite direction, it serves as somewhat of a balance to hyperbolic conceptions of the analyst's role as well as of the therapeutic relationship. For example, in the recent literature, the analyst's position is described in terms of "analytic love" (e.g. Loewald, 1960; Friedman, 2005; Nussbaum, 2005). One analyst writes that his love for his patient is not essentially different from his love for his friends and children (Bach, 2006). Gray's focus on the analyst's observational and cognitive skills in identifying defensive activities just below the surface of consciousness also serves as a balance to the excessive attention to the analyst's countertransference reactions and to the claim that such reactions serve as a reliable guide to the patient's unconscious mental sates.

7 Silberschatz (2005) goes on to say that Control-Mastery theory "has moved beyond its psychoanalytic roots and I view it as an integrative cognitive-psychodynamic-relational theory" (p. 222). However, this view did not appear to be shared by Weiss and Sampson (1986).

8 Although more evident with borderline patients, the incompatibility between intense negative emotional arousal and ability to engage in reflective activity is a general one.

9 It may seem surprising to include self-psychology among ego psychology perspectives on psychotherapy and ego functions. However, it should not be. For one thing, despite his criticisms, Kohut (1984) himself noted the links between self psychology and ego psychology. Most important, similar to ego psychology, self psychology conceptualizes psychopathology in terms self defects, which can readily be seen as ego impairments, and views the central goals of psychoanalytic treatment in terms of "repair" of defects and accretions of psychic structure.

10 However, Balint (1968) cautions, the "basic fault" cannot be "removed, resolved, or undone" (p. 183). Rather, successful treatment at best may enable a more realistic adaptation to one's "basic fault".

11 The sequestered aspects of oneself are often described in the literature as childlike, needy, spontaneously linked to one's organic impulses, authentic, and least de-vitalized by the demands of social conformity; The views of Balint and Ferneczi belong to what Strenger (1989) has referred to as the romantic vision of psychoanalysis.

Occupying a central place in that vision is a conception of psychopathology in terms of developmental defects and arrests that are largely due to environmental failure and a corresponding conception of treatment that focuses on the role of the therapeutic relationship that facilitates developmental growth, even in some cases, psychological "re-birth".

12 The core meaning of this reading bears a strong family resemblance to the Sullivanian formulation of the relationship between the self-system and "not me" experiences.

13 This is one way of understanding Freud's (1914) concept of self-preservative instincts; Still another way of understanding Freud's "where id was, there shall ego be", when id is understood as instinctual drives, is that it addresses the question of psychobiological drives achieving representation in the subjective experience of "I desire" or "I need" or "I fear". For example, how does one get from the biological level of neural firings, hormonal secretion, low blood sugar, to "I am hungry" or "I have sexual desire or a sexual fantasy"; Freud was quite familiar with Kant's writings. His concept of the ego or I can be traced back conceptually to Kant's (1781 [1965]) "transcendental ego" in the sense that in both contexts, the ego or I is a precondition for experience, that is, makes possible experience as *my* experience, as well as the unity of consciousness. As Walsh (1967) writes in his summary of Kant's philosophy, the existence of an I "is the ultimate condition for experience, in the sense of being the logical subject of experience or the point to which all experience relates" (p. 315).

14 Recall that in the Narcissus myth. Narcissus not only falls in love with his own reflection, but also rejects and cannot reciprocate Echo's love for him. That is, his self-absorption prevents him from being able to receive and respond to anything outside himself. Narcissus responds to his reflection as a separate object, suggesting that, for Narcissus, objects are essentially extensions of himself. Thus, ironically, Narcissus falls in love with what he thinks is a separate object but cannot respond to an actual separate object.

15 The classic literary expression of the paralyzing effect of excessive self-reflection on action is depicted in Hamlet.

16 There is evidence that stimulus input from the external world is necessary for intact functioning in different areas ranging from visual perception to overall ego functioning. With regard to the former, there is evidence that eye movements, which contribute to varied stimulus input, are necessary for intact visual perception. Thus, when one eliminates the functional effects of eye movements (through stabilizing the retinal image by inserting a scleral contact lens so that when the eye moves the image [e.g., a square] moves with it) the stimulus one is looking at fragments (Eagle, Bowling, & Klein, 1966; Eagle & Hill, 1969). Although there are individual differences, there is also evidence that deprivation of sensory input interferes with adequate ego functioning (e.g., Miller, 1962). And finally, there is evidence that in dire conditions, such as solitary confinement and concentration camps, the individual's ability to be invested in something outside himself or herself is associated with more intact ego functioning and survival (Eagle, 1981).

17 Note the strong family resemblance between this approach and work on mentalization and reflective capacity. Indeed, the emphasis on understanding how one's mind works can be seen as a particular way of talking about mentalization and self-reflection.

18 It is not clear how repudiation can reduce the danger of excessive excitation. What happens to the pressure for discharge? An interesting question that arises is why insight accompanied by emotion should be more strongly linked to therapeutic change than insight that is primarily intellectual and relatively unaccompanied by emotion (Moran, personal communication). Although widely accepted as a clinical fact, the reasons for this being the case (if it is) are not self-evident. I think a reasonable answer to this

question is that the experience of emotion, including in reaction to an event such as an interpretation, is a marker of *special self relevance* of that event. In contrast, intellectual ideas have an existence independent of the person holding them. That is, whereas ideas have an existence independent of oneself, – in Popper's (1978) words, they have an independent existence in World 3 – emotions (as well as desires and wishes) necessarily take the form of I feel (as well as I desire and I wish). One cannot readily speak of the existence of emotions independent of the person experiencing the emotion.

12

A unified psychoanalytic theory

A basic assumption motivating this book is that the project of seeking integration of different psychoanalytic *schools* and developing a relatively unified psychoanalytic theory of the mind is both possible and desirable. This assumption is far from widely shared in the psychoanalytic community. There are voices that argue for the desirability of the current state of pluralism as well as voices that question the very possibility of integration. In what follows, I review and examine these arguments and then return to the question of why a revised and expanded ego psychology is best suited to serve as a foundation for a unified psychoanalytic theory.

The emergence of psychoanalytic schools

The emergence of new psychoanalytic *schools* can be charitably understood as being triggered by the conviction of an increasing number of critics that existent (and often hegemonic) theory either neglects and/or does not provide an adequate explanatory account of significant aspects of psychological life. As Greenberg (2001) puts it, "each new theory being . . . narrowly focused on a partial truth . . . probes a dimension of our experience that had not been previously investigated" (p. 359). From this perspective, the theoretical formulations associated with each new theory can be seen as efforts to correct the neglect and explanatory deficiencies of extant theory. However, virtually without exception, the theoretical formulations of new psychoanalytic schools are proposed not as accounts to be integrated into existing theory or to the revision and expansion of existing theory, which could potentially contribute to the incremental progressive development of a unified psychoanalytic theory. Rather, they emerge as self-sufficient theories that claim to account for all aspects of the human personality (Rangell, 2007, 2008).[1]

A familiar pattern in the emergence of new psychoanalytic schools is an initial restriction of their explanatory to a limited set of phenomena (e.g., self-disorders; schizoid phenomena). However, over time, the explanatory domain of the new theoretical formulations is expanded to virtually all behavior, or at least, a wide swath of human behavior. In order to buttress these more expansive claims, it is not uncommon for the new "school" to engage in a reductionism in which much of human behavior is accounted for by a limited set of motives, needs, and tendencies that replace the limited set of motives, etc. posited by existing theory. The net result is the replacement of one form of reductionism, most frequently, drive theory reductionism, in which virtually all manifest behavior is seen as directly or indirectly motivated by drives, with the reductionism of the new theoretical "school", in which virtually all manifest behavior is seen as direct or indirect expressions of the particular set of motives and needs emphasized by the particular new "school" in question. Consider as a specific example of the preceding pattern the emergence of Fairbairn's object relations theory. There is little question that Freudian theory fails to provide an adequate account of the role of the object and of object relations beyond their role in drive gratification. The very definition of the object in Freudian theory is "the thing in regard to which the instinct achieves its aim" (Freud, 1915b, p. 122). Indeed on this view, commerce with objects or even the very conception of objects would never develop were they not necessary for drive gratification.

A core claim of object relations theory is that it provides a more accurate account of the role of the object and of object relations (including the nature of the infant-mother bond) in psychological life than is provided by Freudian theory or ego psychology. There is little doubt, as posited by object relations theory, that along with other species, we are inherently, in Fairbairn's (1952) words, object-seeking creatures. However, Fairbairn writes that we are "primarily object seeking (rather *than* pleasure-seeking as in the classic theory)" (p. 82). As a specific expression of that view, Fairbairn (1952) writes that sexual desire serves primarily as a "sign-post to the object" (p. 33).

Thus, Fairbairn effectively excludes the role of pleasure and the distinctive nature of sexual desire in psychological life and reduces their motivational significance to object-seeking needs and behaviors. In doing so, he essentially replaces Freudian reductionism with his own object relational reductionism, in which the primary if not exclusive function of the object is, as Jones (1952) puts it in his Preface to Fairbairn's (1952) book, the provision of object support for the ego. The reductionism takes the additional form of viewing all psychopathology in terms of "the relationships of the ego to its internalized objects" (p. 60).

A similar reductionism is evident in the trajectory of theoretical developments in self psychology, from the defensible and modest claim in Kohut's 1971 and 1977 books, that because the Freudian emphasis on "structural conflict" does not do justice to a set of self phenomena, psychoanalytic theory needs to include a psychology of the self, to the all-encompassing claim in his 1984 book that issues of self-cohesiveness and self-defects underlie all psychopathology. Kohut (1984) writes that "we have begun to consider even the psychoneuroses – Freud's 'transference neuroses'– as specific variants of self disturbances" (p. 80). He also writes: "I am referring here only to narcissistic personality and behavior disorders and am disregarding the fact that I believe the oedipal neuroses, too, should be viewed as self-disorders in a wider sense" (Kohut, 1984, p. 218, fn. 5) (See Chapter 2). Thus, Kohut's claim is that clinical phenomena that appear to be expressions of inner conflict are, upon deeper understanding, revealed to be manifest representations of latent underlying self-defects. Thus, as is the case with object relations theory, the result is reductionism, now a self psychology form of reductionism in which a wide range of behaviors is understood as expressions of self-defects.

Further, virtually all aspects of selfhood discussed in self psychology, for example, continuity of a coherent sense of self over time, regulation of self-esteem, self-soothing capacity, the self-enhancing function, and so on can be understood as ego functions, including the synthetic function of the ego. It is not clear that a separate psychoanalytic school is required to afford adequate recognition to the importance of issues of selfhood.[2]

The preceding pattern of reductionistic theorizing is not new. It has characterized the entire history of psychoanalysis. Theoretical concepts and formulations that may shed light on a particular slice of psychological life are not offered as partial and incremental contributions to the project of an increasingly comprehensive and integrated theory, but rather as wholesale alternatives to existing theory. Thus, one not simply a psychoanalyst, but a Freudian or a Kleinian an Adlerian or a Jungian or a Sullivanian, and so on, with the clear implication that one is dedicated to viewing much of human behavior through the particular lens dictated by one's professed adherence and loyalty to a particular school. Education and training in and affiliation with psychoanalytic institutes oriented toward a particular "school" further crystallizes this tendency.

Any account of the emergence of new *schools* in the history of psychoanalysis would not be complete without reference to the role played by the authoritarian and dogmatic attitudes of the Freudian establishment toward new theoretical formulations that were deemed to be "dissident" or "revisionist", that is, that appear to question or contradict core axiomatic Freudian principles (See Bergmann, 2000; Kirsner, 2009; Richards, 2003, 2017). The dogmatic and authoritarian practices on the part of the psychoanalytic establishment created a situation in which if the views of the "dissidents" were to be heard and represented in psychoanalytic training and education, there was little choice but to establish their own *schools*, their psychoanalytic training institutes, and quite often, their own professional journals.

Given the history of rejection and/or marginalization of "dissident" points of view, one can perhaps understand the preference for pluralism over unity and integration on the part of many psychoanalysts who may equate integration and a more unified theory with a return to dogmatic hegemony. However, this point of view does not appear to take into account a number of problems associated with current pluralism itself. Unfortunately, in certain respects, in reacting against existing dogmatism, the so-called "dissident" *schools* tended to mimic some of the authoritarian attitudes and behaviors of the prevailing hegemonic establishment by installing their own form of dogmatism. Thus, the new *schools* that emerge are often as dogmatic and fixed in their views and practices as the dominant views and practices against which they were rebelling. The result is often not, as some have suggested, a benevolent form of pluralism, but rather, as Cooper (2008) has described it, "a plurality of orthodoxies".

The search for a common ground

It has been argued that despite theoretical differences, partial integration, referred to as the "common ground", has already been achieved in regard to clinical technique. In 1990, Wallerstein argued that the universal acceptance in the psychoanalytic community of the centrality of transference (and presumably of the analysis of transference), despite other theoretical differences, constitutes a common ground among different psychoanalytic schools. He writes that despite theoretical differences, the common ground of psychoanalysis lies in a shared clinical technique. He writes that

> our clinical interventions (apart from differences of style and of theory-drenched languages) reflect a shared analytic method, rest on a shared clinical theory of defense and anxiety, of conflict and compromise, of transference and countertransference, and evoke comparable data of observation, despite our avowed wide theoretical differences.
>
> (p. 11)

Similar to Wallerstein, Kernberg (1993) locates the common ground in clinical work, more specifically, in "an increased focus on the centrality of transference analysis in all psychoanalytic approaches" (p. 660). And in 1995, Gabbard proposed that the (presumed) universal acceptance in the psychoanalytic community of the analyst's countertransference as a valuable, even indispensable, tool for understanding the patient's unconscious mental states constitutes a common ground despite other theoretical differences.

A problem with this claim is that it rests on the assumption that psychoanalysts of different theoretical persuasions all mean the same thing when they refer to transference. However, as Eagle and Wolitzky (1989) have observed, to take increased focus on transference analysis as meaningful evidence of a "common ground", one would have to demonstrate agreement on the definition of transference (what is being transferred?) and on such matters "on which aspects of the patient's behavior are indicative of transference" (p. 31). However, such agreement has not been demonstrated.

There is little evidence that clinical judges can reliably identify transference even when using agreed-upon, specified, criteria. In one of the few studies that directly bear on this issue, Luborsky, Graff, Pulver, and Curtis (1973) investigated whether four expert judges could agree in their ratings of various aspects of transference from a tape-recorded psychoanalysis. The mean interjudges were quite modest at best. The judges, as a group, could not agree very well on either global ratings of amount of transference (mean, r=.26), or evidence for transference (mean, r-.21), or on the degree to which references to object relations were allusions to the transference (mean, r=.31).

Even if Wallerstein's and Gabbard's claims were shown to be valid, this would be a rather anemic form of integration, more a sociological observation regarding analyst's practices (similar to the observation that a certain percentage of analysts use the couch). However, as I have tried to demonstrate elsewhere (Eagle, 2018b), the common ground, particularly with regard to transference, is only apparent. This is so because analysts belonging to different schools conceptualize transference in different ways. For example, Freudian analysts maintain that patients aim to have unconscious infantile wishes gratified by the analyst; self psychology analysts maintain that patients seek unqualified empathic mirroring, and so on. These differences in conceptions of transference reflect underlying differences regarding theories of the mind. It seems unlikely that a genuine common ground in clinical approach could be achieved despite fundamental theoretical differences. However, even if this were possible, it would constitute a rather limited form of integration.

Is integration of different psychoanalytic schools desirable?

There is a widely shared sentiment in the psychoanalytic community that the current pluralism of different *schools* is a desirable state of affairs, one that is liberating and that enriches psychoanalysis. For example, despite stating that psychoanalysis has grown under the impact of "one theoretical excess after another", Greenberg (2001) regards such excess as "inspired" and as "wonderful and surprising" (p. 359).

I suspect that one reason many analysts do not view pluralism as a serious problem is that it may, indeed, be less of a problem in the clinical context. Let us say that an analyst belonging to a particular school, say self psychology, focuses primarily on self phenomena and interprets a wide range of clinical material from the perspective of self psychology theory. And let us say that another analyst belonging to an object relations school focuses primarily on object relational phenomena and interprets a wide range of clinical material from an object relations theory perspective. Insofar as issues of both self and object relations are likely to be of much importance to a wide range of, if not all patients, the analyst's selective focus on these issues and relative neglect of other aspects of the patient's life, the analyst's interventions may nevertheless be therapeutically effective. Thus, a relatively wide range of different coherent narratives may be therapeutically useful so long as they are relevant to at least some critical aspect of the patient's life. (See Glover [1931] on inexact interpretations and Kohut's [1984] comments on this topic.) However, in contrast to the clinical situation, the selective focus and selective theoretical lens do constitute a serious challenge that needs to be met in the context of efforts at developing an integrated psychoanalytic theory of the mind.

Under certain circumstances, however, pluralism may be problematic even in the clinical context. Although a wide range of master narratives that address only partial aspects of the patient's life may be therapeutically useful, it does not follow that *any* coherent master narrative or theoretical perspective will necessarily be therapeutic for all patients. That is, it is reasonable to expect that narratives or interpretations that are not especially relevant to critical aspects of the patient's life and that do not speak to his or her experience and are largely dictated by the analyst's loyalty to a particular theory may not be of much therapeutic value. Thus, therapeutic effectiveness may not be a function solely of the mere coherence of the narrative or theoretical perspective, but also in Freud's (1917) words, of its tallying with what is real in the patient, when one understands "real" in the sense of resonating with the patient's experiences and concerns.[3]

The inescapability of pluralism

Another attitude toward psychoanalytic pluralism focuses not so much on its desirability, but rather on its *inescapability*. The most articulate and highly intelligent spokesperson for this position is Roy Schafer. In a number of his papers and books, Schafer presents a nuanced and philosophically sophisticated case for the inevitability of pluralism and by implication, for the impossibility of meaningful integration among different schools. Although Schafer does not state explicitly that integration is impossible, it is clearly implicit in his description of different schools and his conception of the nature of theory.

In his 1980 paper, Schafer argues that "psychoanalytic theorists of different persuasions have employed different principles or codes – one might say narrative structures – to develop their ways of doing analysis and telling about it" (p. 29). And in his 1979 paper, Schafer writes that insofar as each psychoanalytic school is characterized by "an organized set of beliefs and a corresponding way of defining facts" (p. 347), it is foolish "to ask the naively empirical question 'Well, what are the facts?'" (p. 347). In his 1992 book *Retelling a Life*, Schafer argues that the different psychoanalytic theories that underlie different *schools* should be thought of as different "master narratives" (p. 147), that is, as different perspectives on the clinical material (See also Schafer, 1979).

On this view, each psychoanalytic school is associated with a distinctive master narrative, for example, one for drive theory, one for object relations theory, one for self psychology, and one for ego psychology, and so on. Further, "master narratives"

> are competitive only in that they construct alternative narratives, each with entailments of its own. This conception of the variety of tales to be told in any area of study implies that judgments of right or wrong have no claim on our attention.
>
> (Schafer, 2004, p. 248)

Hence, there is no point in attempting to assess to what degree the different master narratives are supported or refuted by the available evidence insofar as the evidence itself is constituted by and understood through a particular theoretical lens and a particular set of principles or codes. According to this view, it would appear that the project of integration of different master narratives is pointless. Rather, one should simply see them as different perspectives that are incommensurate with each other.

A clear implication of Schafer's view is that different master narratives employ different principles or codes or narrative structures in *interpreting the same given set of phenomena*. However, in his 1979 paper, Schafer writes that "the analysts of each school *elicit and highlight somewhat different analytic phenomena*, which are consistent with, and more or less confirmatory of, fixed assumptions and the methods they define" (p. 348, emphasis added). The statement that each school elicits and highlights somewhat *different* analytic phenomena is striking insofar as any meaningful *comparison* of different theoretical formulations arises primarily in the context of different explanatory accounts of largely *the same set of phenomena* (e.g., the role of the object in psychological life).

Let us say that, as Schafer's comments suggest, one psychoanalytic school focuses on drives and another school on object relations. Insofar as each school focuses on *different* phenomena, we could expect different theoretical accounts. However, this would not rule out integration of these different accounts into a more comprehensive theory that covers both the drive and the object relational phenomena. The problem here is that each school claims to provide, not an account of a limited set of phenomena, but a comprehensive account of the nature of mind, applying its account to the entire personality. Thus, the issue here is not a matter of competing explanatory accounts nor of incommensurate principles or codes in relation to the same phenomena. It is rather, a problem of the blind men and the elephant, that is, a matter of each school mistaking the part for the whole. Thus, contrary to Schafer's position, this sort of problem does not constitute an impassable barrier to integration. It is, in principle, susceptible to an integrative solution.

Another problem with Schafer's position is that it does not address the possibility that two different master narratives, each internally coherent, may contradict each other in particular ways. This may not be of great consequence in the clinical situation insofar as each patient is presumably exposed to an internally coherent story line that at least is in some way relevant to his or her life. However, in the context of a theory of the mind, one cannot claim veridicality for contradictory master story lines – logically, they may both be wrong, but they cannot both be right.

Schafer's attitude toward pluralism is strongly influenced by his views on the philosophy of mind, particularly the philosophy of action. He writes that analytic sessions "would be better conceptualized as thought actions, speech actions, and nonverbal action performed by patient and analyst" and adds that

> actions exist only under a description. This means that to say what you are doing, you inevitably select one of the ways in which it may be stated. For example, writing a letter can also be referred to as writing to a friend or sending birthday wishes or resuming a neglected correspondence, and so on, depending on the beliefs and desires, or more generally, the intentions of the speaker or writer.
>
> (Schafer, 2004, pp. 240–241)

Schafer is suggesting with this example that each psychoanalytic school views the patient's actions under a particular description. Hence, on this view, a comparative assessment of an action is not meaningful. However, Schafer's letter-writing example does not support his position.

That writing a letter can also be referred to as writing to a friend or sending birthday wishes or resuming a neglected correspondence depending on the intentions of the writer simply provides additional and more detailed information about what the writer is doing beyond simply the general information that he or she is writing a letter. In all these descriptions, the action of writing a letter remains constant, that is, is not altered or revised under the different descriptions of writing to a friend, sending birthday wishes, and so on. Furthermore, the different descriptions can be additive rather than alternative or incommensurate accounts of what the writer is doing. Thus, Schafer's letter-writing example hardly serves as an analogy to different master narratives of different schools entailing different closed systems and different incommensurate accounts. Indeed, if anything, the letter-writing example serves as a useful analogy in making the points that each description provides specific information and that the different descriptions and narratives can be meaningfully integrated into a fuller, more informative, richer, and more adequate explanatory account.

Since each of the descriptions of what the letter writer is doing refers back to the writer's *intentions*, it is in a more thorough examination of the letter writer's intentions, including his or her unconscious intentions, that the issue of different master narratives may arise. For example, from the perspective of object relations theory, the action of writing a letter to a friend may be interpreted as an expression of object-seeking; from a self psychology perspective, it may be interpreted as seeking an empathic connection; from a Freudian perspective, it may be interpreted as sublimation, and so on. However, each of these descriptions may constitute relatively accurate, but partial, accounts of what the individual is doing rather than incommensurate master narratives. In short, the fact that actions exist only under a description does not preclude the possibility of integration of different descriptions.

If I understand Schafer's view, this is essentially the philosophical position taken by Rorty (1991), who is highly skeptical of the idea that theory can be understood as a "mirror of nature", that is, as corresponding to a reality independent of one's theoretical construction. For Rorty's form of neo-pragmatism, the function of theory is not correspondence with an independent reality, but advancement of a project in which a community is engaged. Thus, according to Rorty (1991), Einstein's relativity theory on the nature of the universe has no greater claim on truth than a witch doctor's theory of the physical universe. Rather, on Rorty's view, each theory should be assessed in terms of the pragmatic criterion of how well it advances one's project.[4]

Rorty (1991) eschews the idea of objectivity and the pursuit of knowledge for its own sake and argues for a turn to solidarity. He writes:

> The tradition in Western culture which centers around the notion of the search for Truth, a tradition which runs from the Greek philosophers through the Enlightenment, is the clearest example of the attempt to find a sense in one's existence by turning away from solidarity to objectivity.
>
> (p. 21)

One of Rorty's critiques of the "objectivist tradition' is that it "centers around the assumption that we must step outside our community long enough to examine it in the light of something which transcends it, namely, that which it has in common with every other actual and possible human community" (p. 22). Rorty appears to view this position as having reached a kind of dead end. He contrasts it with "those who wish to reduce objectivity to solidarity – call them 'pragmatists' – [and who] do not require either a metaphysics or an epistemology. They view truth as, in William James' phrase, what is good for *us* to believe" (p. 22). Rorty adds:

> For pragmatists, the desire for objectivity is not the desire to escape the limitations of one's community, but simply the desire for as much intersubjective agreement as possible, the desire to extend the reference of 'us' as far as we can.[5] Insofar as pragmatists make a distinction between knowledge and opinion, it is simply the distinction between topics on which such agreement is relatively easy to get and topics on which agreement is relatively hard to get.
>
> (p. 23)

And finally, Rorty writes that according to a pragmatist view, "there is nothing to be said about truth or rationality apart from descriptions of the familiar procedures of justification which a given society – *ours* – uses in one or another area of inquiry" (p. 23). Schafer's position on the role of master narratives in psychoanalytic theories seems quite compatible with the Rortyan view of the nature and function of theory and explanation. For both Schafer and Rorty, the main criterion for evaluating a theoretical account is the pragmatic one of its contribution to the accomplishment of one's project. In the psychoanalytic context, the project is the achievement of therapeutic effectiveness (See Eagle, 1980, on the relationship between veridicality and effectiveness).[6] Although this neo-pragmatic view may be appropriate in the clinical situation, it does not serve one well in the context of attempting to develop an integrated psychoanalytic theory of the mind. However, it may not be appropriate even in the clinical situation. Many patients who come for treatment, particularly psychodynamic treatment, care about and assume that they will be learning some truths about themselves – not master narratives from a particular theoretical perspective or persuasive narratives. As Sass (1992) notes (See also Eagle, 1984), there is little evidence that therapists who in their writing take the position that the provision of coherent and persuasive narratives or "aesthetic fictions" (Geha, 1984) or something akin to text interpretation (Schafer, 2004) is what is offered in treatment share these views with their patients. This disjunction or split between theoretical position and clinical work strikes me as something that is not quite right and that needs to be addressed. Although I am not at all certain I can identify precisely what is not right about it, my strong intuition is that one would be better off as a therapist if one's theoretical views and what one does and what one feels free to share in the clinical situation tend to be of one piece.

Rorty writes that if one wants to get as much intersubjective agreement as possible and wants to extend the reference of "us" as far as possible, one may have to escape the limits of one's community. This would certainly apply to the "communities" of different psychoanalytic schools. One can draw a parallel between reflection on one's perspective on the personal and theoretical levels. In both contexts, one takes one's perspective as an object of reflection. In the former personal context, it is one's subjective experiences, construals, and attributions that are taken as objects of reflection and inquiry. In the theoretical context of different psychoanalytic schools, it is one's theoretical perspectives and assumptions that are objects of reflection, which are often associated with as much affective intensity as one's personal experiences and perspectives.[7] In both contexts, the aim of the reflective process is to make possible a more objective point of view, which consists, at least in large part, in the integration into one's current perspective both one's own prior perspective, as well as other perspectives or viewpoints to be understood.

The most useful discussion of the issue of integration of different perspectives with which I am familiar is found in Nagel's (1986) *The view from nowhere*. Although Nagel's focus is on how to combine the perspective of "a particular person inside the world with an objective view of that same world, the person and his viewpoint included", his discussion is relevant to the issue of different perspectives among different psycho-analytic schools. As Nagel notes, the issue of how to deal with different perspectives is "a problem that faces every creature with the impulse and the capacity to transcend its particular point of view and to conceive of the world as a whole" (p. 3).

The key move that Nagel suggests is the following one:

> To acquire a more objective understanding of some aspect of one's life or of the world, we step back from our initial view of it and form a new conception which has that view and its relation to the world as its objects. In other words, we place ourselves in the world that is to be understood.
>
> (p. 4)

Nagel goes on to say:

> But we can raise our understanding to a new level only if we examine that relation between the world and ourselves which is responsible for our prior understanding, and form a new conception that includes a more detached understanding of ourselves, of the world, and of the interaction between them.
>
> (p. 5)

Consider as a specific example of a particular theoretical perspective a formulation of interpersonal relationships largely in terms of self-selfobject interactions. Instead of taking the position that, along with those of other schools, one's theoretical perspective is a closed system characterized by incommensurate "master narratives", one steps back and reflects on one's theoretical perspective. This exercise would make it clear that although the formulation of selfobject and self-selfobject relationships point to impor-tant phenomena, a significant gap is created by an exclusive emphasis on a particular set of interactions and by an assimilation of other interactions to self-selfobject phenomena. In particular, it becomes clear that interper-sonal relationships cannot be adequately described exclusively in terms of self-selfobject interactions, and that relationships in which another person is not experienced as a selfobject, but as a separate subject are seriously neglected and/or minimized. One may then be motivated to step back from one's "initial view . . . and form a new conception which has that view and its relation to the world as its objects" (Nagel, 1986, p. 4).

An example of such theoretical reflection is seen in the work of Bacal and Newman (1990) and Fosshage (2017), who, although viewing themselves as self psychologists, nevertheless recognize some of the limitations of that perspective. Thus, Bacal and Newman (1990) write that limiting one's account of interpersonal relationships, as self psychology does, to self-selfobject interactions does not take account of object relations that do not fit this description. Fosshage (2017) attempts to expand self psychology theory to include formulations of relational theory. Note that this process parallels the personal challenge that confronts an individual who, through reflecting on his or her construal of, say, an interpersonal interaction, forms a new conception which has the previous construal (and its accompanying affective reactions) as objects of reflection.[8]

Ego psychology and a one-person versus two-person psychology

I anticipate the criticism that an ego psychology perspective, with its focus on the ego, ego functions, and "the I" reverts back to a one-person psychology and neglects the two-person perspective that has emerged during the past few decades. My responses to this anticipated criticism are as follows:

(1) Theoretical formulations should not be evaluated on the basis of the degree to which they adhere to a one-person versus a two-person perspective, but rather on the basis of how adequately they account for the phenomena under investigation.

(2) An expansion of ego psychology that recognizes the importance of relational factors and processes must include recognition of the following: the role of the object relational milieu in the development of ego functions, the interpersonal nature of defense, interpersonal factors in affect regulation, the critical importance of interpersonal and social reality-testing, including interpersonal schemas, and reflection upon the mental states of others.

(3) Many formulations associated with a so-called two-person perspective do not advance our understanding of the nature of the mind. For example, although there is little doubt that mind develops in an interactional

matrix, and that to some significant extent, internalization of interactions with significant others constitute central aspects of one's
personality, it does not follow that mind is understood only through
"the process of interpretive construction" by another (Mitchell, 1998,
p. 471) or that the adult "mind is preexisting but not preorganized" and
awaits organization through interpersonal interaction (Mitchell, 2000)
(See Eagle et al., 2001). Rather, although mind and ego states can vary
over time and situation, including interpersonal situations, the personality consists of representations and structures (e.g., internal working
models [IWM's]; interactional schemas; beliefs and expectations) that
are relatively stable and resistant to change.

Process such as embodied simulation, automatic and unconscious
imitation, unconscious priming of interpersonal cues, reflecting on the
mental states of others, empathic responses in which one is able to take
the perspective of the other, all point to a constant flow of interpersonal
interaction and mutual influence. It is not clear however, that, beyond
the consciousness of Person A and the consciousness of Person B and
their mutual influence, there is some additional entity (e.g., "the third" or
"dyadic consciousness") that is somehow created and that possesses an
ontological status. A meaningful and less obfuscating way of expressing
a two-person psychology is to view it in terms of, in Chodorow's (2004)
words, the "interaction between two individual psychologies" (p. 216).

Some summing up

As we have seen, to a significant extent, different psychoanalytic schools
emerge as a reaction to perceived relative neglect of important phenomena by existing theory. Hence, each school focuses on a particular set of
phenomena that its adherents believe have been neglected or inadequately
accounted for by existing theory. However, although addressing a limited
set of phenomena, it presents itself as a self-sufficient theory. To the extent
that a revised and expanded ego psychology provides an adequate account
of phenomena that are of primary interest to different schools, it would
seem to obviate the need for a plethora of different schools. Unlike the
more limited perspectives of different psychoanalytic schools (i.e., drive
theory, object relations theory, and self psychology), a revised ego psychology provides a superordinate theoretical perspective capable of integrating

a wide range of vital psychological phenomena of primary interest to other schools, as well as of relevant findings from non-psychoanalytic sources.

The claim that a revised ego psychology constitutes the strongest foundation for a unified psychoanalytic theory of the mind also rests on its placement of the "personal element", the "I", at the center of its theory. Whatever factors, including unconscious factors, may influence them, and whatever the nature of explanatory accounts, it is our lived subjective experiences that make one's life meaningful. And it is these lived experiences that constitute the starting point and central phenomena to be elaborated and accounted for in any psychoanalytic theory of the mind. From the perspectives of behaviorism and artificial intelligence theory, virtually everything we do could be accounted without any reference to subjective experience. Were these perspectives sufficient to account for the nature of the mind, psychoanalytic theory would essentially become irrelevant. Thus, and with some irony, despite its emphasis on unconscious processes, what makes psychoanalytic theory relevant, and perhaps indispensable, to an adequate understanding of the nature of the mind is the existence of subjective experience and the attempt to understand its vicissitudes.

Notes

1　Gedo (1989) writes that "experienced clinicians would refuse to alter their convictions on the basis of. . . [research] results. Instead, they would continues to form their psychoanalytic views in direct response to their personal experiences . . . The belief that psychoanalytic theory will make progress by validating the best hypotheses through refined scientific method is implausible" (p. 514). That Gedo intends his comments to be not only descriptive but also prescriptive is made clear when he goes on to say that "what we need are innovative ideas powerful enough to compel acceptance by significant portions of the analytic community" (p. 514). As reflected in the proliferation of psychoanalytic schools, this is precisely the current state of affairs.

2　An important factor, I believe, contributing to the reductionism is what one can refer to as the narcissism of theory-building, that is, the need to claim that one has authored a grand theory that explains virtually everything rather than limit one's claims to modest and incremental contributions.

3　Despite the importance Freud gives to interpretations tallying with what is real in the patient, as we have seen, he was hardly immune to offering interpretations to clinical material that were primarily generated by theoretical assumptions and that had the quality of being imposed on the patient. One must also keep in mind that, as noted previously, Freud (1937) shifted from this position to an emphasis on *constructions* that triggered the patient's *convictions*.

4　I am reminded of the story of a husband and wife who come to the shtetl Rabbi for counseling. The husband tells his story (his master narrative) to which the Rabbi responds, "You're right". The wife then presents her account, which contradicts the husband's account on just about every point. The Rabbi's response to her is also, "You're right". The Rabbi's assistant who hears all this, quite perturbed, turns to the Rabbi and says:

"How can you say 'You're right' to both of them? You are completely contradicting yourself". The Rabbi turns to the assistant and says: "You're right".

5 Extending the reference to " 'us' as far as we can" would seem to be equivalent to escaping, or at least, expanding, the limitation of one's community.

6 As Wakefield (personal communication) and others have noted, it is quite often the case, contra Rorty, that a comprehensive theory that is mainly the product of seeking understanding and attempting to get at the truth of things (i.e., obtaining knowledge for its own sake) and relatively unrelated to a particular pragmatic project, turns out to be remarkably pragmatic in the end.

7 There is evidence that reflective capacity is impaired under conditions of high emotional arousal (Bateman & Fonagy, 2013). Insofar as affiliation with a particular school is often associated with issues of identity and strong emotions, it becomes difficult to step back and subject the theoretical perspective of the psychoanalytic school with which one is identified to reflection.

8 As is suggested by Pine (1990), in trying to get as full a picture of the patient as possible, contemporary analysts seem to be more likely to refer to more than one theoretical approach or school in discussing clinical material (as well as theoretical issues). Despite showing relatively little interest in integration, analysts appear to be more ready to refer to different theoretical perspectives. Thus, there appear to be looser boundaries between different schools. These less rigid boundaries between different schools may suggest that the time is perhaps ripe for efforts at theoretical integration (See Pine, 2011).

References

Abercrombie, H. C., Giese-Davis, J., Sephton, S., Epel, E. S., Turner-Cobb, J. M., & Spiegel, D. (2004). Flattened cortisol rhythms in metastatic breast cancer patients. *Psychoneuroendocrinology, 29*(8), 1082–1092.

Abraham, K. (1913 [1953]). A constitutional basis of locomotor activity. In *Selected papers* (pp. 235–243). New York: Basic Books.

Adam, K. S., Sheldon-Keller, A. E., & West, M. (1996). Attachment organization and history of suicidal behavior in clinical adolescents. *Journal of Consulting and Clinical Psychology, 64*(2), 264–272.

Adams, R. E., & Passman, R. H. (1979). Effects of visual and auditory aspects of mothers and strangers on the play and exploration of children. *Developmental Psychology, 15*(3), 269–274.

Agrawal, H. R., Gunderson, J., Holmes, B. M., & Lyons-Ruth, K. (2004). Attachment studies with borderline patients: A review. *Harvard Review of Psychiatry, 12*(2), 94–104.

Ainsworth, M. D. S., Blehar, M. C., Waters, E., & Wall, S. (1978*). Patterns of attachment: A psychological study of the strange situation.* Hillsdale, NJ: Lawrence Erlbaum.

Alexander, A. A., Roessler, R., & Greenfield, N. S. (1963). Ego strength and physiological responsivity: III. The relationship of the Barron ego strength scale to spontaneous periodic activity in skin resistance, finger blood volume, heart rate, and muscle potential. *Archives of General Psychiatry, 9*(2), 142–145.

Alexander, F. G., & French, T. M. (1946*). Psychoanalytic therapy: Principles and applications.* New York: Ronald.

Allen, J. P., Uchino, B. N., & Hafen, C. A. (2015). Running with the pack: Teen peer-relationship qualities as predictors of adult physical health. *Psychological Science, 10*, 1574–1583.

Allport, G. W. (1937). *Personality: A psychological interpretation.* New York: Henry Holt & Company.

Allport, G. W. (1955). *Basic considerations for a psychology of personality.* London: Yale University Press.

Alson, L. L., Kratchmer, C., Jeznach, A., Bartlett, N. T., Davidson, P. S. R., & Fujiwara, E. (2013). Self-serving episodic memory biases: Findings in the repressive coping style. *Frontiers in Behavioral Neuroscience, 7*, 117.

Alston, W. (1977). Sentence meaning and illocutionary act potential. *Philosophic Exchange, 8*(1), Article 2.

Alvarez-Monjaras, M., McMahon, T. J., & Suchman, N. E. (2019). Does maternal reflective functioning mediate associations between representations of caregiving with maternal sensitivity in a high-risk sample? *Psychoanalytic Psychology, 36*(1), 82–92.

Alvarez-Monjaras, M., Rutherford, H. J. V., & Mayes, L. C. (2019). Personality organization and maternal addiction: A structural-developmental psychodynamic contribution. *Psychoanalytic Psychology*, *36*(4), 321–327.

Anisfeld, M. (1996). Only tongue protrusion modeling is matched by neonates. *Developmental Review*, *16*(2), 149–161.

Anisfeld, M., Masters, J. C., Jacobson, S. W., Kagan, J., Meltzoff, A. N., & Moore, M. K. (1979). Interpreting "imitative" responses in early infancy. *Science*, *205*(4402), 214–219.

Anisfeld, M., Turkewitz, J., Rose, S., Rosenberg, F. R., Sheiber, F. J., Couturier-Fagan, D. A., . . . Sommer, I. (2001). No compelling evidence that newborns imitate oral gestures. *Infancy*, *2*(1), 111–122.

Apfelbaum, B. (1966). On ego psychology: A critique of the structural approach to psychoanalytic theory. *International Journal of Psychoanalysis*, *47*, 451–475.

Appleton, A. A., Buka, S. L., McCormick, M. C., Koenen, K. C., Loucks, E. B., Gilman, S. E., & Kubzansky, L. D. (2011). Emotional functioning at age 7 years is associated with C-reactive protein in middle adulthood. *Psychosomatic Medicine*, *73*(4), 295–303.

Arlow, J. A., & Brenner, C. (1964). *Psychoanalytic concepts and the structural theory*. New York: International Universities Press.

Armstrong, K. (2018). *"I feel your pain": The neuroscience of empathy*. Retrieved from www.psychologicalscience.org/observer/i-feel-your-pain-the-neuroscience-of-empathy

Asendorpf, J. B., & Scherer, K. R. (1983). The discrepant repressor: Differentiation between low anxiety, high anxiety, and repression of anxiety by autonomic – facial – verbal patterns of behavior. *Journal of Personality and Social Psychology*, *45*(6), 1334–1346.

Avenanti, A., Bueti, D., Galati, G., & Aglioti, S. M. (2005). Transcranial magnetic stimulation highlights the sensorimotor side of empathy for pain. *Nature Neuroscience*, *8*(7), 955–960.

Ayduk, O., Mendoza-Denton, R., Mischel, W., Downey, G., Peake, P. K., & Rodriguez, M. (2000). Regulating the interpersonal self: Strategic self-regulation for coping with rejection sensitivity. *Journal of Personality and Social Psychology*, *79*(5), 776–792.

Ayduk, O., Zayas, V., Downey, G., Cole, A. B., Shoda, Y., & Mischel, W. (2008). Rejection sensitivity and executive control: Joint predictors of borderline personality features. *Journal of Research in Personality*, *42*(1), 151–168.

Bacal, H. A., & Newman, K. M. (1990). Personality, psychopathology, and psychotherapy: Theoretical and clinical perspectives. In *Theories of object relations: Bridges to self psychology*. New York: Columbia University Press.

Bach, S. (2006). Getting from here to there: Analytic love, analytic process. Hillsdale, N. J.: Analytic Press.

Bagby, R. M., Taylor, G. J., & Parker, J. D. (1988). Construct validity of the Toronto alexithymia scale. *Psychotherapy and Psychosomatics*, *50*(1), 29–34.

Bagwell, C. L., Newcomb, A. F., & Bukowski, W. M. (1998). Preadolescent friendship and peer rejection as predictors of adult adjustment. *Child Development*, *69*, 140–153.

Balint, M. P. (1937). Early developmental states of the ego. In M. Balint (Ed.), *Primary love and psychoanalytic technique* (pp. 74–90). London: Karnac Books.

Balint, M. P. (1968). *The basic fault: Therapeutic aspects of regression*. London: Tavistock.

Balint, M. P. (1960). Primary narcissism or primary love. *The Psychoanalytic Quarterly*, *29*(1), 6–43.

Bari, A., & Robbins, T. W. (2013). Inhibition and impulsivity: Behavioral and neural basis of response control. *Progress in Neurobiology*, *108*, 44–79.

Barnes, G. W., Kish, G. B., & Wood, W. O. (1959). The effect of light intensity when onset or termination of illumination is used as reinforcing stimulus. *The Psychological Record*, *9*, 53–60.

Barone, L. (2003). Developmental protective and risk factors in borderline personality disorder: A study using the adult attachment interview. *Attachment & Human Development*, *5*(1), 64–77.

Barron, F. (1953). An ego-strength scale which predicts response to psychotherapy. *Journal of Consulting Psychology*, *17*(5), 327–333.

Bastian, M. L., Sponberg, A. C., Suomi, S. J., & Higley, J. D. (2003). Long-term effects of infant rearing condition on the acquisition of dominance rank in juvenile and adult rhesus macaques (Macaca mulatta). *Developmental Psychobiology*, *42*, 44–51.

Bateman, A., & Fonagy, P. (2008). 8-year follow-up of patients treated for borderline personality disorder: Mentalization-based treatment versus treatment as usual. *American Journal of Psychiatry*, *165*(5), 631–638.

Bateman, A., & Fonagy, P. (2009). Randomized control trial of outpatient mentalization-based treatment versus structured clinical management for borderline personality disorder. *American Journal of Psychiatry*, *166*, 1355–1364.

Bateman, A., & Fonagy, P. (2013). Mentalization-based treatment. *Psychoanalytic Inquiry*, *33*(6), 595–613.

Batson, C. D., Fultz, J., & Schoenrade, P. A. (1987). Distress and empathy: Two qualitatively distinct vicarious emotions with different motivational consequences. *Journal of Personality*, *55*(1), 19–39.

Batson, C. D., O'Quin, K., Fultz, J., Vanderplas, M., & Isen, A. M. (1983). Influence of self-reported distress and empathy on egoistic versus altruistic motivation to help. *Journal of Personality and Social Psychology*, *45*(3), 706–718.

Baumeister, R. F., Brataslavsky, E., Muraven, M., & Tice, D. M. (1998). Ego depletion: Is the active self a limited resource? *Personality Processes and Individual Differences*, *74*(5), 1252–1265.

Baumeister, R. F., & Newman, L. S. (1994). How stories make sense of personal experiences: Motives that shape autobiographical narratives. *Personality and Social Psychology Bulletin*, *20*(6), 676–690.

Baumeister, R. F., & Vohs, K. D. (2007). The strength model of self control. *Current Directions in Psychological Science*, *16*(6), 351–355.

Beach, F. A. (1976). Cross-species comparisons and the human heritage. *Archives of Sexual Behavior*, *5*(5), 469–485.

Bean, C. G., Pingel, R., Hallqvist, J., Berg, N., & Hammarström, A. (2019). Poor peer relations in adolescence, social support in early adulthood, and depressive symptoms in later adulthood-evaluating mediation and interaction using four-way decomposition analysis. *Annals of Epidemiology*, *29*, 52–59.

Beckes, L., & Coan, J. A. (2011). Social baseline theory: The role of social proximity in emotion and economy of action. *Social and Personality Psychology Compass*, *5*(12), 976–988.

Bellak, L., Hurvich, M., & Gediman, H. (1973). *Ego function in schizophrenics, neurotics, normals*. New York: Wiley.

Bellak, L., & Meyers, B. (1975). Ego function assessment and analyzability. *International Journal of Psychoanalysis*, *2*, 413–427.

Belsky, J., Friedman, S. L., & Hsieh, K. H. (2003). Testing a core emotion-regulation prediction: Does early attentional persistence moderate the effect of infant negative emotionality on later development. *Child Development*, *72*, 123–133.

Benjamin, J. (1988). *The bonds of love: Psychoanalysis, feminism, & the problem of domination*. New York: Pantheon.

Berger, M. F., Philippakis, A. A., Qureshi, A. M., He, F. S., Estep, P. W., & Bulyk, M. L. (2006). Compact, universal DNA microarrays to comprehensively determine transcription-factor binding site specificities. *Nature Biotechnology, 24*(11), 1429–1435.

Bergmann, M. S. (2000). *The Hartmann era*. New York: Other Press.

Berlyne, D. E. (1950). Novelty and curiosity as determinants of exploratory behavior. *British Journal of Psychology, 41*, 68–80.

Berman, M. G., Yourganov, G., Askren, M. K., Ayduk, O., Casey, B. J., Gotlib, I. H., . . . Jonides, J. (2013). Dimensionality of brain networks linked to life-long individual differences in self-control. *Nature Communication, 4*(1373), 1–7.

Bernier, A., Carlson, S. M., & Whipple, N. (2010). From external regulation to self-regulation: Early parenting precursors of young children's executive functioning. *Child Development, 81*(1), 326–339.

Bertenthal, B. I., & Longo, M. R. (2007). Is there evidence of a mirror system from birth? *Developmental Science, 10*(5), 526–529.

Bien, N., Roebroeck, A., Goebel, R., & Sack, A. T. (2009). The brain's intention to imitate: The neurobiology of intentional versus automatic imitation. *Cerebral Cortex, 19*(10), 2338–2351.

Bion, W. R. (1962). *Learning from experience*. London: Maresfield Reprints, Karnac Books.

Bird, G., Leighton, J., Press, C., & Heyes, C. (2007). Intact automatic imitation of human and robot actions in autism spectrum disorders. *Proceedings of the Royal Society B: Biological Sciences, 274*, 3027–3031.

Bjorklund, D. F., & Kipp, K. (1996). Parental investment theory and gender differences in the evolution of inhibition mechanisms. *Psychological Bulletin, 120*(2), 163–188.

Black, M. (1967). Review of A. R. Couch's explanation and human action. *American Journal of Psychology, 80*, 655–656.

Blair, C., & Raver, C. (2012). Child development in the context of adversity: Experiential canalization of brain and behavior. *American Psychologist, 67*(4), 309–318.

Blair, C., Raver, C., Granger, D., Mills-Koonce, R., & Hibel, L. (2011). Allostasis and allostatic load in the context of poverty in early childhood. *Development and Psychopathology, 23*(3), 845–857.

Blair, R. J. R. (2008). The amygdala and ventromedial prefrontal cortex: Functional contributions and dysfunction in psychopathy. *Philosophical Transactions of the Royal Society of London: Series B, Biological Sciences, 363*(1503), 2557–2565.

Blair, R. J. R., Morris, J. S., Frith, C. D., Perrett, D. I., & Dolan, R. J. (1999). Dissociable neural responses to facial expression of sadness and anger. *Brain, 1222*, 883–893.

Block, J. H., & Block, J. (1980). The role of ego-control and ego-resiliency in the organization of behavior. In W. A. Collins (Ed.), *Development of cognition, affect, and social relations: The Minnesota symposium on child psychology* (Vol. 13). Hillsdale, NJ: Erlbaum.

Bonanno, G. A., & Singer, J. L. (1990). Repressive personality style: Theoretical and methodological implications for health and pathology. In J. L. Singer (Ed.), *Repression and dissociation* (pp. 435–470). Chicago, IL: University of Chicago Press.

Bonomi, C. (2003). Breaking the solid ground of common sense: Undoing "structure" with Michael Balint. *The American Journal of Psychoanalysis, 63*(3), 219–238.

Borelli, J. L., Compare, A., Snavely, J. E., & Decio, V. (2015). Reflective functioning moderates the association between perceptions of parental neglect and attachment in adolescence. *Psychoanalytic Psychology, 32*(1), 23–35.

Botvinick, M., & Cohen, J. (1998). Rubber hands "feel" touch that eyes see. *Nature, 391*, 756.

Bowlby, J. (1969). *Attachment and loss. Vol. 1: Attachment* (2nd ed.). New York: Basic Books.

Bowlby, J. (1973). *Attachment and loss. Vol. 2: Separation*. New York: Basic Books.

Bowlby, J. (1980). *Attachment and loss. Vol. 3: Loss, sadness and depression*. New York: Basic Books.

Bowlby, J. (1988). *A secure base: Clinical applications of attachment theory*. London: Routledge.

Bram, C. (2017, March 12). The story of O: A recollection of a relationship with Oliver Sacks and a life in New York city. *New York Times Book Reviews, 13*.

Brandt, L. W. (1966). Process or structure? *Psychoanalytic Review, 53*, 50–54.

Brenner, C. (1982). *The mind in conflict*. New York: International Universities Press.

Brenner, C. (2002). Conflict, compromise, formation, and structural theory. *Psychoanalytic Quarterly, 71*(3), 397–417.

Brentano, F. C. (1874 [1973]). *Psychologie von empirischen Standpunkt* (O. Kraus, Ed., A. C. Rancurello, D. B. Terrell, & L. L. McAlister, Trans.). Leipzig: Felix Meiner; London: Routledge.

Brethel-Haurwitz, K. M., Cardinale, E. M., Vekaria, K. M., Robertson, E. L., Walitt, B., VanMeter, J. W., & Marsh, A. A. (2018). Extraordinary altruists exhibit enhanced self-other overlap in neural responses to distress. *Psychological Science, 29*(10), 1631–1641.

Breuer, J., & Freud, S. (1893–1895 [1955]). Studies on hysteria. In *Standard edition* (Vol. 2). London: Hogarth Press.

Brody, G. H., Yu, T., Nusslock, R., Barton, A. W., Miller, G. E., Chen, E., Holmes, C., McCormick, M., & Sweet, L. H. (2019). The protective effects of supportive parenting on the relationship between adolescent poverty and resting-state functional brain connectivity during adulthood. *Psychological science, 30*(7), 1040–1049.

Brody, S., Wagner, D., Heinrichs, M., James, A., Hellhammer, D., & Ehlert, U. (2000). Social desirability scores are associated with higher morning cortisol levels in firefighters. *Journal of Psychosomatic Research, 49*, 227–228.

Bromley, A. (1957). Review of: Final contributions to the problems and methods of psychoanalysis. The selected papers of Sándor Ferenczi, M.D. Volume 3. *Psychoanalytic Quarterly, 26*, 112–114.

Broomfield, N. M., & Turpin, G. (2005). Covert and overt attention in trait anxiety: A cognitive psychophysiological analysis. *Biological Psychiatry, 68*(3), 179–200.

Brumariu, L. E., & Kerns, K. A. (2008). Mother-child attachment and social anxiety symptoms in middle childhood. *Journal of Applied Developmental Psychology, 29*(5), 393–402.

Buber, M. (1923). *I and thou* (R. G. Smith, Trans.). Edinburgh: T. & T. Clark.

Bucci, W. (2002). From subsymbolic to symbolic and back: Therapeutic impact of the referential process. In R. Lasky (Ed.), *Symbolization and desymbolization: Essays in honor of Norbert Freedman* (pp. 50–74). New York: Other Press.

Bullock, M. J., Ironsmith, M., & Poteat, G. M. (1988) Sociometric techniques with young children: A review of psychometrics and classification schemes. *School Psychology Review, 17*(2), 289–303.

Busch, F. (2009). On creating a psychoanalytic mind: Psychoanalytic knowledge as a process. *Scandanavian Psychoanalytic Review, 32*, 85–92.

Busch, F., & Joseph, B. (2004). A missing link in psychoanalytic technique: Psychoanalytic consciousness. *The International Journal of Psychoanalysis, 85*(3), 567–572.

Butler, R. A. (1957). The effect of deprivation of visual incentives on visual exploration motivation in monkeys. *Journal of Comparative and Physiological Psychology, 50*(2), 177–179.

Carlson, S. M., Davis, A. C., & Leach, J. G. (2005). Less is more: Executive function and symbolic representation in preschool children. *Psychological Science, 16*(8), 609–616.

Carlson, S. M., Moses, L. J., & Claxton, L. J. (2004). Individual differences in executive function and theory of mind: An investigation of inhibitory control and planning ability. *Journal of Experimental Child Psychology, 87*(4), 299–319.

Carlson, S. M., & Wang, T. S. (2007). Inhibitory control and emotion regulation in preschool children. *Cognitive Development, 22*(4), 489–510.

Carlson, S. M., & Zelazo, P. D. (2011). The value of control and the influence of values. *Proceedings of the National Academy of Sciences of the United States of America, 108*, 16861–16862.

Carmichael, L. (1926). The development of behavior in vertebrates experimentally removed from the influence of external stimulation. *Psychological Review, 33*(1), 51–58.

Carrera, P., Oceja, L., Caballero, A., Muñoz, D., López-Pérez, B., & Ambrona, T. (2012). I feel so sorry! Tapping the joint influence of empathy and personal distress on helping behavior. *Motivation and Emotion, 37,* 335–345.

Carruthers, O., & Smith, P. K. (Eds.). (1996). *Theories of theories of mind.* Cambridge, MA: Cambridge University Press.

Cascio, C. N., Konrath, S. H., & Falk, E. B. (2015). Narcissists' social pain seen only in the brain. *Social Cognitive and Affective Neuroscience, 10*(3), 335–341.

Casey, B., Somerville, L., Gotlib, I., Ayduk, O., Franklin, N., Askren, M., . . . Shoda, Y. (2011). Behavioral and neural correlates of delay gratification 40 years later. *Proceedings of the National Academy of Sciences of America, 108*(36), 14998–15003.

Cash, T. F., Thériault, J., & Milkewicz Annis, N. (2004). Body image in an interpersonal context: Adult attachment, fear of intimacy and social anxiety. *Journal of Social and Clinical Psychology, 23*(1), 89–103.

Caspi, A., Harrington, H., Moffitt, T. E., Milne, B. J., & Poulton, R. (2006). Socially isolated children 20 years later: Risk of cardiovascular disease. *Archives of Pediatrics & Adolescent Medicine, 160*, 805–811.

Caspi, A., & Moffitt, T. E. (2018). All for one and one for all: Mental disorders in one dimension. *American Journal of Psychiatry, 175*(9), 831–844.

Caspi, A., Moffitt, T. E., Newman, D. L., & Silva, P. A. (1996). Behavioral observations at age 3 years predict adult psychiatric disorders: Longitudinal evidence from a birth cohort. *Archives of General Psychiatry, 53*(11), 1033–1039.

Cattaneo, L., Caruana, F., Jezzini, A., & Rizzolatti, G. (2009). Representation of goal and movements without overt motor behavior in the human motor cortex: A transcranial magnetic stimulation study. *Journal of Neuroscience, 29*(36), 11134–11138.

Cerqueira, J. J., Mailliet, F., Almeida, O. F., Jay, T. M., & Sousa, N. (2007). The prefrontal cortex as a key target of the maladaptive response to stress. *Journal of Neuroscience, 27*, 2781–2787.

Chen, X., Striano, T., & Rakoczy, H. (2004). Auditory-oral matching behavior in newborns. *Developmental Science, 7*(1), 42–47.

Chen, Y., Kubzansky, L. D., & VanderWeele, T. J. (2019). Parental warmth and flourishing mid-life. *Social Science and Medicine, 220,* 65–72.

Chester, D. S., Lynam, D. R., Powell, D. K., & DeWall, C. N. (2016). Narcissism is associated with weakened frontostriatal connectivity: A DTI study. *Social Cognitive and Affective Neuroscience, 11*(7), 1036–1040.

Chodorow, N. (2004). The American independent tradition: Loewald, Erikson, and the (possible) rise of intersubjective ego psychology. *Psychoanalytic Dialogues, 14,* 207–232.

Cicchetti, D., & Rogosch, F. (2001). The impact of child maltreatment and psychopathology on neuroendocrine functioning. *Development and Psychopathology, 13*(4), 783–804.

Ciechanowski, P. S., Katon, W. J., Russo, J. E., & Walker, E. A. (2001). The patient-provider relationship: attachment theory and adherence to treatment in diabetes. *The American Journal of Psychiatry, 158*(1), 29–35.

Ciechanowski, P. S., Walker, E. A., Katon, W. J., & Russo, J. E. (2002). Attachment theory: A model for health care utilization and somatization. *Psychosomatic Medicine, 64*(4), 660–667.

Clifton, A., Pilkonis, P. A., & McCarty, C. (2007). Social network in borderline personality disorder. *Journal of Personality Disorders, 21*(4), 434–441.

Coan, J. A. (2008). Toward a neuroscience of attachment. In J. Cassidy & P. R. Shaver (Eds.), *Handbook of attachment: Theory, research, and clinical applications* (2nd ed., pp. 241–265). New York: Guilford Press.

Coan, J. A. (2010). Adult attachment and the brain. *Journal of Social and Personal Relationships, 27*(2), 210–217.

Codd, J., & Myers, L. B. (2009). *A study of coping style and ethnic differences in ratings of self and personal risk* (PhD thesis). Brunel University, London.

Cohen, E. A. (1953). *Human behavior in the concentration camp* (M. H. Braaksma, Trans.). New York: Grosset & Dunlap.

Coifman, K. G., Bonanno, G. A., Ray, R. D., & Gross, J. J. (2007). Does repressive coping promote resilience? Affective-autonomic response discrepancy during bereavement. *Journal of Personality and Social Psychology, 92*(4), 745–758.

Conway, C. C., Raposa, E. B., Hammen, C., & Brennan, P. A. (2018). Transdiagnostic pathways from early social stress to psychopathology: A 20-year prospective study. *Journal of Child Psychology and Psychiatry, 59*(8), 855–862.

Cooke, L., Myers, L. B., & Derakshan, N. (2003). Lung function, adherence and denial in asthma patients who exhibit a repressive coping style. *Psychology, Health, & Medicine, 8*(1), 35–44.

Cooper, A. M. (2008). American psychoanalysis today: A plurality of orthodoxies. *Journal of the American Academy of Psychoanalysis & Dynamic Psychiatry, 36*(2), 235–253.

Costello, E. J., Mustillo, S., Alaattin, E., Keeler, G., & Angold, A. (2003). Prevalence and development of psychiatric disorders in childhood and adolescence. *Archives of General Psychiatry, 60*(8), 837–844.

Cousineau, T. M., & Shedler, J. (2006). Predicting physical health: Implicit mental health measures versus self-report scales. *Journal of Nervous and Mental Disease, 194*(6), 427–432.

Craighero, L., Fadiga, L., Umilta, C. A., & Rizzolatti, G. (1996). Evidence for visuomotor priming effect. *Neuroreport, 8,* 347–349.

Cramer, P. (2001). The unconscious status of defense mechanisms. *American Psychologist, 56*(9), 762–763.

Cramer, P. (2006). *Protecting the self: Defense mechanisms in action.* New York: Guilford Publications.

Cramer, P. (2008). Seven pillars of defense mechanism theory. *Social and Personality Psychology Compass, 2,* 1963–1981.

Cramer, P. (2012). *The development of defense mechanisms: Theory, research, and assessment.* New York: Springer.

Crowell, J., Treboux, D., Gao, Y., Fyffe, C., Pan, H., & Waters, E. (2002). Assessing secure base behavior in adulthood: Development of a measure, links to adult attachment representations, and relations to couples' communication and reports of relationships. *Developmental psychology, 38,* 679–693.

Crowne, D. P., & Marlowe, D. (1964). *The approval motive: Studies in evaluative dependence.* New York: Wiley.

Crusco, A. H., & Wetzel, C. G. (1984). The Midas touch: The effects of interpersonal touch on restaurant tipping. *Personality and Social Psychology Bulletin, 10*(4), 512–517.

Cundiff, J. M., & Matthews, K. A. (2018). Friends with health benefits: The long-term benefits of early peer social integration for blood pressure and obesity in midlife. *Psychological Science, 29*(5), 814–823.

Cutler, S. E., Larsen, R. J., & Bunce, S. C. (1996). A naturalistic study of daily affect. *Journal of Personality, 64*(2), 379–405.

Damasio, A. (2003). *Looking for Spinoza: Joy, sorrow, and the feeling brain.* New York: Harcourt Books.

Damasio, A. (2018). *The strange order of things: Life, feeling, and the making of cultures.* New York: Pantheon Books.

Dapretto, M., Davies, M. S., Pfeifer, J. H., Scott, A. A., Sigman, M., Bookheimer, S. Y., & Iacoboni, M. (2006). Understanding emotions in others: Mirror neuron dysfunction in children with autism spectrum disorders. *Nature Neuroscience, 9*(1), 28–30.

Darwin, C. (1872 [1965]). *The expression of the emotions in man and animals.* Chicago, IL: University of Chicago.

Davidson, R. J., & Sutton, S. K. (1995). Affective neuroscience: The emergence of a discipline. *Current Opinion in Neurobiology, 5*(2), 217–224.

Davidson, R. J. (1983). Hemispheric asymmetry and emotion. In R. J. Davidson & P. Ekman (Eds.), *Questions about emotions* (pp. 39–57). Cambridge, MA: MIT Press.

Davis, K. L., & Panskepp, J. (2018). *The emotional foundations of personality: A neurological and biological approach.* New York: W. W. Norton.

Davis, P. J. (1990). Repression and the inaccessibility of emotional memories. In J. L. Singer (Ed.), *Repression and dissociation* (pp. 387–404). Chicago: University of Chicago Press.

Davis, P. J., & Schwartz, G. E. (1986). Repression and the inaccessibility of affective memories. *Journal of Personality and Social Psychology, 52,* 155–162.

Davison, W., Pray, M., & Bristol, C. (1990). Mutative interpretation and close psychoanalytic monitoring. *Psychoanalytic Quarterly, 59,* 599–628.

Decety, J. (2011). Dissecting the neural mechanisms mediating empathy. *Emotion Review, 3,* 92–108.

Decety, J., & Lamm, C. (2009). Empathy versus personal distress: Recent evidence from social neuroscience. In J. Decety & W. Ickes (Eds.), *Social neuroscience: The social neuroscience of empathy* (pp. 199–213). Cambridge, MA: MIT Press.

Dennett, D. (1987). *The intentional stance.* Cambridge, MA: MIT Press.

Denollet, J., Schiffer, A. A., Kwaijtaal, M., Hooijkaas, H., Hendriks, E. H., Widdershoven, J. W., & Kupper, N. (2008). Usefulness of type D personality and kidney dysfunction as predictors of interpatient variability in inflammatory activation in chronic heart failure. *The American Journal of Cardiology, 103*(3), 399–404.

DePrince, A., Weinzierl, K. M., & Combs, M. D. (2009). Executive function performance and trauma exposure in a community sample of children. *Child Abuse and Neglect, 33,* 353–361.

Derakshan, N., & Eysenck, M. W. (1997). Interpretive biases for one's own behavior and physiology in high-trait-anxious individuals and repressors. *Journal of Personality and Social Psychology, 73*(4), 816–825.

Derakshan, N., Eysenck, M. W., & Myers, L. B. (2007). Emotional information processing in repressors: The vigilance–avoidance theory. *Cognition and Emotion, 21*(8), 1585–1614.

Descartes, R. (1649 [1989]). *The passions of the soul* (S. H. Voss, Trans.). Indianapolis, IN: Hackett Publishing.

Deutsch, H. (1929). The genesis of agoraphobia. *International Journal of Psychoanalysis, 10*, 51–69.

Diamond, L. M., Hicks, A. M., & Otter-Henderson, K. (2006). Physiological evidence for repressive coping among avoidantly attached adults. *Journal of Social and Personal Relationships, 23*, 205–229.

Di Cesare, G., Errante, A., Marchi, M., & Cuccio, V. (2017). Language for action: Motor resonance during the processing of human and robotic voices. *Brain Cognition, 118*, 118–127.

Dimberg, U., Thunberg, M., & Elmehed, K. (2000). Unconscious facial reactions to emotional facial expressions. *Psychological Science, 11*(1), 86–89.

Dimburg, U. (1982). Facial reactions to facial expressions. *Psychophysiology, 19*(6), 643–647.

Dimburg, U., & Thunberg, M. (1998). Rapid facial reactions to emotional facial expressions. *Scandinavian Journal of Psychology, 39*(1), 39–45.

Dodge, K. A., Price, J. M., Bachorowski, J. A., & Newman, J. P. (1990). Hostile attributional biases in severely aggressive adolescents. *Journal of Abnormal Psychology, 99*(4), 385–392.

Doebel, S., & Munakata, Y. (2018). Group influences on engaging self-control: Children delay gratification and value it more when their in-group delays and their out-group doesn't. *Psychological Science, 29*(5), 738–748.

Doidge, N., Simon, B., Brauer, L., Grant, D. C., First, M., Brunshaw, J., . . . Mosher, P. (2002). Psychoanalytic patients in the U.S., CANADA, and Australia: I. DSM-III-R disorders, indications, previous treatment, medications, and length of treatment. *Journal of the American Psychoanalytic Association, 50*(2), 575–614.

Dombrovski, A. Y., Clark, L., Siegle, G. J., Butters, M. A., Ichikawa, N., Sahakian, B. J., & Szano, K. (2010). Reward/punishment reversal learning in older suicide attempters. *American Journal of Psychiatry, 167*, 699–707.

Donahue, J. J., Goranson, A. C., McClure, K. S., & Van Male, L. M. (2014). Emotion dysregulation, negative affect, and aggression: A moderated, multiple mediator analysis. *Personality and Individual Differences, 70*, 23–28.

Eagle, M. N. (1980). A critical examination of motivational explanation in psychoanalysis. *Psychoanalysis and Contemporary Thought, 3*, 329–380.

Eagle, M. N. (1981). Interests as object relations. *Psychoanalysis and Contemporary Thought, 4*, 527–565.

Eagle, M. N. (1984). *Recent developments in psychoanalysis: A critical examination*. New York: McGraw-Hill.

Eagle, M. N. (1985). Benjamin B. Rubinstein: Contributions to the structure of psychoanalytic theory. In J. Reppen (Ed.), *Beyond Freud: A study of modern psychoanalytic theorists* (pp. 83–108). Hillsdale, NJ: Analytic Press.

Eagle, M. N. (1986). Psychoanalysis a hermeneutics. *Behavioral and Brain Sciences, 9*(2), 231–232.

Eagle, M. N. (1998). Freud's legacy: Defenses, somatic symptoms, and neurophysiology. In G. Guttman & I. Stolz-Strasser (Eds.), *Freud and the neurosciences* (pp. 87–101). Vienna: Verlag der Osterreichischen Akademie der Wissenschaften, Austrian Academy of Sciences Press.

Eagle, M. N. (2000). Repression (parts I). *Psychoanalytic Review, 87*(1), 161–187.

Eagle, M. N. (2002). Removal and removal style: Research on a psychoanalytic concept. *Review of Psychology, 2*, 29–37.

Eagle, M. N. (2009, March). *Agoraphobia: A case study*. Franz Alexander lecture presented to the New Center for Psychoanalysis, Los Angeles, CA.

Eagle, M. N. (2011). *From classical to contemporary psychoanalysis: A critique and integration*. New York: Routledge.

Eagle, M. N. (2012). Theories of motivation. In O. Gabbard, B. E. Litowitz, & P. Williams (Eds.), *Textbook of psychoanalysis* (2nd ed., pp. 39–52). Washington, DC: American Psychiatric Publishing.

Eagle, M. N. (2013). *Attachment and psychoanalysis: Theory, research, and clinical implications*. New York: Guilford Press.

Eagle, M. N. (2017). Inner conflict in Fairbairn's theory. In C. Christian, M. N. Eagle, & D. L. Wolitzky (Eds.), *Psychoanalytic perspectives on conflict*. New York: Routledge.

Eagle, M. N. (2018a). *Core concepts in classical psychoanalysis: Clinical, research evidence, and conceptual critiques*. New York: Routledge.

Eagle, M. N. (2018b). *Core concepts in contemporary psychoanalysis: Clinical, research evidence, and conceptual critiques*. New York: Routledge.

Eagle, M. N. (unpublished manuscript). *Why do we need objects?*

Eagle, M. N., Bowling, L., & Klein, G. S. (1966). Fragmentation phenomena in luminous designs. *Perceptual and Motor Skills, 23*, 143–152.

Eagle, M. N., & Hill, L. A. (1969). Do disappearance patterns in low illumination constitute a perceptual phenomenon or a response artifact? *Nature, 224*, 282.

Eagle, M. N., & Wolitzky, D. L. (1989). The idea of process in psychoanalysis. *Psychoanalysis and Contemporary Thought, 12*, 27–72.

Eagle, M. N., Wolitzky, D. L., & Wakefield, J. C. (2001). The analyst's knowledge and authority: A critique of the "new view" in psychoanalysis. *Journal of the American Psychoanalytic Association, 49*(2), 457–489.

Eagle, R. (2007). *Help him make you smile: The development of intersubjectivity in the atypical child*. Lanham, MD: Rowman & Littlefield.

Edelson, M. (1985). *Hypothesis and evidence in psychoanalysis*. Chicago, IL: University of Chicago Press.

Edelstein, R. S., & Gillath, O. (2007). Avoiding interference: Adult attachment and emotional processing bias. *Personality and Social Psychology Bulletin, 34*, 171–181.

Edward, J. (2003). The loving side of the sibling bond: A force for growth or conflict. *Issues in Psychoanalytic Psychology, 25*(2), 27–43.

Ehrenzweig, A. (1967). *The hidden order of art: A study in the psychology of artistic imagination*. Sacramento, CA: University of California Press.

Eigsti, I. M., Zayas, V., Mischel, W., Shoda, Y., Ayduk, O., Dadlani, M. B., . . . Casey, B. J. (2006). Predicting cognitive control from preschool to late adolescence and young adulthood. *Psychological Science, 17*(6), 478–484.

Eisenberg, N., & Fabes, R. A. (1990). Empathy: Conceptualization, measurement, and relation to prosocial behavior. *Motivation and Emotions, 14*, 131–149.

Eisenberg, N., & Okun, M. A. (1996). The relations of dispositional regulation and emotionality to elders' empathy-related responding and affect while volunteering. *Journal of Personality, 64*, 157–183.

Eisenberg, N., Valiente, C., Fabes, R. A., Smith, C. L., Reiser, M., Shepard, S. A., . . . Cumberland, A. J. (2003). The relations of effortful control and ego control to children's resiliency and social functioning. *Developmental Psychology, 39*, 761–776.

Eissler, K. R. (1950). The Chicago institute of psychoanalysis and the sixth period of development of psychoanalytic technique. *Journal of General Psychology, 42,* 103–157.

Eissler, K. R. (1953). The effect of the structure of the ego on psychoanalytic technique. *Journal of the American Psychoanalytic Association, 1,* 104–143.

Ekman, P. (1984). Expression and the nature of emotion. In K. Scherer & P. Ekman (Eds.), *Approaches to emotion* (pp. 319–343). Hillsdale, NJ: Lawrence Erlbaum.

Ekman, P. (1992). Facial expressions of emotion: New findings, new questions. *Psychological Science, 3*(1), 34–38.

Ekman, P., Levenson, R. W., & Friesen, W. V. (1983). Autonomic nervous system activity distinguishes among emotions. *Science, 221*(4616), 1208–1210.

Eng, W., Heimberg, R., Hart, T., Schneier, F., & Liebowitz, M. (2002). Attachment in individuals with social anxiety disorder: The relationship among adult attachment styles, social anxiety, and depression. *Emotion, 1,* 365–380.

Epstein, S. (1994). Integration of the cognitive and psychodynamic unconscious. *American Psychologist, 49,* 709–724.

Erdelyi, M. (2006). The unified theory of repression. *Behavioral and Brain Sciences, 29,* 449–451.

Esterling, B. A., Antoni, M. H., Kumar, M., & Schneiderman, N. (1990). Emotional repression, stress disclosure responses, and Epstein-Barr viral capsid antigen titers. *Psychosomatic Medicine, 52,* 397–410.

Evans, J. St. B. T., & Stanovich, K. E. (2013). Dual-process theories of higher cognition: Advancing the debate. *Perspectives on Psychological Science, 8*(3), 223–241.

Eysenck, M. W., & Derakshan, N. (1999). Self-Reported and other-rated trait anxiety and defensiveness in repressor, low-anxious, high-anxious, and defensive high-anxious groups. *Anxiety, Stress & Coping, 12*(2), 127–144.

Fairbairn, W. R. D. (1952). *Psychological studies of the personality.* London: Tavistock, Routledge & Kegan Paul.

Fan, Y. T., Decety, J., Yang, C. Y., Liu, J. -L., & Cheng, Y. (2010). Unbroken mirror neurons in autism spectrum disorder. *The Journal of Child Psychology and Psychiatry, 51*(9), 981–988.

Fan, Y. T., Wonneberger, C., Enzi, B., de Greck, M., Ulrich, C., Tempelmann, C., . . . Northoff, G. (2011). The narcissistic self and its psychological and neural correlates: An exploratory fMRI study. *Psychological Medicine, 41*(8), 1641–1650.

Farber, L. (1966). *The ways of the will.* New York: Harper & Row.

Fast, I. (1990). Self and ego: A framework for their integration. *Psychoanalytic Inquiry, 10*(2), 141–162.

Feeney, B., & Kirkpatrick, L. (1996). Effects of adult attachment and presence of romantic partners on physiological responses to stress. *Journal of Personality and Social Psychology, 70,* 255–270.

Feng, C., Yuan, J., Geng, H., Gu, R., Zhou, H., Wu, X., & Luo, Y. (2018). Individualized prediction of trait narcissism from whole-brain resting-state functional connectivity. *Human Brain Mapping, 39*(9), 3701–3712.

Fenichel, O. (1945). *The psychoanalytic theory of neurosis.* New York: W. W. Norton.

Ferenczi, S. (1932 [1988]). *The clinical diary* (J. Dupont, Ed.). Cambridge, MA: Harvard University Press.

Ferenczi, S., & Rank, O. (1924 [1956]). *The development of psychoanalysis.* New York: Dover.

Ferrer, E., & Helm, J. L. (2013). Dynamical systems modeling of physiological coregulation in dyadic interactions. *International Journal of Psychophysiology, 88*(3), 296–308.

Ferrier, D. (1876). *The functions of the brain*. New York: G. P. Putnam's Sons.

Ferro, A. (2006). Clinical implications of Bion's thought. *International Journal of Psychoanalysis, 87*(4), 989–1003.

Field, T. (2001). *Touch*. Cambridge, MA: MIT Press.

Field, T. M., Diego, M., & Hernandez-Reif, M. (2010). Preterm infant massage therapy research: A review. *Infant Behavior & Development, 33*(2), 115–124.

Field, T. M., Woodson, R., Greenberg, R., & Cohen, D. (1982). Discrimination and imitation of facial expressions by neonates. *Science, 218*, 179–181.

Fingarette, H. (1963). *The self in transformation: Psychoanalysis, philosophy and the life of the spirit*. New York: Harper & Row.

Fodor, J. A. (1983). *The modularity of mind: An essay on faculty psychology*. Cambridge, MA: MIT Press.

Fonagy, P., & Bateman, A. W. (2006). Mechanisms of change in mentalization therapy of borderline personality disorder. *Journal of Clinical Psychology, 62*(4), 411–430.

Fonagy, P., & Bateman, A. W. (2008). The development of borderline personality disorder – a mentalizing model. *Journal of Personality Disorders, 22*, 4–21.

Fonagy, P., Gergely, G., Jurist, E., & Target, M. (2002). *Affect regulation, mentalization, and the development of the self*. New York: Other Self.

Fonagy, P., Leigh, T., Steele, M., Steele, H., Kennedy, R., Mattoon, G., . . . Gerber, A. (1996). The relation of attachment status, psychiatric classification, and response to psychotherapy. *Journal of Consulting and Clinical Psychology, 64*, 22–31.

Fonagy, P., Steele, H., & Steele, M. (1991). Maternal representations of attachment during pregnancy predict the organization of infant-mother attachment at one year of age. *Child Development, 62*, 891–905.

Fonagy, P., Steele, M., Steele, H., Leigh, T., Kennedy, R., & Mattoon, G. (1995). Attachment, the reflective self, and borderline states: The predictive specificity of the adult attachment interview and pathological emotional development. In S. Goldberg, R. Muir, & J. Kerr (Eds.), *Attachment theory: Social, developmental and clinical perspectives* (pp. 223–279). Hillsdale, NJ: Analytic Press.

Fonagy, P., & Target, M. (2008). Attachment, trauma, and psychoanalysis: Where psychoanalysis meets neuroscience. In E. L. Jurist, A. Slade, & S. Bergner (Eds.), *Mind to mind: Infant research, neuroscience, and psychoanalysis* (pp. 15–49). New York: Other Press.

Fosshage, J. (2017) Emergence of conflict during the development of the self: A relational self psychological perspective. In C. Christian, M. N. Eagle, & D. L. Wolitzky (Eds.), *Conflict and psychoanalysis*. New York: Routledge.

Foxhall, M., Hamilton-Giachritsis, C., & Button, K. (2019). The link between rejection sensitivity and borderline personality disorder: A systematic review and meta-analysis. *The British Journal of Clinical Psychology, 58*(3), 289–326.

Franchi, S. (2011). Radical constructivism's tathandlung, structure, and geist. *Constructivist Foundations, 7*(1), 17–20.

Frank, J. D. (1981). Therapeutic compnents shared by all psychotherapies. In J. H. Harvey & M. M. Parks (Eds.), *Psychotherapy research and behavioral change* (pp. 9–37). Washington, DC: American Psychological Association.

Frankfurt, H. G. (1971). Freedom of the will and the concept of a person. *Journal of Philosophy, 68*(1), 5–20.

Frankl, V. (1959). *Man's search for meaning: An introduction to logotherapy* (I. Lasch, Trans.). Boston: Beacon Press.

Frasure-Smith, N., Lesperance, F., Gravel, G., Masson, A., Juneau, M., & Bourassa, M. G. (2002). Long-term survival differences among low-anxious, high-anxious, and repressive copers enrolled in the Montreal heart attack readjustment trial. *Psychosomatic Medicine, 64,* 571–579.

Freud, A. (1936). *The ego and the mechanisms of defense.* London: Hogarth Press.

Freud, A. (1945). Indications for child analysis. *The Psychoanalytic Study of the Child, 1*(1), 127–149.

Freud, A. (1954). The widening scope of indications for psychoanalysis discussion. *Journal of the American Psychoanalytic Association, 2*(4), 607–620.

Freud, A. (1960). Discussion of Dr. John Bowlby's paper. *Psychoanalytic Study of the Child, 15,* 53–62.

Freud, A., & Dann, S. (1951). An experiment in group upbringing. *The Psychoanalytic Study of the Child, 6,* 127–168.

Freud, S. (1893 [1962]). On the psychical mechanisms of hysterical phenomena. In *Standard edition* (Vol. 3, pp. 25–39). London: Hogarth Press.

Freud, S. (1893 [1888–1893]). Some points for a comparative study of organic and hysterical motor paralysis. In *Standard edition* (Vol. 1, pp. 157–172). London: Hogarth Press.

Freud, S. (1893–1895). Studies on hysteria. In *Standard edition* (Vol. 2). London: Hogarth Press.

Freud, S. (1894). The neuro-psychoses of defense. In *Standard edition* (Vol. 3, pp. 45–61). London: Hogarth Press.

Freud, S. (1895). Project for a scientific psychology. In *Standard edition* (Vol. 1, pp. 295–397). London: Hogarth Press.

Freud, S. (1896, April). The aetiology of hysteria. *21,* 251–282.

Freud, S. (1887–1902). *The origins of psychoanalysis.* New York: Basic Books, 1954.

Freud, S. (1900 [1953]). The interpretation of dreams. In *Standard edition* (Vol. 4–5). London: Hogarth Press.

Freud, S. (1901). Fragment of an analysis of a case of hysteria. In *Standard edition* (Vol. 7, pp. 3–122). London: Hogarth Press.

Freud, S. (1905). Three essays on the theory of sexuality. In *Standard edition* (Vol. 7, pp. 123–245). London: Hogarth Press, 1953.

Freud, S. (1907 [1906]). Delusions and dreams in Jensen's "Gradiva". In *Standard edition* (Vol. 9, pp. 3–95). London: Hogarth Press, 1959.

Freud, S. (1911 [1958]). Psychoanalytic notes on an autobiographical account of a case of paranoia (Dementia Paranoides). In *Standard edition* (Vol. 12, pp. 3–82). London: Hogarth Press.

Freud, S. (1912 [1957]). On the universal tendency to debasement in the sphere of love (Contributions to the psychology of love II). In *Standard edition* (Vol. 11, pp. 177–190). London: Hogarth Press.

Freud, S. (1914 [1957]). On narcissism: An introduction. In *Standard edition* (Vol. 14, pp. 67–102). London: Hogarth Press.

Freud, S. (1915a). The unconscious. In *Standard edition* (Vol. 14, pp. 159–225). London: Hogarth Press.

Freud, S. (1915b). Instincts and their vicissitudes. In *Standard edition* (Vol. 14, pp. 117–140). London: Hogarth Press.

Freud, S. (1916–1917). Introductory lectures on psycho-analysis. *In Standard edition* (Vol. 15–16, pp. 1–482). London: Hogarth Press.

Freud, S. (1920). Beyond the pleasure principle. In *Standard edition* (Vol. 18, pp. 3–643). London: Hogarth Press.

Freud, S. (1921). Group psychology and the analysis of the ego. In *Standard edition* (Vol. 18, pp. 67–143). London: Hogarth Press.

Freud, S. (1922). Neurotic mechanisms in jealousy, paranoia and homosexuality. In *Standard edition* (Vol. 18, pp. 223–232). London: Hogarth Press.

Freud, S. (1923 [1961]). The ego and the id. In *Standard edition* (Vol. 19, pp. 12–66). London: Hogarth Press.

Freud, S. (1924 [1961]). The economic problem of masochism. In *Standard edition* (Vol. 19, pp. 155–170). London: Hogarth Press.

Freud, S. (1925 [1961]). Some additional notes on dream interpretation as a whole. In *Standard edition* (Vol. 18, pp. 125–138). London: Hogarth Press.

Freud, S. (1926 [1925]). Inhibitions, symptoms, and anxiety. In *Standard edition* (Vol. 20, pp. 77–174). London: Hogarth Press.

Freud, S. (1926b). The question of lay analysis. In *Standard edition* (Vol. 20, pp. 183–258). London: Hogarth Press.

Freud, S. (1927 [1930]). Civilization and its discontents. In *Standard edition* (Vol. 21, pp. 59–145). London: Hogarth Press.

Freud, S. (1932). The acquisition of power over fire. *International Journal of Psycho-Analysis, 13*, 405–410.

Freud, S. (1933 [1964]). New introductory lectures on psychoanalysis. In *Standard edition* (Vol. 22, pp. 3–182). London: Hogarth Press.

Freud, S. (1935). The subtleties of a faulty action. In *Standard edition* (Vol. 22, pp. 231–236). London: Hogarth Press.

Freud, S. (1937 [1964]). Constructions in analysis. In *Standard edition* (Vol. 23, pp. 255–269). London: Hogarth Press.

Freud, S. (1940 [1938]). An outline of psychoanalysis. In *Standard edition* (Vol. 23, pp. 139–207). London: Hogarth Press.

Freud, S. (1950 [1895]). Project for a scientific psychology. In *Standard edition* (Vol. 1, pp. 295–391). London: Hogarth Press.

Friedman, L. (1989). Hartmann's "ego psychology" and the problem of adaptation. *Psychoanalytic Quarterly, 58*, 526–550.

Friedman, L. (2005). Is there a special psychoanalytic love? *Journal of the American Psychoanalytic Association, 53*, 349–375.

Frith, C., & Frith, U. (1999). Interacting minds: A biological basis. *Science, 286*(5445), 1692–1695.

Fujiwara, E., Levine, B., & Anderson, A. K. (2008). Intact implicit and reduced explicit memory for negative self-related information in repressive coping. *Cognitive, Affective, & Behavioral Neuroscience, 8*, 254–263.

Funder, D. C., & Block, J. (1989). The role of ego-control, ego-resiliency, and IQ in delay of gratification in adolescence. *Journal of Personality and Social Psychology, 57*(6), 1041–1050.

Gabbard, G. O. (1995). Countertransference: The emerging common ground. *International Journal of Psychoanalysis, 76*, 745–485.

Gabbard, G. O., & Horowitz, M. J. (2009). Insight, transference interpretation, and therapeutic change in the dynamic psychotherapy of borderline personality disorder. *American Journal of Psychiatry, 166*(5), 517–521.

Geraerts, E., Merckelbach, H., Jelicic, M., & Smeets, E. (2006). Long term consequences of suppression of intrusive anxious thoughts and repressive coping. *Behaviour Research and Therapy, 44*(10), 1451–1460.

Gallagher, S. (2008). Direct perception in the intersubjective context. *Consciousness and Cognition, 17*(2), 535–543.

Gallese, V. (2003). The manifold nature of interpersonal relations: The quest for a common mechanism. *Philosophical Transactions of the Royal Society of London, Series B, Biological Science, 358*(1431), 517–528.

Gallese, V. (2006). Intentional attunement: A neurophysiological perspective on social cognition and its disruption in autism. *Brain Research, 1079,* 15–24.

Gallese, V. (2009). Mirror neurons, embodied simulation, and the neural basis of social identification. *Psychoanalytic Dialogues, 19*(5), 519–536.

Gallese, V., Fadiga, L., Fogassi, L., & Rizzolatti, G. (1996). Action recognition in the premotor cortex. *Brain, 119*(2), 593–609.

Gedo, J. (1983). *Portraits of the artist: Psychoanalysis of creativity and its vicissitudes.* New York: Guilford Press.

Geha, R. E. (1984). On psychoanalytic history and the "real" story of fictitious lives. *International Forum for Psychoanalysis, 1,* 221–229.

Geller, J. D., & Farber, B. A. (1993). Factors influencing the process of internalization in psychotherapy. *Psychotherapy Research, 3*(3), 166–180.

Giess-Davis, J., Sephton, S. E., Abercrombie, H. C., Durán, R. E. F., & Spiegel, D. (20Repression and high anxiety are associated with aberrant diurnal cortisol rhythms in women with metastatic breast cancer. *Health Psychology, 23*(6), 645–650.

Gill, M. M. (1982). *Analysis of transference: Volume 1: Theory and technique.* New York: International Universities Press.

Gill, M. M. (1994). *Psychoanalysis in transition.* Hillsdale, NJ: The Analytic Press.

Gill, M. M. (1976c). Metapsychology is not psychology. In M. M. Gill & P. S. Holzman (Eds.), *Psychology vs. metapsychology: Psychoanalytic essays in memory of George S. Klein, psychological issues* (Monograph No. 36, pp. 71–105). New York: International Universities Press.

Gill, M. M., & Hoffman, I. Z. (1982). A method for studying the analysis of aspects of the patient's experience of the relationship in psychoanalysis and psychotherapy. *Journal of the American Psychoanalytic Association, 30,* 137–167.

Gillath, O., Shaver, P. R., & Mikulincer, M. (2005). An attachment-theoretical approach to compassion and altruism. In P. Gilbert (Ed.), *Compassion: It's nature and use in psychotherapy* (pp. 121–147). London: Brunner-Routledge.

Gillick, R. A., & Bone, S. (Eds.). (1990). *Pleasure beyond the pleasure principle.* New Haven, CT: Yale University Press.

Ginzburg, K., Solomon, Z., & Bleich, A. (2002). Repressive coping style, acute stress disorder, and posttraumatic stress disorder after myocardial infarction. *Psychosomatic Medicine, 64*(5), 748–757.

Glover, E. (1931). The therapeutic effect of inexact interpretation: A contribution to the theory of suggestion. *The International Journal of Psychoanalysis, 12,* 397–411.

Goldfarb, W. (1945). Psychological privation in infancy and subsequent adjustment. *American Journal of Orthopsychiatry, 15*(2), 247–255.

Goldin, P. R., McRae, K., Ramel, W., & Gross, J. J. (2008). The neural bases of emotion regulation: reappraisal and suppression of negative emotion. *Biological Psychiatry, 63*(6), 577–586.

Goldman, A. E. (1953). Studies in vicariousness: Degree of motor activity and the autokinetic phenomenon. *The American Journal of Psychology, 66*(4), 613–617.

Goldstein, K. (1959). Abnormal mental conditions in infancy. *Journal of Nervous and Mental Diseases, 128*(6), 538–557.

Goodkind, M., Eickhoff, S. B., Oathes, D. J., Jiang, Y., Chang, A., Jones-Hagata, L. B., . . . Etkin, A. (2015). Identification of a common neurobiological substrate for mental illness. *JAMA Psychiatry, 72*(4), 305–315.

Gordon, R. M., & Cruz, J. (2004). Simulation theory. In *The encyclopedia of cognitive science* (Vol. 4, pp. 9–14). London: The Nature Publishing Group Macmillan Reference Ltd.

Gorrese, A. (2016). Peer attachment and youth internalizing problems: A meta-analysis. *Child & Youth Care Forum, 45*(2), 177–204.

Grafton, S. T., Arbib, M. A., Fadiga, L., & Rizzolatti, G. (1996). Localization of grasp representation in humans by positron emission tomography. *Experimental Brain Research, 112*, 103–111.

Grandin, T. (1992). An inside view of autism. In E. Schopler & G. B. Mesibov (Eds.), *Higher functional individuals with autism: Current issues in autism.* Boston, MA: Springer.

Grandin, T. (1995). How people with autism think. In E. Schopler & G. B. Mesibov (Eds.), *Learning and cognition in autism: Current issues in autism.* Boston, MA: Springer.

Gray, P. (1994). *The ego and the analysis of defense.* New York: Jason Aronson.

Green, A. (1992). A propos de l'observer des bebes: Interview per P. Geissman. *Journal de Psychoanalyse de l'Infant, 12*, 133–153.

Green, A. (2000). Science and science fiction in infant research. In J. Sandler, A. M. Sandler, & R. Davies (Eds.), *Psychoanalytic monographs no. 5. Clinical and observational psychoanalytic research: Roots of a controversy* (pp. 41–72). New York: International Universities Press.

Green, J. D., Sedikides, C., Gregg, A. P. (2008). Forgotten but not gone: The recall and recognition of self-threatening memories. *Journal of Experimental Social Psychology, 44*(3), 547–561.

Greenberg, J. R. (2001). The analyst's participation: A new look. *Journal of the American Psychoanalytic Association, 49*(2), 359–381.

Greenberg, J. R., & Mitchell, S. A. (1983). *Object relations theory in psychoanalysis.* New York: Basic Books.

Greenfield, N. S., Katz, D., Alexander, A. A., & Roessler, R. (1963). The relationship between physiological and psychological responsivity: Depression and galvanic skin response. *Journal of Nervous and Mental Disease, 136*(6), 535–539.

Griskevicius, V., Ackerman, J. A., Cantú, S. M., Delton, A. W., Robertson, T. E., Simpson, J. A., . . . Tybur, J. M. (2013). When the economy falters do people spend or save? Responses to resource scarcity depend on childhood environment. *Psychological Science, 24*, 197–205.

Griskevicius, V., Tybur, J. M., Delton, A. W., & Robertson, T. E. (2011). The influence of mortality and socioeconomic status on risk and delayed rewards: A life history theory approach. *Journal of Personality and Social Psychology, 100*, 1015–1026.

Groddeck, G. (1923 [2015]). *The book of the it.* New York: Ramenio Books.

Groh, A. M., & Haydon, K. C. (2017). Mothers' neural and behavioral responses to their infants' distress cues: The role of secure base script knowledge. *Psychological Science, 29*(2), 242–253.

Gross, J. J. (2013). *Handbook of emotion regulation*. New York: Guilford Press.

Gunderson, J. (2008). Borderline personality disorder: An overview. *Social Work in Mental Health, 6*(1–2), 5–12.

Guntrip, H. (1969). *Schizoid phenomena, object relations and the self*. New York: International Universities Press.

Gustafsson, P. E., Janlert, U., Theorell, T., Westerlund, H., & Hammarström, A. (2012). Do peer relations in adolescence influence health in adulthood? Peer problems in the school setting and the metabolic syndrome in middle-age. *PLoS One, 7*(6), Article e39385.

Haber, M. G., Cohen, J. L., Lucas, T., & Baltes, B. B. (2007). The relationship between self-reported received and perceived social support: A meta-analytic review. *American Journal of Community Psychology, 39*(1–2), 133–144.

Hackman, D. A., Gallop, R., Evans, G. W., & Farah, M. J. (2015). Socioeconomic status and executive function: developmental trajectories and mediation. *Developmental Science, 18*(5), 686–702.

Hagger, M. S., Wood, C., Stiff, C., & Chatzisarantis, N. L. D. (2010). Ego depletion and the strength model of self-control: A meta-analysis. *Psychological Bulletin, 136*(4), 495–525.

Hallowell, E. S., Oshri, A., Liebel, S. W., Liu, S., Duda, B., Clark, U. S., & Sweet, L. H. (2019). The mediating role of neural activity on the relationship between childhood maltreatment and impulsivity. *Child Maltreatment, 24*(4), 389–399.

Hamilton, A. F. (2013). Reflecting on the mirror neuron system in autism: A systematic review of current theories. *Developmental Cognitive Neuroscience, 3*, 91–105.

Hanson, J. L., Hair, N., Shen, D. G., Shi, F., Gilmore, J. H., Wolfe, B. L., & Pollak, S. D. (2013). Family poverty affects the rate of human infant brain growth. *PLoS One, 8*(12), e80954.

Harlow, H. F. (1953). Mice, monkeys, men, and motives. *Psychological Review, 60*(1), 23–32.

Harlow, H. F. (1958). The nature of love. *American Psychologist, 13*, 673–685.

Harlow, H. F. (1959). The development of learning in the Rhesus monkey. *American Scientist, 47*, 459–479.

Harlow, H. F. (1960). Primary affectional patterns in primates. *American Journal of Orthopsychiatry, 30*, 676–684.

Harlow, H. F. (1962). Affectional systems of monkeys, involving relations between mothers and young. In *International symposium on comparative medicine proceedings* (pp. 6–10). New York: Eaton Laboratories.

Harlow, H. F., Blazer, N. C., & McClearn, G. E. (1956). Manipulatory motivation in the infant rhesus monkey. *Journal of Comparative and Physiological Psychology, 49*, 444–448.

Harlow, H. F., & Harlow, M. K. (1969). Effects of various mother-infant relationships on rhesus monkey behaviors. In B. M. Foss (Ed.), *Determinants of infant behavior IV* (pp. 15–36). London: Methuen.

Hartmann, H. (1927 [1964]). Understanding and explanation. In *Essays on ego psychology* (pp. 369–403). New York: International Universities Press.

Hartmann, H. (1939 [1958]). *Ego psychology and the problem of adaptation* (D. Rapaport, Trans.). New York: International Universities Press.

Hartmann, H. (1939 [1964]). Psycho-analysis and the concept of health. *The International Journal of Psychoanalysis, 20*, 308–321.

Hartmann, H. (1947 [1964]). On rational and irrational action. In *Essays on ego psychology*. New York: International Universities Press.

Hartmann, H. (1948). Comments on the psychoanalytic theory of instinctual drives. *Psychoanalytic Quarterly, 17,* 368–388.

Hartmann, H. (1950). Comments on the psychoanalytic theory of the ego. *The Psychoanalytic Study of the Child, 5,* 74–97.

Hartmann, H. (1952). The mutual influences in the development of ego and id. *The Psychoanalytic Study of the Child, 7*(1), 9–30.

Hartmann, H. (1954 [1964]). Problems of infantile neurosis. In *Essays on ego psychology.* New York: International Universities Press.

Hartmann, H. (1955). Notes on the theory of sublimation. *The Psychoanalytic Study of the Child, 10,* 9–29.

Hartmann, H. (1960). *Psychoanalysis and moral values.* New York: International Universities Press.

Hartmann, H. (1964). *Essays on ego psychology.* New York: International Universities Press.

Hauer, K., Trammel, A. D., Ramroth, H., Pfisterer, M., Todd, C., & Oster, P. (2009). Repressive coping in geriatric patients' reports – impact on fear of falling. *Zeitschrift für Gerontologie und Geriatrie, 42,* 137–144.

Hay, D. F., Payne, A., & Chadwick, A. (2004). Peer relations in childhood. *Journal of Child Psychology and Psychiatry, and Allied Disciplines, 45,* 84–108.

Heffernan, M., & Fraley, R. C. (2013). Do early caregiving experiences shape what people find attractive in adulthood? Evidence from a study on parental age. *Journal of Research in Personality, 47,* 364–368.

Heimann, P. (1950). On countertransference. *International Journal of Psychoanalysis, 31,* 81–84.

Hein, G., Lamm, C., Brodbeck, C., & Singer, T. (2011). Skin conductance response to the pain of others predicts later costly helping. *PLoS One, 6*(8), e22759.

Hein, G., Silani, G., Preuschoff, K., Batson, C. D., & Singer, T. (2010). Neural responses to ingroup and outgroup members' suffering predict individual differences in costly helping. *Neuron, 68*(1), 149–160.

Helm, J. L., Sbarra, D. A., & Ferrer, E. (2014). Coregulation of respiratory sinus arrhythmia in adult romantic partners. *Emotion, 14*(3), 522–531.

Hendrick, I. (1942). Instinct and the ego during infancy. *The Psychoanalysis Quarterly, 76*(2), 415–438.

Hendrick, I. (1943). Work and the pleasure principle. *Psychoanalytic Quarterly, 12,* 311–349.

Herbart, J. F. (1825). Psychologie als Wissenschaft. Koenigsberg: A. W. Unzer.

Hermann, I. (1976). Clinging – going-in-search. *The Psychoanalytic Quarterly, 45,* 5–36.

Hickok, G. (2014). *The myth of mirror neurons: The real neuroscience of communication and cognition.* New York: W. W. Norton & Co.

Higley, D., Suomi, S., & Linnoila, M. (1992). A longitudinal assessment of CSF monoamine metabolite and plasma cortisol concentrations in young rhesus monkeys. *Biological Psychiatry, 32,* 127–145.

Hill-Soderlund, A. L., Mills-Koonce, W. R., Propper, C., Calkins, S. D., Granger, D. A., Moore, . . . Cox, M. J. (2008). Parasympathetic and sympathetic responses to the strange situation in infants and mothers from avoidant and securely attached dyads. *Developmental Psychobiology, 50*(4), 361–376.

Hofer, M. A. (1984). Relationships as regulators: A psychobiologic perspective on bereavement. *Psychosomatic Medicine, 46,* 183–197.

Hofer, M. A. (2003). The emerging neurobiology of attachment and separation: How parents shape their infant's brain and behavior. In S. W. Coates, J. L. Rosenthal, & D. S. Schechter (Eds.), *Relational perspectives book series. September 11: Trauma and human bonds* (pp. 191–209). Washington, DC: The Analytic Press, Taylor & Francis Group.

Hofer, M. A. (2006). Psychobiological roots of early attachment. *Current Directions of Psychological Science, 15*, 84–88.

Hoffman, M. L. (1982). Development of prosocial motivation: Empathy and guilt. In N. Eisenberg (Ed.), *The development of prosocial behavior* (pp. 281–338). New York: Academic Press.

Hogan, R. (1969). Development of an empathy scale. *Journal of Consulting and Clinical Psychology, 33*(3), 307–316.

Hogeveen, J., & Obhi, S. S. (2012). Social interaction enhances motor resonance for observed human actions. *Journal of Neuroscience, 32*(17), 5984–5989.

Hoglend, P., Hersoug, A. G., Bogwald, K. P., Amlo, S., Marble, A., Sorbye, O . . . Crits-Christoph, P. (2011). Effects of transference work in the context of therapeutic alliance and quality of object relations. *Journal of Consulting and Clinical Psychology, 79*, 697–706.

Holt, R. R. (1976). Drive or wish? A reconsideration of the psychoanalytic theory of motivation. In M. M. Gill & P. S. Holzman (Eds.), *Psychology versus metapsychology: Essays in memory of George S. Klein.* New York: International Universities Press.

House, J. S., Robbins, C., & Metzner, H. L. (1982). The association of social relationships and activities with mortality: Prospective evidence from the Tecumseh community health study. *American Journal of Epidemiology, 116*(1), 123–140.

Hughes, A. E., Crowell, S. E., Uyeji, L., & Coan, J. A. (2012). A developmental neuroscience of borderline pathology: emotion dysregulation and social baseline theory. *Journal of Abnormal Child Psychology, 40*(1), 21–33.

Hull, C. L. (1943). *Principles of behavior: An introduction to behavior theory.* Oxford: Appleton-Century.

Hull, C. L. (1951). *Essentials of behavior.* New Haven, CT: Yale University Press.

Hurley, S., & Chater, N. (2005). *Perspectives on imitation: From neuroscience to social science. Vol. 1: Mechanisms of imitation and imitation in animals.* Cambridge, MA: MIT Press.

Iacoboni, M., & Dapretto, M. (2006). The mirror neuron system and the consequences of its dysfunction. *Nature Reviews Neuroscience, 7*(12), 942–951.

Inhelder, B., & Piaget, J. (1958). *The growth of logical thinking from childhood to adolescence.* New York: Basic Books.

Jabbi, M., Bastiaansen, J., & Keysers, C. (2008). A common anterior insula representation of disgust observation, experience and imagination shows divergent functional connectivity pathways. *PloS One, 3*(8), e2939.

Jabbi, M., Swart, M., & Keysers, C. (2007). Empathy for positive and negative emotions in the gustatory cortex. *NeuroImage, 34*, 1744–1753.

Jackson, P. L., Meltzoff, A. N., & Decety, J. (2005). How do we perceive the pain of others? A window into the neural processes involved in empathy. *Neuroimage, 24*, 771–779.

Jacobsen, T., Huss, M., Fendrich, M., Kruesi, M. J., & Ziegenhain, U. (1997). Children's ability to delay gratification: Longitudinal relations to mother-child attachment. *Journal of Genetic Psychology, 158*(4), 411–426.

James, W. (1890). *The principles of psychology* (Vol. 1–2). New York: Holt.

Janet, P. (1907). *The major symptoms of hysteria.* New York: Palgrave Macmillan.

Jankowiak-Siuda, K., & Zajkowski, W. (2013). A neural model of mechanisms of empathy deficits in narcissism. *Medical Science Monitor, 19,* 934–941.

Janov, A. (1970). *The primal scream: Primal therapy: The cure for neurosis.* New York: G. P. Putnam's Sons.

Jebb, A. T., Morrison, M., Tay, L., & Diener, E. (2020). Subjective well-being around the world: Trends and predictors across the lifespan. *Psychological Science, 31*(3), 293–305.

Johnson, S. B., Riis, J. L., & Noble, K. G. (2016). State of the art review: Poverty and the developing brain. *Pediatrics, 137*(4), e20153075.

Joireman, J. (2004). Empathy and the self-absorption paradox II: Self-rumination and self-reflection as mediators between shame, guilt, and empathy. *Self and Identity, 3*(3), 225–238.

Jones, E. (1946). A valedictory address. *International Journal of Psychoanalysis, 27,* 7–12.

Jones, E. (1952). Preface. In *To Fairbairn's psychoanalytic studies of the personality.* London: Tavistock, Routledge & Kegan Paul.

Jones, E. (1957). *The life and work of Sigmund Freud* (Vol. 3). London: Hogarth.

Jones, S. S. (2006). Exploration or imitation? The effect of music on 4-week-old infants' tongue protrusions. *Infant Behavior & Development, 29*(1), 126–130.

Jung, W. E. (2003). The inner eye theory of laughter: Mind reader signals cooperator value. *Evolutionary Psychology, 1,* 214–253.

Jurbergs, N., Long, A., Hudson, M., & Phipps, S. (2007). Self-report of somatic symptoms in survivors of childhood cancer: Effects of adaptive style. *Pediatric Blood & Cancer, 49*(1), 84–89.

Jurist, E. L. (2005). Mentalized affectivity. *Psychoanalytic Psychology, 22*(3), 426–444.

Kahan, D., Polivy, J., & Herman, C. P. (2003). Conformity and dietary disinhibition: A test of the ego-strength model of self-regulation. *International Journal of Eating Disorders, 32,* 165–171.

Kahneman, D. (2011). *Thinking, fast and slow.* New York: Farrar, Straus and Giroux.

Kant, I. (1781/1965). *Critique of pure reason* (Trans. N. K. Smith). New York: St. Martin's Press.

Kaplan, G. A., Wilson, T. W., Cohen, R. D., Kauhanen, J., Wu, M., & Salonen, J. T. (1994). Social functioning and overall mortality: Prospective evidence from the Kuopio ischemic heart disease risk factor study. *Epidemiology, 5*(5), 495–500.

Karreman, A., & Vingerhoets, A. J. J. M. (2012). Attachment and well-being: The mediating role of emotion regulation and resilience. *Personality and Individual Differences, 53*(7), 821–826.

Karssen, A. M., Her, S., Li, J. Z., Patel, P. D., Meng, F., Bunney, W. E., & Lyons, D. M. (2007). Stress-induced changes in primate prefrontal profiles of gene expression. *Molecular Psychiatry, 12,* 1089–1102.

Karush, A., Easser, B. R., Cooper, A., & Swerdloff, B. (1964). The evaluation of ego strength: A profile of adaptive balance. *Journal of Nervous and Mental Disorders, 139,* 332–349.

Kazdin, A. E. (2006). Arbitrary metrics: Implications for identifying evidence-based treatment. *American Psychologist, 61,* 42–49.

Kernberg, O. (1965). Notes on countertransference. *Journal of the American Psychoanalytic Association, 13,* 38–56.

Kernberg, O. (1976). Technical considerations re borderline personality organization. *Journal of the American Psychoanalytic Association, 24,* 795–830.

Kernberg, O. (1993). The current status of psychoanalysis. *Journal of the American Psychoanalytic Association, 41*(1), 45–62.

Keyes, K. M., Eaton, N. R., Krueger, R. F., McLaughlin, K. A., Wall, M. M., Grant, B. F., & Hasin, D. S. (2012). Childhood maltreatment and the structure of common psychiatric disorders. *British Journal of Psychiatry, 200*(2), 107–115.

Kidd, C., Palmeri, H., & Aslin, R. N. (2013). Rational snacking: Young children's decision-making on the marshmallow task is moderated by beliefs about environmental reliability. *Cognition, 126*(1), 109–114.

Kilner, J. M., & Lemon, R. N. (2013). What we know currently about mirror neurons. *Current Biology, 23*(23), R1057–R1062.

Kinsbourne, M. (2002). The role of imitation in body ownership and mental growth. In A. N. Meltzoff & W. Prinz (Eds.), *Cambridge studies in cognitive perceptual development. The imitative mind: Development, evolution, and brain bases* (pp. 311–330). Cambridge, MA: Cambridge University Press.

Kirsner, D. (2009). *Unfree associations: Inside psychoanalytic institutes.* London: Process Press.

Kish, G. B., & Barnes, G. W. (1961). Reinforcing effects of manipulation in mice. *Journal of Comparative and Physiological Psychology, 54*(6), 713–715.

Kim, P., Evans, G. W., Angstadt, M., Ho, S. S., Sripada, C. S., Swain, J. E., . . . Phan, K. L. (2013). Effects of childhood poverty and chronic stress on emotion regulatory brain function in adulthood. *Proceedings of the National Academy of Sciences of the United States of America, 110*(46), 18442–18447.

King, L. A., Hicks, J. A., Krull, J. L. & Del Gaiso, A. K. (2006). Positive affect and the experience of meaning in life. *Journal of Personality and Social Psychology, 90,* 179–196.

Klein, G. S. (1969 [1970]). The ego in psychoanalysis: A concept in search of identity. *Psychoanalytic Review, 56*(4), 511–525.

Klein, G. S. (1976). Freud's two theories of sexuality. In M. M. Gill & P. S. Holzman (Eds.), *Psychology versus metapsychology: Psychoanalytic essays in memory of G. S. Klein* (pp. 14–70). New York: International Universities Press.

Klein, M. (1935). A contribution to the psychogenesis of manic-depressive states. *International Journal of Psychoanalysis, 16,* 145–174.

Klein, M. (1952). The origins of transference. *International Journal of Psycho-Analysis, 33,* 433–438.

Klein, M. (1975). *Envy and gratitude and other works 1946–1963* (M. Masud & R. Khan, Eds.). London: The Hogarth Press.

Knafo, D. (2002). Revisiting Ernst Kris's concept of regression in the service of ego and art. *Psychoanalytic Psychology, 19*(10), 24–49.

Knight, R. P. (1952). Borderline states. *Bulletin of the Menninger Clinic, 17,* 1–12.

Kober, H., Mende-Siedlecki, P., Kross, E. F., Weber, J., Mischel, M., Hart, C. L., & Ochsner, K. N. (2010). Prefrontal–striatal pathway underlies cognitive regulation of craving. *Proceedings of the National Academy of Sciences, 107*(33), 14811–14816.

Kochanska, G., Coy, K. C., Tjebkes, T. L., & Husarek, S. J. (1998). Individual differences in emotionality in infancy. *Child Development, 69*(2), 375–390.

Kochanska, G., Murray, K., & Coy, K. C. (1997). Inhibitory control as a contributor to conscience in childhood: From toddler to early school age. *Child Development, 68,* 263–277.

Koffka, K. (1935). *Principles of Gestalt psychology.* London: Lund Humphries.

Köhler, W. (1958). *Die physischen Gestalten in Ruhe und im stationären Zustand. Eine natur-philosophische Untersuchung.* Braunschweig, Germany: Friedr. Vieweg und Sohn (Translated extract reprinted as "Physical Gestalten". In W. D. Ellis (Ed.), *A source book of Gestalt psychology* (pp. 17–54). London: Routledge & Kegan Paul Ltd.

Kohut, H. (1971). *The analysis of the self.* New York: International Universities Press.

Kohut, H. (1977). *The restoration of the self.* New York: International Universities Press.

Kohut, H. (1984). *How does analysis cure?* Chicago, IL: University of Chicago Press.

Kremen, A. M., & Block, J. (1998). The roots of ego control in young adulthood: Links with parenting in early childhood. *Journal of Personality and Social Psychology, 75*(4), 1062–1075.

Kris, E. (1952). *Psychoanalytic explorations in art.* Madison, CT: International Universities Press.

Kubzansky, L. D., Martin, L. T., & Buka, S. L. (2009). Early manifestations of personality and adult health: A life course perspective. *Health Psychology, 28*(3), 364–372.

Lahey, B. B., Rathouz, P. J., Keenan, K., Stepp, S. D., Loeber, R., & Hipwell, A. E. (2015). Criterion validity of the general factor of psychopathology in a prospective study of girls. *Journal of Child Psychology and Psychiatry, and Allied Disciplines, 56*(4), 415–422.

Laing, R. D. (1967). *The politics of experience.* New York: Pantheon.

Laing, R. D. (1999). *The politics of the family, and other essays.* London: Routledge.

Lakoff, G., & Johnson, M. (1999). *Philosophy in the flesh: The embodied mind and its challenge to western thought.* New York: Basic Books.

Lamm, C., Decety, J., & Singer, T. (2011). Meta-analytic evidence for common and distinct neural networks associated with directly experienced pain and empathy for pain. *Neuroimage, 54,* 2492–2502.

Landstedt, E., Hammarström, A., & Winefield, H. (2015). How well do parental and peer relationships in adolescence predict health in adulthood? *Scandinavian Journal of Public Health, 43*(5), 460–468.

Lawson, G. M., Duda, J. T., Avants, B. B., Wu, J., & Farah, M. J. (2013). Associations between children's socioeconomic status and prefrontal cortical thickness. *Developmental Science, 16*(5), 641–652.

Lees-Haley, P. R. (1992). Efficacy of MMPI-2 validity scales and MCMI-II modifier scales for detecting spurious PTSD claims: F, F-K, fake bad scale, ego strength, subtle-obvious subscales, DIS, and DEB. *Professional Issues, 48*(5), 681–688.

Leighton, J., Bird, G., Charman, T., & Heyes, C. (2008). Weak imitative performance is not due to a functional "mirroring" deficit in adults with autism spectrum disorders. *Neuropsychologia, 46*(4), 1041–1049.

Leites, N. (1971). *The new ego.* New York: Science House.

Leonard, J. A., Berkowitz, T., & Shusterman, A. (2006). The effect of friendly touch on delay-of-gratification in preschool children. *Quarterly Journal of Experimental Psychology, 67*(11), 2123–2133.

Lepage, J. F., & Theoret, H. (2007). The mirror neuron system: Grasping others' actions from birth? *Developmental Science, 10*(5), 513–523.

Lepper, M. R., Greene, D., & Nisbett, R. E. (1973). Undermining children's intrinsic interest with extrinsic reward: A test of the "overjustification" hypothesis. *Journal of Personality and Social Psychology, 28*(1), 129–137.

Lessard, J. C., & Moretti, M. M. (1998). Suicidal ideation in an adolescent clinical sample: Attachment patterns and clinical implications. *Journal of Adolescence, 21*(4), 383–395.

Levenson, E. (1998). Awareness, insight, and learning. *Contemporary Psychoanalysis, 34*(2), 239–249.

Levenson, R. W., Ekman, P., & Friesen, W. V. (1990). Voluntary facial action generates emotion-specific autonomic nervous system activity. *Psychophysiology, 27,* 363–384.

Levenson, R. W., & Ruef, A. M. (1992). Empathy: A physiological substrate. *Journal of Personality and Social Psychology, 63*(2), 234–246.

Levine, H. B. (1997). The capacity for countertransference. *Psychoanalytic Inquiry, 17*(1), 44–68.

Levine, M., Glass, H., & Meltzoff, J. (1957). The inhibition process, Rorschach human movement responses, and intelligence. *Journal of Consulting Psychology, 21*(1), 41–45.

Levine, M., & Spivack, G. (1959). Incentive, time conception and self- control in a group of emotionally disturbed boys. *Journal of Clinical Psychology, 15,* 110–113.

Lewis, M. (1992). *Shame: The exposed self.* New York: The Free Press.

Lhermitte, F. (1986). Human anatomy and the frontal lobes. Part II: Patient behavior in complex social situations: The "environmental dependency syndrome". *Annals of Neurology, 19*(4), 335–343.

Lhermitte, F., Pillon, B., & Serdaru, M. (1986). Human autonomy and the frontal lobes. Part I: Imitation and utilization behavior: A neuropsychological study of 75 patients. *Annals of Neurology, 19,* 326–334.

Lichtenberg, J. (1989). *Psychoanalysis and motivation.* Hillsdale, NJ: The Analytic Press.

Lieb, K., Zanarini, M. C., Schmahl, C., Linehan, M. M., & Bohus, M. (2004). Borderline personality disorder. *Lancet (London, England), 364*(9432), 453–461.

Lieberman, A. F. (1999). Negative maternal attributions: Effects on toddlers' sense of self. *Psychoanalytic Inquiry, 19*(5), 737–756.

Lieberman, M. D., Eisenberger, N. I., Crockett, M. J., Tom, S. M., Pfeifer, J. H., & Way, W. M. (2007). Putting feelings into words: Affect labeling disrupts amygdala activity in response to affective stimuli. *Psychological Science, 18*(5), 421–428.

Liston, C., Miller, M. M., Goldwater, D. S., Radley, J. J., Rocher, A. B., Hof, P. R., & McEwen, B. S. (2006). Stress-induced alterations in prefrontal cortical dendritic morphology predict selective impairments in perceptual attentional set-shifting. *Journal of Neuroscience, 26,* 7870–7874.

Little, M. (1951). Countertransference and the patients' response to it. *International Journal of Psychoanalysis, 32,* 32–40.

Liu, L., Feng, T., Suo, T., Lee, K., & Li, H. (2012). Adapting to the destitute situations: Poverty cues lead to short-term choice. *PloS One, 7*(4), e33950.

Livesley, W. J. (1991). The classifying of personality disorder: Ideal types, prototypes, or dimensions. *Journal of Personality Disorders, 3,* 52–59.

Loewald, H. (1951). Ego and reality. *International Journal of Psychoanalysis, 32,* 10–18.

Loewald, H. (1952). The problem of defence and the neurotic interpretation of reality. *International Journal of Psychoanalysis, 33,* 444–449.

Loewald, H. (1960). On the therapeutic action of psychoanalysis. *International Journal of Psychoanalysis, 41,* 16–33.

Loewald, H. (1971). On motivation and instinct theory. *The Psychoanalytic Study of the Child, 26*(1), 91–128.

Loewald, H. (1972). Freud's conception of the negative therapeutic reaction, with comments on instinct theory. *Journal of the American Psychoanalytic Association, 20,* 235–245.

Loewald, H. W. (1975). Psychoanalysis as an art and the fantasy character of the psychoanalytic situation. *Journal of the American Psychoanalytic Association, 23*(2), 277–299.

Loewald, H. (1979). The waning of the Oedipal complex. *Journal of the American Psychoanalytic Association, 27,* 751–775.

Loewald, H. (1980). *Papers on psychoanalysis.* New Haven: Yale University Press.

López-Pérez, B., & Ambrona, T. (2015). The role of cognitive emotion regulation on the vicarious emotional response. *Motivation and Emotion, 39,* 299–308.

López-Pérez, B., Carrera, P., Ambrona, T., & Oceja, L. (2014). Testing the qualitative differences between empathy and personal distress: Measuring core affect and self-orientation. *The Social Science Journal, 51*(4), 676–680.

Lotze, R. H. (1852). *Mediziniche Psychologie oder Physiologie der Seele* (pp. 287–325). Leipzig, Germany: Weidmann'sche Buch-handlung.

Lowenstein, R. (1982). Ego autonomy and psychoanalytic technique. In *Practice and precept in psychoanalytic technique: Selected papers of Rudolph Lowenstein.* New Haven: Yale University Press.

Luborsky, L., Crits-Cristoph, P., & Alexander, K. (1990). Repressive style and relationship patterns- three samples inspected. In J. L. Singer (Ed.), *Repression and dissociation: Implications for personality theory, psychopathology, and health* (pp. 275–298). Chicago, IL: University of Chicago Press.

Luborsky, L., Graff, H., Pulver, S., & Curtis, H. (1973). A clinical-quantitative examination of consensus on the concept of transference. *Archives of General Psychiatry, 29*(1), 69–75.

Lundqvist, L. O., & Dimberg, U. (1995). Facial expressions are contagious. *Journal of Psychophysiology, 9,* 203–211.

Luria, A. R. (1966). *Human brain and psychological processes.* New York: Harper & Row.

Lurquin, J. H., Michaelson, L. E., Barker, J. E., Gustavson, D. E., von Bastian, C. C., Carruth, N. P., & Miyake, A. (2016). No evidence of the ego-depletion effect across task characteristics and individual differences: A pre-registered study. *PLoS One, 11*(2), e0147770.

Luyten, P., Cambell, C., Allison, E., & Fonagy, P. (2020). The mentalizing approach to psychopathology: State of the art and future directions. *Annual Review of Clinical Psychology, 16,* 297–325.

Luyten, P., & Fonagy, P. (2015). The neurobiology of mentalizing. *Personality Disorders: Theory, Research, and Treatment, 6*(4), 366–379.

Ma, F., Chen, B., Xu, F., Lee, K., & Heyman, G. D. (2018). Generalized trust predicts young children's willingness to delay gratification. *Journal of Experimental Child Psychology, 169,* 118–125.

Mahler, M. S. (1968). *On human symbiosis and the vicissitudes of individuation. Vol. 1: Infantile psychosis.* New York: International Universities Press.

Mahler, M. S., Pine, F., & Bergman, A. (1970). The mother's reaction to her toddler's drive for individuation. In E. J. Anthony & T. Benedek (Eds.), *Parenthood: Its psychology and psychopathology* (pp. 257–274). Boston: Little, Brown.

Mahler, M., Bergman, & Pine, F. (1975). *The psychological birth of the human infant: Symbiosis and individuation.* New York: Basic Books.

Main, M., & Goldwyn, R. (1998). *Adult attachment interview scoring and classification manual – 6th version.* Berkeley: University of California, Unpublished manuscript.

Main, M., & Hesse, E. D. (1990). Parents' unresolved traumatic experiences are related to infant disorganized attachment status: Is frightened and/or frightening parental behavior the linking mechanism? In M. Greenberg, D. Cichetti, & M. Cummings (Eds.), *Attachment in the preschool years.* Chicago, IL: Chicago University Press.

Makari, G. (2008). *Revolution in mind: The creation of psychoanalysis.* New York: Harper Collins.

Marcus, E. R. (1999). Modern ego psychology. *Journal of the American Psychoanalytic Association, 47*(3), 843–871.

Marinak, B. A., & Gambrell, L. B. (2008). Intrinsic motivation and rewards: What sustains young children's engagement with text? *Literacy Research and Instruction, 47*(1), 9–26.

Marsh, A. A., Finger, E. C., Mitchell, D. G. V., Schneider, M. R., Sims, C., Kosson, D., . . . Blair, R. J. R. (2008). Reduced amygdala response to fearful expressions in children and adolescents with callous-unemotional traits and disruptive behavior disorders. *The American Journal of Psychiatry, 165,* 712–720.

Mascaro, N., & Rosen, D. H. (2005). Existential meaning's role in the enhancement of hope and prevention of depressive symptoms. *Journal of Personality, 73*(4), 985–1015.

Masling, J., & Cohen, I. S. (1987). Psychotherapy, clinical evidence, and the self-fulfilling prophecy. *Psychoanalytic Psychology, 4,* 65–80.

Mason, W. A., Hollis, J. H., & Sharpe, L. G. (1962). Differential responses of chimpanzees to social stimulation. *Journal of Comparative and Physiological Psychology, 55,* 1105–1110.

Mason, W. A., Saxon, S. V., & Sharpe, L. G. (1963). Preferential responses of young chimpanzees to food and social rewards. *The Psychological Record, 13,* 341–345.

Masterson, J. F. (1981). *The narcissistic and borderline disorders: An integrated developmental approach.* New York: Routledge.

Matheny, A. P., Riese, M. L., & Wilson, R. S. (1985). Rudiments of infant temperament: Newborn to 9 months. *Developmental Psychology, 21*(3), 486–494.

Matte-Gagné, C., & Bernier, A. (2011). Prospective relations between maternal autonomy support and child executive functioning: Investigating the mediating role of child language ability. *Journal of Experimental Child Psychology, 110*(4), 611–625.

Maunder, R. G., Lancee, W. J., Balderson, K. E., Bennett, J. P., Borgundvaag, B., Evans, S., . . . Wasylenki, D. A. (2006). Long-term psychological and occupational effects of providing hospital healthcare during SARS outbreak. *Emerging Infectious Diseases, 12*(12), 1924–1932.

Mayr, E. (1961). Cause and effect in biology. *Science, 134*(3489), 1501–1506.

McDougall, W. (1908). *An introduction to social psychology.* London, UK: Methuen.

McTeague, L. M., Huemer, J., Carreon, D. M., Jiang, Y., Eickhoff, S. B., & Etkin, A. (2017). Identification of a common neural circuit disruptions in cognitive control across psychiatric disorders. *American Journal of Psychiatry, 174*(7), 676–685.

Mead, G. H. (1934). *Mind, self, and society from the standpoint of a social behaviorist* (C. W. Morris, Ed.). Chicago: University of Chicago.

Meehl, P. (1994). Subjectivity in psychoanalytic inference: The nagging persistence of Wilhelm Fliess's Achensee question. *Psychoanalysis and Contemporary Thought, 17*(1), 3–82.

Mehrabian, A., & Epstein, N. (1972). A measure of emotional empathy. *Journal of Personality, 40*(4), 525–543.

Meissner, W. W. (1996). The self-as-object in psychoanalysis. *Psychoanalysis and Contemporary Thought, 19*(3), 425–459.

Meissner, W. W. (1997). The self and the body: I. The body self and the body image. *Psychoanalysis and Contemporary Thought, 20,* 419–448.

Meltzoff, A. N. (1995). Understanding the intentions of others: Re-enactment of intended acts by eighteen month -old children. *Developmental Psychology, 3,* 838–850.

Meltzoff, A. N., & Moore, M. K. (1977). Imitation of facial and manual gestures by human neonates. *Science, 198,* 75–78.

Meltzoff, A. N., & Moore, M. K. (1983). Newborn infants imitate adult facial gestures. *Child Development, 54,* 702–809.

Meltzoff, A. N., & Moore, M. K. (1989). Imitation in newborn infants: Exploring the range of gestures imitated and the underlying mechanisms. *Developmental Psychology, 25*(6), 954–962.

Meltzoff, A. N., & Moore, M. K. (1992). Early imitation within a functional framework: The importance of person identity, movement, and development. *Infant Behavior and Development, 15*, 479–505.

Meltzoff, J., & Levine, M. (1954). The relationship between motor and cognitive inhibition. *Journal of Consulting Psychology, 18*(5), 355–358.

Meltzoff, J., Singer, J. L., & Korchin, S. J. (1953). Motor inhibition and Rorschach movement responses: A test of the sensory-tonic theory. *Journal of Personality, 21*(3), 400–410.

Memedovic, S., Grisham, J. R., Denson, T. F., & Moulds, M. L. (2010). The effects of trait reappraisal and suppression on anger and blood pressure in response to provocation. *Journal of Research in Personality, 44*(4), 540–543.

Meuwissen, A. S., & Carlson, S. M. (2015). Fathers matter: The role of father parenting in preschoolers' executive function development. *Journal of Experimental Child Psychology, 140*, 1–15.

Miano, A., Dziobek, I., & Roepke, S. (2017). Understanding interpersonal dysfunction in borderline personality disorder: A naturalistic dyadic study reveals absence of relationship-protective empathic inaccuracy. *Clinical Psychological Science, 5*(2), 355–366.

Mikulincer, M., Florian, V., & Weller, A. (1993). Attachment styles, coping strategies, and posttraumatic psychological distress: The impact of the Gulf war in Israel. *Journal of Personality and Social Psychology, 64*(5), 817–826.

Milner, J. S. (1988). An ego-strength scale for the child abuse potential inventory. *Journal of Family Violence, 3*, 151–162.

Mischel, W. (1958). Preference for delayed reinforcement: An experimental study of a cultural observation. *The Journal of Abnormal and Social Psychology, 56*(1), 57–61.

Mischel, W. (1961). Preference for delayed reinforcement and social responsibility. *Journal of Abnormal and Social Psychology, 62*, 1–7.

Mischel, W., Ayduk, O., Berman, M. G., Casey, B. J., Gotlib, I. H., Jonides, J., . . . Shoda, Y. (2011). "Willpower" over the life span: decomposing self-regulation. *Social Cognitive and Affective Neuroscience, 6*(2), 252–256.

Mischel, W., & Moore, B. (1973). Effects of attention to symbolically presented rewards on self-control. *Journal of Personality and Social Psychology, 28*, 172–179.

Mischel, W., Shoda, Y., & Peake, P. K. (1988). The nature of adolescent competencies predicted by preschool delay of gratification. *Journal of Personality and Social Psychology, 54*(4), 687–696.

Mischel, W., Shoda, Y., & Rodriguez, M. (1989). Delay of gratification in children. *Science, 244*, 933–938.

Mitchell, J. (2000). *Mad men and medusas*. London: Penguin.

Mitchell, J. (2003). *Siblings*. Cambridge: Polity.

Mitchell, S. A. (1988). *Relational concepts in psychoanalysis: An integration*. Cambridge, MA: Harvard University Press.

Mitchell, S. A. (1993). Aggression and the endangered self. *Psychoanalytic Quarterly, 62*(3), 351–382.

Mitchell, S. A. (1995). *Hope and dread in psychoanalysis*. New York: Basic Books.

Mitchell, S. A. (1998). The analyst's knowledge authority. *Psychoanalytic Quarterly, 67*(1), 1–31.

Modell, A. H. (1975). The ego and the id – fifty years later. *International Journal of Psychoanalysis, 56*, 57–68.

Modell, A. H. (1990). *Other times, other realities: Toward a theory of psychoanalytic treatment*. Cambridge, MA: Harvard University Press.

Modin, B., Ostberg, V., & Almquist, Y. B. (2010). Childhood peer status and adult susceptibility to anxiety and depression. A 30-year hospital follow-up. *Journal of Abnormal Child Psychology, 39*, 187–199.

Modinos, G., Ormel, J., & Aleman, A. (2009). Activation of anterior insula during self-reflection. *PLoS One, 4*(2), e4618.

Moffitt, T. E., Arseneault, L., Belsky, D., Dickson, N., Hancox, R. J., Harrington, H. L., . . . Caspi, A. (2011). A gradient of childhood self-control predicts health, wealth, and public safety. *Proceedings of the National Academy of Sciences, 108*(7), 2693–2698.

Moffitt, T. E., Harrington, H., Caspi, A., Kim-Cohen, J., Goldberg, D., Gregory, A. M., & Poulton, R. (2007). Depression and generalized anxiety disorder: Cumulative and sequential comorbidity in a birth cohort followed prospectively to age 32 years. *Archives of General Psychiatry, 64*(6), 651–660.

Moran, R. (2001). *Authority and estrangement: An essay on self- knowledge*. Princeton, NJ: Princeton University Press.

Morrison, A. P. (1989). *Shame: The underside of narcissism*. Hillsdale, NJ: Analytic Press.

Morrison, I., Llloyd, D., di Pelligrino, G., & Roberts, N. (2004). Vicarious response to pain in anterior cingulate cortex: Is empathy a multisensory issue? *Cognitive, Affective, and Behavioral Neuroscience, 4*, 270–278.

Moss, E. Rousseau, D., Parent, S., St. Laurent. D., & Saintonge, J. (1998). Correlates of attachment at school age: Maternal reported stress, mother-child interaction, and behavior problems. *Child Development, 69*(5), 1390–1405.

Mund, M., & Mitte, K. (2012). The costs of repression: A meta-analysis on the relation between repressive coping and somatic diseases. *Health Psychology, 31*(5), 640–649.

Murray, E. J. (1956). A content-analysis method for studying psychotherapy. *Psychological Monographs, 70*, 1–31.

Myers, L. B. (2010). The importance of the repressive coping style: Findings from 30 years of research. *Anxiety, Stress, and Coping, 23*(1), 3–17.

Myers, L. B., & Brewin, C. R. (1994). Recall of early experience and the repressive coping style. *Journal of Abnormal Psychology, 103*(2), 288–292.

Myers, L. B., Davies, A., Evans, E., & Stygall, J. (2005). How successful are repressors at self-care behaviour? *Psychology and Health, 20*, 188–189.

Nagel, T. (1986). *Thew view from nowhere*. New York: Oxford University Press.

Nagy, E., Compagne, H., Orvos, H., Pal, A. P., Molnar, P., Janszky, I., . . . Bardos, G. (2005). Index finger movement imitation by human neonates: Motivation, learning and left-hand preference. *Pediatric Research, 58*, 749–753.

Newman, D. L., Caspi, A., Moffitt, T. E., & Silva, P. A. (1997). Antecedents of adult interpersonal functioning: Effects of individual differences in age 3 temperament. *Developmental Psychology, 33*(2), 206–217.

Nussbaum, M. C. (2005). Analytic love and human vulnerability: a comment on Lawrence Friedman's "Is there a special analytic love"? *Journal of the American Psychoanalytic association, 53*, 377–383.

Nyström, P. (2008). The infant mirror neuron system studied with high density EEG. *Social Neuroscience, 3*(3–4), 334–347.

Oberman, L., Hubbard, E., Mccleery, J., Altschuler, E., Ramachandran, V., & Pineda, J. (2005). EEG evidence for mirror neuron dysfunction in autism spectrum disorders. *Cognitive Brain Research, 24*, 190–198.

Obhi, S. S., Hogeveen, J., Giacomin, M., & Jordan, C. H. (2014). Automatic imitation is reduced in narcissists. *Journal of Experimental Psychology: Human Perception and Performance, 40*(3), 920–928.

Ochsner, K., & Gross, J. (2005). The cognitive control of emotion. *Trends in Cognitive Sciences, 9*, 242–249.

Ogden, R. S., Moore, D., Redfern, L., & McGlone, F. (2015). Stroke me for longer this touch feels too short: The effect of pleasant touch on temporal perception. *Consciousness and Cognition, 36*, 306–313.

Ogden, T. (1997). *Reverie and interpretation: Sensing something human.* Northvale, NJ: Jason Aronson.

Oldfield, J., Humphrey, N., & Hebron, J. (2015). The role of parental and peer attachment relationships and school connectedness in predicting adolescent mental health outcomes. *Child and Adolescent Mental Health, 21*(1), 21–29.

Ollendick, T. H., Weist, M. D., Borden, M. C., & Greene, R. W. (1992). Sociometric status and academic, behavioral, and psychological adjustment: A five-year longitudinal study. *Journal of Consulting and Clinical Psychology, 60*(1), 80–87.

Olson, S. L., & Lifgren, K. (1988). Concurrent and longitudinal correlates of preschool peer sociometrics: Comparing rating scale and nomination measures. *Journal of Applied Developmental Psychology, 9*(4), 409–420.

Oskis, A., Loveday, C., Hucklebridge, F., Thorn, L., & Clow, A. (2009). Diurnal patterns of salivary cortisol across the adolescent period in healthy females. *Psychoneuroendocrinology, 34*(3), 307–316.

Panksepp, J. B., & Lahvis, G. P. (2007). Social reward among juvenile mice. *Genes, Brain, and Behavior, 6*(7), 661–671.

Parish, M., & Eagle, M. N. (2003). Attachment to the therapist. *Psychoanalytic Psychology, 20*(2), 271–286.

Parker, J. G., & Asher, S. R. (1987). Peer relations and later personal adjustment: Are low-accepted children at risk? *Psychological Bulletin, 102*(3), 357–389.

Passman, R. H., & Erck, T. W. (1978). Permitting maternal contact through vision alone: Films of mothers for promoting play and locomotion. *Developmental Psychology, 14*(5), 512–516.

Passman, R. H., & Longeway, K. P. (1982). The role of vision in maternal attachment: Giving 2-year-olds a photograph of their mother during separation. *Developmental Psychology, 18*(4), 530–533.

Patel, P. D., Katz, M., Karssen, A. M., & Lyons, D. M. (2008). Stress-induced changes in corticosteroid receptor expression in primate hippocampus and prefrontal cortex. *Psychoneuroendocrinology, 33*, 360–367.

Patrick, M., Hobson, R. P., Castle, P., Howard, R., & Maughan, B. (1994). Personality disorder and mental representation of early social experience. *Development and Psychopathology, 6*, 375–388.

Paul, V., Rauch, A., Kugel, H., Horst, L., Bauer, J., Dannlowski, U., . . . Suslow, T. (2012). High responsivity to threat during the initial stage of perception in repression: A 3 T fMRI study. *Social Cognitive and Affective Neuroscience, 7*, 980–990.

Pedersen, S. H., Poulsen, S., & Lunn, S. (2014). Affect regulation: Holding, containing and mirroring. *The International Journal of Psychoanalysis, 95*(5), 843–864.

Peters, J. H., Hock, M., & Krohne, H. W. (2012). Sensitive maintenance: A cognitive process underlying individual differences in memory for threatening information. *Journal of Personality and Social Psychology, 102*(1), 200–213.

Petterson, E., Larsson, H., & Lichtenstein, P. (2016). Common psychiatric disorders share the same genetic origin: A multivariate sibling study of the Swedish population. *Molecular Psychiatry, 21,* 717–721.

Pfaehler, G. T., & Roessler, R. (1965). Ego strength and intravenous glucose tolerance. *Journal of Psychosomatic Research, 8,* 431–439.

Phipps, S., & Srivastava, D. K. (1997). Repressive adaptation in children with cancer. *Health Psychology, 16*(6), 521–528.

Phipps, S., & Steele, R. (2002). Repressive adaptive style in children with chronic illness. *Psychosomatic Medicine, 64*(1), 34–42.

Pine, F. (1990). *Drive, ego, object, and self: A synthesis for clinical work.* New York: Basic Books.

Pine, F. (2011). Beyond pluralism: Psychoanalysis and the workings of mind. *Psychoanalytic Quarterly, 80*(4), 823–856.

Pinto, A., Steinglass, J. E., Greene, A. L., Weber, E. U., & Simpson, H. B. (2014). Capacity to delay reward differentiates obsessive-compulsive disorder and obsessive-compulsive personality disorder. *Biological Psychiatry, 75*(8), 653–659.

Poe, E. A. (1965). The purloined letter. In *The complete tales and poems of Edgar Allen Poe* (H. Allen, Intro.). New York: Random House.

Polan, H. J., & Hofer, M. A. (1999). Psychobiological origins of infant attachment and separation responses. In J. Cassidy & P. R. Shaver (Eds.), *Handbook of attachment: Theory, research, and clinical applications* (pp. 162–218). New York: Guilford Press.

Polan, H. J., & Hofer, M. A. (2008). Psychobiological origins of infant attachment and its role in development. In J. Cassidy & P. R. Shaver (Eds.), *Handbook of attachment: Theory, research, and clinical applications* (pp. 158–172). New York: The Guilford Press.

Popper, K. (1978, April 7). *Three worlds: The Tanney lectures on human values.* Delivered at the University of Michigan.

Portuges, S. H., & Hollander, N. C. (2011). The therapeutic action of resistance analysis: Interpersonalizing and socializing Paul Gray's close process attention. In M. J. Diamond & C. Christian (Eds.), *The second century of psychoanalysis: Evolving perspectives on therapeutic action* (pp. 71–95). London: Karnac.

Posner, D. (1999). *Relationship among attachment styles, empathy, object representations, and alexithymia* (Doctoral dissertation). Derner Institute of Advanced Psychological Studies, Adephi University, New York.

Posner, M. I., & Rothbart, M. K. (2000). Developing mechanisms of self-regulation. *Development and Psychopathology, 12,* 427–441.

Posner, M. I., & Rothbart, M. K. (2007). Research on attention networks as a model for the integration of psychological science. *Annual Review of Psychology, 58,* 1–23.

Prasertsri, N., Holden, J., Keefe, F. J., & Wilkie, D. J. (2011). Repressive coping style: Relationships with depression, pain, and pain coping strategies in lung cancer outpatients. *Lung Cancer (Amsterdam, Netherlands), 71*(2), 235–240.

Press, C., Richardson, D., & Bird, G. (2010). Intact imitation of emotional facial actions in autism spectrum conditions. *Neuropsychologia, 48*(11), 3291–3297.

Priel, B., & Shamai, D. (1995). Attachment style and perceived social support: Effects on affect regulation. *Personality and Individual Differences, 19*(2), 235–241.

Prinstein, M. J., Rancourt, D., Adelman, C. B., Ahlich, E., Smith, J., & Guerry, J. D. (2018). Peer status and psychopathology. In W. M. Bukowski, B. Laursen, & K. H. Rubin (Eds.), *Handbook of peer interactions, relationships, and groups* (pp. 617–636). New York: The Guilford Press.

Quirin, M., Pruessner, J. C., & Kuhl, J. (2008). HPA system regulation and adult attachment anxiety: Individual differences in reactive and awakening cortisol. *Psychoneuroendocrinology, 33,* 581–590.

Racker, H. (1953). A contribution to the problem of counter-transference. *The International Journal of Psychoanalysis, 34,* 313–324.

Racker, H. (1968). *Transference and countertransference*. New York: International Universities Press.

Radley, J. J., Arias, C. M., & Sawchenko, P. E. (2006). Regional differentiation of the medial prefrontal cortex in regulating adaptive responses to acute emotional stress. *Journal of Neuroscience, 26,* 12967–12976.

Ramachandran, V. S., & Oberman, L. M. (2006). Broken mirrors: A theory of autism. *Scientific American, 295*(5), 62–69.

Rangell, L. (2007). *The road to unity in psychoanalytic theory*. New York: Jason Aronson.

Rangell, L. (2008). Reconciliation: The continuing role of theory. *The Journal of the American Academy of Psychoanalysis and Dynamic Psychiatry, 36*(2), 217–233.

Rao, D. G. (1998). *Danger and defense: The technique of close process attention A Festschrift in Honor of Paul Gray* (M. Goldberger, Ed.). Northvale, NJ: Jason Aronson.

Rao, U., Chen, L. A., Bidesi, A. S., Shad, M. U., Thomas, M. A., & Hammen, C. L. (2010). Hippocampal changes associated with early-life adversity and vulnerability to depression. *Society of Biological Psychiatry, 67*(4), 357–364.

Rapaport, D. (1951). The autonomy of the ego. *Bulletin of the Menninger Clinic, 15,* 113–123.

Rapaport, D. (1953). On the psychoanalytic theory of affects. *International Journal of Psychoanalysis, 34,* 177–198.

Rapaport, D. (1956 [1967]). The theory of ego autonomy: A generalization. In M. Gill (Ed.), *The collected papers of David Rapaport* (pp. 722–744). New York: Basic Books.

Rapaport, D. (1959). A historical survey of psychoanalytic ego psychology. *Psychological Issues 1,* 15–17.

Rapaport, D. (1959 [1967]). The theory of attention cathexis: An economic and structural attempt at the explanation of cognitive processes. In M. Gill (Ed.), *The collected papers of Davie Rapaport* (pp. 778–794). New York: Basic Books.

Rapaport, D. (1960). The structure of psychoanalytic theory. *Psychological issues, 2*(2), 1–158.

Rapaport, D. (1967). *The collected papers of David Rapaport*. New York: Basic Books.

Raver, C. C., Blair, C., & Willoughby, M. (2013). Poverty as a predictor of 4-year-olds' executive function: New perspectives on models of differential susceptibility. *Developmental Psychology, 49*(2), 292–304.

Richards, A. D. (2003). Psychoanalytic discourse at the turn of our century: A plea for a measure of humility. *Journal of the American Psychoanalytic Association, 51S,* 73–89.

Richards, A. D. (2017). From favorite persona non-grata: A psychoanalytic journey. *Journal of Psychohistory, 45*(2), 135–139.

Ricoeur, P. (1970). *Freud and philosophy: An essay on interpretation*. New Haven, CT: Yale University Press.

Rizzolatti, G., Fadiga, L., Gallese, V., & Fogassi, L. (1996). Premotor cortex and the recognition of motor actions. *Cognitive Brain Research, 3*, 131–141.

Rizzolatti, G., Fogassi, L., & Gallese, V. (2001). Neurophysiological mechanisms underlying the understanding and imitation of action. *Nature Reviews: Neuroscience, 2*(9), 661–670.

Rizzolatti, G., Semi, A. A., & Fabbri-Destro, M. (2014). Linking psychoanalysis with neuroscience: The concept of ego. *Neuropsychologia, 55*, 143–148.

Rizzolatti, G., & Sinigaglia, C. (2008). *Mirrors in the brain: How our minds share actions and emotions* (F. Anderson, Trans.). Oxford: Oxford University Press.

Rizzolatti, G., & Sinigaglia, C. (2010). The functional role of the parieto-frontal mirror circuit: Interpretations and misinterpretations. *Nature Reviews Neuroscience, 11*(4), 264–274.

Robinson, J. S. (1959). Light onset and termination as reinforcers for rats living under normal light conditions. *Psychological Reports, 5*, 793–796.

Rochat, M. J., Caruana, F., Jezzini, A., Escola, L., Intskirveli, I., Grammont, F., . . . Umiltà, M. A. (2010). Responses of mirror neurons in area F5 to hand and tool grasping observation. *Experimental Brain Research, 204*(4), 605–616.

Roessler, R., Alexander, A. A., & Greenfield, N. S. (1963). Ego strength and physiological responsivity: I. The relationship of the Barron Es scale to skin resistance. *Archives of General Psychiatry, 8*, 142–154.

Roff, J. D., & Wirt, R. D. (1984). Childhood aggression and social adjustment as antecedents of delinquency. *Journal of Abnormal Child Psychology, 12*(1), 111–126.

Roff, M. (1961). Childhood social interactions and young adult bad conduct. *The Journal of Abnormal and Social Psychology, 63*(2), 333–337.

Rolls, E. T., O'Doherty, J., Kringelbach, M. L., Francis, S., Bowtell, R., & McGlone, F. (2003). Representations of pleasant and painful touch in the human orbitofrontal and cingulate cortices. *Cerebral Cortex, 13*, 308–317.

Rolls, E. T., Kringelbach, M. L., & de Araujo, I. E. T. (2003). Different representations of pleasant and unpleasant odors in the human brain. *European Journal of Neuroscience, 18*, 695–703.

Rorty, R. (1991). *Objectivity, relativism, and truth.* Cambridge, MA: Cambridge University Press.

Rosenbach, C., & Renneberg, B. (2014). Rejection sensitivity as a mediator of the relationship between experienced rejection and borderline characteristics. *Personality and Individual Differences, 69*, 176–181.

Rosenblatt, A. D. (1985). The role of affect in cognitive psychology and psychoanalysis. *Psychoanalytic Psychology, 2*, 85–98.

Rosenzweig, E. (2016). With eyes wide open: How and why awareness of the psychological immune system is compatible with its efficacy. *Perspectives on Psychological Science, 11*(2), 222–238.

Rothbart, M. K., Ziaie, H., & O'Boyle, C. G. (1992). Self-regulation and emotion in infancy. In N. Eisenberg & R. A. Fabes (Eds.), *New directions for child development, no. 55: The Jossey-Bass education series. Emotion and its regulation in early development* (pp. 7–23). San Francisco, CA: Jossey-Bass.

Rubinstein, B. B. (1974). On the role of classificatory processes in mental functioning: Aspects of a psychoanalytic theoretical model. *Psychoanalysis & Contemporary Science, 3*, 101–185.

Rubinstein, B. B. (1975). On the clinical psychoanalytic theory and its role in the inference and confirmation of particular clinical hypotheses. *Psychoanalysis & Contemporary Science, 4,* 3–57.

Rubinstein, B. B. (1976). On the possibility of a strictly clinical psychoanalytic theory: An essay in the philosophy of psychoanalysis. In M. M. Gill & P. S. Holzman (Eds.), *Psychology vs. metapsychology: Essays in memory of George S. Klein.* New York: International Universities Press.

Rubinstein, B. B. (1997). *Psychoanalysis and the philosophy of science: Collected papers of Benjamin B. Rubinstein* (R. R. Holt, Ed.). Madison, CT: International Universities Press.

Rustin, M. (2007). Taking account of siblings: A view from child psychotherapy. *Journal of Child Psychotherapy, 33*(1), 21–35.

Rycroft, C. (1972). *A critical dictionary of psychoanalysis.* London: Penguin.

Sackett, G. P., Ruppenthal, G. C., & Davis, A. E. (2002). Survival, growth, health, and reproduction following nursery rearing compared with mother rearing in pigtailed monkeys (Macaca nemestrina). *American Journal of Primatology, 56*(3), 165–183.

Sampson, H. (1976). A critique of certain traditional concepts in the psychoanalytic theory of therapy. *Bulletin of the Menninger Clinic, 40,* 255–262.

Sampson, H., Weiss, J., Mlodnosky, L., & Hause, E. (1972). Defense analysis and the emergence of warded-off mental contents: An empirical study. *Archives of General Psychiatry, 26,* 524–532.

Sandler, J. (1976). Countertransference and role-responsiveness. *International Review of Psychoanalysis, 3,* 43–47.

Sandler, J. (1981). Character traits and object relations. *The Psychoanalytic Quarterly, 50*(4), 694–708.

Sandler, J. (1991). *Foreword to R. Stein's psychoanalytic theories of affect.* New York: Praeger.

Sandler, J., & Sandler, A. M. (1998). *Object relations theory and role responsiveness.* London: Karnac.

Sartre, J. P. (1956). *Being and nothingness: A phenomenological essay on ontology* (H. E. Barnes, Trans.). London: Methuen.

Sass, L. (1992). The epic of disbelief: The postmodernist turn in contemporary psychoanalysis. In S. Kvale (Ed.), *Psychology and postmodernism* (pp. 166–182). Thousand Oaks, CA: Sage.

Sbarra, D. A., & Hazan, C. (2008). Coregulation, dysregulation, self-regulation: An integrative analysis and empirical agenda for understanding adult attachment, separation, loss, and recovery. *Personality and Social Psychology Review, 12*(2), 141–167.

Scarfone, D. (2002). Sexual and actual. In D. Widlocher (Ed.) & S. Fairfield (Trans.), *Infantile sexuality and attachment* (pp. 97–111). London: Karnac.

Schafer, R. (1976). *A new language for psychoanalysis.* New Haven, CT: Yale University Press.

Schafer, R. (1979). The appreciative analytic attitude and the construction of multiple histories. *Psychoanalysis and Contemporary Thought, 2*(1), 3–24.

Schafer, R. (1980). Narration in the psychoanalytic dialogue. *Critical Inquiry, 7*(1), 29–53.

Schafer, R. (2004). Narrating, attending, and empathizing. *Literature and Medicine, 23*(2), 241–251.

Schanberg, S. M., & Kuhn, C. M. (1980). Maternal deprivation: An animal model of psychosocial dwarfism. In E. Usdin & T. Sourkes (Eds.), *Enzymes and neurotransmitters in mental disease* (pp. 373–395). Chichester: Wiley.

Schlam, T. R., Wilson, N. L., Shoda, Y., Mischel, W., & Ayduk, O. (2013). Preschoolers' delay of gratification predicts their body mass 30 years later. *The Journal of Pediatrics, 162*, 90–93.

Schlick, M. (1925 [1985]). *General theory of knowledge* (A. E. Blumberg, Trans.). Chicago, IL: Open Court.

Schury, K., & Kolassa, I. T. (2012). Biological memory of childhood maltreatment: Current knowledge and recommendations for future research. *Annals of the New York Academy of Sciences, 1262*, 93–100.

Schutz-Bosbach, S., Mancini, B., Aglioti, S. M., & Haggard, P. (2006). Self and other in the human motor system. *Current Biology, 16*(18), 1830–1834.

Scult, M. A., Knodt, A. R., Swartz, J. R., Brigidi, B. D., & Hariri, A. R. (2017). Thinking and feeling: Individual differences in habitual emotion regulation and stress-related mood are associated with prefrontal executive control. *Clinical Psychological Science, 5*(10), 150–157.

Sechehaye, M. (1951). *Symbolic realization.* New York: International Universities Press.

Seeman, T. E. (1996). Social ties and health: The benefits of social integration. *Annals of Epidemiology, 6*(5), 442–451.

Seeman, T. E., & McEwen, B. S. (1996). Impact of social environment characteristics on neuroendocrine regulation. *Psychosomatic Medicine, 58*(5), 459–471.

Seeyave, D. M., Coleman, S., Appugliese, D., Corwyn, R. F., Bradley, R. H., Davidson, N. S., . . . Lumeng, J. C. (2009). Ability to delay gratification at age 4 years and risk of overweight at age 11 years. *Archives of Pediatric and Adolescent Medicine, 163*(4), 303–308.

Sephton, S. E., Sapolsky, R. M., Kraemer, H. C., & Spiegel, D. (2000). Diurnal cortisol rhythm as a predictor of breast cancer survival. *Journal of the National Cancer Institute, 92*(12), 994–1000.

Sethi, A., Mischel, W., Aber, J. L., Shoda, Y., & Rodriguez, M. L. (2000). The role of strategic attention deployment in development of self-regulation: Predicting preschoolers' delay of gratification from mother – toddler interactions. *Developmental Psychology, 36*(6), 767–777.

Sherman, D. K., Bunyan, D. P., Creswell, J. D., & Jaremka, L. M. (2009). Psychological vulnerability and stress: The effects of self-affirmation on sympathetic nervous system responses to naturalistic stressors. *Health Psychology, 28*(5), 554–562.

Sherwin-White, S. (2007). Freud on brothers and sisters: A neglected topic. *Journal of Child Psychotherapy, 33*(1), 4–20.

Shimada, S., & Hiraki, K. (2006). Infant's brain response to live and televised action. *Neuroimage, 32*, 930–939.

Shoda, Y., Mischel, W., & Peake, P. K. (1990). Predicting adolescent cognitive and self-regulatory competencies from preschool delay of gratification: Identifying diagnostic conditions. *Developmental Psychology, 26*, 978–986.

Shybut, J. (1968). Delay of gratification and severity of psychological disturbances among hospitalized psychiatric patients. *Journal of Consulting and Clinical Psychology, 32*(4), 462–468.

Silberschatz, G. (2005). The control-mastery theory. In G. Silberschatz (Ed.), *Transformative relationships: The control-mastery theory of psychotherapy* (pp. 3–30). New York: Routledge.

Silverman, D. K. (1998). The tie that binds: Affect regulation, attachment, and psychoanalysis. *Psychoanalytic Psychology*, *15*(2), 187–212.

Silverman, D. K. (1991). Attachment patterns and Freudian theory: An integrative proposal. *Psychoanalytic Psychology*, *8*, 169–193.

Silverman, D. K. (2000). An interrogation of the relational turn: A discussion with Stephen Mitchell. *Psychoanalytic Psychology*, *17*(1), 146–152.

Silverman, I. (2003). Gender differences in delay of gratification: A meta-analysis. *Sex Roles*, *49*(9), 451–463.

Simpson, J. A., & Belsky, J. (2008). Attachment theory within a modern evolutionary framework. In J. Cassidy & P. R. Shaver (Eds.), *Handbook of attachment: Theory, research, and clinical applications* (pp. 131–157). New York: The Guilford Press.

Simpson, J. A., Rholes, W. S., & Nelligan, J. S. (1992). Support seeking and support giving within couples in an anxiety-provoking situation: The role of attachment styles. *Journal of Personality and Social Psychology*, *62*(3), 434–446.

Singer, J. L. (1955). Delayed gratification and ego development: Implications for clinical and experimental research. *Journal of Consulting Psychology*, *19*(4), 259–266.

Singer, J. L., & Sincoff, J. X. (1990). Beyond repression and the defenses. In J. L. Singer (Ed.), *Repression and dissociation* (pp. 471–496). Chicago, IL: University of Chicago Press.

Singer, T., Seymour, B., O'Doherty, J. P., Kaube, H., Dolan, R. J., & Frith, C. D. (2004). Empathy for pain involves affective but not sensory components of pain. *Science*, *303*, 1157–1162.

Singer, T., Seymour, B., O'Doherty, J. P., Stephan, K. E., Dolan, R. J., & Frith, C. D. (2006). Empathic neural responses are modulated by the perceived fairness of others. *Nature*, *439*(7075), 466–469.

Slade, A. (2005). Parental reflective functioning: An introduction. *Attachment and Human Development*, *7*(3), 269–281.

Slade, A., Grienenberger, J., Bernbach, E., Levy, D., & Locker, A. (2005). Maternal reflective functioning, attachment, and the transmission gap: A preliminary study. *Attachment and Human Development*, *7*(3), 283–298.

Smith, J. (1970). On the structural view of affect. *Journal of the American Psychoanalytic Association*, *18*(3), 539–561.

Smith, R. (1992). *Inhibition: History and meaning in the science of mind and brain*. Oakland, CA: University of California Press.

Snyder, H. R., Young, J. F., & Hankin, B. L. (2017). Strong homotypic continuity in common psychopathology-, internalizing-, and externalizing-specific factors over time in adolescents. *Clinical Psychological Science*, *5*(1), 98–110.

Sobhani, M., Fox, G. R., Kaplan, J., & Aziz-Zadeh, L. (2012). Interpersonal liking modulates motor-related neural regions. *PLoS One*, *7*(10), e46809.

Sorce, J. F., & Emde, R. N. (1981). Mother's presence is not enough: Effect of emotional availability on infant exploration. *Developmental Psychology*, *17*(6), 737–745.

Southgate, V., & Hamilton, A. F. (2008). Unbroken mirrors: Challenging a theory of autism. *Trends in Cognitive Sciences*, *12*(6), 225–229.

Spelke, E. S. (1990). Principles of object perception. *Cognitive Science: A Multidisciplinary Journal*, *14*(1), 29–56.

Spezzano, C. (1993). *Relational perspectives book series. Vol. 2: Affect in psychoanalysis: A clinical synthesis*. London: Analytic Press, Inc.

Squires, C. (2002). Attachment and infant sexuality. In D. Widlocher (Ed.), *Infantile sexuality and attachment* (pp. 133–156). New York: Other Press.

Sroufe, L. A., & Waters, E. (1977). Attachment as an organizational construct. *Child Development*, *48*(4), 1184–1199.

Stacks, A. M., Muzik, M., Wong, K., Beeghly, M., Huth-Bocks, A., Irwin, J. L., & Rosenblum, K. L. (2014). Maternal reflective functioning among mothers with childhood maltreatment histories: Links to sensitive parenting and infant attachment security. *Attachment & Human Development*, *16*(5), 515–533.

Staebler, K., Helbing, E., Rosenbach, C., & Renneberg, B. (2011). Rejection sensitivity and borderline personality disorder. *Clinical Psychology & Psychotherapy*, *18*(4), 275–283.

Steger, M. F., Oishi, S., & Kashdan, T. B. (2009). Meaning in life across the lifespan: Levels and correlates of meaning in life from emerging adulthood to older adulthood. *Journal of Positive Psychology*, *4*, 43–52.

Stein, M. B., Simmons, A. N., Feinstein, J. S., Martin, B. S., & Paulus, P. (2007). *Increased amygdala and insula activation during emotion processing in anxiety-prone subjects*. Retrieved from https://ajp.psychiatryonline.org/doi/full/10.1176/ajp.2007.164.2.3.318

Stein, R. (1991). *Psychoanalytic theories of affect*. New York: Praeger.

Stepansky, P. E. (2009). *Psychoanalysis at the margins*. New York: Other Press.

Sterba, R. (1934). The fate of the ego in analytic therapy. *International Journal of Psychoanalysis*, *15*, 117–126.

Stern, D. B. (1985). *The interpersonal world of the infant*. New York: Basic Books.

Stern, D. B. (2003). *Unformulated experience*. Hillsdale, NJ: Analytic Press.

Stich, S., & Nichols, S. (1992). Folk psychology: Simulation or tacit theory? *Mind & Language Special Issue: Mental Simulation: Philosophical & Psychological Essays*, *7*(1–2), 35–71.

Stock, A., & Stock, C. (2004). A short history of ideo-motor action. *Psychological Research*, *68*, 176–188.

Stolorow, R. D., & Lachmann, F. M. (1980). *Psychoanalysis and developmental arrest: Theory and treatment*. New York: International Universities Press.

Stone, L. (1954). The widening scope of indications for psychoanalysis. *Journal of the American Psychoanalytic Association*, *2*, 567–594.

Storr, A. (1988). *Solitude: A new return to the self*. New York: Free Press.

Strachey, J. (1914). Editor's note to on narcissism. In *Standard edition* (Vol. 14, pp. 69–71). London: Hogarth.

Strachey, J. (1915). Editor's note to intsincts and their vicissitudes. In *Standard edition* (pp. 111–116). London: Hogarth.

Strachey, J. (1926). Editor's introduction to Inhibitions, symptoms and anxiety. In *Standard Edition* (Vol. 20, pp. 77–86). London: Hogarth.

Strachey, J. (1934). The nature of the therapeutic action of psychoanalysis. *International Journal of Psycho-Analysis*, *15*, 127–159.

Strachey, J. (1950 [1895]). Editor's introduction to the project for a scientific psychology. In *Standard edition* (Vol. 1, pp. 283–293). London: Hogarth.

Strachey, J. (1962). The emergence of Freud's fundamental hypotheses, appendix to the neuro-psychoses of defence. *Early Psycho-Analytic Publications*, 62–68.

Strachey, J. (1966). *The standard edition of the complete psychological works of Sigmund Freud, volume I (1886–1899): Pre-psycho-analytic publications and unpublished drafts* (pp. 1–411). London: The Hogarth Press and the Institute of Psychoanalysis.

Strenger, C. (1989). The classic and the romantic vision in psychoanalysis. *The International Journal of Psychoanalysis*, *70*(4), 593–610.

Sugarman, A. (2006). Mentalization, insightfulness, and therapeutic action: The importance of mental organization. *International Journal of Psychoanalysis, 87*, 965–987.

Sugarman, A. (2007). Whatever happened to neurosis? Who are we analyzing? And how?: The importance of mental organization. *Psychoanalytic Psychology, 24*(3), 409–428.

Sullivan, H. S. (1950). The illusion of personal individuality. *Psychiatry: Journal for the Study of Interpersonal Processes, 13*, 317–332.

Sullivan, H. S. (1953). *The interpersonal theory of psychiatry*. New York: Norton.

Suomi, S. J., & Harlow, H. F. (1972). Social rehabilitation of isolate-reared monkeys. *Developmental Psychology, 6*(3), 487–496.

Szalai, J., & Eagle, M. N. (1992). The relationship between individual differences in defensive style and concept formation. *British Journal of Medical Psychology, 65*, 47–57.

Tackett, J. L., Lahey, B. B., van Hulle, C., Waldman, I., Krueger, R. F., & Rathouz, P. J. (2013). Common genetic influences on negative emotionality and a general psychopathology factor in childhood and adolescence. *Journal of Abnormal Psychology, 122*(4), 1142–1153.

Tangney, J. P., Baumeister, R. F., & Boone, A. L. (2004). High self-control predicts good adjustment, less pathology, better grades, and interpersonal success. *Journal of Personality, 72*(2), 271–324.

Taylor, S. E., Kemeny, M. E., Reed, G. M., Bower, J. E., &Gruenewald, T. L. (2000). Psychological resources, positive illusions and health. *American Psychologist, 55*, 99–109.

Terrell, G. (1959). Manipulatory motivation in children. *Journal of Comparative and Physiological Psychology, 52*, 705–709.

Thiel, K. J., Okun, A. C., & Neisewander, J. L. (2008). Social reward-conditioned place preference: A model revealing an interaction between cocaine and social context rewards in rats. *Drug Alcohol Dependence, 96*, 202–212.

Thiel, K. J., Sanabria, F., & Neisewander, J. L. (2009). Synergistic interaction between nicotine and social rewards in adolescent male rats. *Psychopharmacology, 204*, 391–402.

Thompson, R. A. (2008). Early attachment and later development: Familiar questions, new answers. In J. Cassidy & P. R. Shaver (Eds.), *Handbook of attachment: Theory, research, and clinical applications* (pp. 348–365). New York: The Guilford Press.

Tini, M., Corcoran, D., Rodrigues-Doolabh, L., & Waters, E. (2003, April). *Maternal attachment scripts and infant secure base behavior*. Paper presented at the Biennial Meetings of the Society for Research in Child Development, Tampa, FL.

Tomarken, A. J., & Davidson, R. J. (1994). Frontal brain activation in repressors and non-repressors. *Journal of Abnormal Psychology, 103*(2), 339–349.

Torre, J. B., & Lieberman, M. D. (2018). Putting feelings into words: Affect labeling as implicit emotion regulation. *Emotion Review, 10*(2), 116–124.

Trezza, V., Baarendse, P., & Vanderschuren, L. (2009). Prosocial effects of nicotine and ethanol in adolescent rats through partially dissociable neurobehavioral mechanisms. *Neuropsychopharmacology, 34*, 2560–2573.

Trezza, V., Damsteegt, R., Achterberg, E. J., & Vanderschuren, L. J. (2011). Nucleus accumbens μ-opioid receptors mediate social reward. *The Journal of Neuroscience, 31*(17), 6362–6370.

Trezza, V., & Vanderschuren, L. J. (2008). Cannabinoid and opioid modulation of social play behavior in adolescent rats: Differential behavioral mechanisms. *European Neuropsychopharmacology, 18*(7), 519–530.

Truax, C. B. (1966). Reinforcement and nonreinforcement in Rogerian psychotherapy. *Journal of Abnormal Psychology, 71*, 1–9.

Tsakiris, M., & Haggard, P. (2005). The rubber hand illusion revisited: Visuotactile integration and self-attribution. *Journal of Experimental Psychology: Human Perception and Performance, 31*(1), 80–91.

Umilta, M. A., Escola, L., Intskirveli, I., Grammont, F., Rochat, M., Caruana, F., . . . Rizzolatti, G. (2008). When pliers become fingers in the monkey motor system. *Proceedings of the National Academy of Sciences of the United States, 105*(6), 2209–2213.

Vaux, A. (1992). Assessment of social support. In H. O. F. Veiel & U. Baumann (Eds.), *The series in clinical and community psychology: The meaning and measurement of social support* (pp. 193–216). New York: Hemisphere Publishing Corp.

Vetere, A., & Myers, L. B. (2002). Repressive coping style and adult romantic attachment style: Is there a relationship? *Personality and Individual Differences, 32*(5), 799–807.

Vicedo, M. (2009). Mothers, machines, and morals: Harry Harlow's work on primate love from lab to legend. *Journal of the History of the Behavioral Sciences, 45*(3), 193–218.

Vicedo, M. (2010). The evolution of Harry Harlow: From the nature to the nurture of love. *History of Psychiatry, 21*(2), 190–205.

Viviani, R., Dommes, L., Bosch, J., Stingl, J. C., & Beschoner P. (2018). The neural correlates of decisions about sadness in facial expressions. *Journal of Neuroscience, Psychology, and Economics, 11*(2), 93–105.

Vivona, J. M. (2009). Leaping from brain to mind: A critique of mirror neuron explanations of countertransference. *Journal of the American Psychoanalytic Association, 57*(3), 525–550.

Vivona, J. M. (2010). Siblings, transference, and the lateral dimension of psychic life. *Psychoanalytic Psychology, 27*, 8–26.

Vrtička, P., Andersson, F., Grandjean, D., Sander, D., & Vuilleumier, P. (2008). Individual attachment style modulates human amygdala and striatum activation during social appraisal. *PLoS One, 3*, e2868.

Waelder, R. (1936 [1930]). The principle of multiple function: Observations on over-determination. *Psychoanalytic Quarterly, 5*, 45–62.

Waelder, R. (1960). *Basic theory of psychoanalysis*. New York: International University Press.

Wakefield, J. C. (1991). Why emotions can't be unconscious: An exploration of Freud's essentialism. *Psychoanalysis and Contemporary Thought, 14*(1), 29–67.

Wakefield, J. C. (1992). Freud and cognitive psychology: The conceptual interface. In J. W. Barron, M. N. Eagle, & D. L. Wolitzky (Eds.), *Interface of psychoanalysis and psychology* (pp. 77–98). Washington, DC: American Psychological Association.

Wakefield, J. C. (2018). *Freud and philosophy of mind: Reconstructing the argument for unconscious mental states*. New York, NY: Palgrave Macmillan.

Wallerstein, R. S. (1990). Psychoanalysis: The common ground. *International Journal of Psychoanalysis, 71*(1), 3–20.

Wallerstein, R. S. (2002). The growth and transformation of American ego psychology. *Journal of the American Psychoanalytic Association, 50*(1), 135–169.

Walsh, W. H. (1967). Immanuel Kant. In P. Edwards (Ed.), *Encyclopedia of philosophy, Vols. 3 & 4* (pp. 305–324). New York: Collier Macmillan.

Wampold, B. E. (2015). How important are the common factors in psychotherapy? An update. *World Psychiatry, 14*, 270–277.

Wang, L., Shi, Z., & Li, H. (2009). Neuroticism, extraversion, emotion regulation, negative affect and positive affect: The mediating roles of reappraisal and suppression. *Social Behavior and Personality, 37*(2), 193–194.

Ward, S. E., Leventhal, H., & Love, R. (1988). Repression revisited: Tactics used in coping with a severe health threat. *Personality and Social Psychology Bulletin, 14*(4), 735–746.

Waters, H., & Rodrigues-Doolabh, L. (2004). *Manual for decoding secure base narratives.* Stony Brook: State University of New York, Unpublished manuscript.

Waters, T. E. A., Brockmeyer, S. L., & Crowell, J. A. (2013). AAI coherence predicts caregiving and care seeking behavior: Secure base script knowledge helps explain why. *Attachment & Human Development, 15*(3), 316–331.

Waters, T. E. A., Raby, K. L., Ruiz, S. K., Martin, J., & Roisman, G. I. (2018). Adult attachment representations and the quality of romantic and parent–child relationships: An examination of the contributions of coherence of discourse and secure base script knowledge. *Developmental Psychology, 54*(12), 2371–2381.

Waters, T. E. A., & Roisman, G. I. (2019). The secure base script concept: An overview. *Current Opinion in Psychology, 25*, 162–166.

Watson, D., & Clark, L. A. (1984). Negative affectivity: The disposition to experience aversive emotional states. *Psychological Bulletin, 96*(3), 465–490.

Watts, T. W., Duncan, G. J., & Quan, H. (2018). Revisiting the marshmallow test: A conceptual replication investigating links between early delay of gratification and later outcomes. *Psychological Science, 29*(7), 1159–1177.

Weinberger, D. A. (1990). The construct validity of the repressive coping style. In J. L. Singer (Ed.), *Repression and dissociation* (pp. 337–386). Chicago, IL: University of Chicago Press.

Weinberger, D. A., Schwartz, G. E., & Davidson, R. J. (1979). Low-anxious, high-anxious, and repressive coping styles: Psychometric patterns and behavioral and physiological responses to stress. *Journal of Abnormal Psychology, 88*, 369–380.

Weiss, J. (1998). Patients' unconscious plans for solving their problems. *Psychoanalytic Dialogues, 8*(3), 411–428.

Weiss, J., & Sampson, H. (1986). *The psychoanalytic process: Theory, clinical observation, and empirical research.* New York and London: Guilford Press.

White, R. W. (1959). Motivation reconsidered: The concept of competence. *Psychological Review, 66*(5), 297–333.

White, R. W. (1960). Competence and the psychosexual stages of development. In *Nebraska symposium on motivation* (pp. 97–141). Lincoln, NE: University of Nebraska Press.

White, R. W. (1963). Ego and reality in psychoanalytic theory. *Psychological Issues, 3*(3, Whole no. 11), 1–210.

Wicker, B., Keysers, C., Plailly, J., Royet, J. P., Gallese, V., & Rizzolatti, G. (2003). Both of us disgusted in my insula: The common neural basis of seeing and feeling disgust. *Neuron, 40*(3), 655–664.

Widlocher, D. (2002). Primary love and infantile sexuality: An eternal debate. In D. Widlocher (Ed.), *Infantile sexuality and attachment* (pp. 1–36). New York: Other Press.

Williams, J. H. (2008). Self-other relations in social development and autism: Multiple roles for mirror neurons and other brain bases. *Autism Research, 1*, 73–90.

Williams, J. H., Whiten, A., Suddendorf, T., & Perrett, D. I. (2001). Imitation, mirror neurons and autism. *Neuroscience and Biobehavioral Reviews, 25*, 287–295.

Wilson, A., & Weinstein, L. (1996). The transference and the zone of proximal development. *Journal of the American Psychoanalytic Association, 44*, 167–200.

Wilson, R. S., & Matheny, A. P. (1983). Assessment of temperament in infant twins. *Developmental Psychology, 19*(2), 172–183.

Wiltink, J., Subic-Wrana, C., Tuin, I., Weidner, W., & Beutel, M. E. (2010). Repressive coping style and its relation to psychosocial distress in males with erectile dysfunction. *The Journal of Sexual Medicine, 7*(6), 2120–2129.

Winnicott, D. W. (1953). Transitional objects and transitional phenomena. *International Journal of Psychoanalysis, 34*, 89–97.

Winnicott, D. W. (1954). Mind and its relation to the psyche-soma. *British Journal of Medical Psychiatry, 27*(4), 201–209.

Winnicott, D. W. (1956). Primary maternal preoccupation. In *The maturational process and the facilitating environment* (pp. 300–305). New York: International Universities Press.

Winnicott, D. W. (1958). *Collected papers: Through pediatrics to psycho-analysis*. London: Tavistock.

Winnicott, D. W. (1960). Ego distortion in terms of true and false self. In D. W. Winnicott (Ed.), *The maturational processes and the facilitating environment* (pp. 140–152). Madison, CT: International Universities Press.

Winnicott, D. W. (1963). Regression as therapy illustrated by the case of a boy whose pathological dependence was met by the parents. *British Journal of Medical Psychology, 36*(1), 9–12.

Winnicott, D. W. (1965). Ego distortion in terms of true and false self. In *The maturational process and the facilitating environment* (pp. 140–152). New York: International Universities Press.

Wittgenstein, L. (1966). Lectures and conversations on aethetics. In C. Barrett (Ed.), *Psychology and religious belief*. Berkeley, CA: University of California Press.

Wolf, E. (1988). *Treating the self: Elements of clinical self psychology*. New York: Guilford.

Wolfe, C. D., & Belle, M. A. (2004). Working memory and inhibitory control in early childhood: Contributions from physiology, temperament, and language. *Developmental Psychobiology, 44*, 68–83.

Wolitzky, D. L. (2000). The conception of transference. In D. K. Silverman & D. L. Wolitzky (Eds.), *Changing conceptions of psychoanalysis: The legacy of Merton M. Gill* (pp. 265–287). Hillsdale, NJ: The Analytic Press.

Wright, A. G., Krueger, R. F., Hobbs, M. J., Markon, K. E., Eaton, N. R., & Slade, T. (2013). The structure of psychopathology: Toward an expanded quantitative empirical model. *Journal of Abnormal Psychology, 122*(1), 281–294.

Yearwood, K., Vliegen, N., Chau, C., Corveleyn, J., & Luyten, P. (2019). When do peers matter? The moderating role of peer support in the relationship between environmental adversity, complex trauma, and adolescent psychopathology in socially disadvantaged adolescents. *Journal of Adolescence, 72*, 14–22.

Young, K. S., Burklund, L. J., Torre, J. B., Saxbe, D., Lieberman, M. D., & Craske, M. G. (2017). Treatment for social anxiety disorder alters functional connectivity in emotion regulation neural circuitry. *Neuroimaging, 261*, 44–51.

Yu (2020, January 26). By the book. *New York Times Book Review*, p. 6.

Zelenko, M., Kraemer, H., Huffman, L., Gschwendt, M., Pageler, N., & Steiner, H. (2005). Heart rate correlates of attachment status in young mothers and their infants. *Journal of the American Academy of Child and Adolescent Psychiatry, 44*, 470–476.

Zilberg, N. J., Wallerstein, R. S., DeWitt, K. N., Hartley, D., & Rosenberg, S. E. (1991). A conceptual analysis and strategy for assessing structural change. *Psychoanalysis and Contemporary Thoughts, 14*, 317–342.

Zweig, A. (1967). Lipps' theory of empathy in aesthetic experience. In P. Edwards (Ed.), *Encyclopedia of philosophy, Vols 3 & 4* (pp. 486–487). New York: Colliers MacMillan.

Index

Page numbers followed by 'n' indicate a note on the corresponding page.